BL 1175 .B445 G67 v.4
Gosvami
Srila Prabhupada-lilamrta.

Śrīla Prabhupāda-līlāmṛta, Volume 4

IN EVERY TOWN AND VILLAGE

kali-kālera dharma—kṛṣṇa-nāma-saṅkīrtana
kṛṣṇa-śakti vinā nahe tāra pravartana

The fundamental religious system in the age of Kali is the chanting of the holy name of Kṛṣṇa. Unless empowered by Kṛṣṇa, one cannot propagate the saṅkīrtana movement.

—*Caitanya-caritāmṛta*

Śrīla Prabhupāda-līlāmṛta, Volume 4

IN EVERY TOWN AND VILLAGE

Around the World
1968–1971

A Biography of
His Divine Grace
A. C. Bhaktivedanta Swami Prabhupāda

Founder-Ācārya of
The International Society for Krishna Consciousness

Satsvarūpa dāsa Goswami

THE BHAKTIVEDANTA BOOK TRUST
Los Angeles · London · Paris · Bombay · Sydney

Readers interested in the subject matter of this book
are invited by the Bhaktivedanta Book Trust
to correspond with the Secretary:

Bhaktivedanta Book Trust
3764 Watseka Avenue
Los Angeles, California 90034

First Printing, 1982: 10,000 copies

Library of Congress Cataloging in Publication Data

Gosvāmī, Satsvarūpa Dāsa, 1939–
Srila Prabhupada-lilamrta

"Books by ....A. C. Bhaktivedanta Swami Prabhupada"
v. 4, p.
Includes index.
CONTENTS —v. 4. Around the World
1968–1971: in every town and village
1. Bhaktivedanta Swami, A. C., 1896–1977. 2. Gurus
—Biography. 3. International Society for Krishna
Consciousness—Biography. I. Title.
BL1175.B445G67 294.5'61'0924 (B) 80-5071
ISBN 0-89213-115-2 (v. 4)

Contents

Foreword

Though I have been a student of the Kṛṣṇa devotional traditions in India for fifteen years, in the late sixties I was influenced by the then common notion among academicians (not to mention the general public) that the movement begun by Bhaktivedanta Swami was simply another watered-down product of an Indian *guru's* attempt to make Hindu teachings attractive to Western youth. The anticult campaigns of the mid-seventies highlighted ISKCON (International Society for Krishna Consciousness) as one of the spurious "cults." However, my research into the validity of such attitudes led me to conclude that the Kṛṣṇa movement in America was more authentically Indian than I had first imagined. When the opportunity presented itself, in 1980, for me to live in Kṛṣṇa temples in California for three weeks, I began an intensive study of ISKCON that has since taken me to fourteen temples throughout America and India. Through living in the temples and speaking at length with ISKCON leaders and devotees, I have come to regard many members of the movement as good friends and their *guru,* Bhaktivedanta Swami, as a man worthy of the attention and acclaim this biographical series affords.

In this volume of Bhaktivedanta Swami's biography, one of the central lessons taught the astute reader is the complexity and depth of the *guru*-disciple relationship. Much of the criticism from parents and anticult groups centers on the authoritarian demand of "cult" leaders for absolute submission from their followers. It is assumed that the leader has personal motives (e.g. power or monetary gain) that drive him to control others, while the surrendered disciples are manipulated, in an unthinking state, by the capricious whim of the spiritual master. In this volume of the life of Bhaktivedanta Swami, we see the foolishness of such an analysis. What springs from page after page is the willing devotion of young men and women to a man whom they admire for his deep faith and humility, not his autocratic or forceful demands. Early in ISKCON's life in America, the very fabric of this fledgling institution was threatened by schismatic teachings of newly ordained ascetics on the *relative* place of the *guru* in the life of faith and in the institution. Bhaktivedanta Swami had to state forcefully the Indian tradition that the *guru's* position is absolute—that of the eternal spiritual father—not simply one of convenience, to be overshadowed by time.

Yet we can see why some of the young devotees were confused as Bhaktivedanta Swami prostrated himself before the images of Kṛṣṇa and of his *guru* in the line of spiritual teachers before him. Such, however, is the character of *paramparā,* or *guru* succession. One's *guru* is the *only* channel through which one's devotion is transmitted faithfully to God, and such is also the case for one's *guru* (though some, like Bhaktivedanta Swami, seem also to have direct access as well). Thus to a mother who exclaims, "You know, these boys actually *worship* you!" Bhaktivedanta Swami responds, "Yes, that is our system. I am also worshiping my Guru Mahārāja." (p.230)

This volume of Bhaktivedanta Swami's biography reveals the religious dimensions of the *guru*-disciple relationship in the varied attempts this remarkable Vaiṣṇava ascetic made to nurture the deepening faith of his new American children in a God and a spiritual tradition foreign to their native soil. From loosely performed rituals to standardized *pūjās* (Deity worship) done according to classic Bengali texts, we see the old master encourage greater attention to the details of worship. From spontaneous but uninformed attempts to celebrate their *guru's* birthday to formal *Vyāsa-pūjās* set in traditional Bengali songs and prayer, Bhaktivedanta Swami's disciples are led into old Indian traditions of honoring one's spiritual master as a part of the act of worshiping God. But what struck me as I read the pages that follow is the model of piety set by Bhaktivedanta Swami himself as he became deeply immersed in the praises of God while singing, or chanting, or dancing. It becomes quite clear that the lesson of the master is not merely what he says, but what he does. And it is also clear that the followers of Bhaktivedanta Swami struggled—not always successfully—to match up to the high standard of living and devotion the mature Bhaktivedanta Swami set.

The reader will marvel at the persistence, ingenuity, and faithfulness to Bhaktivedanta Swami's vision his disciples evidence in their attempt to spread Kṛṣṇa consciousness to every town and village. From the married couples who pioneered the movement in England and accomplished with the aid of the Beatles' Harrison and Lennon (!) what renowned sages from India before them could not, to the disciples who endured the worst that India's climate and cuisine could produce to work long days and nights bringing faith in Kṛṣṇa back to India's own people, the contagious devotion of the master lives on in his spiritual children. Thus the success of ISKCON in these formative years (1969 – 1971) can be understood only when both partners in the *guru*-disciple relationship are given due attention. Nonetheless, it is Bhaktivedanta Swami, with his deep faith, energetic preaching, and persistent ideals, who forms the nucleus of the fledgling community of faith we observe in the early years of ISKCON.

What begins to happen before the careful readers' eyes in this volume is the institutionalization or routinization of ISKCON's dress, ritual behavior, and administrative structure. With the formation of the Governing Body Commission (G.B.C.) to run the practical affairs of the institution (book publication, temple economics, etc.), Bhaktivedanta Swami accomplished something his own master had envisioned but had not accomplished before his death, namely, to provide an administrative structure that could hold together disparate temples in varied locations with their separate leaderships. It is clear after Bhaktivedanta Swami's death in 1977 that the G.B.C. has enabled ISKCON to weather storms from within (including the defection of one of Bhaktivedanta Swami's eleven appointed successors) and from without (e.g. the tax and legal challenges to ISKCON's religious status in California) that would have been impossible without central leadership. We see in this volume the beginnings of that leadership core and the freedom from administrative detail the G.B.C. afforded Bhaktivedanta Swami.

Having interviewed Satsvarūpa dāsa Goswami and visited a farm under his management, I have seen the same devotion expressed for him by his disciples that he expresses here for Bhaktivedanta Swami. That is not surprising when one realizes that even with effective institutional structures like the G.B.C. in place, communities of faith remain vital only so long as there are living models to give expression to ideals and beliefs that can otherwise seem quite remote. Critics of ISKCON who see only the outward trappings of surrender to the *guru* miss the humility before God and *guru* that is demanded of each *guru* as well. This volume is a success not because of some academic standard of objectivity (which few biographers meet in any case), but because of the skillful blend of oral history, documented reminiscences, and transparent admiration, all of which bring Bhaktivedanta Swami to life for the reader as a real (and exceptional) person. We not only sense, but observe that it is complete devotion to God through the person of one's spiritual master that animated ISKCON in its early years and continues to do so now, as evidenced by the author himself. Thus this book reads like a personal yet precise diary relating the formative years of ISKCON and its founder-teacher. And just as in reading a diary, we learn as much from reading between the lines as we do from the events and persons described. This is a fascinating chronicle I urge you to read.

Dr. Larry D. Shinn
Danforth Professor of Religion
Oberlin College
Oberlin, Ohio

Preface

After the disappearance of His Divine Grace A. C. Bhaktivedanta Swami Prabhupāda from this mortal world on November 14, 1977, many of his disciples saw a need for an authorized biography of Śrīla Prabhupāda. The responsibility of commissioning such a work rested with the Governing Body Commission of the International Society for Krishna Consciousness. At their annual meeting in 1978, the GBC resolved that a biography of Śrīla Prabhupāda should be written and that I would be the author.

According to the Vaiṣṇava tradition, if one aspires to write transcendental literature, he must first take permission from his spiritual master and Kṛṣṇa. A good example of this is Kṛṣṇadāsa Kavirāja Gosvāmī, the author of Lord Caitanya Mahāprabhu's authorized biography, *Śrī Caitanya-caritāmṛta*. As Kṛṣṇadāsa Kavirāja has explained:

> In Vṛndāvana there were also many other great devotees, all of whom desired to hear the last pastimes of Lord Caitanya.
>
> By their mercy, all these devotees ordered me to write of the last pastimes of Śrī Caitanya Mahāprabhu. Because of their order only, although I am shameless, I have attempted to write this *Caitanya-caritāmṛta*.
>
> Having received the order of the Vaiṣṇavas, but being anxious within my heart, I went back to the temple of Madana-mohana in Vṛndāvana to ask His permission also.

This transcendental process is further described by His Divine Grace Śrīla Prabhupāda in his commentary on the *Caitanya-caritāmṛta* as follows:

> To write about the transcendental pastimes of the Supreme Personality of Godhead is not an ordinary endeavor. Unless one is empowered by the higher authorities or advanced devotees, one cannot write transcendental literature, for all such literature must be above suspicion, or in other words, it must have none of the defects of conditioned souls, namely mistakes, illusions, cheating, and imperfect sense perception. The words of Kṛṣṇa and the disciplic succession that carries the orders of Kṛṣṇa are actually

> authoritative. . . . One must first become a pure devotee following the strict regulative principles and chanting sixteen rounds daily, and when one thinks he is actually on the Vaiṣṇava platform, he must then take permission from the spiritual master, and that permission must also be confirmed by Kṛṣṇa from within his heart.

So to say the *Śrīla Prabhupāda-līlāmṛta* is an authorized biography does not mean that it is a flattering portrait commissioned by an official body, but that it is an authorized literature presented by one who is serving the order of Kṛṣṇa and *guru* through the disciplic succession. As such, *Śrīla Prabhupāda-līlāmṛta* is not written from the mundane or speculative viewpoint, nor can ordinary biographers comprehend the significance and meaning of the life of a pure devotee of God. Were such persons to objectively study the life of Śrīla Prabhupāda, the esoteric meanings would evade them. Were they to charitably try to praise Śrīla Prabhupāda, they would not know how. But because *Śrīla Prabhupāda-līlāmṛta* is authorized through the transcendental process, it can transparently present the careful reader with a true picture of Śrīla Prabhupāda.

Another important aspect of the authenticity of *Śrīla Prabhupāda-līlāmṛta* is the vast amount of carefully researched information that I am able to focus into each volume. The leading devotees of the Kṛṣṇa consciousness movement, in addition to giving me permission to render this work, have also invited the world community of ISKCON devotees to help me in gathering detailed information about the life and person of Śrīla Prabhupāda. The Bhaktivedanta Book Trust, Prabhupāda's publishing house, has given me his collection of letters, totaling over seven thousand; and scores of Prabhupāda's disciples have granted interviews and submitted diaries and memoirs of their association with Śrīla Prabhupāda. Aside from his disciples, we have interviewed many persons in various walks of life who met Śrīla Prabhupāda over the years. The result is that we have a rich, composite view of Śrīla Prabhupāda, drawn from many persons who knew him in many different situations and stages of his life. The Acknowledgments section in this book lists the persons who are cooperating to bring about *Śrīla Prabhupāda-līlāmṛta.*

Despite the authorized nature of this book and despite the support of my many well-wishers, I must confess that in attempting to describe the glories of our spiritual master, His Divine Grace A. C. Bhaktivedanta Swami Prabhupāda, I am like a small bird trying to empty the ocean by carrying drops of water to the land. The picture I have given of Śrīla Prabhupāda is only a glimpse into his unlimited mercy, and that glimpse has only been possible by the grace of *guru* and Kṛṣṇa.

Satsvarūpa dāsa Goswami

Acknowledgments

Editor: Maṇḍaleśvara dāsa
Research Chief: Baladeva Vidyābhūṣaṇa dāsa
The Gita-nagari Press Supervisors: Maṇḍaleśvara dāsa, Gaura Pūrṇimā dāsa
Editorial Consultant: Jayādvaita Swami
Editorial Assistant: Bimalā-devī dāsī
Production Managers: Ṛkṣarāja dāsa, Gaura Pūrṇimā dāsa
File Manager: Gaura Pūrṇimā dāsa
File Consultants: Memoirs and letters: Aṣṭa-sakhī-devī dāsī
Lectures and conversations: Rukmiṇī-devī dāsī
Compositors: Aṣṭa-sakhī-devī dāsī, Nārāyaṇī-devī dāsī, Gaura Pūrṇimā dāsa
Research: Aṣṭa-sakhī-devī dāsī, Rukmiṇī-devī dāsī
Layout: Sādhana-siddhi dāsa
Copy Editor: Bimalā-devī dāsī
Proofreader: Ṛkṣarāja dāsa
Sanskrit: Agrāhya dāsa
Typists: Ācārya-devī dāsī, Aṣṭa-sakhī-devī dāsī, Nārāyaṇī-devī dāsī

* * *

BBT Production Manager: Rājendranātha dāsa
Indexer: Kīrtana-rasa dāsa
Research: Subhadrā-devī dāsī
Sanskrit: Gopīparāṇadhana dāsa, Kuśakratha dāsa
Copy Editor/Proofreader: Kṣamā-devī dāsī
Proofreader: Rādhā-vallabha dāsa
Patron Donors for Research: Śrīla Bhagavān dāsa Goswami, Prabhupāda-kṛpa Swami, Hari-vilāsa dāsa

Mukunda dāsa Goswami and Kṛṣṇa Gopāla dāsa assisted in gathering interviews.

Special thanks to Śrīla Tamāla Kṛṣṇa Goswami, who provided inspiration and friendship.

Introduction

In *Śrīla Prabhupāda-līlāmṛta Volume 1, A Lifetime in Preparation*, we saw Śrīla Prabhupāda struggling alone to publish *Back to Godhead* magazine, personally typing, editing, visiting the printer, and then distributing the copies on the streets of New Delhi. Working alone in Jhansi, India, Prabhupāda gathered a few part-time followers to create the League of Devotees, an early attempt to enact his vision of introducing people from all nations, races, and levels of society to Kṛṣṇa, the Supreme Personality of Godhead.

In *Volume 2, Planting the Seed*, Śrīla Prabhupāda was still alone as he arrived in America in 1965. But he was filled with faith in Kṛṣṇa and determination to establish Kṛṣṇa consciousness in the West and thus fulfill the desire of his spiritual master and the prediction of the scriptures and previous saints. Young men and women on New York's Lower East Side joined, attracted not so much to Vedic culture as to "Swamiji" and his chanting of Hare Kṛṣṇa. Thus, beginning from a small storefront, Śrīla Prabhupāda introduced the Hare Kṛṣṇa movement to America.

In *Volume 3, Only He Could Lead Them*, we followed Śrīla Prabhupāda to San Francisco's Haight-Ashbury during the hippie heyday of 1967, as he established his Kṛṣṇa consciousness movement there, just as he had done in New York City. Then in May of '67 he appeared to suffer a heart attack and retired to India to recuperate. It became even clearer that the Kṛṣṇa consciousness movement—its life and its growth—depended entirely upon him. Although a few dozen sincere workers were dedicated to his service, they felt helpless and incompetent to do any missionary work—or even to maintain their own spiritual vows to abstain from illicit sex, meat-eating, intoxication, and gambling—unless he were personally present to lead them. *Only He Could Lead Them* ends in December 1967 with Śrīla Prabhupāda's return to America and his young spiritual family.

As Śrīla Prabhupāda would comment several years later, his movement didn't really begin until this return to America in December 1967. His time was limited, he knew—the heart attack had proven that. Now, in whatever time was left, he had to accomplish his mission. And as his International Society for Krishna Consciousness began to grow, it gradually spread beyond its simple and sometimes humorous beginnings to become a spiritual institution considered noteworthy even among world religions.

In the present volume we follow Śrīla Prabhupāda through the years of his greatest active participation in ISKCON, the International Society for Krishna Consciousness, as its sole leader. In 1968, as the present volume opens, Śrīla Prabhupāda has approximately fifty disciples and six ISKCON centers. Although his followers have increased their numbers, most of them are no more than sincere neophytes. Prabhupāda is personally available to each of his disciples, and he continues to manage and maintain each ISKCON center. Then in July of 1970 Śrīla Prabhupāda forms his Governing Body Commission and begins to turn over ISKCON's management to his board of G.B.C. secretaries. Yet even as the present volume ends, we find Prabhupāda still actively guiding the activities of his society, expanded now to six hundred disciples and sixty-five centers.

Although the teachings of Kṛṣṇa consciousness have existed since time immemorial within India's Sanskrit Vedic literatures and are the origin and essence of all religious expression, until Śrīla Prabhupāda began his preaching, Kṛṣṇa consciousness in its original purity had never been widely spread. In the most popular and basic Vedic text, *Bhagavad-gītā*, Lord Kṛṣṇa teaches that He is the Supreme Personality of Godhead and that real religion, real knowledge, and real endeavor can be understood only when one dedicates his life to the loving service of the Lord. Only full surrender to the Supreme can bring one freedom from the laws of *karma* and the cycle of repeated birth and death.

From childhood, Śrīla Prabhupāda worshiped Lord Kṛṣṇa, understanding Him to be the Supreme Personality of Godhead, the source of all existence. And beginning at age twenty-two, after his first meeting with his spiritual master, Śrīla Bhaktisiddhānta Sarasvatī Ṭhākura, Śrīla Prabhupāda became more and more active in spreading the teachings of Lord Kṛṣṇa. Śrīla Prabhupāda was convinced that devotional service to Lord Kṛṣṇa is life's goal and that to engage others in devotional service is the highest welfare activity. And these convictions drove him in his traveling and preaching on behalf of his spiritual master and Kṛṣṇa.

Śrīla Prabhupāda's success in spreading Kṛṣṇa consciousness was due to his being directly empowered by the Supreme Personality of Godhead. *Caitanya-caritāmṛta* states, *kali-kālera dharma—kṛṣṇa-nāma-saṅkīrtana/ kṛṣṇa-śakti vinā nahe tāra pravartana:* "The fundamental religious system in the age of Kali is the chanting of the holy name of Kṛṣṇa. Unless empowered by Kṛṣṇa, one cannot propagate the *saṅkīrtana* movement." Yet although Śrīla Prabhupāda was empowered, his life's story is not one in which success comes neatly and automatically, everything being miraculously enacted by God. Rather, Śrīla Prabhupāda's story is one of *constant attempts on behalf of his spiritual master.* Successes come, but only after great endeavor and faith.

Prabhupāda encountered difficulties in trying to spread love of God in a godless world. He sometimes met opposition from governments, the media, and religionists, including those in India; and even within his own society he met difficulties caused when his neophyte disciples fell to the allurements of the material world. Yet through all difficulties Śrīla Prabhupāda persevered with the sublime tolerance, kindness, and unflinching determination of a pure devotee of Lord Kṛṣṇa.

By material standards it is extraordinary that a person of Śrīla Prabhupāda's age could constantly travel, confront problems and opposition, and simultaneously produce volume after volume of translated Vedic literatures. But material vision cannot comprehend Śrīla Prabhupāda's activities. He was truly a *mahātmā,* as described by Kṛṣṇa in *Bhagavad-gītā:* "The *mahātmās* are always working under the direction of My internal energy." In spreading Kṛṣṇa consciousness, Śrīla Prabhupāda was far from merely a religious zealot trying to increase a sect; his writing, traveling, and preaching were done in pure devotion to Lord Kṛṣṇa and were therefore transcendental. It was Kṛṣṇa Himself, Śrīla Prabhupāda saw, who was bringing the results.

The title of this volume, *In Every Town and Village,* derives from Lord Caitanya's statement,

pṛthivīte āche yata nagarādi grāma
sarvatra pracāra haibe mora nāma

"In every town and village the chanting of My name will be heard." These words, directly spoken by Lord Caitanya, are certainly true; the

Lord's prediction must come to pass. Many Gauḍīya Vaiṣṇavas, however, even as recently as the disciples of Bhaktisiddhānta Sarasvatī, considered the Lord's prediction problematic. The name of Lord Caitanya in every town and village? Should this be taken allegorically? Certainly the Americans, the Europeans, the Africans, the Polynesians, the Mongolians—the uncultured *mlecchas* outside of India—could never become Vaiṣṇavas. Thus Lord Caitanya's words had seemed an enigmatic topic for speculation.

Śrīla Prabhupāda, however, was under orders from his spiritual master, Śrīla Bhaktisiddhānta Sarasvatī, to preach Kṛṣṇa consciousness beyond India. And alone, in 1965, he took the great step and left India, crossed the Atlantic, and began the International Society for Krishna Consciousness in New York City.

Although some of Prabhupāda's Godbrothers had gone to England some thirty years before, they had failed to establish anything and had even concluded that to give Kṛṣṇa consciousness to the Western people was not possible. But Śrīla Prabhupāda, fulfilling Lord Caitanya's prediction, traveled and employed his disciples in traveling, to open centers in New York City, San Francisco, Los Angeles, Boston, Montreal, Buffalo, Seattle. He also sent his disciples abroad, to London, and as described in this volume, they succeeded where Prabhupāda's Godbrothers had failed.

In Every Town and Village tells of Śrīla Prabhupāda's travels, as he carried out the literal meaning of Lord Caitanya's prediction. Prabhupāda's faith in the order of his spiritual master, in the prediction of Lord Caitanya, and in the power of the chanting of Hare Kṛṣṇa to deliver the fallen souls of this age impelled him to travel. Even though from the external point of view traveling became increasingly difficult as he grew older, he continued to travel. He once advised his disciples that they should preach while young and that when older they could retire. But Prabhupāda's deep dedication to his most urgent mission would not allow him to retire. "For a warrior," he said, "to die on the battlefield is glorious—is it not?"

As the present volume explains, Śrīla Prabhupāda traveled not only to enlist new devotees and establish Kṛṣṇa consciousness in new places around the world, but also to maintain what he had already begun. Had he not continued to travel to each temple, instructing his disciples, observing their progress, correcting their mistakes, raising the standard of their Kṛṣṇa consciousness, the devotees would not have been able to continue.

Repeatedly, Prabhupāda had to go around the world.

"In every town and village," therefore, is not a cheap slogan or an allegorical abstraction, especially when we consider the work of Śrīla Prabhupāda. By his faith in Kṛṣṇa, by his selfless dedication to the order of his spiritual master, and by the blessings of Lord Caitanya, he did what no one else could have done. As *Caitanya-caritāmṛta* states, *kṛṣṇa-śakti vinā nahe tāra pravartana:* "Only one empowered by Lord Kṛṣṇa can actually spread the chanting of Hare Kṛṣṇa around the world."

This volume is an account of years of fulfillment in Śrīla Prabhupāda's life, and I invite the reader to relish them. Here are the years of Śrīla Prabhupāda's success—the fulfillment of the "rags to riches" story of one who started alone with nothing but whose movement, writing, and personal life created an astounding and permanent impression on the world. By following Śrīla Prabhupāda through these times, we gain an understanding of his exalted and humble life.

I am unable to describe Śrīla Prabhupāda fully. I have therefore composed an invocation, praying that I be permitted to tell this story purely from the transcendental viewpoint—otherwise it would be ruined and incomprehensible. When properly told, the life of the pure devotee brings the greatest joy and benefit to the hearers.

Invocation

According to Kṛṣṇadāsa Kavirāja, an invocation involves offering obeisances, defining the objective, and bestowing benedictions.

I offer my respectful obeisances to my eternal spiritual master, His Divine Grace A. C. Bhaktivedanta Swami Prabhupāda, whose service is my life and soul. It is for his pleasure that I offer *Śrīla Prabhupāda-līlāmṛta* as an act of devotional service. He has blessed the entire world with Kṛṣṇa consciousness, and he is therefore the best friend of all people and all living entities. He is the most powerful *ācārya*, delivering pure love of God, and he is delivering the message of Lord Caitanya strictly in disciplic succession. No one else has ever spread Kṛṣṇa consciousness as widely as he. I am praying that he will allow me to surmount the difficulties involved in presenting his biography and that he will be pleased with the results. I am convinced that by his good wishes this work can be successful and that if he is not pleased, I am powerless to write anything of merit.

By offering obeisances to my spiritual master, I am offering respects to all other *ācāryas* in the disciplic succession—to Śrīla Prabhupāda's *guru*, Bhaktisiddhānta Sarasvatī Ṭhākura, to his *guru*, and so on, to the six Gosvāmīs, Lord Caitanya, and Lord Kṛṣṇa Himself. Only by the grace of Śrīla Prabhupāda can I bow down in the temple, prostrate at the lotus feet of Gaura-Nitāi, Kṛṣṇa-Balarāma, and Rādhā-Śyāmasundara and have access to Their mercy.

One objective of *Śrīla Prabhupāda-līlāmṛta* is to present the life and teachings of Śrīla Prabhupāda in the transcendental perspective, never portraying Śrīla Prabhupāda as an ordinary man, subject to the modes of nature. Śrīla Prabhupāda was a divinely empowered pure devotee. He was sent to this world by the Supreme Lord just to spread the Kṛṣṇa consciousness movement to people of all nations, races, classes, and creeds and thus to offer everyone the opportunity to become a pure devotee and go back to Godhead.

Another objective of this work is to attract the leaders and influential members of society to appreciate and love Śrīla Prabhupāda. This biography must be honest, factual, and correct in transcendental knowledge, and it must captivate and please the reader. *Śrīla Prabhupāda-līlāmṛta* must enlighten and please and also move the reader to inquire into the writings of Śrīla Prabhupāda. My ultimate objective is that the reader be further moved to take up service to His Divine Grace Śrīla Prabhupāda.

Although it is appropriate while writing an invocation to offer a benediction to the reader, I am fallen and cannot offer any benedictions. Yet I can confidently assure my readers that by reading the life and teachings of Śrīla Prabhupāda they will gain quick access to the mercy of Kṛṣṇa, because it is only by the mercy of a great devotee that anyone gets the mercy of Kṛṣṇa. By reading *Śrīla Prabhupāda-līlāmṛta*, those who associated with and served Śrīla Prabhupāda will refresh their remembrance of him and thus derive ecstasy and rededication to his service. Those who never knew Śrīla Prabhupāda will also be blessed, because according to the Vedic literatures, even a moment's association with the pure devotee can make one's life perfect. To read *Śrīla Prabhupāda-līlāmṛta* is to associate with Śrīla Prabhupāda through the transcendental process of hearing. Therefore, although I myself cannot award any benediction to my readers, this work can do so, as it attracts everyone to Śrīla Prabhupāda.

Thus having made the invocation to this work—offering obeisances, describing my objectives, and offering benedictions—I remain fallen and dumb, begging at the lotus feet of my Guru Mahārāja and waiting for his mercy, which alone can allow this poor writer and poor devotee to speak well.

My dear Śrīla Prabhupāda, my dear Lord Kṛṣṇa, if you think I can be trusted to write correctly, then please allow me to do so. There is a great need for this transcendental literature, as the human beings of Kali-yuga are in a deplorable state of spiritual blindness, with no knowledge of the relief to be gained by service to the pure devotee. The devotees of the Lord and the many sincere followers of Śrīla Prabhupāda are eagerly receiving each successive volume of this work. They want to hear more and more of Śrīla Prabhupāda's activities and instructions, and they want to see them presented expertly so that others may also become attracted to join us in loving, dedicated service to *guru* and Gaurāṅga.

My dear Śrīla Prabhupāda, I know I have to work hard to produce this literature, and I promise to do so. But my efforts will be only a spinning of concocted, empty words unless you become present in these words and bring them to life with transcendental potency.

CHAPTER ONE

Unlimited Opportunity, Limited Time

Montreal
August 1968

Śrīla Prabhupāda was in his room, speaking with several disciples. "So, Annapūrṇā, you have got some news?" he asked. Annapūrṇā was a young British girl. A few months ago her father had written from England that he might be able to provide a house if some devotees came there.

"Yes," she replied.

"So, what is our next program?" She was reticent. "That letter from your father is encouraging?"

"Yes, he encourages me. But he says he can't provide any place if we come there."

Prabhupāda looked disappointed. "That's all right. It is up to Kṛṣṇa. When we go to someone to preach, we have to stand before them with folded hands, with all humility: 'My dear sir, please take to Kṛṣṇa consciousness.' "

"Prabhupāda?" Pradyumna spoke up. "I was reading a book by this big atheist swami."

"Hmm?"

"There are some letters in the back of the book, and I was looking at them . . ."

"Atheist swami's book," Prabhupāda said, "we have nothing to do with."

"I wasn't looking at his philosophy," Pradyumna explained. "I was just looking at the techniques he used when he was in America. He wanted to go to Europe, so he had a man, a rich benefactor, who went on a six-week tour of France, England, Germany, Switzerland, Holland, and then back, arranging lectures. That's how he did most of his tour. He had one or two influential people, and they arranged everything. And the lectures were arranged, and the society . . ."

"So, you can arrange like that?" Prabhupāda asked.

"I was thinking that there would be a Royal Asiatic Society in London. I think Ṭhākura Bhaktivinoda was a member of that."

"But where is Ṭhākura Bhaktivinoda's *saṅga* (association)?" Prabhupāda asked.

"Well," Pradyumna continued, "still there may be some people you could open correspondence with. They might be interested in sponsoring you."

"Is there anything about Kṛṣṇa in that swami's speech?" Prabhupāda asked.

"No."

Prabhupāda sat thoughtfully. In England he would have no place to stay. Pradyumna might talk of influential persons traveling ahead and making all the arrangements, but where were such persons? Here was a shy girl who could barely speak up, whose father would not help, and Pradyumna reading an atheist swami and talking of a Royal Asiatic Society—but nothing practical. Prabhupāda had plans, though. He had asked Mukunda and Śyāmasundara to go to London and try to establish an ISKCON center. They had agreed and would be arriving in Montreal from San Francisco in a few days.

Śrīla Bhaktisiddhānta Sarasvatī, Prabhupāda's own spiritual master, had wanted Kṛṣṇa consciousness in Europe. During the 1930s he had sent his most experienced *sannyāsīs* to London, but they had returned, nothing accomplished. It wasn't possible to teach Kṛṣṇa consciousness to the *mlecchas*, they had complained. Europeans couldn't sit long enough to hear the Vaiṣṇava philosophy. One of the *sannyāsīs* had met Lord Zetland, who had inquired curiously, "Swamiji, can you make me a *brāhmaṇa*?" The *sannyāsī* had assured Lord Zetland he could, certainly, if Zetland would give up meat-eating, intoxication, gambling, and illicit sex. "Impossible!" Lord Zetland had replied. And the *sannyāsīs* had accepted this response as the standard for all Europeans. The *sannyāsīs* had returned to India; Vaiṣṇavism could never take hold in the West.

Prabhupāda had faith that his disciples would succeed; they would help him establish ISKCON centers in Europe, just as they had in North America. Certainly such success would greatly please Śrīla Bhaktisiddhānta Sarasvatī. Prabhupāda told of a man who found a gourd lying on the road and picked it up and then found a stick and a wire and picked them up. In themselves, the three parts were useless. But by putting the gourd, the stick, and the wire together, the man made a *vīṇā* and began to play beautiful music. Similarly, Prabhupāda had come to the West and found some rejected youths lying here and there, and he himself had been rejected by the people of New York City; but by Kṛṣṇa's grace the combination had become successful. If his disciples remained sincere and followed his orders, they would succeed in Europe.

Three married couples—Mukunda and Jānakī, Śyāmasundara and Mālatī (with their infant daughter, Sarasvatī), and Guru dāsa and Yamunā—arrived in Montreal, eager to travel to London. These three couples had begun the temple in San Francisco, where they had had close association with Śrīla Prabhupāda. They had helped Prabhupāda introduce *kīrtana, prasādam,* and Ratha-yātrā among the hippies of Haight-Ashbury. Now they were eager to help him introduce Kṛṣṇa consciousness in London.

Prabhupāda asked the three couples to remain with him in Montreal for a week or two, so that he could train them to perform *kīrtana* expertly. Chanting Hare Kṛṣṇa was not a theatrical performance but an act of devotion, properly conducted only by pure devotees—not by professional musicians. Yet if Prabhupāda's disciples became proficient in their singing, Londoners would better appreciate Kṛṣṇa consciousness.

The thought of these devotees preaching in England made Prabhupāda ecstatic. With their *kīrtana* they would become more popular than the *yogīs*, with their gymnastics and impersonal meditation. As the London program became a tangible fact, Prabhupāda began to reveal more plans. Prabhupāda already seemed to have hundreds of detailed plans for implementing Kṛṣṇa consciousness around the world—he only needed willing helpers.

In the daily *kīrtana* rehearsals, Prabhupāda taught the devotees to chant Hare Kṛṣṇa and other devotional songs, beginning with a slow tempo and building gradually. He would regularly interrupt and have them begin again. Listening carefully as Yamunā led the chanting, Prabhupāda would stop her at times to correct her Sanskrit pronunciation.

After two weeks in Montreal, the London party came together for a final meeting with Prabhupāda. He was sending them to start a center in London to fulfill his spiritual master's dream. The *sannyāsīs* Śrīla Bhaktisiddhānta Sarasvatī had sent to London, Prabhupāda told them, had lectured in a few places, posed for photos with lords and ladies, and then returned to India. But Prabhupāda wanted his disciples to go out boldly, chant the holy name, and attract others to chant.

Lord Caitanya had personally used this method while touring South India. *Caitanya-caritāmṛta* describes that whoever saw Lord Caitanya became ecstatic in love of God; then that ecstatic person would chant the holy name and ask others to chant; and when they saw that person, they too would become ecstatic. Thus the waves of ecstatic love of Kṛṣṇa would increase.

Prabhupāda predicted that when the devotees chanted Hare Kṛṣṇa, the people of London would hear the *mantra*, become devotees, and then enlighten others. Kṛṣṇa consciousness would grow. The only requirement was that the chanting be done purely, without any material motivation. Prabhupāda's enthusiasm was contagious, and as he spoke he filled his disciples with the same contagious enthusiasm.

When Mukunda asked Prabhupāda if he had any specific instructions, Prabhupāda replied with a story. In his youth, he had once seen a movie of Charlie Chaplin. The setting was a formal ball held outdoors, and off from the main dance arena were lanes with benches where couples sat. Some mischievous boys had plastered glue on one of the benches, and a young man and his girl friend came and sat down. "When the young man got up"—Prabhupāda laughed as he told the story—"his tails tore up the middle."

Prabhupāda told how the couple had returned to the dance, unaware of what had happened. But now they drew stares from the other dancers. Wondering why he was suddenly attracting so much attention, the young man went into the dressing room and saw in the mirror his ripped coattails. Deliberately, he then tore his coat all the way up to the collar, returned to his partner, and began dancing exuberantly.

Then another man joined, ripping his own coattails and dancing with his partner, as if to compete with the first couple. One by one, the other dancers followed, ripping their coattails and dancing with abandon.

By the conclusion of the story, the devotees in Prabhupāda's room were all laughing uproariously. But finally their laughter subsided and the meeting ended. Not until the devotees were already at the airport did Mukunda, talking with Śyāmasundara, begin to appreciate and marvel at how expertly Prabhupāda had answered his question. By their bold, enthusiastic, confident preaching, they would attract people. Not everyone would immediately "join in the dancing," as had the people in the Charlie Chaplin film; the devotees might even be considered crazy at first. But they would be offering Kṛṣṇa consciousness, the highest and rarest gift, and intelligent people would gradually appreciate this, even if at first they scoffed.

By Śrīla Prabhupāda's order, his London-bound disciples, holding *kīrtana* in public, would present a profile quite different from the reserved profile of his *sannyāsī* Godbrothers. His Godbrothers had imitated the British ways; but Prabhupāda wanted the British to imitate the Vaiṣṇavas. To appear in the streets of London with shaven heads and *dhotīs* would require boldness. But it would be exciting to chant, carrying out the order of Lord Caitanya. And the people would follow—gradually, but definitely. It was the will of Lord Caitanya.

* * *

Śrīla Prabhupāda's visit to Montreal took place early in the summer of 1968, six months after his return to America. In India, from July to December of 1967, he had recovered his health, and on December 14 he had returned to San Francisco. After a few weeks he had gone to Los Angeles, where a small group of disciples had opened a storefront temple in a middle-class black and Hispanic neighborhood. The storefront was bare and the location secluded. Prabhupāda had stayed there two months, delivering lectures, holding *kīrtanas*, and giving strength and inspiration to his disciples. Although a buzzing in his head had made working difficult, he had found the warm climate and sunshine agreeable and had continued to translate *Śrīmad-Bhāgavatam*, dictating tapes and sending them to Boston for typing.

A reporter from *Life* had come to Śrīla Prabhupāda's apartment and interviewed him for an upcoming *Life* feature, "The Year of the Guru."

When the story had appeared it had mixed Śrīla Prabhupāda and his movement with coverage of other *gurus*. Although the article had carried a large color photo of Śrīla Prabhupāda and favorably described a reporter's visit to the New York ISKCON center, Prabhupāda had said that being grouped with *gurus* who taught concoctions of *yoga* and meditation was not good.

In May, a few months after leaving Los Angeles, Prabhupāda had paid a first visit to his ISKCON center in Boston. There also he had found a few disciples based in a small storefront. He had lectured at many of the local universities, including Harvard and M.I.T. At M.I.T., addressing a gathering of students and faculty, he had challenged, "Where in this university is there a department to teach scientifically the difference between a living body and a dead body?" The most fundamental science, the science of the living soul, was not being taught.

After Boston, Śrīla Prabhupāda had come to Montreal. And after three months in Montreal, Prabhupāda flew to Seattle, where he stayed for one month. Then he briefly visited Santa Fe, New Mexico, where the ISKCON center was a tiny, isolated storefront.

Prabhupāda's reasons for traveling from center to center were to train and convince each disciple and to speak with newcomers. Many young people came to hear, but Prabhupāda found the majority already ruined by illicit sex and drugs. They were "rich men's sons," but they had become hippies, wandering the streets. By Kṛṣṇa's grace, now some of them were being saved.

Even while recuperating in India, Prabhupāda had always thought of returning to America to continue his movement. The Indians had seemed interested only in sense gratification, like that of the Americans. But many American youths, disillusioned with their fathers' wealth, were not going to the skyscrapers or to their fathers' businesses. As Prabhupāda had seen from his stay in New York City and San Francisco, thousands of youths were seeking an alternative to materialism. Frustrated, they were ripe for spiritual knowledge.

The devotees, still neophytes, knew nothing of spiritual life and in most cases very little of material life. But because they were sincerely taking to Kṛṣṇa consciousness, Prabhupāda was confident that their shortcomings would not prevent their spiritual progress. Although naturally beautiful, these Western youths were now dirty and morose; their beauty had become covered. But the chanting of Hare Kṛṣṇa was reviving them,

Prabhupāda said, just as the monsoon revives the land of Vṛndāvana, making it fresh and verdant. And as the Vṛndāvana peacocks sometimes dance jubilantly, so the devotees, having shed their material bonds, were now ecstatically dancing and chanting the holy names. When a reporter asked Prabhupāda if his disciples were hippies, Prabhupāda replied, "No, we are not hippies. We are happies."

More than being a visiting lecturer or a formal guide, Śrīla Prabhupāda was the spiritual father of his disciples. They accepted him as their real father, and he found them devoted and affectionate, far more than his own family had been. These young American boys and girls—"the flower of your country," Prabhupāda called them—had received the blessing of Lord Caitanya and were delivering that blessing to their countrymen. Prabhupāda said it was up to his American disciples to save their country. He was giving them the method, but they would have to implement it.

Śrīla Prabhupāda loved his disciples, and they loved him. Out of love, he was giving them the greatest treasure, and out of love they were following his instructions. This was the essence of spiritual life. On the basis of this love, the Kṛṣṇa consciousness movement would grow. Not surprisingly, some disciples had fallen away to their former, materialistic way of living. But Prabhupāda sought those sincere souls who would stay. That was the important thing, he said. One moon is more valuable than many stars; so even a few sincere workers would accomplish wonderful things. The sincere and intelligent would stay, and Lord Caitanya Mahāprabhu would empower them to carry out His desires for distributing love of Kṛṣṇa. In this way, the devotees' lives would become perfect. Many disciples, in fact, already felt this happening. Kṛṣṇa consciousness worked because they sincerely practiced it and because Śrīla Prabhupāda carefully and patiently tended the growing plants of transcendental loving service he had planted in their hearts.

Los Angeles
October 1968

Śrīla Prabhupāda returned to find the devotees living and worshiping in an exciting location on Hollywood Boulevard. A large *saṅkīrtana* party, organized by his disciple Tamāla Kṛṣṇa, would chant Hare Kṛṣṇa on the streets all day and sell *Back to Godhead* magazines in larger quantities than ever before—as many as two hundred magazines a day, with a collection of over one hundred dollars.

Then one day, shortly after Prabhupāda's arrival, the landlord evicted the devotees from their place on Hollywood Boulevard. With no temple the devotees moved to scattered locations throughout the city. As many evenings as possible, however, they would all gather in someone's garage, lent to them for the evening, and Śrīla Prabhupāda would chant Hare Kṛṣṇa with them and lecture.

Then Prabhupāda rented a former Christian church on La Cienega Boulevard. He introduced a more regulated Deity worship and an increased Sunday love feast. Each week would bring a new, specially planned festival with a big feast and hundreds of guests. These new programs in Los Angeles encouraged Prabhupāda, and he wanted to see them introduced in ISKCON centers throughout the world.

* * *

Śrīla Prabhupāda was planning to go to England. But first he wanted to visit his farm project in West Virginia, and he had also been promising the devotees in San Francisco he would attend their Ratha-yātrā festival in July. This traveling to establish and expand his ISKCON was alone enough to keep him busy; yet he was also always meditating on his work of translating and commenting on Vedic literatures.

In L.A. during December, Śrīla Prabhupāda had begun *The Nectar of Devotion*, a summary study of Rūpa Gosvāmī's *Bhakti-rasāmṛta-sindhu. The Nectar of Devotion* would be a handbook for his disciples, elaborately explaining the science and practice of *bhakti-yoga*. Simultaneous with *The Nectar of Devotion*, he had also begun *Kṛṣṇa, the Supreme Personality of Godhead*, a summary study of *Śrīmad-Bhāgavatam's* Tenth Canto. Visiting the temple only on Sundays, he had spent most of his time at his small rented house on the outskirts of Beverly Hills, where he worked intensely on his two major literary projects.

Prabhupāda's most ambitious literary undertaking, the completion of *Śrīmad-Bhāgavatam*, was to be no less than sixty volumes. He had begun in India in 1959, and all along he had been aware that he was attempting a gigantic task at an advanced age. Now Kṛṣṇa was giving him opportunities both for writing Vedic literatures and for traveling, and he was working at an amazing pace.

a Prabhupāda at the New Vrindaban farm community, June 1968.

orge Harrison chanting
e Kṛṣṇa with the devo-
s in London.

Śrīla Prabhupāda lecturing in the Montreal temple room, Summer 1968.

Śrīla Prabhupāda's arrival at London's Heathrow Airport, September 11, 1969.

Reception in the V.I.P. lounge at Heathrow Airport.

Installation of Rādhā-Londonīśvara, December 14, 1969.

Śrīla Prabhupāda with Tamāla Kṛṣṇa at Regents Park, London.

Installation of Rādhā-Londonīśvara, December 14, 1969. *(continued)*

Śrīla Prabhupāda lecturing in the temple room at the Bury Place temple.

Devotees perform *saṅkīrtana* on Dalhousie Square, Calcutta.

Gala welcome for Śrīla Prabhupāda in Bombay, September 29, 1970.

Above: Śrīla Prabhupāda with Sumati Morarji, head of the Scindia Steamship Company.

Left: Śrīla Prabhupāda and his disciples at Ram Sharanam in Bombay where they stayed during November of 1970.

Below: *Kīrtana* procession through the streets of Surat.

Right: Śrīla Prabhupāda addressing the crowd at Sadhu-samaj, Bombay.

Below: Devotees lead *kirtana* offstage at Sadhu-samaj, Bombay.

Left and below: The site of the Ardha-kumbha-melā, at Prayag.

Left: Pilgrims bathe at the confluence of the Yamunā and Ganges Rivers, Prayag.

Above: Śrīla Prabhupāda with Hanuman Prasad Podar in Gorakhpur, February 1971.

Right: Śrīla Prabhupāda speaks to twenty thousand persons each night at the Bombay *paṇḍal*, March 25-April 14, 1971.

Left and above: At the Calcutta *paṇḍāl,* April 14–24, 1971.

Above left: Śrīla Prabhupāda walks in Red Square, Moscow, June 1971.

Above right: Śrīla Prabhupāda in front of St. Basil's Cathedral.

Left: An initiation ceremony in the Brooklyn temple, July 1971.

Right: Śrīla Prabhupāda's arrival at Kennedy Airport.

Above: Śrīla Prabhupāda on Nairobi television.

Right: Śrīla Prabhupāda preaching in Kenya.

The force driving Prabhupāda was the desire of his spiritual master, Śrīla Bhaktisiddhānta Sarasvatī. As for how much time he had remaining to execute his mission—that was in Kṛṣṇa's hands. Everything was up to Kṛṣṇa: "If Kṛṣṇa wants to kill you, no one can save you; and if Kṛṣṇa wants to save you, no one can kill you." Yet although Prabhupāda was always in transcendental consciousness, beyond the effects of old age, he was aware that he didn't have many more years left. All along he had had the vision of a spiritual movement for all nations and cultures, and to establish this he was racing against time.

Śrīla Prabhupāda's mood of urgency was the natural mood of the Vaiṣṇava preacher—an ambition to engage everyone in loving service to Kṛṣṇa. Without Kṛṣṇa consciousness the bewildered, conditioned souls of Kali-yuga were all heading for the horrible consequences of their sinful lives. Prabhupāda's sense of urgency, therefore, was an expression of his compassion. He wanted to save the gross materialists, who were blind to the existence of the soul. If they wasted their human life, they would suffer millions of years before getting another chance to awaken their Kṛṣṇa consciousness and go back to Godhead.

The heart attack Prabhupāda had endured in 1967 had accelerated his mood of urgency. Although before the heart attack he had often worked like a young man and played the drum for hours, now Kṛṣṇa's warning was clear. The heart attack was to have been the time of his death, Prabhupāda had said, but because his disciples had prayed, "Our master has not finished his work. Please protect him," Kṛṣṇa had spared him. Similarly, on the boat to America in 1965 his heart had almost failed. But then also Kṛṣṇa had saved his life.

The scope of Prabhupāda's work was enormous; even with many years and good health he could never finish. Prabhupāda saw that in future generations many people would come forward to help, and thus, by a combined effort, the Kṛṣṇa consciousness movement would continue to check the forces of Kali-yuga and save the entire world. Caitanya Mahāprabhu had predicted this, and Prabhupāda knew that it must come to pass. But the task of erecting the framework for this universal effort rested on Prabhupāda alone. And he worked tirelessly, knowing that unless he established a complete foundation the entire mission might later collapse.

Beginning with Prabhupāda's first success in New York City in 1966, Kṛṣṇa had shown unlimited opportunities for spreading Kṛṣṇa consciousness. But how much time was there? Only Kṛṣṇa could say; it was up to Him. Prabhupāda remained ever mindful of the vast scope of his mission and the ever-narrowing span of time he had in which to complete it. "I am an old man," he often told his disciples. "I could pass away at any moment."

* * *

Śrīla Prabhupāda would receive several letters a week from the devotees in London. It was now December 1968—the devotees had been in London four months—and still they had no temple, nor even a place where they could live and worship together. Mostly they had been visiting Hindu families, holding *kīrtana* and sharing *prasādam*. Śrīla Prabhupāda had encouraged this, but after hearing a few reports he decided the program was stagnant. The devotees should not expect much from the Hindus, he said. "They have become hodgepodge due to so many years of subjugation by foreigners and have lost their own culture. . . . I am concerned to preach this gospel amongst the Europeans and Americans."

The devotees were jolted, but they knew Prabhupāda was right. Determined to change their tactics, they immediately began lecturing at colleges and universities and chanting in the streets. They were preaching to the British, and it felt right. When they wrote to Prabhupāda that although they had accomplished little they were "planting seeds," Prabhupāda replied,

> Regarding your analogy of sowing Krishna Consciousness seeds, I may inform you that there is a Bengali proverb—Sa bure Meoya Phale. This means that fruits like chestnuts and pomegranates, or similar other valuable fruits and nuts take some time to be fructified. So any good thing comes into our possession after hard struggle and endeavor. So Krishna Consciousness is the greatest of all good fruits. We must therefore have necessary endurance and enthusiasm to get the result. We shall never be disappointed when things are presented in reversed order. Anyway, your honest labor is now coming to be fructified. Always depend upon Krishna and go on working with enthusiasm, patience and conviction.

* * *

Through the spring and summer of 1969, Prabhupāda continued touring his American ISKCON centers. From Los Angeles he had sent

Gaurasundara and Govinda dāsī, a young married couple, to Hawaii; and on their invitation that he come during the mango season, he joined them. But when he got there in March he found that it was not mango season and that his disciples had accomplished little. They had taken jobs and were working full time just to support themselves.

New York City
April 9, 1969

Prabhupāda traveled to New York City, the birthplace of his Kṛṣṇa consciousness society, where his movement had been growing for nearly three years. Although the center was established and his books were being distributed, he still had to visit to strengthen the devotees. His presence gave them determination and courage. For seven months they had carried on without his personal touch, but his visits—when he would sit in his room and reciprocate warmly with them—were vital. Nothing could equal these intimate meetings.

Many devotees, new and old, crowded into Prabhupāda's apartment at 26 Second Avenue. "There was one reporter for the *Honolulu Advertiser*," Prabhupāda said, "—he was putting questions to me. And then he wrote an article: 'The swami is a small man, but he is delivering a great message.' That is true. I am small. But the message—that is not small."

Brahmānanda showed Prabhupāda a globe with markers representing ISKCON centers. "Now there is one in North Carolina," Brahmānanda said.

"Then it becomes fifteen?" Prabhupāda asked. He was smiling and looking directly from one devotee to another. "I want each of you to go and start a center. What is the difficulty? Take one *mṛdaṅga*. Then another person will come and join you—he will take *karatālas*. When I came here, Brahmānanda and Acyutānanda were dancing. And after chanting, hundreds of men will come to your storefront and enjoy chanting and dancing."

"The girls also?" Rukmiṇī asked.

"There is no harm," Prabhupāda said. "Kṛṣṇa does not make distinction—female dress or male dress. I mean to say, the female body is weaker, but spiritually the body does not matter. In the absence of Lord Nityānanda, His wife, Jāhnavī devī, was preaching. First you must understand the philosophy. You must be prepared to answer questions.

Kṛṣṇa will give you intelligence. Just like I was not prepared to answer all these questions, but Kṛṣṇa gives intelligence."

After eight days in his New York City home, Prabhupāda went to Buffalo. At State University of New York at Buffalo, Rūpānuga was teaching an accredited course in Kṛṣṇa *yoga* with some sixty students enrolled, regularly chanting the Hare Kṛṣṇa *mantra* on beads. Prabhupāda stayed for a few days, lecturing and initiating disciples. Then he went to Boston for more initiations and several marriages.

Columbus, Ohio
May 9, 1969

The devotees had arranged for Prabhupāda and Allen Ginsberg to chant onstage at Ohio State University.

Allen had been a friend of the Kṛṣṇa consciousness movement from its first days on the Lower East Side. Shortly after Prabhupāda's arrival in Columbus, he stopped by Prabhupāda's house and discussed philosophy with Prabhupāda for several hours. Allen was friendly with Prabhupāda, as always. But he doubted whether Kṛṣṇa consciousness could become popular in America. "The need," he said, "is for a large, single, unifying religious movement in America."

"So here is Kṛṣṇa," Prabhupāda replied, "—all-attractive. Now you can say, 'Why shall I accept Kṛṣṇa?' But since you ask for a unifying element, then I say, 'Here is Kṛṣṇa.' Now you can analyze: Why should you accept Kṛṣṇa? And I shall reply, 'Why you shall not?' Whatever you want or expect from the Supreme or Unifying, everything is there in Kṛṣṇa."

If Prabhupāda wanted his movement popularized, Allen suggested, he should consider omitting many of the sectarian Hindu aspects, such as the dress, the food, and the Sanskrit.

Kṛṣṇa consciousness, Prabhupāda replied, was not sectarian or Hindu. Lord Caitanya had said that a person could chant *any* name of God—but one must chant. As for the food, Prabhupāda explained that any food was acceptable as long as it was purely vegetarian. And dress—there was no stricture that Americans wear robes and shave their heads. The Hare Kṛṣṇa *mantra*, Prabhupāda added, was a natural sound, not foreign.

Allen objected. The Hare Kṛṣṇa *mantra* sounded foreign; perhaps they should think of an alternative, more American *mantra*.

"This is going on," Prabhupāda replied. "Some people are inclined to one thing and some to others. And it will go on until the end of creation. But our position is that we are searching after the center. And here is the center."

At Ohio State's Hitchcock Hall a thousand students occupied the seats, and a thousand more crowded the aisles and stage. The program began with a *kīrtana* led by Allen Ginsberg. Allen then introduced Prabhupāda, and Prabhupāda lectured. When Prabhupāda began the second and final *kīrtana* of the evening, the students responded wildly. Those seated stood and danced, some jumping in their seats, and those in the aisles and on the stage also joined in. Amid the thunderous *kīrtana* of nearly two thousand voices, Prabhupāda began to dance, jumping up and down on the speaker's dais, his hands raised high. He threw flowers from his garland, and the students scrambled for them. The wildly ecstatic *kīrtana* continued for almost an hour, and then Prabhupāda brought it to a close.

Afterward hundreds of students crowded close around Prabhupāda, asking him questions. Many students continued to chant as they left the hall, and some left crying from the new sensations of spiritual happiness. The next day the ecstatic night of chanting at Hitchcock Hall was the talk of the campus. Prabhupāda was pleased with the evening, and he described the event in a letter to devotees in Los Angeles:

> Yesterday, at the Ohio State University we had a tremendous meeting, and nearly two thousand students were dancing, clapping and chanting along with us. So it is clear that the student community has a nice potential for accepting this philosophy.

* * *

New Vrindaban
May 21, 1969

Accompanied by Kīrtanānanda Swami and Hayagrīva, Prabhupāda then traveled from Columbus to the New Vrindaban farm project in the hills of West Virginia. When their car got stuck in a neighbor's garden near the entrance to the property, Prabhupāda decided to walk the final two miles along the muddy access road that led to the farm. The road soon ended, however, and Prabhupāda and his two guides picked up a footpath, entering the dense forest.

The mid-May trees were still coming into foliage, and the sunlight broke through the branches to a carpet of brilliant purple phlox. Prabhupāda walked quickly ahead of Kīrtanānanda Swami and Hayagrīva, who hurried to keep up. A winding creek repeatedly crossed the path, and Prabhupāda would cross by stepping from stone to stone. The road, he said, would not be difficult to travel by ox cart; the forest was like a jungle, just as he had expected and wanted.

For the past year, Prabhupāda had corresponded with Kīrtanānanda Swami and Hayagrīva concerning New Vrindaban, and this correspondence had established the direction for Kṛṣṇa conscious country living. Prabhupāda had said he wanted the community based on Vedic ideals, everyone living simply, keeping cows, and working the land. The devotees would have to develop these ideas gradually; it would take time. But even in the beginning the keynote should be "simple living and high thinking." Because the community would remain completely aloof from the city, it would at first appear inconvenient and austere. But life would be peaceful, free from the anxieties of the artificial urban society based on hard work for sense gratification. And most important, the members of such a community would be serving Kṛṣṇa and chanting His name.

Prabhupāda spoke little, making his way along the path as if at his own home. They stopped beside the creek, and Prabhupāda sat down on a blanket Kīrtanānanda Swami and Hayagrīva spread for him on the grass. "We are stopping for Kīrtanānanda," Prabhupāda said. "He is tired." Prabhupāda and his party drank water from the creek, rested briefly, and then continued.

As they rounded a curve in the road, Prabhupāda could see a clearing on the ridge ahead. A small frame house and a barn stood at the lower end of the ridge. These two ancient structures, Hayagrīva explained, were the only buildings on New Vrindaban's 120 acres. As no vehicles traveled here, the paths were overrun with high grass. A willow spread its branches close by the old house. The settlement was the picture of undisturbed primitive life.

Prabhupāda liked the simple life at New Vrindaban, and whatever simple thing the devotees offered him he accepted with satisfaction. They served him freshly ground wheat cereal cooked in milk, and he said it was wonderful. When he saw the kitchen's dirt floor covered with cow dung, he approved, saying it was just like in an Indian village.

Prabhupāda also liked his room in the attic, directly above the temple room. He brought out the small Rādhā-Kṛṣṇa Deities he had been traveling with for the last month and a half and had his servant, Devānanda, improvise an altar on a small table to one side of the room. Arranging his two trunks as a desk and placing a picture of his spiritual master on one of the trunks, Prabhupāda immediately resumed his usual schedule.

He would take his late-morning massage sitting outside and then bathe with warm water in an improvised outdoor shower stall. Kīrtanānanda Swami prepared Prabhupāda's usual lunch of *dāl*, rice, and *capātīs*—plus some local pokeweed. The previous summer, Kīrtanānanda Swami and Hayagrīva had picked and canned blackberries, which they now served Prabhupāda as blackberry chutney. The *capātīs* were from freshly milled whole wheat, and everything was cooked over a wood fire. The best fuel for cooking, Prabhupāda said, was cow dung; wood was second, gas third, and electricity last.

Prabhupāda spent much of the day out of doors, under a persimmon tree about a hundred feet from the house. There he would sit and read at a low table one of the men had built. Often he would look up from his reading and gaze across the deep valley to the distant ridge, where the forest met the sky.

In the late afternoon, devotees would gather under the persimmon tree with Prabhupāda, sitting and talking with him until after sunset. They saw Prabhupāda's living with them as a practical demonstration of New Vrindaban's importance; if he, the greatest devotee, could be satisfied living simply and chanting Hare Kṛṣṇa in this backwoods setting, then they should follow his example.

Comparing New Vrindaban to the Vṛndāvana in India, Prabhupāda said that New Vrindaban was in some ways better, since Vṛndāvana, India, was now congested with worldly men. Five hundred years ago the Gosvāmī followers of Lord Caitanya had excavated the sites of Kṛṣṇa's pastimes in Vṛndāvana, and only pure devotees had lived there. But in recent years Vṛndāvana had become a place for materialists and impersonalists. New Vrindaban, however, should admit only the spiritually inclined. In Vedic society, Prabhupāda said, everyone had been satisfied to live like this, in a small village beside a river. Factories were unnecessary. Prabhupāda wanted this Vedic way of life for the entire world, and New Vrindaban could serve as a model for the benefit of the masses.

New Vrindaban had no phone, and mail had to be fetched by a

two-mile walk. In this, Prabhupāda said, New Vrindaban was like Vṛndāvana, India—both Vṛndāvanas lacked in modern amenities. This "difficulty," however, coupled well with the Vaiṣṇava philosophy that modern amenities were not worth the trouble required to get them. A devotee, accepting whatever nature provides, spends his time and energy in spiritual life.

New Vrindaban's only cow was a black and white crossbreed named Kāliya, and Prabhupāda would drink a little of her milk morning, noon, and night. "I haven't tasted milk like this in sixty-five years," he said. One day, he predicted, New Vrindaban would have many cows, and their udders would be so full that the dripping milk would muddy the pastures. Although people in the West were blind to their great sin of cow slaughter and its grievous karmic reactions, he said, New Vrindaban would demonstrate to the world the social, moral, and economic advantages of protecting the cow and utilizing her milk, rather than killing her and eating her flesh.

Prabhupāda wanted the New Vrindaban devotees to build cottages. He wanted many buildings, even if at first they were primitive, and he gave a plan for a simple structure of baked mud. He also wanted a Kṛṣṇa conscious school, and the country, he said, would be the best place for it. "The city is made by man, and the country is made by God," Prabhupāda said, paraphrasing the British poet Cowper. The young students should learn reading, writing, and arithmetic, and at the same time they should become pure devotees. In their play they could imitate the pastimes of Kṛṣṇa and His cowherd boyfriends, with one child massaging Kṛṣṇa, another wrestling with Kṛṣṇa—just as in the spiritual world. The women in New Vrindaban, Prabhupāda said, should care for the children, clean the temple, cook for the Deities, and churn butter.

He had many plans for New Vrindaban, and he was giving only idea seeds, with few details. "You develop it to your heart's content," he told Kīrtanānanda Swami. An ideal Vedic community with the members producing all their own food and necessities was what Prabhupāda wanted. Unless the devotees at New Vrindaban could become self-sufficient, he said, there was no use in their occupying such a big piece of land.

Even before Prabhupāda's visit to New Vrindaban, he had requested Kīrtanānanda Swami and Hayagrīva to plan for seven temples on the property. These seven temples should be named after the major temples of old Vṛndāvana: Madana-Mohana, Govindajī, Gopīnātha, Rādhā-Dāmodara, Rādhā-ramaṇa, Śyāmasundara, and Rādhā-Gokulānanda.

Prabhupāda said he would personally secure Rādhā-Kṛṣṇa Deities for each temple.

It was inevitable that Prabhupāda leave New Vrindaban; letters from London, Los Angeles, and San Francisco compelled him to travel. On the day of his departure, the New Vrindaban devotees teased him, saying he couldn't go. Kīrtanānanda Swami went so far as to say they would block his way on the road. But Prabhupāda corrected him, "You can't do that to the spiritual master."

Accompanied by Kīrtanānanda Swami and the New Vrindaban devotees, Prabhupāda walked along the forest path. The New Vrindaban countryside was verdant, the summer air hot and moist. Prabhupāda was silent. He had come here to encourage his disciples, and he himself had also become encouraged. Here was simple village life as Kṛṣṇa Himself had lived it, depending on the land and the cow. That cow Kāliya had given such nice milk. New Vrindaban's cows were not ordinary; they knew they would not be killed. So far only a few devotees were here, but by Kṛṣṇa's grace more would come.

Prabhupāda and Kīrtanānanda Swami walked together along the forest path, saying little, but their mutual understanding was deep. Prabhupāda hadn't given him many specific instructions: a few words while sitting or walking together outdoors, a gesture, a facial expression of pleasure or concern. Kīrtanānanda Swami could understand, however, that New Vrindaban was very dear to his spiritual master and should become dear to him also. Prabhupāda assured him that because the devotees of New Vrindaban were centered on chanting Hare Kṛṣṇa, serving the Deities, and protecting the cows, Kṛṣṇa would bless them with success. The community was already successful, and Kṛṣṇa would continue to protect the devotees against all impediments and difficulties.

At the end of the two-mile walk, Prabhupāda, surrounded by his followers, stood beside the car that was to take him to the airport in Pittsburgh, from where he would fly to Los Angeles. His suitcases, which had come out on a horse-drawn cart, were loaded into the car's luggage compartment, and Prabhupāda got in the back seat. Amid cries of "Hare Kṛṣṇa!" and "Prabhupāda!" the car pulled out onto the country highway, and Prabhupāda continued chanting Hare Kṛṣṇa on his beads.

* * *

Prabhupāda had been hearing regularly from his six disciples in London. Having little money and living as separate couples in different parts of the city, they found their greatest inspiration in Prabhupāda's letters. They would repeatedly read his instructions and dream of when he would one day visit them in London. Although in San Francisco Kṛṣṇa consciousness had been fun for the three couples, in England it was becoming more and more difficult. The devotees, being foreigners, were not allowed to earn a salary, and except for a few contacts they knew no one. Although unable to live together, they were trying to maintain their morale and Kṛṣṇa consciousness.

Yamunā: *I had to move to a Jamaican ghetto, the top floor of one of the buildings. It was awful. Day after day after day I would sit and listen to a tape of Prabhupāda singing. It was a beautiful tape he had just done in Los Angeles. And I would pray to him, "Please come. Please come."*

Mukunda: *Letters—that's what kept us alive. Prabhupāda would write and say, "I am coming." Two or three times he wrote to say, "I am coming by March." And we would write back and say we wanted to get a place first. We really felt it wouldn't be right for him to come unless we had a place first. He wrote a letter to my wife: "I was planning to come by March, but your husband is not allowing me. What can I do?"*

The devotees in London had not seen Prabhupāda in four months, and still there was no date set for his visit. Although they sometimes became discouraged and talked of going back to America, they persevered. Prabhupāda had promised he would come when they got a temple, and that promise helped them remember that they were personally serving him. They felt that *he* was doing the work and they were his assistants. His absence was only external. By his instructions, whether written, spoken, or remembered in the heart, he was always with them. He was constantly directing them.

While trying out various schemes to popularize Kṛṣṇa consciousness in London, Śyāmasundara arranged for a program to which he invited many of London's prominent citizens. About one hundred people responded to Śyāmasundara's formal invitation—one member of Parliament, a few government officials, but mostly young people.

The devotees served a feast and showed a film of Śrīla Prabhupāda walking by Stowe Lake in Golden Gate Park. Prabhupāda had sent a tape recording specifically for the evening, and the devotees highlighted it as the evening's special attraction, even though they hadn't had time to hear it in advance. Guru dāsa started the tape, and suddenly there was Prabhupāda's voice.

"Ladies and gentlemen, please accept my greetings in the happy year of 1969, and blessings of Śrī Kṛṣṇa, the Supreme Personality of Godhead, for your kindly participating in this happy meeting of Kṛṣṇa consciousness."

Although Prabhupāda had recorded the tape in the quiet of his room in Los Angeles, the devotees were astonished to feel Prabhupāda's direct presence, preaching Kṛṣṇa consciousness to the English.

"Lord Caitanya informed us that the absolute Supreme Personality of Godhead can descend in transcendental sound vibration, and thus when we chant Hare Kṛṣṇa *mantra* offenselessly we immediately contact Kṛṣṇa and His internal energy. Thus we become immediately purified from all dirty things in our heart."

The guests sat listening politely as Prabhupāda described the soul's travail of transmigrating from body to body and the path of the soul's liberation through chanting Hare Kṛṣṇa, Hare Kṛṣṇa, Kṛṣṇa Kṛṣṇa, Hare Hare/ Hare Rāma, Hare Rāma, Rāma Rāma, Hare Hare. Kṛṣṇa consciousness was "transcendentally colorful and full of transcendental pleasure." Chanting could be done anywhere—on the street, in the park, or at home. Prabhupāda concluded his talk.

"But to assemble and sit together we require a place for congregation. Therefore a temple of the Kṛṣṇa consciousness movement is required to be established in various centers in the world, irrespective of the particular country's culture, philosophy, and religion. Kṛṣṇa consciousness is so universal and perfect that it can appeal to everyone, irrespective of his position. Therefore I fervently appeal to you all present in this meeting to extend your cooperation for successful execution of this great movement. Thanking you once more."

There was a pause, and then Prabhupāda began playing the harmonium and singing Hare Kṛṣṇa. Afterward he again spoke.

"My disciples in London have very eagerly asked me to visit there, and I am also very anxious to see you all. So as soon as there is opportunity, I shall go with my *saṅkīrtana* party, who are now engaged in Los Angeles. And that will be a great pleasure, for you all to meet together. That is all."

Only a few weeks after this meeting the group received their first important publicity: a photo of the six devotees and little Sarasvatī appeared with an article by the famous columnist Atticus in the *Sunday Times.* Guru dāsa was quoted as saying, "Hare Kṛṣṇa is a chant which sets God dancing on your tongue. Try chanting 'Queen Elizabeth' and see the difference." The article described the missionary group from America as "very gentle people, a bit unworldly, but not at all ingenuous." Citing their renunciation of illicit sex and intoxication, the article commented, "Tame you might think, but they look very well on it. And what's likely to earn them a public is their chanting." Within a few days the same article appeared in the *San Francisco Chronicle,* but with a new headline: "Krishna Chants Startle London." Prabhupāda was pleased when he saw the headline. Indeed, his *gṛhastha* disciples had succeeded where his *sannyāsī* Godbrothers had failed. Although several of Prabhupāda's scholarly Godbrothers had lectured around England over the last thirty-five years, only one person, an elderly English lady named Elizabeth Bowtell, had shown interest.

Yamunā had written Prabhupāda to find out if they should visit Mrs. Bowtell (she had received the name Vinoda-vāṇī dāsī), and Prabhupāda had replied, "The history of this Vani dasi is that she is an old lady, and has a house and has hung a sign, Gaudiya Math, but that is all." If they liked, Prabhupāda had said, they could pay her a courtesy call and see if she would let them use her place for *kīrtanas.* One of the men had gone to see her at her home, several hours out of the city. But from behind her closed door she had refused to meet with him unless he brought an introductory letter from the Gaudiya Math in New Delhi. Vinoda-vāṇī dāsī was the fruit of thirty-five years of *sannyāsīs'* preaching in England, whereas in four months Prabhupāda's young American missionaries were "startling London."

After months of living scattered throughout the city, the devotees met a landlord who allowed them to stay together rent free in a vacant warehouse at Covent Garden. The devotees improvised a temporary temple and soon recruited their first three British devotees. The newcomers at once took to the full Kṛṣṇa conscious regimen, including the *dhotī* and shaved head—and loved it.

The devotees, thrilled to see their group expanding and Prabhupāda's potency working, decided to phone Prabhupāda from their landlord's office. The telephone was a conference phone, and Prabhupāda's voice came over the little loudspeaker on the desk. The devotees sat around the desk, listening tensely.

"Prabhupāda," Mukunda said, "we have some new *brahmacārīs* here."

"Oh, are they cooking *capātīs*?" Prabhupāda asked from across the ocean. The devotees laughed uncontrollably, then hushed to hear more.

"No," said Mukunda. "But they will be now." The devotees each told Prabhupāda how they missed him, and he said he missed them too and would come as soon as they could get a place.

After allowing the devotees three months in the warehouse at Covent Garden, the landlord announced that he needed to use the space and the devotees would have to move. The couples moved to three separate locations, and again their strong group spirit dissipated.

Prabhupāda began sending two or three letters a week to the scattered couples, praising them for their sincere determination. The devotees would gather regularly, if only to show one another their latest letters. Prabhupāda wrote to Mukunda of his desire to preach Kṛṣṇa consciousness in the West, specifically London.

> So far as I am concerned, I always wish only to expedite my mission of life to spread Krishna Consciousness in the Western part of the world. I am still firmly convinced that if I can establish this movement through the help of all the boys and girls who have now joined with me, then it will be a great achievement. I am old man, and there has already been warning, but before I leave this body, I wish to see some of you very strong in Krishna Consciousness understanding. I am very glad and proud also that you six boys and girls, although you have not been able to establish a nice center in London, still you have done your best. And the news has reached far away in India that my disciples are doing very nice work in Krishna Consciousness. So that is my pride. I have received a letter from my Godbrother informing me that it has been advertised in India that in Vietnam also somebody is spreading Hare Krishna Movement. So there is no need to be disappointed. You go on with your work as best as Krishna gives you the opportunity, and there is no cause of your anxiety. Everything is going smoothly. But since you are now separated, the strength of your activities appears to be a little disturbed. Now you try to assemble together in the same spirit as you were doing, and in that case, temple or no temple, your movement will go on progressively. We are not much concerned about the temple because temple worship is not primary factor in this age. Primary factor is Sankirtan. But sometimes we want a center where people may gather and see, so a temple is required secondarily. So try your best immediately to live together. I am very much eager to see that you are again living together.

For Śrīla Prabhupāda's disciples, his instruction that they preach in London was much more binding than any other obligation. He was in their hearts, and they thought of him constantly. In carrying out his orders and trying to please him, they were constrained not by force or law but by love. To please the spiritual master is to please the Supreme Personality of Godhead; and for Prabhupāda's sincere disciples, to please him seemed the end in itself.

* * *

Los Angeles
June 23, 1969

After leaving New Vrindaban, Śrīla Prabhupāda visited his center in Los Angeles, where he installed Deities of Rādhā and Kṛṣṇa. Although, as he had told his disciples in London, the "primary factor" was *saṅkīrtana*, Deity worship was also necessary. In his writings Prabhupāda had discussed the need for Deity worship, and he had gradually introduced higher and higher standards of Deity worship in each of his ISKCON centers. Los Angeles, having become the model ISKCON center, was the natural place for him to introduce a more opulent and demanding standard for worshiping Rādhā and Kṛṣṇa.

While more than a hundred devotees and guests sat in the spacious hall, Prabhupāda bathed and dressed the little forms of Rādhā and Kṛṣṇa, then placed Them on the altar. He was inviting Rādhā and Kṛṣṇa to descend, to give his disciples the opportunity to serve Them. He was offering his disciples Rādhā and Kṛṣṇa, with faith that his disciples would not neglect Them. If the devotees somehow lost their enthusiasm, Prabhupāda explained in his lecture, then the worship would become like idol worship.

"If there is no life, then it is idol worship. Where there is life, feeling, then you think, 'Where is Kṛṣṇa? Here is Kṛṣṇa. Oh, I have to serve Him. I have to dress Him. I have to serve Rādhārāṇī. She is here. Oh, I just have to do it very nicely and, as far as possible, decorate Her to the best capacity.' If you think like this, then you are Kṛṣṇa conscious. But if you think that it is a brass-made doll or idol, then Kṛṣṇa will reciprocate with you accordingly. If you think that this is a brass-made idol, then it will remain brass-made idol to you forever. But if you elevate yourself to a higher platform of Kṛṣṇa consciousness, then Kṛṣṇa—this very

Kṛṣṇa—will talk with you. This Kṛṣṇa will talk with you."

With each visit to each center, Prabhupāda gave the devotees more service, deepening their commitment to Kṛṣṇa. All the various services were actually the spiritual master's responsibility, he said, and when a disciple cleaned the temple or performed any service, he did so as the spiritual master's assistant. And any job done improperly was the spiritual master's anxiety. If the devotees whimsically changed the Deity worship or neglected the temple, then Prabhupāda, more than any disciple, would feel distress.

Whenever Prabhupāda saw a disciple eager to take on more of the anxiety of preaching Kṛṣṇa consciousness, he would assign that devotee greater responsibility. Anxiety for serving Kṛṣṇa, Prabhupāda said, was the greatest satisfaction. As Bhaktivinoda Ṭhākura had stated, "The trouble I encounter in Your devotional service I will consider the greatest happiness."

Satisfaction for the devotee, Prabhupāda explained, lay in pleasing the previous spiritual masters, and that was best accomplished by preaching to the fallen souls. To the degree that the devotees carried out that order, they would satisfy their spiritual master and subsequently feel satisfaction themselves. Prabhupāda gave the example of Kṛṣṇa and the *gopīs*. When the *gopīs* pleased Kṛṣṇa in the *rāsa* dance, Kṛṣṇa smiled, and when the *gopīs* saw Kṛṣṇa's smile their happiness and beauty increased a million times. When Kṛṣṇa saw the newly increased beauty of the *gopīs* He became more pleased, and thus the happiness and beauty of the *gopīs* increased even more. This loving competition increased on and on unlimitedly.

Even in dealings between spiritual master and disciple a sense of loving competition prevailed, each wanting to serve the other, neither seeking service for himself. Prabhupāda was increasing the duties and responsibilities in each of his ISKCON centers, and sincere disciples were coming forward to accept those responsibilities; thus everyone was feeling satisfaction. This was pure devotional service—to be free from all material desires and to serve Kṛṣṇa as directed by the spiritual master and the scriptures.

When Prabhupāda said that his disciples would become happy by serving Kṛṣṇa, he spoke from his own deep realization of that ecstasy. Whenever he installed a Deity in one of the temples, his ecstasy was greater than that of any of his disciples. At the Ratha-yātrā festivals in Golden Gate Park or any public preaching function, he was the most enlivened. He, more than any of his disciples, wanted the public to come and chant and dance in the temple and see the Deity of Kṛṣṇa, and when they did, he was the most pleased. And if a disciple fell away, Prabhupāda was the most displeased.

Nor was Prabhupāda aloof from the details of temple management: the cost of things, how the devotees were being received in public, how each disciple was advancing. Although his disciples saw him as the most exalted Vaiṣṇava and intimate associate of Lord Kṛṣṇa, they knew he was always available to guide them in their services. He was their leader, but he was with them. He was far above them, but he remained close to them. Only rarely did he leave them behind—as at the Los Angeles Deity installation, when he began to cry, speaking directly to Kṛṣṇa: "Kṛṣṇa, I am most rotten and fallen, but I have brought this thing for You. Please take it." Except for such rare moments, Prabhupāda's disciples saw him preaching and serving along with them.

* * *

San Francisco
July 25, 1969

The day before the Ratha-yātrā festival, Prabhupāda arrived at the San Francisco airport, where a crowd of fifty chanting devotees greeted him. Reporters stepped forward with what to them was an important, relevant question: "Swami, what is your opinion on the recent manned U.S. moon landing?"

"Shall I flatter you or tell the truth?" Prabhupāda asked.

The truth, they said.

"It is a waste of time because it does not benefit you if you cannot live there. The time could have been better spent in Kṛṣṇa consciousness. We must go beyond this universe to the spiritual sky, which is eternal, beyond birth, death, old age, and disease." The *San Francisco Chronicle* printed a picture and story: "Ecstasy in Concourse B."

On the day of the Ratha-yātrā parade, a hundred devotees and a crowd of one thousand gathered on Haight Street before the tall cart. The deities of Jagannātha, Subhadrā, and Balarāma, from their elevated platform within the cart, smiled down upon the crowd. A group of devotee-musicians seated themselves within the cart, made last-minute checks of their loudspeaker system, and began *kīrtana.* In the center of the cart, just beneath the deity platform, a red upholstered *vyāsāsana* awaited Prabhupāda's arrival.

As Prabhupāda's car approached he could hear the cries of the devotees, and as he stepped from the car he saw them all bow down in obeisances. Folding his hands and smiling, he acknowledged his enthusiastic disciples, and he looked around with pleasure at the large crowd that had already gathered. Turning toward the cart, he beheld the deities on their throne, the same deities who had inaugurated Ratha-yātrā in America two years before. They were beautifully dressed and garlanded, and multicolored pennants and thick garlands of carnations decorated their cart. Ratha-yātrā was becoming more wonderful each year. Prabhupāda bowed down before Jagannātha, Subhadrā, and Balarāma, and his disciples all bowed with him.

As Prabhupāda took his seat on the cart the *kīrtana* began again, and the cart, pulled with two long ropes by dozens of men and women, slowly began to move forward. Buckets of burning frankincense poured aromatic clouds from the deities' platform above Prabhupāda's head, as slowly the cart moved along the road to the park.

"How many people are behind us?" Prabhupāda asked, turning to Tamāla Kṛṣṇa, who rode beside him on the cart and had been leading the *kīrtana.* Tamāla Kṛṣṇa climbed back and surveyed the crowd as far as he could see.

"Five thousand!"

"Sing 'Jaya Jagannātha,' " Prabhupāda said, and Tamāla Kṛṣṇa then changed the chant from Hare Kṛṣṇa to "Jaya Jagannātha! Jaya Jagannātha!"

Throughout the parade Prabhupāda sat serenely watching, his right hand in his bead bag. The large crowd consisted mostly of young hippies but also included businessmen dressed in suits and ties, elderly persons with their grandchildren and families, and a few stray dogs. A mixed Sunday crowd.

Suddenly devotees in front began shouting, "Stop the cart! Stop the cart!" Ahead, the low arch of a park bridge spanned the roadway. The devotees managed to stop the 35-foot-high cart just before it reached the bridge. Although the parade appeared to have reached an unforeseen impasse, the chanting continued unabated. The previous year the procession had taken this same route—with a smaller cart—and even then Śyāmasundara had had to climb up and saw off the spire. This year, however, Nara-Nārāyaṇa had devised a collapsible dome with a crank to lower the canopy and superstructure. When Prabhupāda had heard of these plans, he had asked, "Are you sure you want to depend on mechanical means? It could be a disaster." Now the time to lower the canopy had come, and the crank wouldn't work.

With the cart stopped before the bridge, the chanters gathered in greater numbers, facing Prabhupāda and Lord Jagannātha. Under the bridge at least a thousand voices sang together, creating an incredible echo. Then Prabhupāda stood, raised his arms to the crowd, and began dancing.

Bhavānanda: *Everyone went wild. The sound was so uproarious you were deafened under that bridge. Prabhupāda was dancing, jumping on the cart.*

Nara-Nārāyaṇa: *He was dancing, and as he danced his feet crushed the flowers. His garland broke and flowers began cascading everywhere as he danced up and down. He was leaping very deliberately, almost like slow motion.*

Tamāla Kṛṣṇa: *Prabhupāda was jumping up and down, and the people went crazy seeing him in complete ecstasy. He kept jumping and slowly turned around until he was face to face with Lord Jagannātha.*

Prabhupāda sat down and still the car didn't go, and the people were roaring.

"What do they want?" Prabhupāda asked Tamāla Kṛṣṇa.

"I think they want to see you dance again, Śrīla Prabhupāda," Tamāla Kṛṣṇa replied.

"Do you think so?"

"Yes." He then got up and started dancing again. The white wool cap pushed to the back of his head, his arms extended, with the right hand still clutching the *japa* bead bag, his right forefinger extended, and long robes flowing.

The ecstatic chanting and dancing continued. After about fifteen minutes, Nara-Nārāyaṇa finally got the crank to work, and down came the canopy. Again the cart moved forward, under the bridge and on through the park. The crowd had grown now to ten thousand. This was much bigger than any Kṛṣṇa conscious festival ever held before.

Bhavānanda: *Many of these people who attended Ratha-yātrā were intoxicated. We were not intoxicated, of course, but we were higher than they. That we could understand. Everyone was smiling, everyone was laughing, everyone was in ecstasy, everyone was dancing, everyone was chanting. And we were doing it more than anyone. We were doing more chanting, more laughing and smiling, and feeling more freedom. We were free to have a shaved head, free to wear a* dhotī, *free to blow a conchshell, free to spin around on the street and jump up. Even if you were a hippie you couldn't be more far out than the* ratha *cart and Jagannātha, because no one looks more far out than Him. The hippies had come dressed up in outfits with big feathers in their hair and everything, but they were dim compared to Jagannātha.*

The parade route ended at an oceanside dance hall, The Family Dog Auditorium, where the devotees had prepared ten thousand feast plates of *prasādam*—fruit salad, apple chutney, *halavā*, and watermelon slices. Although the cart had stopped, the chanting continued, as Prabhupāda led the crowd inside the auditorium to a temporary stage and altar the devotees had erected among the bizarre trappings of the dance hall. A giant silk screen of Lord Caitanya covered the hall's Tibetan *maṇḍala*, and pictures of Lord Viṣṇu and Śrīla Bhaktisiddhānta Sarasvatī were on the stage. The Jagannātha deities now looked down from their high platform above Prabhupāda's seat, and a garlanded statue of Lord Kṛṣṇa stood on a marble pillar.

Prabhupāda began speaking, and the crowd quieted. He quoted a song by Narottama dāsa Ṭhākura: "My dear Lord Caitanya, please be merciful upon me. I do not find anyone as merciful as You." Drawing the audience's attention to the large silkscreen of Lord Caitanya, Prabhupāda described the Lord's merciful distribution of the holy name of God. Lord Caitanya, he said, was teaching the same thing Lord Kṛṣṇa had taught in *Bhagavad-gītā:* "My dear sons, do not suffer in this abominable condition of material existence. Come back to Me. Come back to home. Enjoy eternal, blissful life, a life of knowledge."

Prabhupāda explained the simplicity of Kṛṣṇa consciousness:

"Lord Caitanya appeared five hundred years ago to establish the direct principles of *Bhagavad-gītā*. He showed that even if you do not understand the process of religion, then simply chant Hare Kṛṣṇa, Hare Kṛṣṇa, Kṛṣṇa Kṛṣṇa, Hare Hare/ Hare Rāma, Hare Rāma, Rāma Rāma, Hare Hare. The results are practical. For example, when we were chanting Hare

Kṛṣṇa all the members who are assembled here were joining in, but now when I am talking about philosophy some are leaving. It is very practical. You can see. The Hare Kṛṣṇa *mantra* is so enchanting that anyone in any condition can take part. And if he continues to chant, gradually he will develop his dormant love of God. It is very simple.

"We are requesting everyone to chant the Hare Kṛṣṇa *mantra* and take *prasādam*. When you are tired of chanting, the *prasādam* is ready; you can immediately take *prasādam*. And if you dance, then all bodily exercise is Kṛṣṇa-ized. And all of the attempts of the *yoga* processes are attained by this simple process.

"So chant, dance, take *prasādam*. Even if you do not at first hear this philosophy, it will act, and you will be elevated to the highest platform of perfection."

* * *

In the middle of a winter of struggle came a fortunate break for the London devotees: a meeting with George Harrison of the Beatles. For a long time the devotees had been thinking of ways to get the Beatles to chant Hare Kṛṣṇa. To the Beatles' Apple Records Studio they had once sent an apple pie with *Hare Krishna* lettered on it. Another time they had sent a wind-up walking apple with the Hare Kṛṣṇa *mantra* printed on it. They had even sent a tape of one of their *kīrtanas* and had received a standard rejection letter from Apple Records. So it seemed to be Kṛṣṇa's special arrangement when Śyāmasundara suddenly met one of the most sought-after celebrities in the world, George Harrison.

In a crowded room at Apple Records, Śyāmasundara, shaven-headed and wearing robes, sat hoping for a chance to have a few words with someone connected with the Beatles. Then George came down the stairs from a conference. As he entered the room, he saw Śyāmasundara. Walking over and sitting down beside Śyāmasundara, he asked, "Where have you been? I've been trying to meet the Hare Kṛṣṇa people for the last couple of years." Śyāmasundara and George talked together for an hour, while everyone else hovered around. "I've really been trying to meet you people," George said. "Why don't you come to my place tomorrow?"

The next day Śyāmasundara went to George's for lunch, where he met the other Beatles: Ringo Starr, John Lennon, and Paul McCartney. They all had questions, but George was especially interested.

George: *I had a copy of the Hare Kṛṣṇa album with Śrīla Prabhupāda singing Hare Kṛṣṇa with the devotees. I'd had the record at least two years. But I got it the week it was pressed. I was open to it. You attract those things. So I used to play that a lot of the time. I was chanting the Hare Kṛṣṇa* mantra *long before I met Śyāmasundara, Guru dāsa, and Mukunda. I was just pleased to hear the Hare Kṛṣṇa* mantra *and have a copy of the record.*

And I knew about Prabhupāda because I had read all the liner notes on that album. Having been to India I could tell where the devotees were all coming from, with the style of dress and shaved heads. I had seen them on the streets of Los Angeles and New York. Having read so many books and looking for yogīs, *my concept of the devotees wasn't like the other people, who think the devotees have all escaped from a lunatic asylum in their pajamas. No, I was aware of the thing and that it was a pretty heavy one, much more austerities than other groups—like no coffee, chocolate, or tea.*

Śyāmasundara continued to see George regularly, and they soon became friends. George, who had been practicing a *mantra* given him by Maharishi Mahesh Yogi, began to hear for the first time about *bhakti-yoga* and the Vedic philosophy. He talked openly to Śyāmasundara, Guru dāsa, and Mukunda of his spiritual quest and his realizations of *karma.*

George: *A* yogī *I met in India said, "You are really lucky. You have youth, fame, fortune, health, but at the same time that's not enough for you. You want to know about something else." Most people don't even get to the point where they realize there's something beyond that wall. They are just trying to get up on top of that wall, to be able to eat and have a nice house and be comfortable and all that. But I was fortunate enough to get all that in time to realize there's something else to life, whereas most people get worn out just trying to attain material things.*

After a visit to Haight-Ashbury in 1967 George had begun to feel guilty for his role in promulgating the LSD culture. He had had the impression that the hippies of Haight-Ashbury were creative craftsmen, but when he saw them drugged, dirty, and hopeless—"a West Coast extension of the Bowery"—he felt partly responsible. He decided to use his influential position by writing and singing songs about something more than psychedelics and sex. He was also feeling an increasing interest in Indian spirituality, due, he felt, to *karma* from his previous lives.

George: *I feel at home with Kṛṣṇa. I think that's something that has been there from a previous birth. So it was like the door was opening to me at that time, but it was also like a jigsaw puzzle and I needed all these little pieces to make a complete picture. And that is what has been happening by the devotees and Swami Bhaktivedanta coming along, or some devotee giving me a book or my hearing that album. It's all been slowly fitting together.*

And these are some of the reasons why I responded to Śyāmasundara and Guru dāsa when they first came to London. Let's face it, if I'm going to have to stand up and be counted, then I'll be with these guys rather than with those over there. It's like that. I'll be with the devotees rather than with the straight people who are the so-called saints.

George offered to help the devotees get a building in London, and he and Śyāmasundara spoke of making a Hare Kṛṣṇa record. But Śyāmasundara never pressed him.

George was the glamorous superstar, the "quiet, serious Beatle," the fabulous guitarist and singer who had access to all the greats, to presidents and queens, wherever he went. And Śyāmasundara had a glamor of his own. He was tall, six feet two, and although shaven-headed, strikingly handsome. And he was a Vaiṣṇava, fully dedicated to the Indian spirituality George was so fond of.

When Prabhupāda heard about George, he took seriously the possibility that George might fully take up Kṛṣṇa consciousness. Carrying this to its logical conclusion, Prabhupāda envisioned a world revolution in consciousness—spearheaded by the Kṛṣṇa conscious Beatles.

> It is understood from your letter that Mr. George Harrison has a little sympathy for our movement, and if Krishna is actually satisfied on him surely he will be able to join with us in pushing on the Samkirtan movement throughout the world. Somehow or other the Beatles have become the cynosure of the neighboring European countries and America also. He is attracted by our Samkirtan Party and if Mr. George Harrison takes the leading part in organizing a huge Samkirtan Party consisting of the Beatles and our ISKCON boys, surely we shall change the face of the world so much politically harassed by the maneuvers of the politicians.

For the London devotees, George's friendship heightened the excitement of Prabhupāda's coming to London. Now that a world-famous personality was waiting to meet Prabhupāda, they felt perhaps they had another way to please him and to make preaching in London a success.

George, by his association with Kṛṣṇa consciousness and by dint of his own spiritual evolution, began to express his devotion to Lord Kṛṣṇa in his songs. Reading Prabhupāda's *Bhagavad-gītā As It Is*, he could appreciate the superiority of the personal conception of God over the impersonal. Guru dāsa showed George the verse in the *Gītā* where Kṛṣṇa says that He is the basis of the impersonal Brahman. George liked the concepts of Kṛṣṇa consciousness, but he was wary of showing exclusive devotion to Prabhupāda and Kṛṣṇa. The devotees, therefore, dealt with him accordingly, so as not to disturb him.

On January 11 Śrīla Prabhupāda wrote another letter to the devotees in London, expressing more ideas of how George could best serve Kṛṣṇa.

> I am so glad that Mr. Harrison is composing songs like "Lord whom we so long ignored." He is very thoughtful. When we actually meet, I shall be able to give him thoughts about separation from Krishna, and they will be able to compose very attractive songs for public reception. The public is in need of such songs, and if they are administered through nice agents like the Beatles, it will surely be a great success.

Prabhupāda cautioned the devotees not to simply depend on George for help but to try to find a building themselves and rent it. George did want to help, however, and again he suggested the devotees make a record on the Apple label. An old favorite idea of the London devotees had been to get the Beatles to make a record chanting Hare Kṛṣṇa; if the Beatles did it, the *mantra* would certainly become world famous. George liked the idea, but he preferred that the devotees sing it and he produce it on the Apple label. "You guys make the money, rather than we get it," he said. "Let's make a record."

So the devotees went over to George's house for a chanting session. George dubbed in his guitar, and a few weeks later the devotees returned and heard their tape. George was ready to try a session at the studio, so the devotees agreed to meet him and his musician friend Billy Preston at Trident Studios on St. Anne's Alley. They recorded for a few hours; the tape sounded good. George and Śyāmasundara agreed on a date for the actual recording.

On the day of the recording about a dozen devotees, including some newly recruited Britishers, assembled at E.M.I. recording studios on Abbey Road. When the first group of devotees arrived in George's Mercedes, a crowd of teenagers began singing Hare Kṛṣṇa to the tune popularized by the rock musical *Hair*. While Yamunā applied Vaiṣṇava *tilaka* to the foreheads of the recording technicians, Mālatī began unpacking the picnic baskets of *prasādam* she had brought, and some of the other devotees put up pictures of Kṛṣṇa and lit incense. The studio was Kṛṣṇa-ized.

With Paul McCartney and his wife, Linda, operating the control console, the recording session began. Everyone worked quickly, making Side One of the 45 rpm record in about an hour. George played organ, and Mukunda played *mṛdaṅga*. Yamunā sang the lead with Śyāmasundara backing her, and the other voices blended in a chorus. And to make it come out exactly right, everyone concentrated on Prabhupāda and prayed for spiritual strength.

On the fourth take, everything went smoothly, with Mālatī spontaneously hitting a brass gong at the end. Then they recorded the flip side of the record: prayers to Śrīla Prabhupāda, Lord Caitanya and His associates, and the six Gosvāmīs. Afterward, George dubbed in the bass guitar and other voices. The devotees, engineers—everyone—felt good about it. "This is going to be big," George promised.

As the record went into production the devotees returned to their regular work, still living separately. Prabhupāda set the time of his arrival for early September. He would go to Hamburg and then come to London, he said—even if there was no temple. Miraculously, only two months before Prabhupāda's arrival, things began to come together.

Guru dāsa met a real estate agent with a building on Bury Place, near the British Museum; the devotees could move in immediately. An ideal location, forty-one pounds a week, and immediate occupancy—it was wonderful. Mukunda wrote Prabhupāda asking him for money for the down payment. Prabhupāda agreed. Śyāmasundara got a letter from George on Apple Corporation Ltd. stationery stating that Apple would guarantee payments if the devotees defaulted. Within a week, the devotees had a five-story building in central London.

But when the devotees went to live at their new center on Bury Place, city officials said they did not have the proper housing permits. The red tape could take weeks, even months. Again the devotees were without a place to live and worship together. Śyāmasundara, however, on faith that everything would work out, began constructing a temple room of California redwood in the building.

John Lennon then suggested to Śyāmasundara that the devotees come and live with him at Tittenhurst, a large estate he had recently purchased near Ascot. He needed some renovation done, and if the devotees would help he would give them a place to live. "Can our *guru* also stay there?" Śyāmasundara asked. John agreed, and the devotees moved into the former servants' quarters at John's estate.

Only a few weeks before Prabhupāda's arrival the record, "Hare Krishna Mantra," was released. Apple Records staged a promotion and brought press reporters and photographers in a multicolored bus to a blue and white pavilion where the devotees had gathered with George.

The first day the record sold seventy thousand copies. Within a few weeks the devotees appeared on the popular TV show *Top of the Pops,* singing "their song."

John Lennon's estate, formerly owned by the Cadbury family, consisted of seventy-six acres of lawn and forest, with a large manor and many smaller buildings. John and his wife, Yoko, lived in the manor. The servants' quarters, where Prabhupāda and the devotees were to live, were four separate apartments in a single narrow building near the manor. About fifteen devotees moved in, reserving one apartment for Prabhupāda and his servant.

John wanted the devotees to tear out the hardwood walls and floors in the main house and replace them with new walls and black and white marble tile floors. While this renovation was beginning, Īśāna, who had recently arrived from Canada, began with a few helpers to convert the old music recital hall into a temple, complete with *vyāsāsana* for Śrīla Prabhupāda. The devotees worked day and night on Prabhupāda's quarters, the temple room, and Prabhupāda's *vyāsāsana.* With such energy did they work that John and Yoko could see that the devotees were obviously in love with their spiritual master. When the devotees were making a tape to send to Prabhupāda in Germany, Īśāna asked John if he had anything he wanted to say to their *guru.* John smiled and said he would like to know Prabhupāda's secret that made his followers so devoted.

The stage was set. The time had come for the principal character to enter. Lord Kṛṣṇa's pure devotee was at last coming to England. For the six devotees who had pioneered Kṛṣṇa consciousness in London, it had been a long struggle. But now it seemed that all their once-impossible dreams were coming true. They had found a place for Prabhupāda to live in, and they had obtained a temple in the center of London. This was Kṛṣṇa's blessing.

CHAPTER TWO

London: A Dream Fulfilled

London
September 11, 1969

With the cooperation of Apple Records and Lufthansa German Airlines, the devotees arranged a reception for Prabhupāda at London's Heathrow Airport. As soon as Prabhupāda descended the stairs of the airplane, he was escorted to a car and driven to a V.I.P. lounge, bypassing the formalities of immigration and customs. As Prabhupāda stepped from the car, the devotees ran out of the terminal and offered obeisances on the wet pavement, while Śrīla Prabhupāda looked down on them, smiling. The devotees rose, brushing wet macadam from their *dhotīs* and *sārīs*, and joyfully surrounded Prabhupāda as he entered the lounge.

Inside the terminal Prabhupāda confronted a mass of reporters and cameramen and several dozen friends of the devotees. A clean cloth covered one of the lounge sofas, and vases with yellow gladioluses sat on either side. Prabhupāda walked over to the sofa and sat down, and Śyāmasundara garlanded him with red and white carnations. Prabhupāda began leading *kīrtana.*

The devotees were oblivious to all but Prabhupāda, and the reporters resigned themselves to simply standing and observing while the devotees sang and danced ecstatically. The eager devotees were unabashed during the *kīrtana*, and their shouts of "Haribol!" and "Jaya Prabhupāda!" as well as blasts from a conchshell, punctuated the regular chanting of Hare Kṛṣṇa.

After the *kīrtana* the reporters remained at a distance as Prabhupāda spoke affectionately to almost each devotee seated before him. "Where is Jānakī?" he asked. "Oh, yes, how are you? Vibhāvatī, how is your daughter? Actually you are all my fathers and mothers. You are taking such care . . ."

For the devotees, only they and Prabhupāda were present in the lounge, and they strained to catch everything he did or said. They couldn't have cared less about any outsider's reaction. Finally, Mukunda invited the reporters to come forward: "If any of you gentlemen have any questions, you can ask them of Prabhupāda."

The reporters, moving in: "What do you think of this reception?"

Prabhupāda: "I am not very much fond of reception. I want to know how people give reception to this movement. That is my concern."

Devotees in unison: "Haribol!"

Reporter: "Is this a very special welcome for you, or is this a performance you go through each day?"

Prabhupāda: "No, wherever I go, I have got my disciples. In Western countries I have got now about twenty centers, especially in America. So the American boys are very enthusiastic. I think in Los Angeles and San Francisco I got a very great reception. In the Ratha-yātrā festival about ten thousand boys and girls followed me for seven miles."

Devotees: "Haribol!"

Sun reporter: "What do you try to teach, sir?"

Prabhupāda: "I am trying to teach what you have forgotten."

Devotees (laughing): "Haribol! Hare Kṛṣṇa!"

Sun reporter: "Which is what?"

Prabhupāda: "That is God. Some of you are saying there is no God. Some of you are saying God is dead. And some of you are saying God is impersonal or void. These are all nonsense. I want to teach all the nonsense people that there is God. That is my mission. Any nonsense can come to me—I shall prove that there is God. That is my Kṛṣṇa consciousness movement. It is a challenge to the atheistic people: This is God. As we are sitting here face to face, you can see God face to face, if you are sincere and if you are serious. That is possible. Unfortunately, you are trying to forget God. Therefore you are embracing so many miseries of life. So I am simply preaching that you become Kṛṣṇa conscious and be happy. Don't be swayed by these nonsense waves of *māyā*, or illusion."

When a reporter asked if the singing was "essential to the sustenance of your faith," Prabhupāda answered at length, describing the cleansing effect of chanting Hare Kṛṣṇa. He quoted *Śrīmad-Bhāgavatam's* declaration that anyone without God consciousness has no good qualities. "Test any of our students," Prabhupāda said, "—how they are good, how they are advanced. Test it. Bring anyone in the world and compare with any one of our boys. You will find how much difference there is in their character and their feeling and their consciousness. If you want a peaceful society, then you must make people God conscious, Kṛṣṇa conscious. Everything will be automatically resolved. Otherwise your so-called United Nations will not help."

The reporters asked about Billy Graham, the moon landing, the war in Ireland, and the whereabouts of Prabhupāda's wife and children. They asked him to turn his head toward them, and they clicked away with their cameras. They thanked him, and the reception dispersed.

Prabhupāda went from the building to the gleaming white Rolls Royce awaiting him outside, courtesy of John Lennon. Prabhupāda entered the back seat and sat crosslegged. The limousine was equipped with darkened windows and a lavish interior, including a television. The devotees had become so confused in their excitement that none of them had thought to join Prabhupāda, and the chauffeur whisked him away to Tittenhurst. Prabhupāda sat silently, except for his occasionally audible chanting, as the chauffeur headed through the winding roads leading away from the airport.

He was in England. His father, Gour Mohan, had never wanted him to come to England. Once an uncle had told Gour Mohan that his son should go to England to become a barrister. But Gour Mohan had said no; if his son went there the meat-eaters, drinkers, and sex-mongers might influence him. But now, seventy years later, Prabhupāda had indeed come to London—not to be influenced by the Englishmen but to influence them. He had come to teach them what they had forgotten.

And he was off to a good start, under Kṛṣṇa's special care. When he had had to live alone in New York City without any money, that had been Kṛṣṇa's mercy. And now he was entering England in a chauffeured limousine, also Kṛṣṇa's mercy. Accepting the ride as part of Kṛṣṇa's plan, Prabhupāda remained deeply fixed in his purpose of carrying out the order of his spiritual master, whatever circumstances awaited.

As they turned onto Route 4, proceeding toward Slough, Prabhupāda saw factories and warehouses and then the flat countryside, with orchards, fields, and grazing horses. The grey, chilly weather hinted of winter ahead.

After about twenty minutes Prabhupāda reached the wealthy neighborhood of Ascot and soon, appearing on the left, the high redwood fence surrounding the Lennon estate.

Prabhupāda had arrived before his disciples. But those who had remained at the manor excitedly received him and showed him to his room on the second floor of the servants' quarters. The small room was chilly and damp, with a low table for a desk and wall-to-wall carpeting made from pieces of rug taken from the other rooms. The adjoining room was bare and even smaller. Prabhupāda sat down at his low desk. "Where is everyone?" he asked. As he leaned back and gazed out the window he saw rain just beginning to fall.

When George, John, and Yoko dropped by after Prabhupāda's lunch, Śyāmasundara invited them to come up and meet Prabhupāda. George turned to John and asked, "Do you want to go up?" The bearded, bespectacled master of Tittenhurst, hair down to his shoulders, assented. Yoko also was curious. So up they all went to Prabhupāda's little room.

Smiling graciously from behind his desk, Prabhupāda asked his guests to enter and be seated. Here were two of the most famous people in England, and Kṛṣṇa wanted him to speak to them. Prabhupāda removed his garland and handed it to Śyāmasundara, indicating that he should put it around George's neck.

"Thank you," said George. "Hare Kṛṣṇa."

Prabhupāda smiled. "This is Kṛṣṇa's blessing."

"Hare Kṛṣṇa," George replied again.

"Yes," Prabhupāda said, "there is a verse in *Bhagavad-gītā: yad yad ācarati śreṣṭhas tat tad evetaro janaḥ/ sa yat pramāṇaṁ kurute lokas tad anuvartate.* The idea is that anything which is accepted by the leading persons, ordinary persons follow them. *Yad yad ācarati śreṣṭhaḥ. Śreṣṭhaḥ* means 'leading persons.' *Ācarati* means 'act.' Whatever leading persons act, people in general follow them. If the leading person says it is nice, then it is all right—the others also accept it. So by the grace of God, Kṛṣṇa, you are leaders. Thousands of young men follow you. They like you. So if you give them something actually nice, the face of the world will change."

Although George and John were about the same age as most of Prabhupāda's disciples, Prabhupāda considered them *śreṣṭhas*, respected leaders. "You are also anxious to bring some peace in the world," Prabhupāda continued. "I have read sometimes your statement. You are anxious also. Everyone is. Every saintly person should be anxious to bring in peace in the world. But we must know the process." He explained the "peace formula" according to *Bhagavad-gītā:* only those who recognize the Supreme Personality of Godhead as the proprietor of everything, the object of all sacrifices, and the friend of everyone can find peace.

Prabhupāda then told the two Beatles even more directly what he had already hinted at: they should learn Kṛṣṇa consciousness and help teach it to the world. "I request you to at least understand this philosophy to your best knowledge," he said. "If you think it is nice, pick it up. You are also willing to give something to the world. So try this. You have read our books, this *Bhagavad-gītā As It Is*?"

John: "I've read bits of the *Bhagavad-gītā*. I don't know which version it was. There's so many different translations."

Prabhupāda: "There are different translations. Therefore I have given this edition, *Bhagavad-gītā As It Is*."

Prabhupāda explained that the material world is a place of misery. Nature is cruel. In America President Kennedy was thought to be the most fortunate, happy man, honored throughout the world. "But within a second"—Prabhupāda loudly snapped his fingers—"he was finished. Temporary. Now what is his position? Where is he? If life is eternal, if the living entity is eternal, where he has gone? What he is doing? Is he happy, or is he distressed? He is born in America, or China? Nobody can say. But it is a fact that, as living entity, he is eternal. He is existing."

Prabhupāda explained the transmigration of the soul. Then again he requested, "Try to understand it, and if it is nice you take it up. You are after something very nice. Is my proposal unreasonable?" The two Beatles glanced at one another but didn't answer. Prabhupāda gave a soft, amused laugh. "You are all intelligent boys. Try to understand it."

Prabhupāda spoke of the importance of music in the *Vedas*. "The *Sāma Veda*," he said, " is *full* of music. Followers of the *Sāma Veda* are always in music. Through musical vibration they are approaching the Supreme." He then sang slowly three verses from *Śrīmad-Bhāgavatam:*

matir na kṛṣṇe parataḥ svato vā
mitho 'bhipadyeta gṛha-vratānām
adānta-gobhir viśatāṁ tamisraṁ
punaḥ punaś carvita-carvaṇānām

na te viduḥ svārtha-gatiṁ hi viṣṇuṁ
durāśayā ye bahir-artha-māninaḥ
andhā yathāndhair upanīyamānās
te 'pīśa-tantryām uru-dāmni baddhāḥ

naiṣāṁ matis tāvad urukramāṅgrhiṁ
spṛśaty anarthāpagamo yad-arthaḥ
mahīyasāṁ pāda-rajo-'bhiṣekaṁ
*niṣkiñcanānāṁ na vṛṇīta yāvat**

Then Prabhupāda asked his guests what philosophy they were following.

"Following?" John asked.

"We don't follow anything," Yoko said. "We are just living."

"We've done meditation," said George. "Or I do my meditation, *mantra* meditation."

They began to ask questions—the same questions Prabhupāda had heard so many times before. After hearing Prabhupāda's explanation of Brahman, the all-pervading spiritual energy of the Supreme Personality of Godhead, Yoko doubted whether Brahman could remain pure and not deteriorate in time. Prabhupāda advised that she would have to become a serious student before she could actually understand spiritual philosophy.

John and Yoko, being devoted eclectics, had difficulty accepting Prabhupāda's concept of Vedic authority.

---

* "Because of their uncontrolled senses, persons too addicted to materialistic life make progress toward hellish conditions and repeatedly chew that which has already been chewed. Their inclinations toward Kṛṣṇa are never aroused, either by the instructions of others, by their own efforts, or by a combination of both.

"Persons who are strongly entrapped by the consciousness of enjoying material life, and who have therefore accepted as their leader or *guru* a similar blind man attached to external sense objects, cannot understand that the goal of life is to return home, back to Godhead, and engage in the service of Lord Viṣṇu. As blind men guided by another blind man miss the right path and fall into a ditch, materially attached men led by another materially attached man are bound by the ropes of fruitive labor, which are made of very strong cords, and they continue again and again in materialistic life, suffering the threefold miseries.

"Unless they smear upon their bodies the dust of the lotus feet of a Vaiṣṇava completely freed from material contamination, persons very much inclined toward materialistic life cannot be attached to the lotus feet of the Lord, who is glorified for His uncommon activities. Only by becoming Kṛṣṇa conscious and taking shelter at the lotus feet of the Lord in this way can one be freed from material contamination." (*Śrīmad-Bhāgavatam*, 7.5.30-32)

John: "We still have to keep sifting through, like through sand, to see who's got the best."

Prabhupāda: "No. One thing you try to understand. Why these people—if Kṛṣṇa is not the supreme authority—why they are taking Kṛṣṇa's book and translating? Why don't you try to understand?"

George: "I'm not saying Kṛṣṇa isn't the Supreme. I believe that. There is a misunderstanding about the translation of the Sanskrit *Gītā* into English. And I was saying that there are many versions, and I think we thought you were trying to say your version, your translation, was the authority and that the other translations were not. But we didn't really have misunderstanding as to the identity of Kṛṣṇa."

Prabhupāda: "That's all right. If you believe Kṛṣṇa is the Supreme Lord, if that is your version, then you have to see who is most addicted to Kṛṣṇa. These people are twenty-four hours chanting *Kṛṣṇa.* And another person, who has not a single word *Kṛṣṇa*—how can he become a devotee of Kṛṣṇa? How can he, who does not utter even the name of Kṛṣṇa, become a representative of Kṛṣṇa? If Kṛṣṇa is authority—and that is accepted—therefore those who are directly addicted to Kṛṣṇa, they are authorities."

After more than an hour of conversation, Prabhupāda distributed some *prasādam* to John, George, Yoko, and the few disciples in his room. If these *śreṣṭhas* were to take up Kṛṣṇa consciousness, that would be good for them and many others also. He had done his duty and provided them the opportunity. It was Kṛṣṇa's message, and to accept it or not was now up to them.

John said he had something to do, and he excused himself. As everyone was leaving, Yoko, walking down the stairs, turned to John and said, "Look at how simply he's living. Could you live like that?"

In the evening Prabhupāda sat with the three couples—Śyāmasundara and Mālatī, Guru dāsa and Yamunā, and Mukunda and Jānakī. After a year's separation they were happily with Prabhupāda, and he was happy to be with them. The love they shared and their mutual satisfaction at being together was based on a unifying desire to establish Lord Caitanya's *saṅkīrtana* movement in this important city. Now that Prabhupāda had come to London, work would not slacken; it would increase under his expert guidance. Prabhupāda could daily instruct the men on organizing more London preaching, and they could report to him as necessary.

The women could also directly serve him, cleaning his quarters, washing and ironing his laundry, and cooking his meals.

"No one can afford a house like this in England anymore," Prabhupāda said. "England has gone down. Now these young boys own a place like this. And we are here."

"Prabhupāda," Śyāmasundara spoke up, "our record sold fifty thousand copies yesterday."

"Oh!" Prabhupāda's eyes widened. "Very big business!"

Prabhupāda said that their money and energy should go toward opening the temple in the city. Now they were living comfortably on this aristocratic estate in the suburbs, and certainly they should try to involve these important celebrities in Kṛṣṇa consciousness as far as possible. But the main business should be to open a temple in the city. Bhaktisiddhānta Sarasvatī had preferred to establish temples in the cities, where the people were. Of course, if John could give this place to Kṛṣṇa and if the devotees could maintain cows and cultivate the land, as in New Vrindaban, then that would be a different matter. They would have to see what Kṛṣṇa desired.

Prabhupāda was sorry that some of his disciples were obliged to work full time renovating the estate in exchange for their stay. *Brāhmaṇas* and Vaiṣṇavas, he said, had the serious work of cultivating spiritual knowledge and teaching it to others, and they deserved the respect and support of the rest of society. The arrangement at Tittenhurst seemed more business than charity. But they should tolerate it as a temporary situation.

Prabhupāda talked with Śyāmasundara, Mukunda, and Guru dāsa about their struggle to get housing permits and renovate the temple downtown. Śyāmasundara had been right, Prabhupāda said, to begin renovating the temple; Kṛṣṇa would protect their investment. When Prabhupāda learned they had secured a series of public lectures that would commit him to three months in London, he smiled. He would be glad to stay and preach in England, he said, for as long as it took to open the London center.

Prabhupāda commended his six London pioneers on succeeding where his *sannyāsī* Godbrothers had failed. He told them that because they had chanted Hare Kṛṣṇa with faith, they had succeeded. They were not great scholars or renunciants, yet they had faith in the holy name and the order of their spiritual master. Prabhupāda said that he also was not a great scholar, but that he had staunch faith, the real requirement for spiritual success.

A devotee could go many places and accomplish many things, Prabhupāda said, but unless he was free of material motives he would not be able to implant the seed of *bhakti* into the hearts of others. Prabhupāda cited Śivānanda, who had gone alone to Hamburg and tried his best, with faith in his spiritual master. Now Kṛṣṇa was blessing Śivānanda with a little success: a storefront temple, newly recruited devotees, an interested professor, and other guests coming and chanting. Even one lone preacher could accomplish many things for Kṛṣṇa, provided the preacher was free from sense gratification and the desire for profit, adoration, and distinction.

Śrīla Prabhupāda rose early, about one A.M., and began dictating his latest book, *Kṛṣṇa, the Supreme Personality of Godhead. Kṛṣṇa*, begun in Los Angeles eight months before, was a summary of *Śrīmad-Bhāgavatam's* Tenth Canto. Starting in 1959 with the First Canto, Prabhupāda had been translating each successive verse, giving a roman transliteration, Sanskrit-English synonyms, the English translation, and then his commentary. *Kṛṣṇa,* however, was all in English, with translation and commentary blended together as transcendental stories.

In his verse-by-verse translation of the *Bhāgavatam*, Prabhupāda was still working on the Third Canto, so to reach the Tenth Canto could take many years. But he was uncertain how many years longer he would live, and the thought of passing away without giving the world an authorized, readable account of the Tenth Canto had been unbearable. Being the account of Lord Kṛṣṇa's earthly pastimes, the Tenth Canto was the climax of *Śrīmad-Bhāgavatam* and the richest nectar of transcendental literature. Now Prabhupāda had enough manuscript pages to print a first volume, complete with the many color illustrations he had commissioned his artists to paint. To print such a book would be expensive, and Prabhupāda had no money. But he depended fully on Kṛṣṇa, and translated quickly in the quiet of early morning.

At 4:30 Prabhupāda's secretary, Puruṣottama, entered, followed by Yamunā dāsī. Puruṣottama offered *ārati* to Prabhupāda's small Rādhā-Kṛṣṇa Deities while Yamunā watched, eager to learn. Prabhupāda sang prayers, accompanying himself on the harmonium.

During Prabhupāda's *maṅgala-ārati* ceremony, the other dozen or so disciples assembled for their own *maṅgala-ārati* at the temple. As they walked the damp pathway to the temple they felt the cold air and heard the bell and Prabhupāda's singing. They could see through the predawn mist the light coming from Prabhupāda's window on the second floor, and the building looked like a lantern in the dark. The sound of the harmonium drifted mystically through the trees.

Later that morning some of the devotees brought Prabhupāda several news articles about his London arrival. The *Daily Sketch*, with its headline "Enter His Divine Grace Abhaya Charan Bhaktivedanta Swami," carried a foot-high photo of Prabhupāda playing *karatālas*. The *Sun's* story, "Happiness is Hare Krishna," appeared with a photo of Prabhupāda and the devotees. And the *Daily Mirror* showed Sarasvatī and one of the adult devotees.

The Daily Telegraph, however, carried a different kind of article: "Hindu Temple Protests." "Conversion of office premises in Bloomsbury into a Hindu temple is being investigated by the Ministry of Public Buildings and Works," the article began. The devotees' neighbors at Bury Place had apparently complained about the renovation that had been going on for the past two weeks. The article quoted a Camden council member: "If their planning application is not granted, it will cost them a lot of money."

Prabhupāda said the devotees should do everything they could to prevent delays or obstacles to their establishing the temple and installing Deities of Rādhā and Kṛṣṇa. He suggested they go daily into the city, work carefully and persistently with the officials, and secure the authorization. Meanwhile, Śyāmasundara should continue his remodeling work at Bury Place.

For Prabhupāda, such diplomatic and legal strategy was as spiritual as translating *Kṛṣṇa* or singing before his Deities. He was serious, heavy; and his disciples sensed this as he looked at them with full concentration, his intelligent gaze penetrating to see if they understood his directions. This heaviness of the *guru* was an essential part of their relationship with him. They were young men, inexperienced, and he was sending them on a mature assignment that required both transcendental and worldly expertise.

Serving as Prabhupāda's menial messengers and workers, his disciples imbibed his gravity. And they too became heavy. They too became dedicated servants of their *guru*. To bungle an important order because of naiveté or carelessness would be a spiritual disqualification. Prabhupāda had often told them a Vaiṣṇava is not a retired person who only sleeps and eats and chants Hare Kṛṣṇa. Rather, a Vaiṣṇava fights for Kṛṣṇa, as did Arjuna and Hanumān. And as the devotee tries his best, working in full surrender, Kṛṣṇa supports and protects him.

Dawn arrived, and time for Prabhupāda's morning walk. The cold September night shrouded the morning in heavy fog. Some of the low-lying grounds were waterlogged this time of year, and even in the higher plots the long grass would remain wet until mid-morning. "This climate," Prabhupāda admitted, "is not at all suitable for me." But having heard of the beauty of the grounds, he insisted on taking his usual morning walk.

Tittenhurst dated back to the 1770s, when the estate had been renowned for its many varieties of trees and shrubs—one of the most unusual collections in England. Even now, cypresses, weeping beech, austin poplars, royal palms, redwoods, varieties of pines, monkey puzzle trees, and orchards of cherry and apple graced the stately grounds. One cypress stood more than 125 feet tall, and the redwoods grew even taller. Bushes and vines grew in dense thickets. Close by the main house were hundreds of rhododendrons, a formal rose garden, and several fountains. The estate had its own lake, stocked with goldfish and perch, and at a far end of the property stood a row of greenhouses for grapes and peaches. Designed so as to be abloom in every season, the grounds had been carefully kept for generations, a recent owner having employed more than twenty gardeners. John, however, was deliberately allowing the grass to go uncut.

Prabhupāda walked out into the morning mist, onto the long, wet grass. Dressed almost entirely in black, he wore a Russian hat with earmuffs and black rubber Wellington boots. A black, full-length overcoat, given him by the devotees in Germany, covered his robes and sweater, leaving only glimpses of saffron cloth.

As Prabhupāda walked, accompanied by several of his disciples, he passed a fountain near the main house and entered a grove. The path narrowed, with vines and bushes close in, and led them into an open meadow, once a well-tended lawn but now a field of high grass. Bulldozers had excavated an area which according to rumor would soon be a helicopter landing field.

At the bottom of the sloping meadow, Prabhupāda entered an orchard. Many leaves had fallen from the trees, and the sun's first rays now revealed shavings of autumn gold at Prabhupāda's feet. He stood under one of the trees, and the diffused sunlight made the sky beyond the branches glow golden. "In my childhood," he said, "there were so many names given to me. My maternal uncle called me Nandu, because I appeared the day after Kṛṣṇa appeared and there was a great celebration on that day. I was called Nandu because I was born the day after Kṛṣṇa. And I was also called Govardhana. One of my sisters used to call me Kacha. I've been called so many names. As children we were all very beautiful. There are always so many names given to them. But all these names — they are all dead and gone." He turned and began to walk again, saying nothing more on the subject.

Prabhupāda mentioned the British economy, which he said was sinking into the sea because of the pound's devaluation. So many British lords had gained their wealth by exploiting other nations; now, having exhausted their good *karma,* they were suffering the results of their sins. They were too poor to maintain their great estates. "They used to have seventeen men working full time just on the garden," Prabhupāda exclaimed, "and now they cannot even pay the taxes. So they have to give the whole thing up. And it is falling into the hands of the *śūdras.*"

Īśāna asked Prabhupāda, "How is it that a person like me, from such a degraded background, can come to Kṛṣṇa consciousness?"

"Because you are intelligent," Prabhupāda replied.

"I don't understand."

"Because you are intelligent," Prabhupāda repeated.

Īśāna's wife, Vibhāvatī, asked, "What is the meaning of *spiritual master*?"

"Actually I am not your spiritual master," Prabhupāda replied. "That title is simply a formality. You should think of me as your spiritual father, your eternal father."

As they walked past a tractor, Kulaśekhara remarked, "The tractor is a very wonderful invention, isn't it?"

Prabhupāda turned to Kulaśekhara. "This tractor is the downfall of the Indian village system."

"Why is that? It does the work of ten men."

"Yes," Prabhupāda said. "Previously, the young men of the village would be engaged in plowing the field. Then this tractor came along and did the work of all those young men, and they had nothing to do. So they went to the cities to try to find work, and they fell into illusion."

Stopping beside a clump of yellowed grass, Prabhupāda asked, "Why is this yellow grass different?" No one answered. "The other grass is green," he said, "but this is yellow. What is the reason?" Still no one answered. "This yellow grass is drying up," Prabhupāda explained, "because the roots are not attached. Therefore it is yellow. Similarly, when we detach ourselves from Kṛṣṇa, then we will dry up."

They walked to a spot where the grass grew almost six feet high. Stopping at a path the tractor had cut, Prabhupāda smiled. "Oh, we can go through there?" And he strode ahead with his cane into the head-high jungle of grass and weeds. He walked until he came to a low hill that had been cleared, and he stopped. As he stood there, surrounded by the sea of grass and a few disciples, Kulaśekhara asked about the song Prabhupāda had been singing earlier that morning.

"The song," Prabhupāda said, "is about Lord Caitanya Mahāprabhu. He would rise, and He would go out at this time of morning, when the sun has risen but is not yet in the sky." As Prabhupāda spoke, the mist was already dissipating, and the golden glow in the sky had moved higher above the horizon. Prabhupāda raised his hands and swayed from side to side. "In this way," he said, "Caitanya Mahāprabhu would dance in the morning."

As they returned by the main house John Lennon stood gazing out through the glass doors, watching. Prabhupāda, walking with a cane, dressed in his black coat and his Wellingtons, looked like the gentleman of the estate out for his morning walk. Stopping now and then, he would look at certain trees, touching their bark, rubbing their leaves, inspecting them closely. At the beginning of the walk, a devotee had picked a rose and handed it to him, and he still held it in his hand with care. He had walked for an hour. Everywhere the scenery had been beautiful, and everywhere he had instructed his followers in Kṛṣṇa consciousness.

As Prabhupāda approached the building where he lived, he met little Sarasvatī. Taking her hand, he walked along with her to the foot of the stairs, where they stopped. Prabhupāda was halfway up the stairs when he turned and saw Sarasvatī standing in the doorway, watching. He beckoned and called to her, "Come on," and she crawled up the stairs after him.

When Sarasvatī came into Prabhupāda's room, he asked her, "So, are you old enough to go to *gurukula*?"

"No," she said, shaking her head.

"Come here, I am going to put a stamp on your forehead, and then we are going to put you in a red mailbox and send you to *gurukula*."

Sarasvatī began to cry, "Mālatī! Mālatī! I don't want to go!" and ran and hid behind her mother.

"Come on, Sarasvatī," Prabhupāda coaxed. "Come sit on my lap, and I will give you some *prasādam*." She came and sat on Prabhupāda's knee. "Now get me the stamps, Puruṣottama," he teased. "We are going to send her to *gurukula*." Sarasvatī shrieked and ran to Mālatī.

To Śrīla Prabhupāda, Sarasvatī was a pure spirit soul, but because she was in a small child's body he didn't teach her philosophy; he teased her, gave her *prasādam*, and treated her with the affection of a grandfather. But through her attachment to him, she would become attached to Kṛṣṇa.

After breakfast, when the sun had warmed the air, Prabhupāda opened his windows, sat down at his harmonium, and sang *bhajanas*. As he sang with closed eyes, his head shaking, he played the harmonium, and Yamunā sat at the bottom of the stairs, crying tears of appreciation. Prabhupāda had been singing for a while when he stopped and called for Yamunā. "Do you enjoy my *kīrtana*?" he asked.

"Yes,"she nodded, "very much."

"The prayers of Narottama dāsa Ṭhākura," he said. "This sound is above the material platform. It is directly from the spiritual platform. And there is no need of understanding the language. It is just like a thunderburst. Everyone can hear the sound of thunder—there is no misunderstanding. Similarly, these songs are above the material platform, and they crack like thunder within your heart. Why don't you come here every day during my chanting?"

"That would be wonderful!"

"Yes," said Prabhupāda, "from now on we will record." And every morning after that, Prabhupāda sang, and Puruṣottama and Yamunā would come to his room and record.

"What is your favorite *bhajana*?" Yamunā asked.

"What's yours?" Prabhupāda returned.

"Lord Caitanya's *Śikṣāṣṭakam* prayers."

"My favorite," said Prabhupāda, "is *Hari hari viphale*." He recited the gist of the prayer in English: " 'O Lord Hari, I have spent my life uselessly. Although I have taken this rare human birth, I have not worshiped Rādhā and Kṛṣṇa, and so I have knowingly drunk poison.' There is so much depth of meaning in Narottama dāsa Ṭhākura's prayers."

Puruṣottama: *Once Prabhupāda was sitting alone in his room. I walked by, and I heard him singing a prayer I'd never heard before. And I went in. Of course everyone knows he sings—he can sing very beautifully, very greatly inspired—but I'd never heard him sing as beautifully as he did that one time. I'd heard him sing many, many times in many temples, but I'd never heard him sing as beautifully as this. I felt very honored to hear it, very privileged. It was beautiful. When he was done, he just got up and said, "Let's go now."*

Prabhupāda also chanted one chapter of *Bhagavad-gītā* daily for eighteen days. "Anywhere *Bhagavad-gītā* is chanted," he said, "that place becomes a *tīrtha* (a holy place)."

Puruṣottama reported to the devotees in the United States these activities of Śrīla Prabhupāda.

> He is singing prayers a lot, and much of it is being recorded. I must admit that the tapes of songs and prayers he is making now are the best ones I have ever heard. Wait until you hear them when we get back. As the *Bhagavatam* says, "Drink deep this nectar, O man of piety, and you shall be taken from this mortal frame!"

The women cooking for Prabhupāda were serving him American desserts: apple pie, doughnuts, glazed cookies. Prabhupāda would smile, but he would only nibble at his dessert. One afternoon he said, "These sweets are very nice, but no one has made me *sandeśa*." None of the devotees knew how to make Bengali sweets, so Prabhupāda took them into the kitchen and taught them to make *sandeśa*. Although they had watched carefully, their first attempts produced *sandeśa* that was dry and grainy. But Prabhupāda accepted it, preferring the *sandeśa*—which Kṛṣṇa Himself used to eat—to the Western confections.

For the devotees at Tittenhurst, to have Prabhupāda living among them was again to witness Kṛṣṇa's pure devotee as he engaged constantly in ecstatic devotional service with his body, mind, and words. They could see how Prabhupāda was speaking and acting in Kṛṣṇa consciousness at every moment, and his presence confirmed that the most exalted platform of pure devotional service was a reality. His disciples felt bliss and renewed determination just being with him.

Prabhupāda's hosts, John and Yoko, also had the valuable opportunity to be near Prabhupāda, although they chose to keep apart. Remaining together in their own world, they mingled but rarely with the devotees. Prabhupāda's men continued to work under John's managers, and John was content to let the Swami and his entourage stay. When the head gardener asked John how to treat the devotees, he said, "Let them please themselves." On hearing of certain activities in the main house, Prabhupāda commented about the bad influence women sometimes have on men, but he kept out of John and Yoko's affairs. He had his own affairs in Kṛṣṇa consciousness.

* * *

Having been whisked from the airport to Tittenhurst, Prabhupāda had seen little of London, and one day he asked Śyāmasundara to take him on a tour of the city. Prabhupāda had grown up in British Calcutta hearing London praised as the seat of Britain's world empire, so when he saw how small many of London's historic landmarks were he was particularly surprised. At Buckingham Palace he remarked, "We have many houses in Calcutta bigger than this." The Thames, celebrated in the writings of British authors he had studied in college, was a disappointment also. "It's a canal," he said. "It's only a canal. In my mind I thought it was bigger than the Ganges."

But the most interesting sight was the building at 7 Bury Place. City officials had recently granted the devotees permission to occupy the temple. That part of the battle was won. Now Śyāmasundara and his few helpers had to finish the remodeling. On seeing the temple's location near the British Museum and Madame Tussauds Wax Museum, Śrīla Prabhupāda became even more anxious that Śyāmasundara fix an opening date as soon as possible.

* * *

In September Śrīla Prabhupāda wrote to Satsvarūpa about his stay at Tittenhurst Park.

> Here there is a nice big hall, exactly suitable for a temple. I have begun to give lectures here on specific days, but there are no outsiders coming.

Prabhupāda wanted to preach to the "outsiders," and if they wouldn't come to him, he would go to them. His first outside meeting, arranged by the devotees, was at Camden Town Hall, in the heart of London, and was well attended, both by Britishers and by Indians. After Prabhupāda's brief lecture—only about fifteen minutes—a lively question-and-answer session began.

Woman: "Would you say Kṛṣṇa is God or Kṛṣṇa is love?"

Prabhupāda: "Without love, how can Kṛṣṇa be God?"

Woman: "No, I asked *you.*"

Prabhupāda: "Yes. That is the real position. *Kṛṣṇa* means 'all-attractive.' Anything which is all-attractive you generally love."

Man: "Then the particle of the Supreme Being, man, is also all-love?"

Prabhupāda: "Yes, you are part and parcel of Kṛṣṇa. You want to love somebody, and Kṛṣṇa wants to love you. This is loving exchange. But instead of loving Kṛṣṇa, you are trying to love something else. That is your trouble. The love is there in you and Kṛṣṇa, and when the love will be exchanged between you and Kṛṣṇa, that will be your perfection of life."

Man: "Thank you."

Indian woman: "Would it matter if I worshiped any other? Would it matter whether I worshiped Kṛṣṇa or Śiva or Christ or Buddha? Would it matter?"

Prabhupāda: "If you worship Śiva, you'll get Śiva. If you worship Kṛṣṇa, you'll get Kṛṣṇa. Why do you expect Kṛṣṇa by worshiping Śiva? What is your idea?"

Indian woman: "My idea is, would it matter?"

Prabhupāda: "Don't you suppose if you purchase a ticket for India you'll go to India? How can you go to America?"

Indian woman: "This is not the point."

Prabhupāda: "This *is* the point. That is explained in *Bhagavad-gītā: yānti deva-vratā devān pitṝn yānti pitṛ-vratāḥ.*"

Indian woman: "But my point is . . ."

Prabhupāda: "Your point, you understand. Why don't you understand the description of *Bhagavad-gītā*? If you worship demigods like Śiva and others, you will go there. If you worship Kṛṣṇa, you'll go to Kṛṣṇa. What is the difficulty to understand?"

Indian woman: "Do you think that Śiva is a demigod?"

Prabhupāda: "Yes, why not?"

Indian woman: "But Kṛṣṇa says that it doesn't matter the way you worship. All means have the same goal, and you will reach the same goal. 'You can take the different paths, but you will come to Me eventually.' "

Prabhupāda: "Try to understand. Suppose you have to go to the forty-second floor of a building. And you are going up one after another. So the goal is the forty-second story, but you cannot claim that after going a few steps, 'I have come to the goal, the forty-second story.' The path is one—that's all right—but you have to reach the ultimate goal. You do not know what is the ultimate goal. You simply say all paths reach to this goal. But you do not know what is the ultimate goal."

A young hippie stood up and shouted, "Hey, Swamiji!" People in the audience turned around and looked. "You said if we're not careful, in the next life we'll become a dog. But I want to tell you that I don't mind if I become a dog in my next life."

"You have my blessings," said Prabhupāda, and the young man sat down.

One-night lectures in scattered places around the city proved further the need of a temple. Prabhupāda had experienced a similar situation in New York City in 1965. At that time also he had had no temple. His audiences would listen respectfully and then disperse, and he would never see them again. To become Kṛṣṇa conscious, however, a person needed to hear about Kṛṣṇa repeatedly, and for that a temple was required. Once Prabhupāda had his temple established in London, thousands would be able to come and hear about Kṛṣṇa, take *prasādam*, and appreciate the lovely Deity form of the Lord. A temple would provide guests with regular, intimate contact with the devotees of the Lord, and this was essential. In the absence of a temple, however, Prabhupāda was prepared to go on lecturing all over London. Kṛṣṇa's teachings, Kṛṣṇa's *kīrtana*, and Kṛṣṇa's *prasādam* were absolute good; they would act regardless of the external situation.

Conway Hall was a five-hundred-seat auditorium in Red Lion Square in central London. By arranging a series of twelve lectures over the next three months, the devotees hoped to oblige Prabhupāda to stay in England at least that long. Guru dāsa had drawn up a list of lecture titles and printed fifty thousand handbills. Admission would be two shillings and sixpence.

The first night at Conway Hall about a hundred people attended.

Prabhupāda sat on a cushion atop a table, leading *kīrtana*, while his disciples sat on the floor. Yamunā played harmonium, and Mukunda and Kulaśekhara played *mṛdaṅgas*. Prabhupāda's Rādhā-Kṛṣṇa Deities stood on Their altar on a separate table beside Prabhupāda. A Hare Kṛṣṇa *mantra* banner hung against the back wall.

Guru dāsa had billed tonight's lecture "Teachings of the *Vedas*," and Prabhupāda explained that Vedic teachings can be understood only by hearing them from self-realized saints. After Prabhupāda's lecture the audience gave a sustained round of applause. Prabhupāda answered questions and had Yamunā lead a final *kīrtana*. The next day Prabhupāda wrote to a Dr. Shyam Sundar das Brahmacari in India: "I spoke for about one hour, and after that they continued clapping, which confirms their appreciation."

At the second Conway Hall engagement, when Prabhupāda stood during the *kīrtana* and began to dance, the devotees onstage joined him, dancing in a circle. Īśāna played his trumpet, and even Sarasvatī, her diapers showing beneath her short dress, jumped up and down in ecstasy. Each week would bring another Conway Hall meeting, and Prabhupāda's dancing became a regular feature.

One night at Conway Hall an Englishman stood and asked, "Why is it you don't try to help the people of your own country? Why did you come so far? Why don't you simply approach the big politicians? There are big politicians to try to help *there*."

Prabhupāda: "You are a great politician. Therefore, I am approaching you. Is that all right?"

Another man asked: "If this is the absolute truth, how come there's so many people in London but not so many people are in attendance here?"

Prabhupāda: "When you are selling diamonds, you don't expect many customers. But if you are giving cut glass, the fools will come. We have a very precious thing—this Kṛṣṇa consciousness movement. Don't expect that all the foolish people will take to it. Some sincere souls have come. You please also take it."

Prabhupāda felt encouraged by the response of the English. Regularly the audiences would join in the chanting and dancing.

> In London things are going on nicely, and last evening we had a meeting in Conway Hall and several hundred persons were joining us in chanting

> and dancing. After the meeting one reporter from the biggest London newspaper came behind the stage to get further information about our movement for publication in his paper. So I am very encouraged to see the nice reception that the people and the news medias are giving to our activities in London.

Late in October Prabhupāda spoke at the English Speakers Union to a predominantly Indian audience.

He began his talk, "Although we are a small gathering today, this is a very important meeting. India has got a message. You are all respectable Indians present here in an important city of the world, London, and I have come here with an important mission. It is not the same mission as Indians generally have who come here and to other foreign countries—to beg something. I have come here to *give* something. So you please try to cooperate with me."

On October 30 Prabhupāda lectured at Oxford Town Hall. His talk was basic, although embellished with more Sanskrit quotes than usual. His disciples had not expected much of a response from the Oxford students, yet the hall was filled. And when Prabhupāda stood and gestured for everyone to raise their hands and dance, practically the entire audience responded. While Mukunda played the huge pipe organ and hundreds joined the chanting, Prabhupāda held his arms high and began powerfully jumping up and down.

> Yesterday we had a very successful meeting at Oxford at the Town Hall. About 350 boys, girls, old men, ladies and gentlemen participated and we made them all dance and chant with us, every one. After the meeting, many boys and gentlemen came to congratulate me.

Prabhupāda received an invitation to appear on Britain's most popular TV talk show, "Late Night Line-Up." The interviewer, accustomed to snappy repartee, tried to engage Prabhupāda in his style of conversing, avoiding long, philosophical answers.

"Swamiji," he asked, "do you have a concept of hell in your religion?"

"Yes," Prabhupāda replied. "London is hell."

The host appeared stunned, as if beaten at his own game from the start. Prabhupāda continued, "It is always damp, cloudy, and raining. In India the sun is always shining."

The interviewer was still at a loss for words, and Prabhupāda, perhaps sensing the man's embarrassment, added, "Of course, it is a very great credit to the English people to have established such a great civilization in such a climate."

There were other questions, and Prabhupāda talked for an hour, explaining the Kṛṣṇa consciousness movement and philosophy. The next day a London newspaper announced, "Swami Calls London Hell."

The "Hare Krishna Mantra" record was still high on the charts in England and throughout the continent, and this fame led a Dutch television company to invite Prabhupāda's disciples to Amsterdam, all expenses paid, to do a show. They would have only five minutes of air time, but Prabhupāda accepted it. "Five minutes," he said, "is sufficient. We will preach the whole philosophy of Kṛṣṇa consciousness in five minutes."

Prabhupāda and his party took the ferry from Dover across the English Channel to France and then traveled by train to Amsterdam. The television studio, located outside the city, was in a modern, air-conditioned building, with constant loudspeaker announcements, artificial plants, a TV in every room—but no windows.

The receptionist brought Prabhupāda and his disciples to a windowless room with painted concrete walls. "In India," Prabhupāda said, "we wouldn't consider living in a place without windows and fresh air. I want to sit by a window." So the devotees checked through the entire building until finally, in the third-floor hallway, they found a window. Moving their chairs with them, they went with Prabhupāda and sat by the window.

"By the year 2000, no one will see the light of day," Prabhupāda said. "Cities will be forced to live underground. They will have artificial light and food, but no sunlight."

The producer of the program arrived, surprised to find that "the Swami" was also going to be part of the act. The surprise was a pleasant one, and he welcomed Prabhupāda to his show. "Now, what I want you and your group to do," he explained, "is to sing your record, 'Hare Krishna Mantra.' You don't have to actually sing out loud. We're going to play your record, and you mime. Pretend you're playing those instruments. Pretend you're singing." He allowed that afterward Prabhupāda could speak—for two minutes.

Just before Prabhupāda and the devotees went onstage, they had to wait in the wings while a local Dutch group danced around, pretending to play their saxophones, trumpets, and drums. Then the producer brought in a table with a cushion on it for Prabhupāda and seated the devotees around Prabhupāda on the floor.

The cameras began, the record played, and the devotees started to mime. Suddenly clouds, produced by dry ice, rolled in on the set—a "mystical" effect. As the devotees disappeared under clouds of carbon dioxide, only Prabhupāda remained clearly visible. Seeing the special effect unsuccessful, the producer motioned the devotees to stand and dance beside the Swami.

The song ended, and a camera closed in on Prabhupāda. "Now you have two minutes, Swamiji," the producer said. Prabhupāda began.

"We have been chanting this Hare Kṛṣṇa *mantra.* This is a transcendental sound vibration, nondifferent from the Lord. The Lord's name and His form are the same. Please chant this sublime sound, and your life will become perfect. You'll become happy, and you'll realize your true nature—that you are an eternal servant of God, Kṛṣṇa. This process is called *bhakti-yoga*, and we request everyone to take to this chanting. Thank you very much."

Prabhupāda was pleased as his disciples' record continued to be a hit in Europe.

> The Hare Krishna record is selling very nicely. Yesterday, it sold 5,000 copies, and this week it is on the chronological list as #20. They say next week it will come to be #3, and after that it may come to #1. So they are very much hopeful of this record.

To Satsvarūpa in Boston Prabhupāda wrote,

> The Hare Krishna record is going on in England nicely, and I heard that in Australia it stands 4th on the list of 50 important records.

"Hare Krishna Mantra" became the number one song in West Germany, number one in Czechoslovakia, and among the top ten all over Europe and even in Japan. With the income from the record, the devotees began paying their bills and financing the renovations of the Bury Place temple.

Sometimes the devotees would perform at concerts with professional groups, and sometimes they would receive invitations to appear in nightclubs. After one particularly late and nasty nightclub engagement, Yamunā went to Prabhupāda and told him what the place had been like. Prabhupāda called for all the devotees. "These places," he explained, "are not good for *brahmacārīs*. The principle is that we have to make devotees. So we have to think where we are going. If we are going somewhere to preach but we can't make any devotees there, what is the use? So we have to think like that." He said he wasn't forbidding them to preach in the nightclubs, but he told them to be careful.

One of the devotees asked if showing slides of Kṛṣṇa mixed in with psychedelic slides was permissible. Prabhupāda said no. Kṛṣṇa should be on a throne or an altar. If they watered Kṛṣṇa consciousness down, it would become idol worship.

Not since Prabhupāda had first left India in 1965 had he preached to Indians as extensively as now. Indians would always attend his lectures, and even if they didn't dance and chant they appreciated Kṛṣṇa consciousness. Even before Prabhupāda's arrival in England, a few Indians had stepped forward to help the devotees, and now the majority of Prabhupāda's occasional guests at Tittenhurst were Indians. Bringing their families, they would sit and chat with Prabhupāda, often inviting him to their homes for dinner.

Kedar Nath Gupta: *Prabhupāda agreed to come to our house. We received him with a warm welcome, and many other people also came to hear him. He was very much pleased to see that we had our family Deities of Rādhā and Kṛṣṇa, given by my mother. And he commented, "I am very much pleased to come to this place and see that Rādhā and Kṛṣṇa are here."*

He gave a very nice lecture and told that the purpose of the human form of life is self-realization. He said one should be inquisitive to know who he is. All those assembled who had come to hear him were very much pleased and impressed by his lecture. After his lecture, I did the ārati, *and we offered the foodstuffs to the Deity. And then we distributed* prasādam *to everyone. Prabhupāda took the* prasādam, *and he was very much pleased to take* prasādam *in our house. As he was leaving I requested him, "When can I see you next?" He said, "You can see me any time you want."*

Sometimes there would be disagreements over philosophy, but Prabhupāda's arguments were always convincing. The Indians were respectful to Prabhupāda and repeatedly invited him to their homes. One of Britain's most prominent and respected Indians visited, Praful Patel, as did many businessmen with the means to help Prabhupāda's mission. But few were willing to sacrifice.

* * *

The second moon landing by American astronauts was scheduled for mid-November, only a few weeks away. For months the moon shots had received much press coverage, and Prabhupāda would speak of them often. Almost a year ago in Los Angeles he had answered a reporter's queries on the possibility of man's landing on the moon: "Just like we are going from one place to another by motorcar or by airplane, this mechanical process will not help us go to the moon planet. The process is different, as described in the Vedic literature. One has to qualify. According to our literature, our information, it is not possible. In this body we cannot go there."

At Tittenhurst Prabhupāda often brought up the moon landing while talking with his disciples. "The moon landing was a hoax," he said one evening in his room, "for they cannot go to the moon. The moon planet, Candraloka, is a residence of the demigods, higher beings than these drunkards and cow-eating slaughterers who are trying to inhabit it. You cannot think this travel is allowed—like when I migrated from India to the U.S. The moon planet cannot be visited so quickly. It is not possible."

Śrīla Prabhupāda's disciples accepted his statements. He was giving not simply his opinion but the verdict of the Vedic scriptures. Because he accepted Vedic authority over modern science, so did his disciples—but not Puruṣottama.

Detecting Puruṣottama's dubious mentality, Prabhupāda would often joke lightly in Puruṣottama's presence. Someone would ask a question—"Where is Jānakī?"—and Prabhupāda would reply, "Oh, Jānakī has gone to the moon." Then everyone, except Puruṣottama, would laugh.

The devotees knew of Puruṣottama's difficulty—he was an American, and proud that the Americans were conquering space—and they knew that Prabhupāda was joking about it. Puruṣottama was up on the latest scientific advancements. He was impressed by NASA's achievements and astronaut Neil Armstrong's "giant step for mankind."

Although Puruṣottama went on with his duties, he became sullen, and Prabhupāda noted his lack of enthusiasm. One morning Puruṣottama and Yamunā were together with Prabhupāda in his room. Puruṣottama had several day's growth of beard and was wearing the same orange sweater he had slept in, whereas Yamunā was neat and clean. Although she had only two simple cotton *sārīs,* she would always put on a freshly washed and ironed one before going to see Prabhupāda. Looking at his two servants, Prabhupāda said, "Yamunā, you have so many *sārīs*. They are all so beautiful."

Yamunā looked up at Prabhupāda in surprise. "I don't have so many, Śrīla Prabhupāda."

"No," he said, "you are wearing a new piece of cloth every day. It's so nice. You're always looking so neat and clean—and your *tilaka.* Puruṣottama, what do you think? Who do you think has the best *tilaka*?" Puruṣottama didn't answer. "Beautiful *tilaka,*" Prabhupāda said, "means beautiful person."

About six o'clock that same evening, Yamunā was cooking *purīs* and potatoes for Prabhupāda when she heard him ring the servant's bell. Leaving the ghee on the fire, she ran up to Prabhupāda's quarters. He talked with her about the lecture he would give that evening and eventually asked, "When will *prasādam* be ready—before the discourse?"

"Yes, Śrīla Prabhupāda. I'm . . ." Yamunā smelled smoke. "Oh!" she gasped. "Please excuse me, Prabhupāda! I've left some ghee on the fire!" Rushing downstairs, she found the kitchen filled with black smoke. She couldn't see the stove. "Puruṣottama! Puruṣottama!" she cried. Puruṣottama arrived, and together they groped through the smoke. Somehow Puruṣottama extinguished the fire before it caused serious damage.

Puruṣottama and Yamunā were covered with soot. Their faces were black, and Puruṣottama's orange sweater, his robes, and Yamunā's *sārī* were all blackened. Suddenly Prabhupāda rang the servant's bell, and they both hurried upstairs to tell him about the fire. When Jānakī returned downstairs and saw the mess, she ran upstairs to Prabhupāda's room, where Yamunā and Puruṣottama stood, still covered with soot, before Prabhupāda.

"What has happened here?" Jānakī burst out.

Prabhupāda looked at her soberly and said, "Today Puruṣottama has gone to the moon."

"What?" Jānakī asked.

Prabhupāda repeated, "Yes, our Puruṣottama has gone to the moon."

"Prabhupāda," Puruṣottama said, "I am a *brahmacārī*. Why are you saying these things?"

"Being a *brahmacārī* is no restriction from going to the moon. Anyone can go," Prabhupāda said, winking.

* * *

The devotees regularly encountered John and Yoko. Although originally interested in a business relationship, John was inclined toward the devotees, but his friends advised him not to get involved with the Swami and his group. So he remained aloof.

Īśāna dāsa: *I was in the kitchen working, and John was sitting at the piano. He had a piano in the kitchen, a great upright piano with all the varnish removed—bare wood. And in this way he was sitting at the piano, playing Hare Kṛṣṇa. The man was actually a great musician, and he played Hare Kṛṣṇa in every musical idiom you could think of—bluegrass music or classical music or rock-and-roll or whatever. He would go at will from one idiom to another, always singing Hare Kṛṣṇa. It was so natural for him, and one could see that he was a musical genius. And in this way he was entertaining me, and he was obviously really enjoying it. So anyway, while this piano-playing was going on with great vigor and enthusiasm, this chanting Hare Kṛṣṇa, his wife, Yoko Ono, appeared in a nightgown or what have you and said, in a very distressed tone, "Please, John, I have a* terrible *headache. Can't you stop that sort of thing and come upstairs with me?"*

George was different. He was drawn to Prabhupāda. When one of the devotees had asked, "Why out of all the Beatles are only you interested?" George had replied, "It's my *karma*. One of the things in my sign is the spiritual side."

George Harrison: *Prabhupāda just looked like I thought he would. I had like a mixed feeling of fear and awe about meeting him. That's what I liked about later on after meeting him more—I felt that he was just more like a friend. I felt relaxed. It was much better than at first, because I hadn't been able to tell what he was saying and I wasn't sure if I was too worldly to even be there. But later I relaxed and felt much more at ease with him, and he was very warm towards me. He wouldn't talk dif-*

ferently to me than to anybody else. He was always just speaking about Kṛṣṇa, and it was coincidental who happened to be there. Whenever you saw him, he would always be the same. It wasn't like one time he would tell you to chant the Hare Kṛṣṇa mantra *and then the next time say, "Oh, no, I made a mistake." He was always the same.*

Seeing him was always a pleasure. Sometimes I would drop by, thinking I wasn't planning to go but I better go because I ought to, and I would always come away just feeling so good. I was conscious that he was taking a personal interest in me. It was always a pleasure.

George was attracted to Kṛṣṇa, and he liked to chant. Even before meeting Prabhupāda, he had learned something of Kṛṣṇa from Maharishi Mahesh Yogi, from the autobiography of Paramahansa Yogananda, and from traveling in India. But Prabhupāda's instructions in particular impressed upon him that Lord Kṛṣṇa was the Absolute Truth, the origin of everything.

George: *Prabhupāda helped me to realize the multifaceted way to approach Kṛṣṇa. Like the* prasādam, *for example. I think it is a very important thing,* prasādam, *even if it's only a trick. Like they say, the way to a man's heart is through his stomach. Well, even if it's a way to a man's spirit soul, it works. Because there is nothing better than having been dancing and singing or just sitting and talking and then suddenly they give you some food. It's like it's a blessing. And then when you learn to touch Him or taste Him, it's important.*

Kṛṣṇa is not limited. And just by Prabhupāda's being there and pouring out all this information, I was moved. It's like the mind is stubborn, but it's all Kṛṣṇa. That's all you need to know—it's all Kṛṣṇa. This world is His material energy too—the Universal Form. And in Prabhupāda's books there are these pictures showing Kṛṣṇa in the heart of a dog and a cow and a human being. It helps you to realize that Kṛṣṇa is within everybody.

Although Prabhupāda might have been teaching some higher aspect, what came through to me a lot was a greater understanding of how Kṛṣṇa is everywhere and in everything. Prabhupāda explained about the different aspects of Kṛṣṇa, and he provided a meditation where you could see Kṛṣṇa as a person everywhere. I mean, there isn't anything that isn't Kṛṣṇa.

Prabhupāda saw George as a "nice young boy," and a devotee of Kṛṣṇa. According to the *Bhāgavatam*, no matter what a person may be materially, if he is a nondevotee and never utters the holy name of God he cannot possess *any* good qualities. Many swamis and *yogīs* in India, even some who considered themselves Vaiṣṇavas, had no faith in or understanding of the holy names of Kṛṣṇa. But George liked to chant Hare Kṛṣṇa, and he had put the holy name of Kṛṣṇa in his songs, which were tremendously popular all over the world. So he was serving Kṛṣṇa through his music, and that made all the difference.

> Mr. George Harrison appears to be a very intelligent boy, and he is, by the Grace of Krishna fortunate also. On the first day, he came to see me along with John Lennon, and we had talks about 2 hours. He wanted to talk with me more, but he has now gone to his sick mother in Liverpool.

Prabhupāda also saw George as a rich man, and Lord Caitanya had strictly instructed devotees in the renounced order not to mix with worldly men. But Lord Caitanya had also taught that a devotee should accept any favorable opportunity for propagating Kṛṣṇa consciousness.

> If this boy cooperates with our movement, it will be very nice impetus for after all, he is a monied man. These monied men have to be very cautiously dealt with in spiritual life. We have to sometimes deal with them on account of preaching work; otherwise, Lord Chaitanya Mahaprabhu has strictly restricted to mix with them for Krishna Conscious people. But we get instruction from Rupa Goswami that whatever opportunity is favorable for pushing on Krishna Consciousness we should accept.

Prabhupāda dealt with George cautiously, but encouraged him to chant the Lord's name, take His *prasādam,* and surrender all his works to Him.

When the devotees in the U.S. heard of Prabhupāda's dealings with the Beatles, some of them exaggerated the closeness of the relationship, especially in the case of John Lennon. Prabhupāda heard of this and immediately stopped it.

> Regarding the booklet you and Gargamuni are sending, in the introductory portion signed by you and Gargamuni you have said that I am "personally instructing John Lennon and George Harrison in the yoga of ecstasy." This is not very satisfactory. Of course, George Harrison sometimes comes to see me and naturally I instruct him on the bhakti yoga. But the statement in the letter gives hint as if I have been invited by them for this. If this comes to their notice, they may take some objection which

> will not go to our credit. These things should not be publicly advertised, and I do not know why this has been done. Anyway, if you have not distributed many of them, you just try to take out the portion which is not a fact.

George: *Prabhupāda never really suggested that I shouldn't do what I was doing. I heard that at different times he would say to the devotees that I was a better devotee because of my songs and the other things I was doing. He never actually said that to me, but I always heard that. And the good thing for me was that I didn't have a feeling that I needed to join full time. I think it would have spoiled it if he had always been on at me, saying, "Why don't you pack in doing what you are doing and go and live in a temple somewhere?" He never made me feel any different, like I wasn't quite in the club. He was never like that.*

I'm a plainclothes devotee. It's like that. I saw my relationship—that I should help when and where I could, because I know people in society. It's like any half-decent person; you just try and help each other a little bit.

He was always pleased with me, because anything I did was a help. I mean not just to the Kṛṣṇa temple as such, but just to anything spiritual that I did, either through songs or whatever—it pleased him. He was just always very friendly. He was always chanting, and at times he said that to me—just to keep chanting all the time, or as much as possible. I think once you do that, you realize the chanting is of benefit.

There are some gurus *who go around making out that they are "it," but Prabhupāda was saying, "I am the servant of the servant of the servant of Kṛṣṇa," which is really what it is, you know. He wasn't saying, "I am the greatest," and "I am God," and all that. With him it was only in the context of being a servant, and I liked that a lot. I think it's part of the spiritual thing. The more they know, then the more they actually know that they are the servant. And the less they know, the more they think they are actually God's gift to mankind.*

So although he was obviously a very powerful individual, very spiritually advanced, he always retained that humbleness. And I think that is one of the most important things, because you learn—more than all the words he says—you learn really from the example of how he lives and what he does.

*　　　*　　　*

The *Daily Sketch* reported, "Krishna people dine out at John and Yoko's place." A photograph showed the devotees seated out of doors, taking *prasādam*.

> Lunch time at Tittenhurst Park, stately home of John Lennon and Yoko Ono—and some of the Lennons' house guests take their places in yesterday's sunshine.
>
> The picnickers are followers of the Indian Swami, His Divine Grace Abhay Charan Bhaktivedanta.
>
> They have adopted the ways of the East, from their clothes and shaven heads right down to the Indian curry they eat with their fingers.
>
> Which is all rather out of character for a place like Tittenhurst Park, which cost John £150,000 and covers sixty acres of most exclusive Sunninghill near Royal Ascot race course.

Prabhupāda and his people and John and Yoko and theirs made an odd combination. Two days after Prabhupāda's arrival at Tittenhurst, John and Yoko had flown to Canada to perform with the Plastic Ono Band at Toronto's Rock-N-Roll Revival at Varsity Stadium. In October John and Yoko had recorded "Wedding Album" and begun work on a film, *Rock-and-Roll Circus*, and John had recorded "Cold Turkey." Although John was usually shy, the devotees working at the main house found him openhearted and generous with his possessions. He invited the devotees to stay permanently at Tittenhurst and farm. Whatever he had, he said, he would share with them.

One day Yoko asked Yamunā if a devotee couple could stand in for her and John onstage at a London theater. She and John had previously appeared there dressed in only a burlap bag and were supposed to make another appearance, but Yoko thought perhaps a devotee couple could take their place. The crowd, she said, might never know the difference, and even if they did, it would be a hilarious publicity stunt for the devotees. Politely declining, Yamunā explained why devotees could never do such a thing. When she told Prabhupāda, he was adamant: none of his disciples would go. For days afterward, he condemned this sensuality.

John invited Prabhupāda to the manor to hear his recent recording of "Cold Turkey." Although such a song held little interest for Prabhupāda, John whimsically wanted him to hear it. Taking the opportunity to preach to the great man of the world, Prabhupāda went. Within John's main sitting room, Prabhupāda sat on the couch before the fireplace.

The tape was ready on the large sixteen-track machine that had recorded it, and as Prabhupāda sat patiently, John began to work the controls.

But the machine wouldn't play. John began cursing under his breath, turning knobs and pushing buttons. Although only Puruṣottama had accompanied Prabhupāda, two other devotees hid outside beneath the windows, listening. When they peeked in and saw John struggling with the machine, they began giggling in the shadows.

"Oh," Prabhupāda said, "so your machine is not working. Well, never mind. We have also made some recording, and we would like to play this music for your pleasure." John resigned himself to listening to Prabhupāda's singing, and Prabhupāda was saved from the "Cold Turkey."

Prabhupāda kept his visit short. As he was leaving, he saw on the wall framed, life-size photos of John and Yoko naked. He also saw black and white silhouettes of a man and woman in various positions of sexual intercourse. On returning to his room, he commented, "It is not good for us to continue staying here." He asked Mukunda to find him an apartment in London. The Bury Place renovations were still incomplete, and Prabhupāda said he preferred to be in the city so that he could oversee the work. The natural setting of Tittenhurst was pleasant, but Prabhupāda's hosts' way of life and his were incompatible.

One day John and Yoko, dressed in black, came to visit Prabhupāda. Acknowledging him to be a great *yogī* with mystic power, they asked him to use his powers to arrange with Kṛṣṇa that they be reunited after death. Prabhupāda was disappointed.

"This is not my business," he said. "Kṛṣṇa provides you with life, and He takes it away in the form of death. It is impossible that you can be united after death. When you go back home, back to Godhead, you can be united with Kṛṣṇa. But husband and wife—this is simply a mundane relationship. It ends with the body at the time of death. You cannot pick up this kind of relationship again after death."

* * *

At one end of the estate lived a bricklayer and his wife in a small, neglected Georgian house. Hired by John to build a recording studio on the property, the bricklayer had only recently moved to Tittenhurst. A tough, burly man, he never spoke to the devotees, until one day he asked several of them if they believed in ghosts.

"Oh, yes," Kulaśekhara said. "Prabhupāda says there are ghosts."

"I don't believe," the bricklayer said. "My wife is having dreams, but I don't believe in ghosts."

The bricklayer's wife revealed that both she and her husband had been hearing "something" at night. Last night they had gone running to John Lennon's house, terrified, complaining of sounds: chains rattling, boot heels pounding, and the noise of something "like a body being dragged across the floor." The bricklayer had seen his wife violently shaken by the shoulders, although no one else was there.

When the devotees told Prabhupāda, he said, "You tell John Lennon that if he wants we can get rid of these ghosts." Mukunda relayed the message, but John had already invited his friend, a white witch, to come and exorcise the ghost.

The warlock visited the bricklayer's cottage, and a few devotees tagged along. Over the fireplace in the main room they found a carving of a person with a ghost coming out of his forehead, and on the opposite wall, mahogany runes. "These are ancient witch runes," the warlock said, shaking his head. "I can't do anything here."

When John asked the devotees to try their method, Prabhupāda directed them. At the bricklayer's cottage they should sprinkle water offered to Kṛṣṇa in the doorways, blow conchshells, and then have *kīrtana.* A group of devotees went, and Kulaśekhara led the *kīrtana.* After half an hour of chanting, Kulaśekhara felt a great release of pressure within the room, and the *kīrtana* became ecstatic. The devotees returned to their engagements, assuring John that the ghosts would not return, and the bricklayer and his wife moved in again.

The next morning Prabhupāda passed the old cottage on his walk. "So, how is the ghost?" he asked.

"No news, Prabhupāda," Kulaśekhara replied.

The following morning Prabhupāda again asked, "How is the ghost? Would they like to have him back?"

Years ago in India, Prabhupāda said, when he was running his chemical business, he had detected ghosts in the building at night.

"What did you do?" one of the devotees asked.

"I simply chanted Hare Kṛṣṇa, and the ghosts would go away." Prabhupāda then opened his eyes wide and gestured with both hands, mimicking the frightened workers in the plant who had come running to him: "Bābājī! Bābājī! There is ghost! There is ghost!" The devotees laughed.

"Actually," Prabhupāda said, "there are many ghosts here. Especially over by the stable areas. They are attached to this place. But they will not harm you if you just chant Hare Kṛṣṇa."

* * *

Prabhupāda was anxious to leave Tittenhurst, and by late October some of the devotees had moved to Bury Place. Prabhupāda no longer had any business at Tittenhurst. Mr. Lennon was an influential person who had seemed interested in Kṛṣṇa, but now there was no point in Prabhupāda's staying on at the estate.

Yoko and her ex-husband, Dan, now John's manager, were also pressing John to be rid of the devotees. Dan complained that the devotees were trying to take over the place. The devotees, on the other hand, complained to John that Dan and Yoko were misrepresenting them. On one side were Dan and Yoko, on the other the devotees. John was in the middle; he had to choose.

John told Mukunda that as far as he was concerned he got along fine with the devotees, but the people around him were having difficulty. He would give the devotees a couple more weeks to move to their new temple in the city. The devotees were already in the process of moving to Bury Place, and Mukunda had found an apartment for Prabhupāda a short drive from the temple. In a few days everything would be ready for Prabhupāda to move.

On the day Prabhupāda left Tittenhurst, he stopped at his car and said, "I want to say good-bye to a few friends first." He then took a last walk through the grounds, giving careful attention to the trees, sometimes touching their leaves, just as on his morning walks. Then he left. The next day a severe storm swept through the Tittenhurst estate, breaking windows and uprooting trees.

* * *

November 3, 1969

Prabhupāda moved into his furnished apartment on Baker Street, a ten-minute drive from the Bury Place temple. After two months in London, he was anxious to see his temple open, and Śyāmasundara was working hard, although progressing slowly.

For the temple's interior Śyāmasundara had an artistic concept taken from photographs he had seen of the Ajanta Caves, South Indian temples with walls and ceilings of carved stone. His inspiration was to produce a similar effect using California redwood he and Mukunda had shipped to England a year ago. On first hearing the plans, Prabhupāda had asked, "Why make it so artistic?" But Śyāmasundara had been so set on the idea that Prabhupāda had permitted him. With the ceiling partly finished, there was no turning back.

Śyāmasundara toiled day and night, yet each day the temple design seemed to grow more elaborate, with the walls and floor fashioned of solid redwood and the ceiling lined with redwood arches. Śyāmasundara took great care to see that each piece fit exactly into place. As Śyāmasundara inched along, devotees joked that the room looked like an upside-down boat. But Prabhupāda encouraged him, telling him it was very beautiful.

Prabhupāda often allowed his disciples to work as they liked. He reasoned that they were raising the money and could spend it in Kṛṣṇa's service as they pleased. He also did not care to interfere in every detail of a disciple's service, especially when that disciple was strongheaded and had ideas that were not harmful or obstructive. All Prabhupāda's disciples were ultimately under his absolute decision, but he was often lenient—"eighty-percent lenient," he would sometimes say.

Śyāmasundara particularly thrived on having his own big projects. He had arranged for the Mantra-Rock Dance in San Francisco, built the first Ratha-yātrā carts, established a friendship with George Harrison, and now he was designing a temple. Prabhupāda allowed it—watchfully, like a father.

Consulting the Vedic calendar, Prabhupāda chose December 14 for the temple-opening celebration. And despite predictions from Śyāmasundara and others that the deadline would be impossible to meet, Prabhupāda ordered invitations printed immediately. The devotees had tremendous work to do, and little time. Not only did they have the temple to complete, but also Prabhupāda's quarters on the second floor and the kitchen in the basement. Faced with their tight deadline, they worked harder.

As Prabhupāda was anxious about the temple opening, he was also anxious about publishing the first volume of *Kṛṣṇa*. But he had no money.

According to printers' estimates, the book would cost about $19,000. Prabhupāda told Śyāmasundara to ask his friend George for a donation. Śyāmasundara, who had always been careful not to ask George for money, was hesitant. But Prabhupāda insisted, and Śyāmasundara gave in.

George agreed, but regretted it afterward. Then Śyāmasundara began to feel sorry. After all, he hadn't really wanted to ask George, and George hadn't really wanted to be asked. When Prabhupāda heard of this, he invited George to see him.

George told Prabhupāda that every day people were asking him for his money. But when Prabhupāda explained the importance of the *Kṛṣṇa* book and how George's donation would be devotional service to Kṛṣṇa, George dismissed his regrets. He also agreed to write a foreword to the volume.

George: *I didn't really think I was qualified to write the foreword to Prabhupāda's book. But one way of looking at it is, because I am known, it would help. But from the other point of view, it could really hinder, because not everyone wants to listen or to believe what I say. There are a lot of people who would be put off just because I'm saying it. I mean, if I picked up a book on Kṛṣṇa and the foreword was written by Frank Zappa or somebody like that, I would think, "God, maybe I don't want to know about it."*

So I thought that although he asked me, maybe Prabhupāda didn't really want me to write the foreword. But it was one of those things I couldn't get out of. Everybody had their minds made up, "You're writing the foreword, and that's it." So I just did it.

When Śrīla Prabhupāda asked to watch the moon landing, the devotees rented a television and placed it in Prabhupāda's living room. Prabhupāda took his massage as usual, sitting in a chair before the television.

Puruṣottama announced, "Well, Prabhupāda, it's about time, so I'll turn on the television, and soon we'll be getting some pictures from the astronauts out in space."

A reporter was speaking from Cape Canaveral, Florida: "We are just about to get the first pictures of this historic occasion." The picture appeared fuzzy, then cleared. The spacecraft had landed on the moon. As the astronauts emerged from the ship, they slowly eased themselves down onto the moon's surface. Puruṣottama was in ecstasy.

Dhanañjaya: *I was attempting to massage Prabhupāda's head and at the same time watch the program. All of a sudden, as the men were landing, Prabhupāda motioned for me to sit in front of him, so I came around. As soon as I sat down, Prabhupāda started to massage my head. I was quite embarrassed. "You have forgotten how to massage properly?" he asked. "This is how you do it." He massaged my head for about two minutes.*

Then I stood behind Prabhupāda and again began massaging his head. By this time, the astronauts were moving across the landscape. They had gotten out their little American flag and were sticking it in the ground and were jumping up and down. Apparently they were defying gravity, because every time they jumped up they would float through the air and then gently land again. There was a lot of jubilation and sounds from them.

"So, Puruṣottama," Prabhupāda asked, "they have come to the moon?"

"Yes, Prabhupāda," Puruṣottama said excitedly. "They've landed on the moon!"

Prabhupāda smiled.

Dhanañjaya: *Again, Prabhupāda motioned me to the front. I moved around and sat down. I thought he wanted me to massage him from the front. But again he put his hands on my head and massaged. He said, "Can't you learn this simple thing, massaging my head?" I had been watching the television and not giving my full attention to my service. I tried again, but again Prabhupāda said, "You still don't know how to do this." I said, "Well, Prabhupāda, I am trying my hardest." He laughed and said, "That is all right. Continue."*

Prabhupāda asked Puruṣottama, "So, what can you see?"

"They're exploring the moon's surface," he said.

"So, what is there?"

"Well, it looks like they have landed inside a crater somewhere, and the ground is sandy with some rocks. Oh, look, they're showing some shadows from some of the rocks that are lying around!"

"That's all you can see? There are no people? There are no trees? There are no rivers? There are no buildings?"

"No," Puruṣottama replied. "The moon is barren."

"They have not landed on the moon," Prabhupāda said emphatically. "This is not the moon."

Later when Mālatī brought in Prabhupāda's lunch, he said, "What Mālatī has done, she has made this little *kicharī* for Kṛṣṇa, and that is far greater than what they have done."

Even though Prabhupāda's quarters were incomplete and temple renovation made 7 Bury Place noisy and hectic, Prabhupāda decided to move in. "I am not attached to a comfortable apartment," he said. "My attachment is to living in the association of devotees." He was moving into the temple at a time when the record sales were low and the devotees were having to purchase supplies piecemeal, whenever they got money. Yet with Prabhupāda living with them and supervising their work, they were satisfied.

Tamāla Kṛṣṇa arrived from Los Angeles, and in addition to supervising much of the construction, he began taking the devotees out daily to chant on the streets and sell *Back to Godhead* magazines. Yamunā was sewing curtains from morning until night. Īśāna, Śyāmasundara, and others were working every possible hour on the renovation. And every day Prabhupāda would walk through the building to see the progress.

With only one week left until the opening, Śyāmasundara still labored on the temple ceiling. He had not even begun the altar. Again the other devotees complained to Prabhupāda that Śyāmasundara was too slow, but Prabhupāda replied, "He wants to make it artistic. Let him do it."

Śyāmasundara, this time on his own, asked George for a donation for an altar. George gave two thousand pounds, and Śyāmasundara picked out a slab of golden sienna marble and two slabs of red marble. Although Prabhupāda had a pair of seventeen-inch carved wood Deities of Rādhā and Kṛṣṇa, he didn't plan to use Them. And the size of the altar Śyāmasundara was building clearly required larger Deities.

One day a Mr. Doyal phoned, representing a large London Hindu society. He had heard the devotees wanted Rādhā-Kṛṣṇa Deities, and he had a pair he would donate. When Prabhupāda heard the news, he sent Tamāla Kṛṣṇa, Mukunda, and Śyāmasundara to Mr. Doyal's home to see the Deities.

Rādhā and Kṛṣṇa were white marble and stood about three feet high. Never before had the devotees seen such large Deities, and they offered obeisances. When they returned to the temple and told Prabhupāda, he said, "Take me there at once!"

Śrīla Prabhupāda, accompanied by Śyāmasundara, Mukunda, and Tamāla Kṛṣṇa, arrived by van at Mr. Doyal's home. Prabhupāda entered the living room and sat down. The Deities, covered by a cloth, stood on a table in the corner. Tamāla Kṛṣṇa was about to unveil Them when Prabhupāda checked him: "No. That's all right." Prabhupāda sat and spoke with Mr. Doyal, asking him about his work and where he had come from in India, and he met Mr. Doyal's family. Prabhupāda and his host chatted while the devotees listened.

"Swamiji," Mr. Doyal said at length, "I want to show you my Deities."

"Yes," Prabhupāda replied, "I will see Them after some time."

Prabhupāda began to speak about his Kṛṣṇa consciousness mission, and after a while Mr. Doyal again requested, "Please take a look at these Deities." And with that he walked over and unveiled Rādhā and Kṛṣṇa.

"Oh, yes," Prabhupāda said, folding his hands respectfully. Mr. Doyal explained that he had ordered the Deities from India for his own use, but in transit a tiny piece of Rādhārāṇī's finger had chipped off; therefore, according to Hindu tradition, the Deities could not be installed.

"Tamāla Kṛṣṇa," Prabhupāda said. "See how heavy these Deities are."

Tamāla Kṛṣṇa, placing one hand at Rādhārāṇī's base and the other around Her shoulder, lifted Her. "Not so heavy," he said.

"Śyāmasundara," Prabhupāda said. "See how heavy is Kṛṣṇa." The Deities were actually heavy for one man to carry, but the devotees understood Prabhupāda's intention.

"Not bad," Śyāmasundara said, holding Kṛṣṇa a few inches off the table.

"Yes," Prabhupāda said conclusively, "I think They're all right. Let us take Them. We have our van." And suddenly Prabhupāda was leaving, with his disciples following, carefully carrying Rādhā and Kṛṣṇa. Prabhupāda thanked Mr. Doyal.

"But Swamiji! Swamiji!" protested Mr. Doyal, who was not prepared for this sudden exit. "Please, we will arrange to bring Them. Our society will bring Them." But Prabhupāda was already out the door and leading his men to the van.

"Please wait," Mr. Doyal persisted. "We have to fix Them first, then you can take Them."

"We have an expert man," Prabhupāda said. "He can fix these things." Prabhupāda was assuring Mr. Doyal and at the same time directing his disciples. He opened the door of the van, and Śyāmasundara and Tamāla Kṛṣṇa slowly entered, cautiously setting Rādhā and Kṛṣṇa within. Tamāla Kṛṣṇa knelt in the back to hold the Deities secure, while Śyāmasundara got into the driver's seat.

"Now drive," Prabhupāda said. And off they went, with Prabhupāda smiling from the window to Mr. Doyal and his family, who stood together on the curb.

Śyāmasundara had driven but a few blocks when Prabhupāda asked him to stop the van. Turning around in his seat, Prabhupāda began offering prayers: *Govindam ādi-puruṣaṁ tam ahaṁ bhajāmi* . . . He looked long at Kṛṣṇa, who was white with a slight bluish cast, and at the exquisite white Rādhārāṇī by His side. "Kṛṣṇa is so kind," he said. "He has come like this." Then he had Śyāmasundara continue driving slowly back to the temple.

Carefully, Prabhupāda supervised his disciples' carrying the Deities up to the second floor. The devotees were astounded and delighted to see Prabhupāda in such an animated and intense state, bringing Rādhā and Kṛṣṇa into Their temple. He had the Deities placed in a curtained-off section of his own room, and then he sat at his desk.

Prabhupāda smiled. "Kṛṣṇa has played a great trick." In the *Mahābhārata* also, he said, there are incidents where Kṛṣṇa plays tricks. One such trick was Kṛṣṇa's agreeing to be on the side of the general He saw first in the morning. The two opposing generals, Arjuna and Duryodhana, had both come to Kṛṣṇa's tent early in the morning as Kṛṣṇa slept. They had agreed that one of them would stand at Kṛṣṇa's head and the other at Kṛṣṇa's feet and that they would wait until Kṛṣṇa awoke. Duryodhana chose to stand by Kṛṣṇa's head, while Arjuna chose His feet. Kṛṣṇa awoke and saw Arjuna.

"That was one great trick that was played by Kṛṣṇa," Prabhupāda said. "Similarly, this is a great trick." He told how Kṛṣṇa had also tricked Mother Yaśodā when she had tried to discipline Kṛṣṇa. He had run away, and she had run after Him, caught Him, and tried to tie Him with ropes. "But every time she came with more rope," Prabhupāda said, "it was just a little too short. Kṛṣṇa can play any kind of trick. Another such trick has been played. They made so much effort to bring these Deities here, thinking They will be for their Hindu Centre. But all the time Kṛṣṇa wanted to come here. So this chip on the Deity's hand is just Kṛṣṇa's trick. And we have caught Them."

"Prabhupāda," Mukunda said, "you kidnapped Kṛṣṇa."

"Yes," Prabhupāda said. "Once I was in the bank, and the manager had some scheme. But I foiled his scheme. So he said to me, 'Mr. De, you should have been a politician.' " Prabhupāda laughed. Then he became grave and asked the devotees not to talk about the incident. Many people would not understand how he could install a chipped Deity. The devotees agreed to keep the secret, but they had no doubt that

Prabhupāda's love for Kṛṣṇa was transcendental to Hindu customs; Rādhā and Kṛṣṇa had come to London on Prabhupāda's desire.

"How do you dress big Deities like this?" Yamunā asked. "They already have clothes on."

Prabhupāda said, "You bring me some cloth."

"What kind of cloth, Prabhupāda? What should the clothes look like?"

"Like in the pictures," he replied.

"Well, there are so many different pictures," she said. "Sometimes Kṛṣṇa has a ruffled skirt on, and sometimes He has a *dhotī* on, and sometimes He has a big crown on."

"Kṛṣṇa looks very beautiful in saffron," Prabhupāda said. "So you bring me some silk *dhotīs* in yellow and saffron color."

Yamunā collected six silk *sārīs* with silver and gold borders, and Prabhupāda indicated the design he wanted and told Yamunā how to arrange the crowns. With only a few days remaining before the installation ceremony, Yamunā began working almost continuously at her sewing machine. Several times a day Prabhupāda would come to see her progress.

Śyāmasundara had completed most of the altar, except for Lord Jagannātha's altar and the canopy over Rādhā and Kṛṣṇa's throne. Both the canopy and Lord Jagannātha's altar would be supported by four heavy wooden columns more than six feet high. Two rear columns would hold a marble slab for the Jagannātha deities to stand on, and two front columns were now supporting Rādhā and Kṛṣṇa's large velvet canopy. The columns were big and heavy; Śyāmasundara called them "elephant-leg columns." The columns now stood in place on the altar, although Śyāmasundara hadn't had a chance to secure them. The day before the installation Śyāmasundara collapsed upstairs in exhaustion.

On opening day many guests, Indians especially, crowded the temple, responding to flyers and advertisements. Apple Records had supplied a professional florist, who had decorated the room with floral arrangements. A BBC television crew was on hand to videotape the ceremony. While most of the devotees held *kīrtana*, Prabhupāda, behind a curtain at the other end of the temple, bathed Rādhā and Kṛṣṇa.

The plan was that after the bathing ceremony the Deities would be placed on the altar and Yamunā would dress Them. Once they were dressed and enthroned, the curtain would open for all the guests to behold Śrī Śrī Rādhā and Kṛṣṇa. Prabhupāda would lecture, and then everyone would feast. But because of Śyāmasundara's oversight, the installation almost became a disaster.

Prabhupāda had finished bathing the Deities and They had been placed on the marble altar, when suddenly the "elephant-leg columns" tottered. The canopy above the Deities began to collapse. Prabhupāda, seeing the danger, jumped onto the altar and seized the heavy columns in a split second. With great strength he held the two front pillars in place. "Get this out of here!" he shouted. While Prabhupāda's arms protected the Deities, the men removed the canopy, and then two men at a time carried each of the pillars away. The Deities remained unharmed.

While Prabhupāda was behind the curtain rescuing Rādhā and Kṛṣṇa, on the other side of the curtain guests and reporters awaited the unveiling of the Deities. Unaware of the mishap, the guests saw only men emerging from behind the curtain carrying large pillars and a canopy. The BBC camera crew began filming the canopy and pillars as they appeared from behind the curtain, taking them to be part of a ceremonial procession.

The few devotees behind the curtain with Prabhupāda were amazed. But there was no time now for apologies or appreciations. Yamunā dressed the Deities, Prabhupāda hurrying her. When at last everything was ready, Prabhupāda opened the main curtain, revealing the graceful forms of Lord Kṛṣṇa and Rādhārāṇī to the temple full of guests. A devotee began to offer *ārati*, while Prabhupāda, wearing a saffron *cādar* and a garland of carnations, stood to one side, reverentially looking upon Rādhā and Kṛṣṇa as their worshiper and protector.

This was the culmination of months of effort. Actually, years of planning had preceded this auspicious occasion. One hundred years before, Bhaktivinoda Ṭhākura had hoped for the day when Kṛṣṇa consciousness would come to England, and Śrīla Bhaktisiddhānta Sarasvatī had also desired it. Now that an authorized temple of Rādhā and Kṛṣṇa was preaching Kṛṣṇa consciousness in London, it was a historic occasion for Gauḍīya Vaiṣṇavism; a long-standing order of the previous *ācāryas* had been fulfilled. Prabhupāda had sent invitations to several of his Godbrothers in India. None of them had been able to come, of course, but at least they should have been pleased to learn that this dream of Śrīla Bhaktisiddhānta Sarasvatī's had been fulfilled.

Prabhupāda was seventy-three. He had now opened twenty-one temples in three years. Recently he had told some of his disciples that they should try to form a governing body for ISKCON, to relieve him of the management and allow him to concentrate fully on presenting Kṛṣṇa conscious literature. This literature could be introduced all over the world into homes, schools, and colleges for the benefit of everyone. It would be in such literature that he would live on. How much time he had left in this world he didn't know, he said, but he wanted to go on serving and trying to please his Guru Mahārāja, life after life.

Nevertheless, despite Prabhupāda's desire to retire from active work and absorb himself in writing books, here he was installing Deities in a new temple and protecting Them from his disciples' carelessness. Had he not been present, the celebration would have been a disaster. So many hardworking disciples, and they still needed his personal guidance.

ISKCON was just beginning to grow. Prabhupāda wanted to open not just twenty-one temples, but at least 108. His world traveling and book printing were just beginning, and, like everything else, the number of disciples would increase. The prestige of his movement would increase, and with it opposition from the atheists. Kṛṣṇa consciousness was growing, and Prabhupāda was in the forefront. "All around I see bright," he said. "That is the glory of Kṛṣṇa." He saw himself as a servant of his spiritual master; the bright future was in Kṛṣṇa's hands.

Prabhupāda called for Śyāmasundara. Although Prabhupāda was angry at first because of the near-disaster on the altar, he admitted that his disciples had done their best. The temple was beautiful, he told Śyāmasundara; he liked it. He then asked that a sign be placed out front with gold letters on a blue background:

RADHA-KRISHNA TEMPLE

This temple was constructed with great labor and effort
by Shyamasundar das Adhikary

On the day of Prabhupāda's departure from London, he distributed some of his personal effects, such as sweaters and scarves, to his disciples. He then went downstairs alone into the temple to see the Deities. He offered fully prostrated obeisances on the floor for a long time and then stood, looking at Rādhā and Kṛṣṇa.

Yamunā: *Prabhupāda was looking at the Deities with complete devotion. He loved those Deities. He had commented about Their exquisite beauty and how They complemented each other—how sometimes Rādhārāṇī looked more beautiful but how Kṛṣṇa's moonlike face and eyes were shining. Prabhupāda saw me and matter-of-factly said, "If you prac-*

tice what I have taught you and follow the instructions of how I have taught you to worship the Deity, and if you read the books that we have printed, it is sufficient for you to go back to Godhead. You need not learn anything new. Simply practice what I have taught you, and your life will be perfect." *Then he left—just left.*

CHAPTER THREE

A Threat Against ISKCON

Boston
December 21, 1969

More than one hundred of Prabhupāda's disciples and followers are in the lobby of the International Terminal of Boston's Logan Airport. Kīrtanānanda Swami has come from New Vrindaban with a truckload of devotees. The devotees from New York are here with a large banner: NEW YORK ISKCON WELCOMES SRILA PRABHUPADA. Most of the devotees wear heavy coats over their *dhotīs* and *sārīs* and are chanting Hare Kṛṣṇa; some play drums and cymbals. A few babies and children are present. Waiting passengers can only watch, startled.

Prabhupāda's plane is late, and the devotees continue chanting, often leaping into the air with outstretched arms. They haven't seen Prabhupāda in a long time, and they are waiting, expecting to see him at any moment. Oblivious of the proprieties of being in public, the devotees chant emotionally, building almost to uncontrolled ecstasy. The state police step in to tell the biggest devotee, Brahmānanda, "Cool it!" The chanting falls away to a murmur of *japa:* Hare Kṛṣṇa, Hare Kṛṣṇa, Kṛṣṇa Kṛṣṇa, Hare Hare/ Hare Rāma, Hare Rāma, Rāma Rāma, Hare Hare.

The plane from London arrives! The devotees are unable to see the passengers entering in the glassed-in immigration and customs area because the bottom six feet of the glass wall is painted black. Straining to see over the top, the devotees press forward, chanting, feverish, some almost hysterical. Suddenly they see Prabhupāda's raised hand with bead bag on the other side of the wall! They can see only his raised hand and bead bag. They go wild.

Fearlessly, with drums and *karatālas,* the *kīrtana* explodes again: Hare Kṛṣṇa, Hare Kṛṣṇa, Kṛṣṇa Kṛṣṇa, Hare Hare/ Hare Rāma, Hare Rāma, Rāma Rāma, Hare Hare. Advaita is tearfully smashing the *karatālas* together and chanting. Brahmānanda, jumping up and down, trying to glimpse into the customs room, is crying uncontrollably and yelling, "Prabhupāda! Prabhupāda!"

Śrīla Prabhupāda, free of customs, suddenly appears before them. Kīrtanānanda Swami, reserved until now, leaps around airport chairs and runs to him. Everyone is pushing and running, trying to be where Prabhupāda is.

Prabhupāda's saffron robes are wrinkled from the long flight, and he wears a knit sweater. He holds his white plastic attaché case in his left hand and again raises his right arm with forefinger and thumb extended from the bead bag. He smiles wonderfully, beaming to his children. Devotees cheer and cry: "All glories to Prabhupāda!"

As he walks toward a saffron-covered sofa in the airport lounge, the devotees move with him in an ecstatic wave, pressing in close. He sits down. Paramānanda, from New Vrindaban, comes forward with his infant son, the first boy born in ISKCON, and holds him forward to Prabhupāda for blessings. Prabhupāda is smiling, and the devotees are completely, unabashedly blissful.

"Where is Hayagrīva?" Prabhupāda asks. The question is repeated by the devotees, and big Hayagrīva lurches through the crowd, grumbling and falling flat at Prabhupāda's feet in obeisance. One by one, the leaders of the various ISKCON centers come forward and place garland after garland around Prabhupāda.

Prabhupāda looks beyond the wall of devotees at the newsmen with their cameras and at the baffled, curious, and disdainful onlookers. A bystander says, "I think he must be some kind of politician."

"So"—Prabhupāda begins speaking—"the spiritual master is to be worshiped as God. But if he is thinking that he is God, then he is useless. My request is, please don't take Kṛṣṇa consciousness as a sectarian religion. . . ." Prabhupāda explains that Kṛṣṇa consciousness is a great science, culminating in pure love of God. "These boys and girls had never heard of Kṛṣṇa before," Prabhupāda continues, "but now they have taken it up so naturally—because it is natural." Prabhupāda says that he is an old man yet he is sure that even if he passes away his students will continue the Kṛṣṇa consciousness movement. The potency of this movement is such that it can awaken awareness of God within anyone's heart.

After the lecture Prabhupāda stands and is escorted outside, where a limousine waits to drive him off through the newly fallen snow.

Riding joyfully in the car with Prabhupāda were Kīrtanānanda Swami, Brahmānanda, Satsvarūpa, and Puruṣottama. A professional chauffeur drove. Prabhupāda talked of London. It was an old, aristocratic city, he said, and the temple was in a very influential area near the British Museum. "The location is—what it is called—downtown?"

They passed a large billboard advertising a restaurant and lounge: CONTINENTAL. On seeing the billboard, Prabhupāda said, "*Cintāmaṇi*—what is that? Oh, no, Continental."

The devotees looked at one another: "*Cintāmaṇi.*" Prabhupāda had thought that the sign had read *Cintāmaṇi,* meaning the spiritual gems that make up the transcendental land of Kṛṣṇaloka. But Prabhupāda himself was *cintāmaṇi,* pure and innocent, coming to the cold, dirty city of Boston yet always thinking of Kṛṣṇa wherever he was. How fortunate to be with him! Satsvarūpa glanced at the professional chauffeur. "Drive carefully," he said.

Prabhupāda spoke softly from the back seat, while the devotees in front peered back, barely able to see him in the darkness and completely awed by his friendly yet inconceivable presence. "The other day," he said, "I told George Harrison that if he thought his money belonged to him, that was *māyā.*"

At the Sumner Tunnel the limousine pulled up at an automatic toll booth. The driver threw a coin into the chute, and the red light turned green. Prabhupāda asked if sometimes people drove through without paying, and Brahmānanda replied that an alarm would go off. They moved ahead into the Sumner Tunnel, usually an eerie, nerve-racking place—but not when riding with Prabhupāda.

"I told George to give his money to Kṛṣṇa," Prabhupāda said, "not that he had to give it to Kṛṣṇa by giving it to me, necessarily, but that somehow or other he must spend all of his money for Kṛṣṇa."

"But you are the only way to Kṛṣṇa," Brahmānanda said.

Prabhupāda laughed lightly. "Yes," he admitted, "at least in the West."

This was the great privilege of being able to ride with Prabhupāda: to hear him say little things or serious things and to see his fathomless expression or his kind smiling. It was a rare opportunity.

"I am representing unadulterated teachings," Prabhupāda continued. "Kṛṣṇa says in *Bhagavad-gītā*, 'Surrender to Me,' and I say, 'Surrender to Kṛṣṇa.' It is very simple. So many swamis come and present themselves as Kṛṣṇa, and it is all spoiled. But I say, 'Surrender to Kṛṣṇa.' I do not say anything new or adulterated. Kṛṣṇa says, 'Surrender to Me,' and I say, 'Surrender to Kṛṣṇa.' "

Prabhupāda asked Brahmānanda if fifty thousand copies of *Back to Godhead* magazine were being printed. Brahmānanda answered that they were. "Good," Prabhupāda replied. Turning his attention to Satsvarūpa, Prabhupāda asked how the composing machine was working, and Satsvarūpa said that hundreds of pages were being composed each month. Prabhupāda asked Kīrtanānanda Swami about New Vrindaban. New Vrindaban would improve, Prabhupāda said; the only thing wrong was that it got "blocked up" in the winter.

Each devotee in the car felt completely satisfied by his brief exchange with Prabhupāda, and they rode with him intoxicated in spiritual bliss.

Most of the devotees had raced ahead to the temple on Beacon Street and were waiting excitedly. The limousine pulled up, and again the devotees were unrestrained in their adoration of their spiritual master. Regally Prabhupāda walked up the walkway, onto the porch steps, through the front door, and into the vestibule, where he gazed around at the purple walls and the pink and green doorways. Surrounded by cheers and loving looks, he smiled.

The second-floor parlor, now the temple room, was filled with more than 150 disciples and guests, and they could see Prabhupāda's form rise into view as he came up the stairs. He still carried his white attaché case in his left hand and his bead bag in his right. And although he had just come out of the winter's night, he wore no coat, only cotton robes and a sweater. He appeared radiant.

Prabhupāda approached the altar. He seemed to notice everything: the small Rādhā-Kṛṣṇa Deities enthroned beneath a red velvet canopy, the larger deities of Jagannātha, Subhadrā, and Balarāma on a raised shelf above the picture of Lord Caitanya and His *saṅkīrtana* party, even the brass *ārati* paraphernalia, brightly shining on the small table near the altar. Turning to his secretary and traveling companion, Puruṣottama, he asked, "What do you think, Puruṣottama? Isn't this very nice?"

Crossing the room, Prabhupāda sat on the red velvet *vyāsāsana*. He spoke, and the audience was attentive. After praising the London center, the Deity worship there, the expertly made *purīs* for Rādhā and Kṛṣṇa, he turned toward the altar and said, "If you clean the Deities' utensils, your heart will become cleansed." By polishing the Deities' paraphernalia, he said, the devotees were cleaning their spiritual master's heart also. As he spoke, focusing simply and purely on devotion to the Deity, the devotees suddenly realized the importance of this aspect of their Kṛṣṇa consciousness. "Who has made these clothes?" Prabhupāda asked, glancing at Rādhā and Kṛṣṇa's little flounced dresses.

"Śāradīyā," a few devotees called out.

Prabhupāda smiled, "Thank you very much." Then he threw back his head and laughed. "Is Śāradīyā still fighting with her husband?"

The devotees and guests laughed, while Śāradīyā covered her face with her hands. "Don't fight with your husband," Prabhupāda said. "He is a good boy. Anybody that comes to Kṛṣṇa consciousness is good." He then asked to see the rest of the house.

A hundred devotees, straining to see and hear Prabhupāda's responses, followed him as he went downstairs. Although the crowd surrounded him, he remained relaxed and unhurried. He entered the press room, a long hall directly beneath the temple room. A large old offset press, a paper cutter, a folder, and flats of paper stock filled the room, which smelled like a print shop. Advaita, the press manager, bowed down in his green khakis before Prabhupāda. He rose up smiling, and Prabhupāda stepped forward and embraced him, putting his arm around Advaita's head. "Very good," he said.

Standing before the printing press, Prabhupāda folded his palms together and offered a prayer to his spiritual master: "Jaya Oṁ Viṣṇupāda Paramahaṁsa Śrī Śrīmad Bhaktisiddhānta Sarasvatī Gosvāmī Mahārāja Prabhupāda kī jaya!" Advaita asked Prabhupāda to give the press a transcendental name. "ISKCON Press," Prabhupāda said matter-of-factly, as if it had already been named.

"Keep all the machines very clean," Prabhupāda said, "and they will last a long time. This is the heart of ISKCON."

"You are the heart of ISKCON, Prabhupāda," a devotee said.

"And this is *my* heart," said Prabhupāda.

Leaving the main press room, Prabhupāda toured the other press facilities. Squeezing in, ducking under, standing on tiptoes, the crowd of devotees followed him step by step. He peeked into a little cubbyhole where a devotee was composing type. The typesetters, he said, should proceed very slowly at first, and in that way they would become expert. Turning to Advaita, he said, "Everyone in India who speaks Hindi has a Gita Press publication. So everyone who speaks English should have an ISKCON Press publication."

Compared to most authors, Prabhupāda's literary contribution was already substantial. But he wasn't just "an author." His mission was to flood the world with literature glorifying Lord Kṛṣṇa. Prabhupāda's ISKCON was now three years old, yet his disciples were only beginning to execute his plans for printing and distributing transcendental literature.

Printing was an important step—the first step. Months ago Prabhupāda had written,

> The press must work on continuously, and we shall produce immense volumes of literature. If the press goes on nicely, I shall be able to give you material for publishing a book every two months. We have got so much material for the Krishna consciousness movement.

And just prior to coming to Boston he had written,

> *Samkirtan* and distributing *Back to Godhead* and our other literatures is the fieldwork of this movement. Temple worship is secondary.

Now ISKCON was printing fifty thousand copies of *Back to Godhead* per month, and Prabhupāda hoped to increase the sales more and more.

Standing in the crowded, chilly basement, surrounded by devotees, press machines, and transcendental literature, Prabhupāda described how he wanted ISKCON Press to operate. He said that after dictating a tape he would mail it to Boston to be transcribed. The transcription should take no more than two days. During the next two days, someone would edit the transcribed manuscript. Then another editor would take two days to edit the transcript a second time. A Sanskrit editor would add diacritical markings, and the manuscript would be ready for composing.

Prabhupāda said he could produce fifteen tapes—three hundred manuscript pages—every month. At that rate, ISKCON Press should produce a book every two months, or six books in a year. Prabhupāda wanted to print at least sixty books. Therefore his press workers would have plenty to do for the next ten years. If the devotees simply printed his books incessantly, he said, even if they had to work twenty-four hours a day in shifts, it would give him "great delight." He was ready, if necessary, to drop all his activities except for publishing books.

This was the special nectar the press devotees were hankering to hear. Printing books was Prabhupāda's heart; it was the thing most dear to him.

During Prabhupāda's week in Boston, Puruṣottama continued as secretary and servant, out of duty. His difficulties in London had increased. Doubtful and morose, he came before Prabhupāda two days before their departure.

Puruṣottama: *I had decided to leave in London. I just felt like there were different things I wanted to do. But I felt obligated to stay with him, because he needed me there. It was my job to at least get him back to the States. I felt that he needed someone to travel with him. And I just felt that I should complete that, have everything in order, so I couldn't say to myself that I had just quit when he needed me like that in a foreign country.*

I didn't tell anybody. I didn't speak against him or anything. I performed my duties, but in my attitude I let him know I was really getting kind of distant the last few days. I didn't bow down to him. I would come in, but I just wouldn't bow down to him.

He entered Prabhupāda's room. He didn't bow down. He stood. He was too uncomfortable to sit, because of the gravity of what he would say. Prabhupāda looked up from his desk. "Yes, Puruṣottama?"

Puruṣottama: *I went in to see him. I knew I was going to leave, and it kind of made me sick to do it. Anyway, I told him I have a lot of questions about the movement, the moon, and everything. I just don't believe all of this. He was very congenial about the whole thing. He took it nicely.*

He said to me, "If you have questions, why don't you ask me?" And I said, "You yourself have said that we should only ask questions to somebody we feel we can believe or trust." He looked very hurt. He knew what I was saying. I felt like I really hurt him. I didn't mean it to be so defiant, but there I was.

He said, "I've noticed that you haven't been well lately. You've had some problems?"

I said, "Well, I haven't been trying to hide it." I guess I was trying to prepare him for what was coming. I wanted to leave that night. So I said, "I want to leave." But he said to me, "You've been with me so long, and now you're so anxious to go? You can't even stay a night?" He said, "Why don't you stay at least till my plane leaves." That was two days later. I said, "O.K., I'll do that then."

I was going to go back to New York. Actually I didn't have the money for the ticket, and he gave me the money, he gave me the bus fare. I really appreciated that. I could have borrowed some money from someone else, but he said, "Well, you take it, and you can pay me back later." And I did. I gave it back the next week.

He was very gracious about the whole thing. Actually I could see that he had a very special loving way of looking at the world. I felt that sometimes I could see things in a loving way, like he did, and I realized that I got that viewpoint from him—you know, that little loving spirit. He had that, and I kind of caught some of that from him. And that's one of the things I always remember about him. And I know that through his movement I came to believe in God. Before I met him, I didn't believe in God.

After Puruṣottama left, Prabhupāda spoke with Bhavānanda about Puruṣottama's doubts concerning the moon landing and his consequent doubts of Kṛṣṇa consciousness. "I can understand that he might not accept it because I said it, but how could he disbelieve the Vedic *śāstras*?"

Boston's weather was miserable. When the rain stopped, the snow fell, and when the snow stopped, the rain came again. Prabhupāda tried taking a walk in the front yard, Bhavānanda beside him with the umbrella, watching cautiously to guard him from falling on the ice. But after a week of Boston's nasty December weather, Prabhupāda's cold was getting worse. He would go to Los Angeles.

* * *

Los Angeles
February 25, 1970

On the auspicious occasion of Bhaktisiddhānta Sarasvatī Ṭhākura's appearance day anniversary, the Los Angeles devotees received permission to enter their new temple on Watseka Avenue. The rooms had not even been cleaned, and the large hall was bare; but the devotees brought in Prabhupāda's *vyāsāsana* from the old temple on La Cienaga, and

Prabhupāda had them place on it a large picture of his spiritual master. Standing before his spiritual master, Prabhupāda offered *ārati,* while some fifty disciples gathered around him, chanting Hare Kṛṣṇa and dancing in the otherwise empty hall.

After the *ārati,* Prabhupāda directed his disciples in offering flowers to the picture of Bhaktisiddhānta Sarasvatī. Then, still standing before the *vyāsāsana,* he said he had nothing to offer his spiritual master on this day except his own disciples. He then read aloud the names of all his disciples.

Taking his seat on a low *vyāsāsana* beside the large *vyāsāsana* of Bhaktisiddhānta Sarasvatī Ṭhākura, Prabhupāda gave a short history of his Guru Mahārāja, son of Bhaktivinoda Ṭhākura and powerful *ācārya* of the mission of Caitanya Mahāprabhu. As Prabhupāda recalled his first meeting with his spiritual master, he told how Bhaktisiddhānta Sarasvatī had told him to teach Kṛṣṇa consciousness to the English-speaking world. This large new temple, Prabhupāda said, had been provided by Bhaktisiddhānta Sarasvatī as a gift for the devotees to use in Kṛṣṇa's service. They should not become attached to the opulence, Prabhupāda said, but they should use this wonderful place for preaching. As he spoke, he wept.

"Now bring them *prasādam*!" Prabhupāda called. And the feast began. While devotees sat on the floor in rows, Prabhupāda from his *vyāsāsana* directed the servers, having them bring another *samosā* to one devotee, more chutney to another, and so on. He watched over all of them, encouraging them to take Kṛṣṇa's *prasādam.*

That afternoon Prabhupāda toured the buildings. In addition to the main hall, which he would have the devotees convert into a temple, he saw the equally large lecture hall. These rooms, plus a three-room apartment, ample separate quarters for male and female devotees, a parking lot, and a front lawn, made this the finest physical facility in all of ISKCON. "We don't require such a nice place for ourselves," Prabhupāda told the temple president, Gargamuni. "We are prepared to live anywhere. But such a nice place will give us opportunity to invite gentlemen to come and learn about this Kṛṣṇa consciousness."

The cost of the building had been $225,000, with a $50,000 down payment. Prabhupāda had had more than $10,000 in his book fund, but that was exclusively for printing books. So although he usually didn't like to deal personally in such negotiations, he had made an exception in this case and had asked the other temples to donate to the new "world headquarters" in Los Angeles. He had even mailed snapshots of the buildings to various temple presidents around the world. Thus he had collected the down payment, and on Śrīla Bhaktisiddhānta Sarasvatī's appearance day ISKCON became the legal owner.

This was the only temple ISKCON actually owned—all the other buildings were leased or rented—and Prabhupāda wanted to design everything himself. Hiring professionals would be too expensive, but Prabhupāda had plenty of disciples eager to do the renovation. Karandhara knew a little carpentry, plumbing, and general construction, and he could learn more by experience. Bhavānanda had been a professional designer, and he was filled with Prabhupāda's enthusiasm to transform the plain church into a dazzling palace for the Supreme Personality of Godhead. "First you make my apartment," Prabhupāda told Bhavānanda. "Let me move in, and then we will work on the temple room."

Bhavānanda: *We picked out a part of the Los Angeles temple for Prabhupāda's quarters, and Karandhara built a bathroom. When Prabhupāda came up to the rooms, he said, "This will be my sitting room. This will be my bedroom." And when he came to a third room, with a skylight, he said, "This will be my library."*

Prabhupāda had told me once in Boston that as a child he had lived in a palace with blue walls, red marble floors, and orange and gold trim—the Mulliks' house in Calcutta. So we painted the walls of his sitting room blue, and I put in a white tile floor. The drapes were burnt-orange satin with gold cords and gold fringe. Prabhupāda liked this color scheme very much.

In the bedroom I asked Prabhupāda where he wanted his bed, and he said, "Put the bed in the middle of the room." We had put down a rug, and Prabhupāda said, "Now you should get sheets and cover the rug with them. In India they have rugs like this, nice rugs, and they cover them with sheets. And on special days they take the sheets off. Otherwise they would become ruined." So I went out and bought sheets.

Prabhupāda was in his sitting room when I came in and started putting the sheet over the rug in the bedroom. Prabhupāda came in and said, "Yes, this is very nice. Again I have introduced something new. This is something new for all of you—sheets on rugs." Then he told me, "Now make sure there are no wrinkles in the sheet." I was on my hands and knees on the rug, and Prabhupāda also got down on his hands and knees right next to me. We were both pressing out the wrinkles from the sheet, and when we got to the end, Prabhupāda folded the sheet under the rug.

He was very happy there, because it was our own place. We had never had our own place before.

In the temple room Prabhupāda showed Karandhara where to build the three altars. He indicated the measurements and instructed that before each altar should be a pair of doors and over them the symbols of Visnu: a conchshell over the altar for *guru* and Gaurāṅga; a wheel and club over Rādhā and Kṛṣṇa's altar in the center; and a lotus over Lord Jagannātha's. The spiritual master's *vyāsāsana* was to go at the opposite end of the temple, facing Rādhā and Kṛṣṇa. The walls should be yellow, which Prabhupāda said was in the mode of goodness. The ceiling should be covered with a canopy, and there should be chandeliers.

Once the altars were completed, Prabhupāda wanted to bring the Deities, even though much of the renovation was yet unfinished. After constructing an umbrella-covered cart and decorating it with flowers, the devotees brought the Deities in procession from the old temple on La Cienaga Boulevard to Their new home.

Bhavānanda: *The first time he came into the temple room after his morning walk, he went to the* guru-*Gaurāṅga altar and paid his obeisances. We all paid our obeisances. Then he stood up, and he went to Rādhā and Kṛṣṇa, and then paid obeisances, then to Jagannātha, and we all followed. Then we walked back and he sat on his* vyāsāsana, *and he told us, "Now you line up facing each other from the* vyāsāsana *to Rādhā and Kṛṣṇa, face each other. This way, that way, one way you look is* guru, *and the other way God. And then back and forth that way. Always leave this aisle," he said, "so I can see."*

The Deity was the king, Prabhupāda said, and all the temple residents were His personal servants. The temple, therefore, should be like a palace. An elaborate temple was important for preaching, Prabhupāda explained, because most people, especially Westerners, were not inclined to undergo any austerities for obtaining spiritual life. There was an Indian saying, No one listens to a poor man. Were the devotees to advertise classes on *bhakti-yoga* in such-and-such empty field under a certain tree, Prabhupāda said, no one would come. But a clean, beautiful building with chandeliers and comfortable rooms would attract many people to visit and become purified.

The temple was also for those who wanted to live there as Kṛṣṇa conscious devotees. Devotees, Prabhupāda said, should be willing to live and sleep anywhere. But as the loving, protecting father of his disciples, Prabhupāda took great care to establish a large temple and an adequate dormitory facility. He was making a home for his family. To see that his spiritual children had a place to live and practice their devotional service was just another aspect of his mission.

A special feature of the new temple was Śrīla Prabhupāda's garden. The devotees had excavated a large patch of concrete behind the temple, filled it in with earth, surrounded it with a cinder-block wall, and planted a lawn with flower gardens all around.

Karandhara: *I had dug some beds along the inside perimeter and planted a plant here and a plant there. But Prabhupāda said, "No, plant something everywhere. Everywhere there should be something growing. Everywhere there is a place, you plant something. Let there be growing everywhere." He wanted it overgrown like a jungle, a tropical area where plants just grow luxuriantly everywhere.*

Śrīla Prabhupāda always enjoyed sitting in the garden in the evening with the fresh, cool evening air and the fragrance of the flowers. The topics of conversation in the garden were as varied as Śrīmad-Bhāgavatam*—all different subjects. Sometimes there would be lively conversations with guests or devotees, and sometimes Prabhupāda would spend the entire time just chanting, with very little conversation. Sometimes Prabhupāda would just have somebody read from the* Kṛṣṇa *book.*

Prabhupāda said that his mother maintained a garden on the roof of their house when he was young and that he would go up there in the evenings and play. He remembered that. He always remembered what he liked to do as a child. You would hear him reminisce with pleasure about it. Many times he would comment, "My mother maintained a garden on the roof of our residence, and as a child I would go there in the evening and play. Now I also have such a nice place to come."

Under Prabhupāda's personal direction, the Los Angeles center became a model for the rest of ISKCON. At the morning *Bhāgavatam* class, for example, he had the devotees responsively chant the Sanskrit *mantras* after him, and he asked that this become the standard program in all his temples. In May 1970, he wrote to each of his twenty-six temple presidents throughout North America and Europe, inviting them to visit him at Los Angeles.

> Now at the present moment, I am concentrating my energy in this Los Angeles Center as ideal for all other centers in respect of Deity worship, Arotrik, Kirtan and other necessary paraphernalia. As I have curtailed my moving program, I wish that you may come here at your convenience and stay here for a few days and see personally how things are going on; and by meeting with me personally for necessary instruction, I hope simultaneously in all Centers the activities will be of the same standard.

The temple presidents who visited Prabhupāda, most of them young men in their twenties, came with practical as well as philosophical questions. They came with their notebooks, writing down everything from the temple schedule to color schemes, noting the tunes used in the *kīrtanas*, learning how to manage a *saṅkīrtana* party. And perhaps most important of all, they would note the things Prabhupāda did and the words he spoke personally to them. The temple presidents would then return to their own centers—in Berkeley or Hamburg or Toronto or Sydney—glowing with ecstasy and ready to implement dozens of new standards they had imbibed from Prabhupāda at the Los Angeles world headquarters.

Although Prabhupāda still spoke of expanding his movement more and more, he seemed content to stay in Los Angeles, reaching the rest of the world through his temple presidents, his *saṅkīrtana* parties, and his books. New plans were unfolding, however, and Prabhupāda again spoke of a governing body, twelve hand-picked disciples to manage all of ISKCON's affairs. He also spoke of initiating more *sannyāsīs* and taking them with him to India to train as itinerant preachers. And to insure that his books were regularly and properly printed, he wanted to form a special committee in charge of book publication.

Sometimes managing his worldwide religious movement, sometimes leading the growing group of devotees in chanting Sanskrit *mantras* in the Los Angeles temple, and sometimes sitting alone and translating in the pre-dawn hours, Prabhupāda lived happily in Los Angeles.

One day a record arrived from London. The London devotees, who with George Harrison's help had already produced an album, had now also released a new single, "Govinda." The song consisted of verses Prabhupāda had taught them from *Brahma-saṁhitā*, each verse ending with the refrain *govindam ādi-puruṣaṁ tam ahaṁ bhajāmi*. Prabhupāda asked that the record be played during the morning program in the temple. The next morning, after he had entered the temple room, bowed down before the Deity, and taken his seat on the *vyāsāsana* to begin the class, the record began.

Suddenly, Prabhupāda became stunned with ecstasy. His body shivered, and tears streamed from his eyes. The devotees, feeling a glimmer of their spiritual master's emotion, began to chant Hare Kṛṣṇa as if chanting *japa*. The moments seemed to pass slowly. Finally Prabhupāda spoke: "*Govindam ādi-puruṣaṁ tam ahaṁ bhajāmi.*" He was again silent. Then he asked, "Is everyone all right?" The response was a huge roar: "Jaya Prabhupāda!" And he began the *Śrīmad-Bhāgavatam* class.

* * *

Vaiṣṇavera kriyā-mudrā vijñe na bujhaya: "No one can understand the mind of a Vaiṣṇava." Only a pure devotee can understand another pure devotee perfectly. But by observing the main activities of Prabhupāda's life, we can see that whatever he did was pure service to Lord Kṛṣṇa and was a perfect example of how to surrender to Kṛṣṇa. He taught by precept and by example. Often encouraging, even praising his disciples, he always pushed them into more and more participation in the blissful *saṅkīrtana* movement of Lord Caitanya. But he also exposed the faults of his disciples, and these faults were sometimes great and painful to see, both for him and for his disciples.

One day, as Prabhupāda came into his quarters at the Los Angeles temple, he saw that one of the devotees cleaning his room had placed his picture upside down. A simple mistake. But it indicated something wrong in the disciple's mentality. Every morning the devotees sing prayers to the spiritual master honoring him as the direct representative of God. How could any sincere disciple not notice that he is standing God's representative upside down?

Then a more serious discrepancy. Prabhupāda went to the temple, greeted the Deities, and went to take *caraṇāmṛta*, the scented water from the bathing of the Deities. It was part of his daily schedule. After his morning walk, he would return to the temple and offer obeisances to the Deities while the "Govinda" record was being played. A devotee would then offer him a few drops of *caraṇāmṛta* in his right palm, and he would sip it. He had mentioned this item of devotional service in *The Nectar of Devotion:* "Scented with perfumes and flowers, the water comes gliding down through His lotus feet and is collected and mixed with yogurt. In this way this *caraṇāmṛta* not only becomes very tastefully flavored, but also has tremendous spiritual value. . . . The devotees who come to visit and offer respects to the Deity take three drops of *caraṇāmṛta* very submissively and feel themselves happy in transcendental bliss."

On this particular morning, however, as Śrīla Prabhupāda took *caraṇāmṛta,* he frowned. Someone had put salt in it! He walked the length of the temple room, took his seat on the *vyāsāsana,* and before a room full of a hundred devotees, asked, "Who has put salt in the *caraṇāmṛta*?" A young girl in a *sārī* stood and with a nervous smile said she had done it.

"Why have you done it?" Prabhupāda asked gravely.

"I don't know," she giggled.

Prabhupāda turned to Gargamuni: "Get someone responsible."

Everyone present felt Prabhupāda's anger. The unpleasant moment marred the pure temple atmosphere. A disciple worships Kṛṣṇa by pleasing Kṛṣṇa's representative, the spiritual master; therefore to displease the spiritual master was a spiritual disqualification. The spiritual master was not merely a principle; he was a person—Śrīla Prabhupāda.

When ISKCON Press in Boston misprinted Prabhupāda's name on a new book, he became deeply disturbed. The small paperback chapter from the Second Canto of *Śrīmad-Bhāgavatam* bore his name on the cover as simply A. C. Bhaktivedanta. Omitted was the customary "His Divine Grace" as well as "Swami Prabhupāda." Śrīla Prabhupāda's name stood almost divested of spiritual significance. Another ISKCON Press publication described Prabhupāda as "*ācārya*" of ISKCON, although Prabhupāda had repeatedly emphasized that he was the founder-*ācārya.* There had been many *ācāryas,* or spiritual masters, and there would be many more; but His Divine Grace A. C. Bhaktivedanta Swami Prabhupāda was the sole founder-*ācārya* of the International Society for Krishna Consciousness.

To make matters worse, when Prabhupāda first opened the new *Bhāgavatam* chapter, the binding cracked and the pages fell out. Prabhupāda glowered.

The devotees in Boston, hearing of Prabhupāda's anger, knew at once that their mistake in misprinting Śrīla Prabhupāda's name was a serious oversight. Minimizing the spiritual master's position was a grave offense, and they had even published the offense. The serious implications were difficult for the devotees to face, and they knew they would have to rectify their mentality before they could make spiritual progress. Prabhupāda criticized the mentality behind these mistakes, and his criticisms were instructive to his disciples. Unless *he* instructed them about the absolute position of the spiritual master, how would they learn?

At the beginning of the *Śrīmad-Bhāgavatam* class one morning, Prabhupāda called on one of the women devotees: "Nandarāṇī." She stood respectfully. "Do you chant sixteen rounds every day?"

"Well, I try to, Prabhupāda."

"This is the problem," Prabhupāda said, turning to the temple president. If Nandarāṇī, one of the senior, responsible women, wasn't chanting regularly, then certainly the new women under her weren't either. This was the managers' fault. Prabhupāda had praised and encouraged his disciples for laboring hard to renovate the temple and for going out daily into the streets to chant and distribute magazines. But for a devotee to not chant the prescribed rounds was to neglect the most important instruction.

What Nandarāṇī hadn't said was that the temple authorities had told her that chanting all her sixteen rounds wasn't necessary, as long as she worked. They had told her this, even though Prabhupāda clearly instructed his disciples at initiation to always chant at least sixteen rounds daily.

Then another incident. During the morning class, Prabhupāda was discussing Sārvabhauma Bhaṭṭācārya, an associate of Lord Caitanya. Looking among the devotees, he asked, "Who can tell me who is Sārvabhauma Bhaṭṭācārya?" No one spoke. Prabhupāda waited. "*None* of you can tell me who is Sārvabhauma Bhaṭṭācārya?" he asked. One girl raised her hand; she had "read something about him"—that was all.

"Aren't you ashamed?" Prabhupāda looked at the men. "You should be the leaders. If the men cannot advance, then the women cannot advance. You must be *brāhmaṇas*. Then your wives will be *brāhmaṇas*. But if you are not *brāhmaṇas*, then what can *they* do?" Without improving their chanting and without reading Kṛṣṇa conscious literature, Prabhupāda said, they would never attain the purity necessary for preaching Lord Caitanya's message.

While the local anomalies were weighing heavily on Śrīla Prabhupāda, he learned of strange things his disciples in India had written in their letters, and he became more disturbed. One letter to devotees in America reported that Prabhupāda's Godbrothers in India objected to his title

Prabhupāda. According to them, only Bhaktisiddhānta Sarasvatī should be called Prabhupāda, and they referred to Prabhupāda as "Swami Mahārāja." Prabhupāda also learned that some of his disciples were saying he was not the only spiritual master. They were interested in reading Bhaktisiddhānta Sarasvatī's books—as if to discover some new teaching Prabhupāda had not yet revealed.

Prabhupāda regarded these remarks as dangerous for ISKCON. Advancement in spiritual life was based on implicit faith in the spiritual master, and to Prabhupāda these new ideas indicated a relative conception, as opposed to the absolute conception, of the spiritual master. Such a conception could destroy all he had established; at least, it could destroy the spiritual life of anyone who held it.

Though sometimes ignorant, his disciples, he knew, were not malicious. Yet these letters from India carried a spiritual disease transmitted by several of Prabhupāda's Godbrothers to his disciples there. Prabhupāda had already been troubled when some of his Godbrothers had refused to help him secure land in Māyāpur, the birthplace of Lord Caitanya. Although he had asked them to help his inexperienced disciples purchase land, they had not complied. In fact, some of them had worked against him. Prabhupāda had written to one of his Godbrothers, "I am so sorry to learn that there is a sort of conspiracy by some of our Godbrothers as not to give me a place at Māyāpur."

Prabhupāda was sensitive to any threat to ISKCON. His accepting the name Prabhupāda, his teaching that the disciple must approach the spiritual master as the direct representative of Kṛṣṇa, without attempting to jump over him to the previous spiritual masters—these things he had carefully explained to his disciples. But now a few irresponsibly spoken remarks in India were weakening the faith of some of his disciples. Perhaps this insidious contamination that was now spreading had precipitated the blunders at ISKCON Press and even the discrepancies in Los Angeles. Talks about the relative position of the spiritual master could only be the workings of *māyā*, the Lord's illusory energy. *Māyā* was attempting to bewilder the devotees of ISKCON. That was her job: to lead the conditioned souls away from Kṛṣṇa's service.

The recent events began to hamper Prabhupāda's writing. He had been working quickly in Los Angeles and had recently finished the second and final volume of *Kṛṣṇa*. And on the very tape on which he had dictated the last chapter of *Kṛṣṇa*, he had immediately begun a summary of the

Eleventh Canto of *Śrīmad-Bhāgavatam*. Gradually, however, his writing stopped.

Karandhara: *Prabhupāda's translating would require a great deal of concentration. He would have two or three of his big* Bhāgavatam *volumes opened up and sometimes a number of other small books, which he would refer to for something or other. He would sit, wearing his glasses and speaking into his dictating machine, and he would be completely absorbed in reading. Sometimes he would make a brief note, then look into one of his books, then open another book, turn back to another page, make a note, and then dictate. It required a great deal of concentration. I think that's why Prabhupāda did most of it at night, after he would rise from his late evening nap. From one or two in the morning until six or seven in the morning he would be absorbed. It was quiet at that time, and he could become absorbed.*

But when Prabhupāda became disturbed about the problems in ISKCON, it inhibited his work. He was spending his time discussing with visiting devotees or myself or whoever was there. Then he would spend more time thinking matters over or pondering the problem, and he wouldn't be able to concentrate on his translating. These difficulties disturbed him, and he would think about them and say, "I have not been able to concentrate. I have been thinking about this problem."

Although the spiritual master suffers for his disciples' mistakes, Prabhupāda's perspective was not simply negative. He continued chanting and lecturing in the temple and inviting the leaders of his movement to visit him in the ideal center of Los Angeles; but he also corrected the diseased mentality wherever it appeared. When, for example, Guru dāsa wrote from London to say that they had allowed an Indian guest to lecture in the temple while sitting on Prabhupāda's *vyāsāsana*, Prabhupāda immediately wrote back, correcting him.

> I am surprised how you allowed Mr. Parikh to sit on the Vyasasana. You know that Vyasasana is meant for the representative of Vyasadeva, the Spiritual Master, but Mr. Parikh does not come in the Parampara to become the representative of Vyas, neither does he have any sound knowledge of Vaisnava principles. I understand from your letter that sometimes discussions on Aurobindo philosophy are done by Mr. Parikh from the Vyasasana, so I am a little surprised how did you allow like this. I think you should rectify immediately all these mistakes as stated by you in the last two lines

> of your letter, "I think the best thing to do is to stop his class. Nonsense ought not to be tolerated."

In a letter from Paris, Tamāla Kṛṣṇa asked Prabhupāda philosophical questions about the perfection of the spiritual master, and Prabhupāda answered fully, but sternly.

> A Spiritual Master is always liberated. In any condition of His life He should not be mistaken as an ordinary human being. This position of the Spiritual Master is achieved by three processes. One is called *sadhan siddha.* That means one who is liberated by executing the regulative principles of devotional service. Another is *kripa siddha,* one who is liberated by the mercy of Kṛṣṇa or His devotee. And another is *nitya siddha* who is never forgetful of Kṛṣṇa throughout his whole life. These are the three features of the perfection of life.
>
> So far Narada Muni is concerned, in His previous life He was a maidservant's son, but by the mercy of the devotees He later on became *siddha* and next life He appeared as Narada with complete freedom to move anywhere by the grace of the Lord. So even though he was in His previous life a maidservant's son there was no impediment in the achievement of His perfect spiritual life. Similarly any living entity who is conditioned can achieve the perfectional stage of life by the above mentioned processes and the vivid example is Narada Muni.
>
> So I do not know why you have asked about my previous life. Whether I was subjected to the laws of material nature? So, even though accepting that I was subjected to the laws of material nature, does it hamper in my becoming Spiritual Master? What is your opinion? From the life of Narada Muni it is distinct that although He was a conditioned soul in His previous life, there was no impediment of His becoming the Spiritual Master. This law is applicable not only to the Spiritual Master, but to every living entity.
>
> So far I am concerned, I cannot say what I was in my previous life, but one great astrologer calculated that I was previously a physician and my life was sinless. Besides that, to corroborate the statement of *Bhagavad-gita* "sucinam srimatam gehe yogabhrasta 'bhijayate," which means an unfinished yogi takes birth in rich family or born of a *suci* or pious father. By the grace of Krishna I got these two opportunities in the present life to be born of a pious father and brought up in one of the richest, aristocratic families of Calcutta (Kasinatha Mullik). The Radha Krishna Deity in this family called me to meet Him, and therefore last time when I was in Calcutta, I stayed in that temple along with my American disciples. Although I had

> immense opportunities to indulge in the four principles of sinful life because I was connected with a very aristocratic family, Krishna always saved me, and throughout my whole life I do not know what is illicit sex, intoxication, meat-eating or gambling. So far my present life is concerned, I do not remember any part of my life when I was forgetful of Krishna.

Prabhupāda thought some of his leaders had become entangled in ISKCON management and were trying to gain control for themselves. In the classes he would speak of this only indirectly, as he had when he had exposed that the devotees weren't chanting and reading enough. Consequently, most devotees were unaware of Prabhupāda's anxiety. But occasionally, while sitting in his room or in the garden, Prabhupāda would express his concern. He wanted his disciples to manage ISKCON, but to do so they must be pure. Only then would he be able to concentrate on writing books. In June he wrote to Brahmānanda,

> Now my desire is that I completely devote my time in the matter of writing and translating books, and arrangement should now be done that our Society be managed automatically. I think we should have a central governing body for dealing with important matters. I have already talked with Gargamuni about this. So if you come back by the Rathayatra festival, we can have a preliminary meeting at San Francisco in this connection.

* * *

In July Prabhupāda visited San Francisco for the fourth annual ISKCON Ratha-yātrā. It was the biggest festival ever, with ten thousand people joining in the procession through Golden Gate Park to the beach. Prabhupāda felt ill and didn't join the parade until about midway. He danced in the road before the carts, as a hundred disciples encircled him, chanting and playing *karatālas* and *mṛdaṅgas*.

Afterward, Prabhupāda wanted to ride in the cart, just as he had done the year before, but some of his disciples restrained him. A gang of hoodlums, they said, had caused trouble earlier, and for Prabhupāda to ride on the cart might be dangerous. He disagreed, but finally relented and rode in his car to the beach.

At The Family Dog Auditorium on the beach Prabhupāda began his lecture. "I want to thank you all for coming. Although I am not well, I felt it my responsibility to come, as you have so kindly attended Lord

Jagannātha's Ratha-yātrā festival. I felt it my duty to come and see you and address you." His voice was frail.

Later in his apartment in San Francisco, Prabhupāda complained that he had not been allowed to ride in the cart. As leader of the Hare Kṛṣṇa movement, he should have ridden on the cart. Not only had his disciples refused him, but several disciples had prominently ridden on the cart—as if in his place.

Prabhupāda asked the many temple presidents assembled for the Ratha-yātrā to meet and discuss forming a governing body to manage ISKCON. The devotees met and then reported that they thought only one of them should be elected the chief representative.

They hadn't understood. The strength should be in a group, Prabhupāda said, not in a single individual. Since he was ISKCON's founder-*ācārya*, what need was there for another single leader? He asked them to meet again.

* * *

Returning to Los Angeles, Prabhupāda announced he would award several of his disciples the *sannyāsa* order. The devotee community excitedly prepared for the festival. The *sannyāsīs*, Prabhupāda said, would leave their temples to travel and preach. It was an unprecedented change for ISKCON, a sensation, and the devotees loved it.

Although Prabhupāda was awarding *sannyāsa* to some of his most advanced disciples, he also said the *sannyāsa* initiation was to purify these disciples and to rid them of their entanglement in material desires. He set the initiation for the end of July, two weeks later.

One day in Los Angeles, a visiting devotee speaking with Prabhupāda in his room humbly asked why Prabhupāda hadn't answered his questions in a recent letter. Prabhupāda remembered no such letter. Inquiring from his secretary, Prabhupāda discovered that his secretary often showed incoming letters to certain temple leaders, who at their discretion would sometimes withhold letters they considered petty or too disturbing.

Prabhupāda was outraged. How dare they come between him and his other disciples? How could they presume to make such decisions on their own? How could a disciple censor his spiritual master's mail?

Although Prabhupāda reprimanded the devotees involved, the incident only increased the already heavy burden on his mind. Again the thought of spiritual disease transmitted in letters from India disturbed him. He found no one close to him in Los Angeles with whom he could speak confidentially about this serious minimization of the spiritual master. As his anxiety affected him bodily, he fell ill and stopped eating.

Karandhara: *I'd heard some things, but in the spirit of "going on" it had all been glossed over. And Prabhupāda didn't talk much about it either. One time, though, I was in his room, right after the* sannyāsīs *had left Los Angeles, and he asked me if I understood what had gone on. I said, "Well, I think so." But I didn't really know very much.*

At that time the devotees who were going out on saṅkīrtana *were in the alleyway chanting, and Prabhupāda was at his desk. Hearing the* kīrtana, *he turned back, looking in the direction of the devotees below his window, and smiled. Then he turned to me. "They're innocent," he said. "Do not involve them in this business."*

Karandhara still didn't understand, and he wondered what not to involve them in. He did know, however, that a shadow was hanging over the heads of the *sannyāsīs*.

Prabhupāda requested three trusted disciples to come be with him in Los Angeles.

Rūpānuga: *I was in Buffalo and the phone rang. Someone said, "Śrīla Prabhupāda is on the telephone." I said, "What? You're kidding!" It wasn't Śrīla Prabhupāda, but it was his servant, Devānanda. Devānanda said, "Śrīla Prabhupāda wants you to come to Los Angeles." I said, "What's wrong?" He said, "Well, he doesn't want . . ." Then he said, "Śrīla Prabhupāda wants to talk about it* now."

So Śrīla Prabhupāda got on the phone, and as soon as I heard him on the line, I paid my obeisances. Then I said, "Śrīla Prabhupāda, what's wrong?" He said, "You didn't know I was ill?" I said, "No!" He said, "You should come immediately."

Then I said, "Uh . . . uh . . . Śrīla Prabhupāda, let me speak to Devānanda." I didn't know what was going on, so I asked Devānanda, "Tell me what's going on." Then he said, "Śrīla Prabhupāda said he will talk with you when you come. He will explain everything."

Bhagavān dāsa: *One day after coming back from* saṅkīrtana, *I received a call from Rūpānuga, who told me he was on his way to Los Angeles, having received a call from Prabhupāda that there was some disturbance there. He couldn't tell me more, but he said he would call me when he returned.*

This set my mind reeling. I sat in the chair, hot and sweaty after coming back from saṅkīrtana, *my mind absorbed in thinking of Prabhupāda and what could be going on. I called Los Angeles to talk to Prabhupāda's secretary, Devānanda, who told me he couldn't really say anything at that point. I was hoping somehow or other I would get more information of the situation, but after waiting some time, I went in to take my shower.*

I was in the shower when all of a sudden someone banged on the door. "Prabhupāda is on the telephone. He wants to speak with you." I was sure there was some misunderstanding—how is it possible that the spiritual master could be on the telephone? Anyway, I ran out of the shower, all wet, and picked up the telephone and said, "Hello?"

There was a long pause. Then all of a sudden I heard Śrīla Prabhupāda's voice on the other end: "Bhagavān dāsa?"

"Yes," I said. "Śrīla Prabhupāda, please accept my humble obeisances. How can I serve you?" I was completely stunned. Then Prabhupāda's voice came slowly on the phone, "There are many things that you will do, but the first thing is that you must come here immediately." I said, "Of course, Śrīla Prabhupāda, I will be there right away." And with that we both hung up.

I managed to gather the money together to take the flight to Los Angeles. And when I got on the plane in Detroit, it just so happened that Rūpānuga was also on the same plane. We sat together and discussed what could possibly be happening in Los Angeles to cause Śrīla Prabhupāda so much distress.

When we arrived at the airport, Karandhara picked us up and told us that some of the older devotees had been plotting against Prabhupāda and that that day Prabhupāda had given several of the men sannyāsa *and sent them away to preach. This was all quite amazing to me, and I didn't really know what to make of it.*

When we came into Prabhupāda'a room, he looked distressed and was rubbing his head, complaining of the blood pressure that was caused by the conspiracy.

Tamāla Kṛṣṇa: *I had written Śrīla Prabhupāda a lengthy letter from Paris, describing how we wanted to expand our preaching efforts in*

Europe, and suddenly I received a telegram from His Divine Grace that said, "Received your letter 26 July. Come Los Angeles immediately." I was quite surprised, and I remember disentangling myself that very day and leaving that night, even though I was in charge of the activities there.

When I arrived in Los Angeles, I found Rūpānuga, Bhagavān, Kīrtanānanda Swami, and Karandhara. I was in a very enthusiastic, blissful mood from having done so much saṅkīrtana, *and I had no idea of any difficulty. But these devotees were all in a heavy, sober, somber mood, and they tried to explain to me what was going on. But actually I could not get a very clear understanding. I had arrived in the late afternoon, and I could not see Śrīla Prabhupāda.*

Early the next morning, when Prabhupāda was informed that I had arrived, he called for me before maṅgala-ārati. *I went up to his quarters, and when I came through the door, Prabhupāda was sitting in his room with his head downward. He looked up, and he appeared to be almost ill. He was gaunt and looked very sorrowful. He said meekly, just as I was bowing down, "Have they told you?"*

Of course, I hadn't really understood everything, but in reply to his question I said, "Yes, they have told me some things." And Prabhupāda said, "Can you help me?" So I answered, "Yes, Śrīla Prabhupāda." He said, "Can you take me out of here?" I said, "Yes, Śrīla Prabhupāda."

Of course, I didn't feel that I could help Śrīla Prabhupāda, but I could understand that I had to say yes. How can you say, "No, I won't"? But how far could I help? It's like lifting the heaviest object in the world. The guru *is so heavy, and yet I had to say yes.*

So Prabhupāda asked me next, "Where will you take me?" And I said, "Well, we can go to Florida." He said, "No, that is not far enough." I said, "I could take you to Europe." He said, "No, that also will not be good. The problem may be there also." So anyway, we didn't conclude where to go at that time. But Prabhupāda said, "It is like a fire here. I must leave at once. It has become like a fire."

Prabhupāda confided in Rūpānuga, Tamāla Kṛṣṇa, and Bhagavān about the various incidents: his mail withheld, his name misprinted, his riding in the Ratha-yātrā parade restricted. He mentioned these and other indications that certain persons wanted to move him into the background, out of the reach of his disciples. He didn't want to stay in Los Angeles, he didn't want to stay in the United States, he didn't even want to go to Europe. He wanted to leave the arena of his disciples' offenses. But before leaving, he wanted to complete his plans for establishing a governing body to manage ISKCON. To this end he dictated the following on July 28:

> I, the undersigned, A. C. Bhaktivedanta Swami, disciple of Om Visnupad Paramhansa 108 Sri Srimad Bhaktisiddhanta Sarasvati Gosvami Maharaj Prabhupada, came in the United States in 1965 on September 18th for the purpose of starting Krishna Consciousness Movement. For one year I had no shelter. I was travelling in many parts of this country. Then in 1966, July, I incorporated this Society under the name and style the International Society for Krishna Consciousness, briefly ISKCON. . . . Gradually the Society increased, and one after another branches were opened. Now we have got thirty-four (34) branches enlisted herewith. As we have increased our volume of activities, now I think a Governing Body Commission (hereinafter referred to as the GBC) should be established. I am getting old, 75 years old, therefore at any time I may be out of the scene, therefore I think it is necessary to give instruction to my disciples how they shall manage the whole institution. They are already managing individual centers represented by one president, one secretary and one treasurer, and in my opinion they are doing nice. But we want still more improvement in the standard of Temple management, propaganda for Krishna consciousness, distribution of books and literatures, opening of new centers and educating devotees to the right standard. Therefore, I have decided to adopt the following principles and I hope my beloved disciples will kindly accept them.

Prabhupāda then listed the names of the twelve persons who would form the G.B.C.:

1. Sriman Rupanuga Das Adhikary
2. Sriman Bhagavandas Adhikary
3. Sriman Syamsundar Das Adhikary
4. Sriman Satsvarupa Das Adhikary
5. Sriman Karandhar Das Adhikary
6. Sriman Hansadutta Das Adhikary
7. Sriman Tamala Kṛṣṇa Das Adhikary
8. Sriman Sudama Das Adhikary
9. Sriman Bali Mardan Das Brahmacary
10. Sriman Jagadisa Das Adhikary
11. Sriman Hayagriva Das Adhikary
12. Sriman Kṛṣṇadaṣ Adhikary

> These personalities are now considered as my direct representatives. While I am living they will act as my zonal secretaries and after my demise they will be know as Executors.

Prabhupāda further described the role of the *sannyāsīs:*

> I have already awarded Sannyas or the renounced order of life to some of my students and they have also got very important duties to perform in this connection. The Sannyasis will travel to our different centers for preaching purpose as well as enlightening the members of the center for spiritual advancement.

Prabhupāda's legal document went on to set forth general directions for the G.B.C. secretaries. They should travel regularly to the temples in their respective zones to insure that each devotee chanted sixteen rounds and followed a regulated schedule and that the temples were clean. His twelve G.B.C. secretaries would relieve him of management, and they would rectify present and future difficulties within the society. That rectification, Prabhupāda's document explained, would be possible only when the devotees in each temple engaged fully in regulated devotional service: rising early for *maṅgala-ārati* at four-thirty, attending *Śrīmad-Bhāgavatam* class and reciting the Sanskrit verses, and chanting in the streets and distributing *Back to Godhead* magazines and other Kṛṣṇa conscious literature. This emphasis on strictly following Kṛṣṇa conscious principles would supersede all material formulas for management. The G.B.C. would insure that in their appointed zones all the devotees were properly engaged. There would be no *māyā.*

The next day Prabhupāda drafted another significant statement, naming Bhagavān, Rūpānuga, and Karandhara trustees of his Bhaktivedanta Book Trust.

> The Bhaktivedanta Book Trust account will be used to publish my books and literature and to establish Temples throughout the world, specifically three temples are to be established, one each in Mayapur, Vrndavana, and Jagannath Puri.

Since returning to America in 1967, Prabhupāda had often said he would stay permanently in America as the adopted son of his disciples. Now he revealed new plans. He spoke of going to India to preach and to establish large ISKCON temples. For the devotees, who based their activities mostly in small rented houses, Prabhupāda's constructing cathedrallike buildings in India was inconceivable. In India, Prabhupāda said, he would teach his disciples how to preach and how to establish temples.

Prabhupāda picked a team, including two newly initiated *sannyāsīs*, to accompany him to India. In the future, he said, more disciples could join him, for India would become an important field for Kṛṣṇa consciousness. Prabhupāda wrote Satsvarūpa and Uddhava in Boston:

> You are all my children, and I love my American boys and girls who are sent to me by my spiritual master and I have accepted them as my disciples. Before coming to your country I took sannyas in 1959. I was publishing B.T.G. since 1944. After taking sannyas I was more engaged in writing my books without any attempt to construct temples or to make disciples like my other God-brothers in India.
>
> I was not very much interested in these matters because my Guru Maharaj liked very much publication of books than constructing big, big temples and creating some neophyte disciples. As soon as He saw that His neophyte disciples were increasing in number, He immediately decided to leave this world. To accept disciples means to take up the responsibility of absorbing the sinful reaction of life of the disciple.
>
> At the present moment in our ISKCON campus politics and diplomacy has entered. Some of my beloved students on whom I counted very, very much have been involved in this matter influenced by Maya. As such there has been some activity which I consider as disrespectful. So I have decided to retire and divert attention to book writing and nothing more.

On July 31 Prabhupāda wrote Brahmānanda and Gargamuni, explaining why he was leaving for India.

> In order to set example to my other Sannyasi students I am personally going to Japan with a party of three other Sannyasi students. Although it is beyond my physical condition, still I am going out so that you may learn the responsibility of Sannyas. . . .
>
> I am fervently appealing to you all not to create fracture in the solid body of the Society. Please work conjointly, without any personal ambition. That will help the cause.

> It is the injunction of the Vedas that the Spiritual Master should not be treated as ordinary man even sometimes the Spiritual Master behaves like ordinary man. It is the duty of the disciple to accept Him as a Superhuman Man. In the beginning of your letter your comparison of the soldier and the commander is very appropriate. We are on the battlefield of Kurukshetra—one side Maya, the other side Kṛṣṇa. So the regulative principles of a battlefield, namely to abide by the order of the commander, must be followed. Otherwise it is impossible to direct the fighting capacity of the soldiers and thus defeat the opposing elements. Kindly therefore take courage. Let things be rightly done so that our mission may be correctly pushed forward to come out victorious.

Prabhupāda wrote other letters revealing his plans to travel to India.

> Our life is very short. The Kṛṣṇa consciousness movement is not meant for fulfilling one's personal ambition, but it is a serious movement for the whole world. I am therefore going to the Eastern hemisphere, beginning from Japan. We are going four in a party and all of us are Sannyasis. In this old age I am going with this party just to set an example to my disciples who have taken recently the Sannyas order.

In preparation for Prabhupāda's trip to India, Prabhupāda's secretary, Devānanda, now Devānanda Swami, asked him questions from the immigration form, mechanically reading the questions and filling in the answers as Prabhupāda replied. "Have you ever committed any criminal acts?" Devānanda asked, reading from the form.

Prabhupāda's eyes widened: "You are asking your spiritual master if he did anything criminal?" And he turned to Bhagavān: "You see, I am simply surrounded by people I cannot trust. It is a dangerous situation."

Prabhupāda sat in his garden the night before his departure. "Don't be disturbed," he told the disciples with him. "We are not going backward. We are going forward. I will reveal everything to you. I will rectify." His strong words and criticisms, he said, had been to enlighten his disciples, to warn them and show them the subtleties of *māyā*.

Karandhara mentioned that the temple leaders had arranged that only a few devotees go with Prabhupāda the next day to the airport. "Where did this idea come from?" Prabhupāda asked. "*Śrīmad-Bhāgavatam* instructs that when a saintly person leaves your company, all present should follow the departing vehicle as far as possible, until it is out of sight."

So the next day the devotees all accompanied Prabhupāda, chanting and dancing behind him through the long corridors of Los Angeles International Airport. After many months with them, he was now leaving. Devotees cried.

Prabhupāda, dressed in new garments, his head freshly shaven, looked effulgent. He sat in the departure lounge, head held high, as grave and unfathomable as ever. He was embarking on a new adventure for Lord Caitanya. He was old and might not return, he said, but his disciples should continue the Kṛṣṇa consciousness movement seriously. "If you follow this new schedule," he said, "you will keep *māyā* from attacking." And then he left them.

* * *

En route to Japan Prabhupāda stopped overnight in Hawaii. He stayed in a motel, and Gaurasundara and Govinda dāsī came to talk with him. Govinda dāsī wanted Prabhupāda to stay and install their Deities of Rādhā and Kṛṣṇa in the temple. If Gaurasundara agreed, Prabhupāda said, he would stay a few days longer to perform the Deity installation. "Let me consult," Gaurasundara replied. And the next day Prabhupāda flew on to Japan. From Japan Prabhupāda wrote Govinda dāsī.

> It is very encouraging to learn that people inquired about me and were eager to hear my speaking. I could have stayed one or two more days, there was no hurry, but you did not make any arrangement. I personally proposed to Gaurasundara that I shall install the Deities, and he replied that, "Let me consult." But he never informed me of the result of that consultation and with whom he had to consult. So this is the present situation in our ISKCON Society. It is clear that a great mischievous propaganda was lightly made and the effect has created a very unfavorable situation and I am very much afflicted in this connection. Still there is time to save the Society out of this mischievous propaganda and I hope all of you combine together to do the needful.

At the Tokyo airport Prabhupāda was greeted by executives of Dai Nippon Printing Company, the printers of *Kṛṣṇa, the Supreme Personality of Godhead* and the twenty thousand monthly copies of *Back to Godhead*. Prabhupāda and his entourage rode in a limousine, courtesy of Dai Nippon, to a small private apartment about forty-five minutes from the temple.

Prabhupāda had developed a severe cough and several other symptoms of ill health, due, he said, to his disciples' behavior. Yet despite his illness he would talk for hours of his concern for ISKCON, especially with his traveling G.B.C. secretary, Tamāla Kṛṣṇa.

Soon after their arrival in Japan, Prabhupāda's secretary received a disturbing call from a devotee attending the society-wide Janmāṣṭamī celebration at New Vrindaban. Four of the newly initiated *sannyāsīs* had arrived, the devotee said, and were teaching a strange philosophy. Devotees were confused. Prabhupāda had left America, the *sannyāsīs* were saying, because he had rejected his disciples. The *sannyāsīs* were blaming themselves and other disciples for not realizing that *Prabhupāda was actually Kṛṣṇa!*

When Prabhupāda heard this, he said, "That is why I did not go. I knew this would happen. This is impersonalism." He defined the Māyāvāda (impersonal) misconception of the *guru* and Kṛṣṇa. If one says that the *guru* is God, or if the *guru* himself says that he is God, that is Māyāvāda philosophy.

For the Māyāvādīs, spiritual realization is realization of one's identity with Brahman, the all-pervading spirit. Despite their austerities and their detachment from materialistic society, and despite their study of *Vedānta-sūtra* and the commentaries of Śaṅkara, they mistakenly think that Kṛṣṇa's body, name, pastimes, service, and devotees are all facets of *māyā*, or illusion; therefore they are called *Māyāvādīs.* A Māyāvāda spiritual master does not reveal to his disciple the holy name of Kṛṣṇa, the holy pastimes of Kṛṣṇa, or the transcendental form of Kṛṣṇa, since the Māyāvādī considers all these *māyā.* Instead, the *guru* explains the oneness of all things, teaching the disciple that the concept of separate existence and ego is illusion. The Māyāvādīs sometimes compare the *guru* to a ladder. One uses the ladder to reach a higher position, but if the ladder is no longer needed one kicks it away.

Coughing intermittently and speaking with physical discomfort, Prabhupāda explained the Māyāvādīs' dangerous misconceptions. The impersonalists held a cheap, mundane view of the *guru*, the *guru's* worship, and the *guru's* instructions. If one says that the *guru* is God and God is not a person, then it follows logically that the *guru* has no eternal personal relationship with his disciples. Ultimately the disciple will become equal to the *guru*, or in other words he will realize that he, too, is God.

Arguing from the Vedic scripture, Prabhupāda refuted the Māyāvādīs' claims. The individual souls, he said, are Kṛṣṇa's eternal servants, and this master-servant relationship is eternal. Service to Kṛṣṇa, therefore, is spiritual activity. Only by serving the *guru*, however, can a disciple fully revive his eternal relationship with Kṛṣṇa. The Vedic literature gives paramount importance to serving the spiritual master. He is the representative of God, the direct, manifest link to God. No one can approach God but through him. Lord Kṛṣṇa says, "Those who are directly My devotees are actually not My devotees. But those who are devotees of My servant (the spiritual master) are factually My devotees."

For hours Prabhupāda drilled his disciples. He would pose a Māyāvāda argument, then ask his disciples to defeat it. If they failed, he would defeat it himself. He stressed that the relationship between the spiritual master and disciple was eternal—not because the *guru* was Kṛṣṇa, but because he was the confidential *servant* of Kṛṣṇa, eternally. A bona fide spiritual master never says that he is Kṛṣṇa or that Kṛṣṇa is impersonal.

The devotees began to understand how the offenses of minimizing Śrīla Prabhupāda's position were products of Māyāvāda philosophy. For the Māyāvādī, to increase devotion to the *guru* is unnecessary; if individual relationships are all ultimately illusion, why increase the illusion? If the master-servant relationship is ultimately illusion, then the less the disciple sees his *guru* as master and himself as servant, the more he is advancing. The Māyāvāda philosophy was a subtle and insidious poison.

At least Prabhupāda had been spared the pain of being personally present in New Vrindaban to witness the Māyāvāda rantings of certain of his disciples and the appalling display of ignorance of most of the others. He had his small entourage and was on his way to preach in India. While here in Tokyo, he would try to obtain many *Back to Godhead* magazines and *Kṛṣṇa* books to take with him.

Prabhupāda observed Janmāṣṭamī at his apartment by having disciples read aloud to him from *Kṛṣṇa, the Supreme Personality of Godhead* throughout the day. If they kept reading, he said, they might be able to finish the book in one day. The devotees had decorated Prabhupāda's room with leaves and flowers strung from the ceiling and along the walls, and Prabhupāda sat on a thin mattress behind his low desk, hearing the pastimes of Kṛṣṇa. At nine P.M., after fasting all day, the devotees were still reading to him when he asked if they would be able to finish the book by midnight. The devotees replied that they would not.

"Then you stop, and I will read." Prabhupāda opened a Sanskrit volume of the Tenth Canto of *Śrīmad-Bhāgavatam* and, for the next two hours, chanted the Sanskrit verses. "You cannot understand the Sanskrit," he said, "but I know you can feel. The verses are so potent that just by hearing one can be purified."

During the reading, Kīrtanānanda Swami and Kārttikeya Swami cooked a feast in the kitchen. At midnight the devotees served Śrīla Prabhupāda the Janmāṣṭamī feast. Taking only a few bites, he watched his disciples eat heartily.

The next day was Vyāsa-pūjā, Prabhupāda's seventy-fourth birthday, and he went to the Tokyo ISKCON temple. The temple was only two rooms—one for living, one for worshiping—with Japanese grass mats on the floor. Prabhupāda sat to the right of the altar, looking at Lord Jagannātha, while his disciples sat on the floor before him, singing *Gurv-aṣṭaka* prayers glorifying the spiritual master. None of them, however, knew exactly how to conduct the Vyāsa-pūjā ceremony, and after a while they ended the *kīrtana*. In the painfully awkward moments that followed, the devotees realized they were supposed to do something special. But what?

Prabhupāda appeared angry: "Don't you have *puṣpa-yātrā*? Isn't *prasādam* ready?" The devotees looked at one another. "This is not Vyāsa-pūjā," Prabhupāda said. "You have not been to Vyāsa-pūjā before? Don't you know how to celebrate the Vyāsa-pūjā, how to honor the spiritual master?" One of the *sannyāsīs* began to cry. "Tamāla Kṛṣṇa," Prabhupāda said, "didn't you see how I observed my Guru Mahārāja's birthday? Where is *puṣpa*?" (*Puṣpa* is Sanskrit for "flowers.")

Puṣpa? Puṣpa? Tamāla Kṛṣṇa decided Prabhupāda must mean *puṣpānna*, a fancy rice dish. "I'm not sure," he said.

"What kind of Vyāsa-pūjā is this with no *puṣpa*?" Prabhupāda asked.

"We can get some, Prabhupāda," Tamāla Kṛṣṇa offered.

Tamāla Kṛṣṇa grabbed Sudāmā. "Prabhupāda wants *prasādam*. He wants *puṣpānna* rice." They ran into the kitchen and hurriedly started the rice.

Meanwhile, in the temple the devotees struggled through their version of a Vyāsa-pūjā ceremony. Kīrtanānanda Swami stood and began to read aloud from the introduction of *Kṛṣṇa, the Reservoir of Pleasure*, which included a short biography of Prabhupāda. But Prabhupāda interrupted, scolding his disciples for concocting and for acting improperly. "If you don't know," he said, "then why didn't you ask me how to do this properly?"

The Japanese guests present didn't understand English, but they could see the spiritual master was disturbed. Prabhupāda explained that in devotional service everything must be done properly, according to the *paramparā* method, without concocting. "We will observe Vyāsa-pūjā again tomorrow," he said. "Come to my room. I will tell you what to do."

The next day, after a simple, traditional ceremony, the devotees felt ecstatic. Afterward they agreed: when one displeases his spiritual master, there is no happiness; but as soon as the spiritual master is pleased, the disciple becomes blissful.

The Janmāṣṭamī–Vyāsa-pūjā festival in New Vrindaban had become a nightmare. Hundreds of devotees had converged there from the East Coast, with many others from California and even Europe. They had come for a blissful festival, but instead had found Śrīla Prabhupāda's newly initiated *sannyāsīs* expounding a devastating philosophy.

The *sannyāsīs*, speaking informally to groups here and there, would explain how the devotees had offended Prabhupāda and how he had subsequently withdrawn his mercy. The *sannyāsīs* revealed their special insights that Prabhupāda was actually God, that none of his disciples had recognized him as such, and that all of them, therefore, beginning with the *sannyāsīs,* were guilty of minimizing his position. And that was why Prabhupāda had left for India; he had "withdrawn his mercy" from his disciples.

The devotees were devastated. None of them knew what to say in reply. The *sannyāsīs*, by their preaching, had projected gloom everywhere, which was proper, they said; everyone should feel guilty and realize that they had lost the grace of their spiritual master. No use trying to cheer one another up by chanting Hare Kṛṣṇa or eating a feast; everyone should accept the bitter medicine.

Although Prabhupāda had given his disciples three volumes of *Śrīmad-Bhāgavatam*, as well as *Bhagavad-gītā As It Is*, *The Nectar of Devotion, Teachings of Lord Caitanya,* and other literature, none of the devotees were well-versed in them. Many devotees wondered if the philosophy the *sannyāsīs* were preaching was correct, but none of them knew enough of the scriptures to immediately refute it. The devotees turned to the new G.B.C. men, Prabhupāda's appointed leaders and guardians of ISKCON. The G.B.C., along with other senior devotees, began carefully searching through Prabhupāda's books to ascertain exactly what he had said about the position of the spiritual master.

Then Hayagrīva announced that a letter had just arrived from Śrīla Prabhupāda in Tokyo. As soon as the devotees all gathered under the pavilion roof to hear, Hayagrīva read aloud: "My dear Sons and Daughters . . ." and then Prabhupāda listed almost all the New Vrindaban residents. The devotees immediately felt a wave of hope. Just to hear Prabhupāda say "My dear Sons and Daughters" was a great relief.

Hayagrīva continued to read: "Please accept my blessings."

Prabhupāda hadn't rejected them!

The letter went on to say that Śrīla Prabhupāda was pleased with the work of the New Vrindaban devotees, and he promised to come and visit them. Soon he would send for other devotees to join him in India, he said. As he described what preaching in India would be like, the devotees became caught up in the momentum of Śrīla Prabhupāda's preaching spirit. They cheered. They felt blissful.

Then Prabhupāda specifically referred to the difficulty facing ISKCON: "Purge out of New Vrindaban the non-Vrindaban atmosphere that has entered." His letter turned the tide against the Māyāvāda teachings.

The G.B.C. then called a meeting of all disciples in the temple room. Reading selections from *The Nectar of Devotion*, they established that the spiritual master, although not God, should be honored as much as God because he is the confidential servant of God. Several senior devotees spoke their heart's convictions, citing examples from their association with Prabhupāda to prove that he had not rejected them—he was too kind. The *sannyāsīs* might *feel* rejected because of their own guilt, someone said, but they should not project their guilt on others.

The false teachings, however, had dealt a blow from which many devotees would need time to recover. Newcomers at the festival were especially unsettled. But the cloud of gloom that had hung over New Vrindaban now lifted, thanks to Śrīla Prabhupāda's timely letter.

The *sannyāsīs* admitted their confusion. The G.B.C. then phoned Kīrtanānanda Swami in Tokyo and told him that Prabhupāda's letter had resolved most of the problems, but that the *sannyāsīs* still held their misconceptions. Hearing this, Prabhupāda felt his suspicions confirmed.

Certain disciples had been contaminated by the poisonous philosophy from India. Consequently, material desires for power and control had overwhelmed them, even in Prabhupāda's presence.

Turning to Tamāla Kṛṣṇa, Sudāmā, and the three *sannyāsīs* with him, Prabhupāda asked what they thought should be done. With the previous day's philosophic drilling still sharp in their minds, they suggested that anyone teaching Māyāvāda philosophy should not be allowed to stay within ISKCON. Prabhupāda agreed. If these *sannyāsīs* continued to preach Māyāvāda philosophy, he said, they should not be allowed to stay in his temples but should go out and "preach"on their own. Tamāla Kṛṣṇa conveyed this message to the G.B.C. in the U.S., and Prabhupāda was satisfied that the problem would be adjusted. He had created his G.B.C. to handle such matters.

On September 2 Prabhupāda wrote Haṁsadūta in Germany.

> Regarding the poisonous effect in our Society, it is a fact and I know where from this poison tree has sprung up and how it affected practically the whole Society in a very dangerous form. But it does not matter. Prahlad Maharaj was administered poison, but it did not act. Similarly Lord Kṛṣṇa and the Pandavas were administered poison and it did not act. I think in the same parampara system that the poison administered to our Society will not act if some of our students are as good as Prahlad Maharaj. I have therefore given the administrative power to the Governing Body Commission.

To Hayagrīva in New Vrindaban Prabhupāda wrote,

> I am very glad to know that the GBC is actively working to rectify the subversive situation which has been weakening the very foundation of our Society. All you members of the GBC please always remain very vigilant in this connection so that our Society's growth may go on unimpeded by such poisonous elements. Your preaching in New Vrindaban as well as intensified study of our literatures with seriousness is very much encouraging. Please continue this program with vigour and reestablish the solidity of our movement.
>
> From the beginning I was strongly against the impersonalists, and all my books stressed on this point. So my oral instruction as well as my books are all at your service. Now you GBC consult them and get a clear and

> strong idea. Then there will be no more disturbance. The four Sannyasis may bark, but still the caravan will pass.

Prabhupāda wrote Satsvarūpa in Boston,

> I am very glad to know that you are not affected by the propaganda of the Sannyasis that I am displeased with all the members of the Society—I am never displeased with any member.

The worst was over, Prabhupāda thought. For months this problem had upset him and his writing. Relentlessly he had instructed his disciples, for their own benefit and for the benefit of his movement. The disease had taken its toll, and that was unfortunate. But the devotees were being forced to turn to Prabhupāda's books and apply their teachings, and that was the positive outcome. Now they should clearly understand the position of the spiritual master and never again be led astray by false philosophies or sentiment.

Prabhupāda's main business in Tokyo was with Dai Nippon. Considering him an important author and a venerable religious monk, they had provided him a car and apartment. Each morning they sent a private car to drive Prabhupāda to Imperial Palace Park, where he could take his morning walk. Prabhupāda liked the neatly planted trees and gravel walks, and he appreciated the habits of the Japanese people. As he would pass, elderly ladies would bow to him from the waist, and others would fold their hands respectfully, acknowledging his being a holy man.

On the morning of Prabhupāda's meeting with Dai Nippon, he came out of his apartment with Tamāla Kṛṣṇa and Devānanda Mahārāja and got into the back seat of a Dai Nippon company car. The car proceeded through the early-morning streets, and Prabhupāda chanted his Gāyatrī *mantra* silently.

A Dai Nippon junior executive escorted Prabhupāda and his two disciples into an elevator and up to a spacious room with a long conference table. Prabhupāda's guide cordially offered him a seat at the table, and Prabhupāda sat down, with Tamāla Kṛṣṇa and Devānanda Mahārāja on either side. Soon there entered Dai Nippon's six top executives, including the corporation president. Each stood behind his respective chair, and each in turn, beginning with the president, bowed slightly from the waist and presented his calling card. Addressing Prabhupāda as "Your Divine Grace," they introduced themselves, announced their posts, and took their seats.

"We are very honored to have you here," the president began. "You are a great religious author, and it is our great privilege to be publishing your books." After the president had spoken briefly, tea was served. Prabhupāda requested hot milk. Conversation was informal, and Prabhupāda spoke of the importance of his mission and his Kṛṣṇa conscious literature. No one discussed business, however, and the Dai Nippon executives soon excused themselves. They would meet again the next morning.

When Prabhupāda was again alone in the room with his disciples and the junior executive who had escorted him, he asked the young Japanese, "So what is your goal in life?" By way of answer, the man gathered up all the business cards that lay scattered before Prabhupāda on the table and stacked them, with the president's on top, then the first vice-president's, and so on, putting his own card in its place on the bottom. He then dramatically removed his card from the bottom of the stack and slapped it on top—a graphic answer to Prabhupāda's question.

Prabhupāda smiled. To become president of the company, he said, was temporary. All material life was temporary. He explained on the basis of *Bhagavad-gītā* that the body was temporary and that the self was eternal. All the identities and positions people hankered after were based on the bodily conception of life and would one day be frustrated. The purpose of life, therefore, was not to become the temporary president of a temporary corporation within the temporary material world, but to realize the eternal soul's relationship with the Supreme Personality of Godhead and gain eternal life. Prabhupāda spoke for almost half an hour while the man listened politely.

At the next day's meeting, negotiations began. The conference room was different, the table smaller, and three of Dai Nippon's international sales representatives sat opposite Prabhupāda. Prabhupāda presented his price: $1.35 per book.

"Oh, Your Divine Grace," one of the salesmen exclaimed, "it is not possible for us to give this price. We will lose too heavily. We cannot afford it." They explained their position, quoting paper costs and other expenses.

Prabhupāda began to speak about his mission. ISKCON's book distribution, he said, was a charitable work for the benefit of all humanity. ISKCON distributed these books for whatever donations people were able to make, and he received no profit or royalties. It was spiritual education, the most valuable literature. "In any case," Prabhupāda said in closing, "you deal with my secretary in this regard." And he sat back in his chair. The burden was on Tamāla Kṛṣṇa.

Tamāla Kṛṣṇa began by saying that Prabhupāda had been too kind, because ISKCON could actually never pay such a high price. He then quoted a price forty cents lower per book than Prabhupāda's quote. "Mr. Tamāla,"—the salesmen were again upset—"please reconsider your point."A polite argument ensued.

Suddenly Prabhupāda interrupted, presenting himself as an impartial third party. He said he would settle the difference that had arisen between his secretary and the salesmen. "I have heard both sides," he said, "and I feel that the price should be $1.25 per book. That's all."

"Yes, Your Divine Grace," the salesmen agreed, "that is right."

After further negotiations, Prabhupāda agreed on a contract that included a reprint of Volume One and a first printing of Volume Two of *Kṛṣṇa, the Supreme Personality of Godhead*, two issues of *Back to Godhead*, a Hindi issue of *Back to Godhead*, and a new book, *Śrī Īśopaniṣad*. ISKCON had to pay only $5,000 cash, and Dai Nippon would deliver everything on credit.

Prabhupāda held a feast at his apartment for the Dai Nippon executives, who especially liked the *samosās* and *pakorās*. They presented Prabhupāda with a watch and continued to see to his comfort during his stay in Tokyo. Prabhupāda also met a Canadian-born Japanese boy, Bruce, who was seriously interested in Kṛṣṇa consciousness. Prabhupāda invited him to come and join him in India, and the boy eagerly agreed.

CHAPTER FOUR

India: Dancing White Elephants

Calcutta
August 29, 1970

For the first time in almost three years, Prabhupāda returned to India—to Calcutta, his hometown. Although it was late and the journey from Tokyo had been twelve hours, Prabhupāda felt happy as he descended the stairway from the airplane. Acyutānanda and Jayapatāka, his only American disciples in India, were standing on the airfield, and as they saw him approaching in his saffron silk robes, they bowed down. Prabhupāda smiled and embraced them. They ushered him to a flower-bedecked car and accompanied him to the terminal building, where he entered the V.I.P. lounge.

Some of Prabhupāda's Godbrothers and old Calcutta friends were present to receive him, and a *kīrtana* party from the Chaitanya Math was chanting. The reception was large and festive. As the room resounded with Hare Kṛṣṇa, Prabhupāda took his seat. The sound of the *kīrtana*, the many pictures of Kṛṣṇa, and the smell of incense and jasmine flowers combined with Prabhupāda's transcendental presence to transform the drab airport into a heavenly scene.

Indians crowded forward to place flower garlands around Prabhupāda's neck, and as the garlands piled higher, Prabhupāda removed them. But the garlands kept coming, and again they piled up, almost covering Prabhupāda's face. The American devotees watched in fascination as the Bengali *brahmacārīs* played their *mṛdaṅgas* with exotic rhythms. The people in the crowd pressed in closer to touch Prabhupāda's feet and ask his blessings, and Prabhupāda smiled, seeming quite at home. When the *kīrtana* ended, he began to speak.

"I am coming back to the city after three years. Hare Kṛṣṇa. I have been around the world and have found that happiness and peace cannot be established in this world by materialistic advancement. I have seen Japan, which is highly advanced in machines and technology. Yet there is no real happiness there. But the people of India, even if they do not understand the significance of *saṅkīrtana*, they enjoy listening to it. My advice to the Indians is that if you advance only in science and technology, without paying attention to *hari-nāma*, then you will remain forever backward. There is tremendous strength in *hari-nāma*. . . ."

Reporter: "You have said, and I quote, 'Even communism, if it is without *kṛṣṇa-nāma*, is void.' Why do you say that?"

Prabhupāda: "Why do you refer to communism in particular? Without Kṛṣṇa consciousness, everything is void. Whatever you do, Kṛṣṇa must remain in the center. Whether you are communist or capitalist or anything else—it doesn't matter. We want to see whether your activities are centered around Kṛṣṇa."

Reporter: "Right now there is too much turmoil in Bengal. What is your advice to us at this time?"

Prabhupāda: "My advice is to chant Hare Kṛṣṇa. This is the piece of advice to both the capitalists and the communists. All animosity between them will cease completely, and all their problems will be solved, if they take this advice."

The crowd, affirming Prabhupāda's words, began to shout, "*Sādhu! Sādhu!*"

Prabhupāda sat in the back seat, on his way from the airport to the home of Mr. Das Gupta on Hindustan Road. Outside the car window the familiar scenes of Calcutta passed by. For the newcomers riding with him, however, Calcutta was foreign and unfamiliar. Gaunt, loitering cows and street dogs, small horses pulling huge loads, barefoot ricksha-wālās, open shops with exotic foods, dense crowds of pedestrians, the sultry heat, and the incredible traffic—these, although familiar to Prabhupāda, plunged the disciples who had flown with him into culture shock. Tamāla Kṛṣṇa looked nervously at the driver, who swerved in and out of traffic, honking his horn. Prabhupāda laughed softly. "Tamāla Kṛṣṇa, how do you like this driving?"

Acyutānanda and Jayapatāka, however, were acclimatized to Calcutta and had learned to appreciate its culture. They had met high-class, cultured Bengalis who accepted them as *sādhus* despite their American birth. They had preached in many homes and had attracted curious crowds by chanting in public. They had not, however, achieved a solid foothold for ISKCON. But now Prabhupāda had come to change that. He would preach wonderfully, just as he had done in America, and his disciples were eager to serve as his instruments. He would be their vital force, their inspiration, for he was empowered by Lord Caitanya.

Prabhupāda reached the home of Mr. Das Gupta at almost midnight. Many people wanted to see him, and when Devānanda Mahārāja tried to turn them away Prabhupāda said, "No, no, let them come in." Prabhupāda's sister, Bhavatarini, arrived with an array of special dishes she had cooked.

"We can't eat now," one of the *sannyāsīs* protested. "It's late at night."

"No," Prabhupāda said, "we must eat everything. Whatever my sister cooks, we have to eat. This is her favorite activity. She likes to cook for me and feed me. Everyone must take *prasādam*." The devotees at the Chaitanya Math had also cooked a feast, and as Prabhupāda was honoring the *prasādam* prepared by his sister the *prasādam* from the Chaitanya Math arrived. He took a little and induced his followers to eat sumptuously.

It was 1:00 A.M. Prabhupāda sat in his room with Acyutānanda, Jayapatāka, and Devānanda Mahārāja. He explained how irresponsible letters from his disciples in India had perpetrated within ISKCON a deep misunderstanding of the spiritual master's position. He quoted the verse *sākṣād-dharitvena samasta-śāstraiḥ* and explained it: "The *guru* is on an equal level with Hari, the Supreme Personality of Godhead. He is not God, but he is the dearmost servant of God."

Prabhupāda continued preaching to his disciples, clearing away any misconceptions about the spiritual master's position. All the past unpleasant events, he said, were now being rectified. The devotees should continue working together with new life and vigor.

Acyutānanda asked Prabhupāda if he could take *sannyāsa*. The Indians, he said, would respect a *sannyāsī* more. Prabhupada agreed that *sannyāsa* would help Acyutānanda's preaching, and he said that Jayapatāka should also take *sannyāsa*. The ceremony would be in a week, on Rādhāṣṭamī.

The *Amrita Bazar Patrika* carried a front-page news story of Prabhupāda's arrival. A photo showed Prabhupāda walking, with his hand in his bead bag, surrounded by young *sannyāsīs* carrying *daṇḍas*.

> Many VIP's have come to Dumdum Airport before but never have we seen gaiety and celebrations of this magnitude. . . . It was difficult to imagine that he was 75 years old because he was completely fresh after this long journey. With a little smile on his face, he blessed one and all with the word, "Hari Bol!"

Prabhupāda wrote to the devotees in Japan,

> In India, from the very moment we stepped down from the airplane, there is good propaganda work going on. . . . The boy Bruce is improving and becoming more interested. He has now sacrificed his hairs for Kṛṣṇa—that is a good sign.

Calcutta was in political turmoil. A group of communist terrorists, the Naxalites, had been rioting, murdering prominent businessmen and threatening the lives of many others. Many wealthy Marwari industrialists were leaving the city for Delhi and Bombay. Aside from the terrorists, Bengali college students were growing unruly. But the older people of West Bengal, comprising most of Prabhupāda's visitors, were alarmed by the violence and unrest. The only shelter, Prabhupāda told them, was Kṛṣṇa.

> People are in very much perturbed condition. All of them are expecting me to do something for ameliorating the situation, but I am simply advising them to chant Hare Kṛṣṇa because this transcendental sound is the only panacea for all material diseases.

Prabhupāda saw no need to fabricate a special program for the social problems of Calcutta. Chanting Hare Kṛṣṇa was "the only panacea for all material diseases." The question was how best to use his American disciples to give this panacea to the Indians. Prabhupāda had his party of ten devotees, and he had asked his leaders in the West for twenty more within the month. He had ordered $60,000 worth of books and magazines from Dai Nippon, and his *sannyāsīs* were going daily into the streets to perform *kīrtana.*

The *saṅkīrtana* party was getting a good response. Shaven-headed Westerners, wearing *śikhās,* Vaiṣṇava *tilaka*, and saffron robes, playing *karatālas* and *mṛdaṅgas*, chanting Hare Kṛṣṇa with heart and soul, quoting Sanskrit verses from *Bhagavad-gītā*, affirming Lord Kṛṣṇa to be the Supreme Personality of Godhead—for the Bengalis this was sensational, and hundreds would gather to watch. Prabhupāda knew the great appeal his disciples would have; everyone would want to see them. He therefore affectionately called them his "dancing white elephants."

These same devotees, who had grown to love chanting Hare Kṛṣṇa in the streets of San Francisco, Los Angeles, and New York, were now going into an exhausting heat never encountered in America and chanting on Dalhousie Square for several hours daily. Crowds would press in closely, sometimes teasing, laughing, or scoffing, but more often looking on with deep amazement.

Prabhupāda's idea was that when Indians saw young Western people adopting the principles of Kṛṣṇa consciousness the faith of the Indians in their own culture would increase. Prabhupāda explained to his disciples how formerly, during the time of Mahārāja Yudhiṣṭhira, India had been a Kṛṣṇa conscious state. For the last thousand years, however, India had been under foreign subjugation, first under the Moguls and then under the British. As a result, the intelligentsia and, to a lesser degree, the masses of India had lost respect for their own culture. They were now pursuing the materialistic goals of the West, and they saw this as more productive and more practical than religion, which was only sentimental.

Westerners living as renounced Vaiṣṇavas could, as Prabhupāda was well aware, turn the heads and hearts of the Indians and help them regain faith in their own lost culture. It was not a material tactic, however, but a spiritual strength. Prabhupāda stressed that the devotees must be pure in their actions; this purity would be their force.

The chanting in Dalhousie Square and along Chowringee had gone on for about ten days when Prabhupāda decided to stop it. The street *kīrtana*, although an excellent method of preaching, was not the most effective method for India, he said. There were many professional *kīrtana* groups in Bengal, and Prabhupāda didn't want his disciples to be seen like that—as professional performers or beggars. He wanted them to preach in a way that would bring them closer to the more intelligent, respectable Indians, and he unfolded his new plan.

He called it "Life Membership." His disciples would invite Indians interested in supporting and associating with ISKCON to become members. A membership fee of 1,111 rupees would entitle the member to many benefits, such as copies of Śrīla Prabhupāda's books and free accommodation in ISKCON centers around the world.

Speaking one evening in a private home before a group of wealthy businessmen, Prabhupāda initiated his life membership program. After lecturing, he invited his audience to become ISKCON life members, and several Calcutta merchants immediately signed.

B. L. Jaju: *I was really overwhelmed by the simplicity of Prabhupāda's nature. He told me how he had been carrying on his regular business when his* guru *had told him that four hundred years back Caitanya Mahāprabhu had said that Hare Rāma, Hare Kṛṣṇa would be chanted all throughout the world. He said that that was the job given to him by his spiritual master and that he would have to go to America and do it.*

I found no snobbery in him. He was very simple. And he was telling, as if my brother was telling to me, simply how he went to U.S.A., how he started, and how gradually he planned to have this Kṛṣṇa consciousness throughout the world.

Seeing his disciples who had changed their lives, I began to think, "Why not I? In my humble way, I should do something, without worrying what other people are doing." I found that imperceptibly he was affecting my life. My wife and even my son were really surprised when they found that these white people, whom we thought could never turn to Kṛṣṇa consciousness, had changed so much. So we thought we also must try to follow better the teaching of the Gītā.

Whether at a life member's home, at a formal lecture before a large audience, or in his own room, Prabhupāda continued speaking from *Bhagavad-gītā* and *Śrīmad-Bhāgavatam* about Kṛṣṇa and Kṛṣṇa consciousness. Of this he never tired. A guest would ask a question, and Prabhupāda would begin his answer by having one of his disciples read a relevant verse from the *Gītā*. Then he would explain it. If the guest was unsubmissive and wanted to challenge, Prabhupāda would argue.

Sitting at his low desk, occasionally drinking water from his *loṭā*, Prabhupāda would talk hour after hour. The temperature rose to 100 degrees, and as Prabhupāda sat in his room preaching, he wore no shirt, only a simple top cloth, which left his arms, shoulders, and part of his chest bare. Sometimes the devotees sitting with him would be sick or sleepy or otherwise inattentive, and sometimes they would excuse themselves, returning hours later to find him still preaching. Guests also came and went. Yet except for a nap after lunch, Prabhupāda kept preaching, often throughout the day and into the night. Never bored with his subject matter, he would speak as long as there was an interested hearer.

His audiences varied. Sometimes he would speak to a room of husbands and wives, all cultured and well dressed, and sometimes he would speak to one lone old man. Sometimes his audience listened quietly, or argued, or even when appreciating showed their misunderstanding. Sometimes a guest would ask him why he criticized Bengal's reputed saints and politicians, and he would explain on the basis of *Bhagavad-gītā* that the real *sādhu* always glorifies Kṛṣṇa.

Prabhupāda often related his preaching to events of particular interest to his audience, such as Calcutta's political unrest or the downfall of Vedic culture. Yet his concern for local affairs was only the practical necessity of the moment, for he was beyond India. He was thinking of people, places, and activities all around the world. In answering his letters, he would deeply ponder matters in England, Australia, Hawaii, or New Vrindaban. And beyond this, he would always be thinking of Kṛṣṇa. He wanted to glorify Kṛṣṇa throughout the world; India happened to be his present field.

The devotees in India had the privilege of closely observing Prabhupāda in his preaching. His superior tolerance and kindness both inspired them and, by contrast, exposed to them their own inadequacies. As newcomers to India, the devotees were still greatly involved with the practical affairs of living in Calcutta. Weather, disease, and culture shock distracted their minds from Kṛṣṇa consciousness. But Prabhupāda's presence, his preaching, and his example reminded them that reality was beyond the body.

Sometimes the devotees criticized certain of Prabhupāda's visitors. They met Indians who sat with Prabhupāda and presented a facade of godliness but who later smoked cigarettes and showed other signs of low character. Once a group of devotees complained to Prabhupāda about these hypocritical Indians, but Prabhupāda told them the story of the bee and the fly. The bee, he explained, always looks for honey, and the fly for a nasty sore or infection. The devotee should be like the honeybee and see the good in others, not like the fly, looking for the faults.

Prabhupāda's disciples discovered that the best way to learn to live in India was to follow exactly what Prabhupāda did. When taking *prasādam* with him at someone's home, they would eat the same foods as he, and in the same order. When he would finish, they would finish; and when he would wash his hands, they would wash. Life in India was strange, even bewildering, and Prabhupāda's disciples did not have Prabhupāda's vision of his mission in India. But they were following him, like little ducks, wherever he went.

As the devotees came closer to Prabhupāda and witnessed more of his unique qualities, they came to love him more than ever. Sitting in his room on a white cushion and leaning back on the white bolster, Prabhupāda appeared golden-hued and regal, despite his simple surroundings. The devotees could see that he was unaffected by his surroundings, whether in Los Angeles, where he had lived comfortably amid opulence, or in Calcutta. He was at home in India, but he was not just another Indian, not even just another Indian *sādhu*. He was unique. And he was theirs.

* * *

From Prabhupāda's first day in Calcutta he had thought of going to Māyāpur, the sacred birthplace of Lord Caitanya. Bhaktivinoda Ṭhākura, father of Śrīla Prabhupāda's spiritual master and pioneer in spreading Lord Caitanya's teachings beyond India, had longed for the day when Americans and Europeans would join with their Bengali brothers in Māyāpur, chanting the holy names. Prabhupāda wanted to purchase land, establish a Māyāpur center for his Western disciples, and fulfill the dream of his spiritual predecessors. He had written to one of his Godbrothers,

> I wish to go to Mayapur to pay my respects to our Beloved Spiritual Master His Divine Grace Sri Srila Prabhupada as well as to complete the purchase of the land. So if Jagmohan Prabhu will accompany us to finish this transaction it will be very kind of him and I hope you will kindly request him to accompany us.

The followers of Lord Caitanya accept Māyāpur, one hundred and ten miles north of Calcutta, to be identical with Vṛndāvana. Five thousand years ago Lord Kṛṣṇa lived in Vṛndāvana, performing His childhood pastimes, and five hundred years ago Lord Kṛṣṇa appeared in Māyāpur as Lord Caitanya. For the Gauḍīya Vaiṣṇavas, therefore, Māyāpur and Vṛndāvana are the two most dear and sacred places on earth. What better place for ISKCON to have its world headquarters than in Māyāpur! But despite various attempts over the past several years, Śrīla Prabhupāda had still not acquired property there.

He had gone to Māyāpur with Acyutānanda in 1967, seen a plot of land, and asked Acyutānanda to try and get it. But Acyutānanda and the Muhammadan owner had never reached an agreement. Some of Prabhupāda's Godbrothers had temples and property in Māyāpur, but they wouldn't help. Some even seemed to be working against him. When Prabhupāda had written one of his Godbrothers in Māyāpur asking him to help Acyutānanda secure land, the Godbrother's secretary had replied that he was unable to do so. The secretary had remarked, "One must be very fortunate to get land in Mayapur."

Prabhupāda criticized his Godbrothers' uncooperative spirit. He was becoming impatient. "Why are we not able to get the land in Mayapur?" he asked his disciples. "This is dragging on for three hundred years!" Again he wrote one of his Godbrothers.

> Regarding propagating the Name of Sri Mayapur as Birthplace of Lord Caitanya, it is going on regularly in our different literatures and books. If you kindly take the trouble of coming here conveniently, I can show you how we are giving publicity to the Birthsite of Lord Caitanya. Perhaps you know that I begged from His Holiness Sripad Tirtha Maharaj a little piece of land at Mayapur for constructing a home for my Western disciples, but he refused the proposal. Srila Bhaktivinode Thakur wanted that the American and European devotees would come to Mayapur, and the prophecy is now fulfilled. Unfortunately they are loitering in the streets of Calcutta without having a suitable place at Mayapur. Do you think it is all right?

Accompanied by a small party of men, Prabhupāda took the train to Navadvīpa, just across the Ganges from Māyāpur. There they were met by members of the Devananda Math. Riding in rickshas to the Devananda Math, the devotees were charmed by the rural atmosphere of Navadvīpa. Everything was lush from the rainy season, and the devotees found their romantic expectations of India now being fulfilled as they proceeded along roads lined with tropical vegetation. At the Devananda

Math Prabhupāda and his disciples were given special *prasādam* and good accommodations.

Then the rains returned. Day after day the rains came, and the Ganges rose higher and higher, until crossing the swift river into Māyāpur became impossible. Since the rains were not likely to abate soon, Prabhupāda decided to leave. He and his disciples boarded an early-morning train to Calcutta.

The tracks were flooded. Repeatedly the train had to stop—once for more than eight hours. The heat and the crowds of passengers constantly passing through the car made the wait torturous for the devotees. Prabhupāda asked one of his disciples to take a ricksha and try to arrange better transportation. Nothing was available. At last the train continued toward Calcutta, only to stop at the next station, where all the passengers changed to another train. Finally Prabhupāda reached Calcutta and Mr. Das Gupta's home.

"Maybe Lord Caitanya does not want us to establish our headquarters in Māyāpur," Prabhupāda said. The two purposes in his mind—establishing a place in Calcutta and purchasing land in Māyāpur—he had not accomplished.

Prabhupāda continued holding programs in people's homes and talking with guests in his room. One day a Mr. Dandharia visited Prabhupāda and mentioned Bombay's upcoming Sadhu Samaj, a gathering of the most important *sādhus* in India. It was to be held at Chowpatti Beach and promised to be a big affair. Mr. Dandharia requested Prabhupāda to attend, and Prabhupāda accepted.

* * *

Bombay
October 1970

Responding to Śrīla Prabhupāda's request for more disciples to join him in India, a group of twenty American devotees traveled to Brussels and took an inexpensive flight aboard a propeller-driven craft to Bombay. At the airport, while the devotees were wondering where they should go, Mr. Kailash Seksaria, a wealthy Bombay businessman and nephew of Mr. Dandharia, approached them with a letter from Prabhupāda. Mr. Seksaria had arranged for several cars, and he escorted the devotees to his home in an affluent Bombay residential area on Marine Drive. He fed them and provided them with living quarters.

Two days later a telegram arrived informing the devotees and their host that Prabhupāda would be arriving the next day. Prabhupāda arrived at the Bombay airport and, after an enthusiastic reception, rode with Mr. Seksaria to his home.

Marine Drive runs along the seashore, and the houses lining it belong to the very rich. Mr. Seksaria's residence was seven stories, and he offered Śrīla Prabhupāda the first floor, with its large rooms overlooking the Arabian Sea.

Bombay, Prabhupāda said, was India's most materialistic city. It was the nation's movie capital and the city where, more than in any other Indian city, the people wore Western dress. The "gateway to India," it boasted the most industries, the most businesses, and the most billboards. It was a cosmopolitan melting pot of cultures and religions but had none of the Naxalite terrorism of Calcutta or the heavy political atmosphere of New Delhi. Nor did it have the aristocratic families who worshiped Lord Caitanya and His *saṅkīrtana* movement. But it had its own advantages for preaching, Prabhupāda said. It was a city of wealth, with many pious citizens who were intelligent and quick to adopt a good idea. He predicted Bombay would be a favorable city for Kṛṣṇa consciousness.

Prabhupāda's first Bombay preaching engagement was at a gathering of *sādhus*, a *paṇḍāl* in an open field just a few blocks from Mr. Seksaria's home. Prabhupāda's disciples had also been invited, and they arrived several hours before Prabhupāda. The array of Indian *sādhus*, sitting onstage in long rows, startled the devotees. Some of the *sādhus* were bearded, some shaven-headed, some with long matted hair and holding tridents, some covered with ashes, some adorned with beads and clay markings. The devotees were amazed, and many of the *sādhus*, on seeing the white-skinned Vaiṣṇavas, were also amazed.

When the devotees came onstage and began their *kīrtana*, the audience responded by clapping in rhythm and chanting. Afterward, on the advice of Mr. Seksaria, the devotees took their *kīrtana* out into the streets, and many in the audience followed.

That evening the devotees returned to the *paṇḍāl* with Prabhupāda. Prabhupāda sat on a raised platform, and his disciples sat at his feet. After having three of his disciples speak in English, Prabhupāda spoke in Hindi, while the audience of more than five hundred listened silently. After his lecture he came down from the platform, and a crowd gathered around him, touching his feet and following him to his car.

When Prabhupāda heard from his disciples of their spontaneous *kīrtana* through the streets of Bombay, he said they should go to the busiest bazaars and chant daily. So they did. Wherever large numbers of people gathered, the devotees would go and chant. They were strong, youthful, exuberant, and faithful, and they would chant in the streets for three or four hours each day.

Although Prabhupāda did not physically go into the streets chanting with his disciples, he was with them by his instructions and by his presence before they went out in the morning and when they returned in the evening. They were chanting because he had told them to. And they knew that chanting was the natural activity of the soul; everyone should chant. The devotees knew that at the end of life they would go back home, back to Godhead. And better than that, at the end of the day they would go back to Marine Drive to Prabhupāda, who would smile and encourage them.

Radio stations and newspapers took note of the Western devotees chanting in the city. One article appeared in the October 10 edition of the *Times of India:*

> A group of Americans, including women with babes in arms, belonging to the International Society for Krishna Consciousness (ISKCON) has been moving around Bombay during the past few days chanting Hare Krishna Hare Krishna, Krishna Krishna Hare Hare, or Hare Rama Hare Rama, Rama Rama Hare Hare, to the accompaniment of cymbals, castanets, and drums (mridangams).
>
> ... Can the materialistic West, or at any rate, a microscopic part of it, have turned at last to embrace the spiritualism of the east? I met several of the Kirtan-chanting Americans (who have come here to attend the seventh All-India Conference at the Bharat Sadhu Samaj which begins here today) and was at once struck by their sincerity and utter surrender to the cult they have adopted. The Vaishnavas of Mathura could not be so guileless, I thought, as this band of Bhakti enthusiasts.

* * *

The sand of Chowpatti Beach was fine and clean. The audience numbered in the thousands. *Sādhus* sat onstage, Prabhupāda and his followers among them. It was twilight. The sky above the Arabian Sea was cloudy, and a pleasant breeze was stirring.

There had already been two lectures expounding the Māyāvāda philosophy, and now it was time for Prabhupāda to speak—the last scheduled speaker of the evening. The audience was eager to hear him; his accomplishments in the West had caused great curiosity, especially now that he had arrived in Bombay and his devotees were chanting daily in public. Prabhupāda's disciples, bored and exasperated by the preceding two hours of Hindi oratory, could scarcely wait any longer for Prabhupāda to speak. But Prabhupāda, instead of addressing the audience, turned to his disciples and said, "Begin chanting."

As soon as the devotees began the *kīrtana*, little Sarasvatī stood and began to dance. Following her, the other devotees rose and began to dance. As the *kīrtana* came alive with *mṛdaṅgas* and *karatālas*, the dancing and chanting of the devotees seemed to disturb some of the *sādhus* onstage, who rose one by one and left. The audience, however, responded enthusiastically, many of them standing and clapping. After five minutes of ecstatic *kīrtana*, the devotees spontaneously jumped down onto the sand and headed toward the audience. Thousands in the crowd rose to their feet and began to move along with the devotees in a dance, backward and forward.

Indians began crying in uncontrolled happiness, overwhelmed by the genuine *kṛṣṇa-bhakti* of these foreigners. Never before had such a thing happened. Policemen and press reporters joined in the chanting and dancing. Chowpatti Beach was in an uproar of Hare Kṛṣṇa *kīrtana*, as Prabhupāda and his disciples showed the potency of Lord Caitanya's *saṅkīrtana* movement.

After about ten minutes the *kīrtana* ended, though a tumultuous unrest pervaded the talkative crowd. Fifteen minutes elapsed before all the people returned to their seats and the program could continue. The devotees had left the stage and taken their seats on the ground level, leaving Prabhupāda alone onstage. Prabhupāda's voice echoed over the public-address system.

"Ladies and gentlemen, I was requested to speak in Hindi, but I am not very much accustomed to speak in Hindi. Therefore, the authorities in this meeting have allowed me to speak in English. I hope you will follow me, because it is Bombay and most people will be speaking English. The problem is, as this evening's speaker, His Holiness Swami Akhaṇḍānandajī spoke to you, how we can make everyone accustomed to take up good habits—*sad-ācāra*? I think in this age, Kali-yuga, there are many faults."

Prabhupāda went on to explain the power of Lord Caitanya's movement to clean the hearts of everyone. He referred to the two great rogues whom Lord Caitanya had delivered, Jagāi and Mādhāi.

"Now we are saving, wholesale, Jagāis and Mādhāis. Therefore, if we want peace, if we want to be situated on the *sad-ācāra* platform, then we must spread the *hari-nāma mahā-mantra* all over the world. And it has been practically proven. The American and European Vaiṣṇavas who have come here, who have chanted Hare Kṛṣṇa *mantra*—they were cow-flesh eaters, they were drunkards, they were illicit sex mongers, they were all kinds of gamblers. But having taken to this Kṛṣṇa consciousness movement, they have given up everything abominable. *Sad-ācāra* has come automatically. They are no more meat-eaters, they are no more gamblers, they are no more illicit sex mongers, they are no more intoxicators. They do not even take tea, they do not even take coffee, they do not even smoke, which I think is very rare to be found in India. But they have given up. Why? Because they have taken to this Kṛṣṇa consciousness."

Prabhupāda ended his talk after about five minutes.

"I do not feel that I have to say very much. You can see what is the result of Kṛṣṇa consciousness. It is not something artificial. It is there in everyone. I have not done anything magical. But this Kṛṣṇa consciousness is present in all of us. We simply have to revive it."

The audience responded with cheers and a great round of applause. Prabhupāda, with greater force and eloquence than the long-winded Māyāvādīs, had shown the essence of spiritual life—ecstatic chanting of the holy names. And he had offered the living testimony of his American disciples.

For the next week, Prabhupāda and his disciples were the talk of Bombay, and they began receiving many invitations to speak and perform *kīrtana* throughout the city. The *Times Weekly's* coverage of the Sadhu Samaj spotlighted the memorable presence of Śrīla Prabhupāda and his disciples.

> A group of twenty Americans, members of the Hare Krishna delegation, took over the dais. The air was filled with the beating of mridangas, the clash of cymbals and the music of the maha-mantra. Swaying from side to side, their tufts of hair tossing in the breeze they chanted: Hare Krishna . . .
>
> One greying reporter whom I had always regarded as a particularly unsen-

timental person said to me in an emotion-choked voice: "Do you realize what is happening? Very soon Hinduism is going to sweep the West. The Hare Krishna movement will compensate for all our loss at the hands of padres through the centuries."

About twenty-five newsmen came to a press conference on the fifth floor of Mr. Seksaria's residence. Prabhupāda sat with his disciples on a large mattress and answered questions, and the devotees showed a film of the San Francisco Ratha-yātrā. The reporters asked about New Vrindaban. They questioned the devotees: Why had they become *sādhus*? Why had they left their country?

The next day the press was full of stories of Prabhupāda and his movement. The *Times of India* picked up on a particular angle: "U.S. MILLIONAIRE'S SON SEEKS SOLACE IN KRISHNA SOCIETY." The article told of Girirāja's renouncing his father's wealth to join Prabhupāda's movement. One newspaper quoted Girirāja: "My father works hard and earns fabulous money. He also fights with my mother. My sisters ran away from the house. Thus, in spite of material comforts, nobody is happy." Quoting Śyāmasundara: "My father is very rich, but he has to take sleeping tablets every night." And there were other articles.

Soon letters appeared in the letters column of the *Times of India.*

> As far as my knowledge goes, these foreign Hindus of the Hare Krishna movement cannot be equal to the native original brahmanas and Hindus. They will have to be relegated to the lower castes. It is significant to see one of the newly converted sadhus, Sri Gopal dasa, formerly Charles Poland of Chicago, stated that he was a construction worker formerly. Doing sudra's work, it would thus become necessary to allot the three lower castes to these foreign converts according to their profession.

Another letter stated, "The Hare Krishna movement is just a sporadic fad of sentimentalists."

Prabhupāda said these letters should be answered, and he personally outlined replies, delegating their writing to specific disciples. Within a few days, Prabhupāda's replies appeared in the press.

> In India even amongst the brahmanas in different provinces there is no social intercourse. So if they are socially accepted or not doesn't matter.

For example, amongst the qualified legal practitioners in different provinces there may not be social intercourse, but that does not mean they are not qualified lawyers. This is a cultural movement, and if the whole world accepts this cult, even though Indian brahmanas do not accept it will do no harm at all. . . . We are not striving for social or political unity, but if Krishna consciousness is accepted there will automatically be political, social and religious unity. . . .

The fact that one of our boys was a construction worker does not mean that he belongs to the sudra community. The sudra community is the less intelligent class or illiterate class who have no information of the value of life. In America even the highest cultured and educated person can go to work as an ordinary construction worker because they accept the dignity of labor. So although a boy was working as a construction worker in America, he is not a sudra.

But even if he is accepted as a sudra, Lord Krishna says that anyone who comes to Him is eligible to be elevated to the highest position of going back to home, back to Godhead.

In a letter signed by Girirāja, Prabhupāda refuted the charge that his movement was a "sporadic fad of sentimentalists."

. . . How can our movement be sporadic when this science was taught in the Gita five thousand years ago and instructed to the sun-god millions of years before that? How can it be called sporadic when our activity is sanatana-dharma, the eternal occupation of the living entity? Would faddists give up all meat-eating, intoxicants, illicit sex, and gambling for over five years now? Would faddists give up friends, family, and money and get up at 4:00 A.M. daily, ready to go to any country in the world and preach in any conditions immediately on the request of their spiritual master?

Prabhupāda saw all news coverage of the Kṛṣṇa consciousness movement as an aid to propagating Kṛṣṇa consciousness. Even by criticizing the Kṛṣṇa consciousness movement, he said, the papers were broadcasting the holy name of Kṛṣṇa. And Kṛṣṇa's name was absolute.

Mr. Seksaria held a special program for many important dignitaries of Bombay. Although he had expected no more than two hundred persons, many more came. They were Bombay's elite—the women dressed in expensive silk *sārīs* and wearing gold and jewels , the men in silk Nehru-collared suits or white starched *dhotīs* and *kurtās*.

Prabhupāda held *kīrtana* with his disciples, and then he spoke, briefly and gravely. "You are all very intelligent persons," he said. "You are all very learned and educated. You are all very great persons. I beg you—I take the straw of the street between my teeth, and I beg you—just chant Hare Kṛṣṇa. Please chant Hare Kṛṣṇa."

After his talk, Prabhupāda left, and the devotees showed slides of the Hare Kṛṣṇa movement's activities around the world. They also made their first public life membership appeal, and Mr. G. D. Somani, one of India's leading industrialists, as well as Mr. Seksaria, signed on as members.

Although Prabhupāda was happy to see the number of ISKCON's life members increasing, that his shipment of books from Dai Nippon had not yet arrived made him anxious. The devotees were promising life members books, but where were these books? Every day the problem became more and more pronounced.

Prabhupāda learned of a Calcutta port strike. His books had apparently arrived, but the ship, unable to unload cargo in Calcutta, had left port. He worried that the ship would unload the books in some other Indian port. The exact whereabouts and condition of the books, however, remained unknown. Prabhupāda was greatly concerned. He decided to send a competent disciple, Tamāla Kṛṣṇa, to Calcutta to try and retrieve the books. Meanwhile he would continue preaching, depending on Kṛṣṇa.

* * *

Amritsar
October 21, 1970

Accompanied by a group of disciples (seven men and two women), Prabhupāda began the two-day train ride from Bombay to Amritsar. Years ago Prabhupāda had traveled as a preacher in India alone, riding the trains to Jhansi, Delhi, Kanpur, Calcutta, and Bombay to publish *Back to Godhead* and solicit support. After only five years in the West, he now had the great advantage of sincere disciples, and now the Indians were taking notice.

He had stationed Acyutānanda Swami, Jayapatāka Swami, Haṁsadūta, and others in Calcutta; Tamāla Kṛṣṇa, Śyāmasundara, and others in Bombay. His disciples would make life members and try to establish permanent ISKCON centers in two of India's major cities. His Kṛṣṇa consciousness movement was beginning in India, and he wanted to travel with his disciples wherever there was an opportunity to preach. Just as he had worked in America—never settling comfortably in one place, but always traveling, speaking about Kṛṣṇa, meeting new people and offering them devotional service—so he would also work in India.

The train arrived at Kurukṣetra station. "Near here," said Prabhupāda, "Lord Kṛṣṇa spoke *Bhagavad-gītā* five thousand years ago. They say it does not exist—a mythological place. It is a symbol of the field of the body and the senses, they say. It is an allegorical place. But here we are at the station." As he spoke, the sun was setting, and a bright, orange sky shone over the flat land. "How can they say Kurukṣetra is not a real place?" he continued. "Here it is before us. And it has been a historical place for a long, long time."

When the train arrived at Amritsar station, members of the Vedanta Sammelan committee received Prabhupāda and escorted him and his disciples to a park on the outskirts of the city. They showed him the large *paṇḍāl* the Niketan Ashram had erected for the Vedanta Sammelan and assigned him and his disciples their quarters—three small rooms. Prabhupāda took one room, the two women the second room, and four of the men crowded into the third, leaving three men to sleep outdoors on cots. The first night in the northern climate was cold. Available bedding was meager, and none of the devotees had brought warm clothing.

At four the next morning the devotees congregated in Śrīla Prabhupāda's room for *maṅgala-ārati* and *kīrtana* before the Deities of Rādhā and Kṛṣṇa—the same Deities who had been traveling with Prabhupāda for the past one and a half years. Despite the austere conditions, the devotees felt fortunate to have such intimate contact with Prabhupāda and Rādhā-Kṛṣṇa. Prabhupāda played *mṛdaṅga,* leading the chanting of prayers to the spiritual master. Afterward, he had the *pūjārī* distribute to each devotee a bit of the fruit and sweetmeats that had just been offered to the Deities. It was still before sunrise, and the room was chilly. As the devotees sat huddled beneath a naked bulb, Prabhupāda had them read aloud from *Śrīmad-Bhāgavatam.*

That same morning Prabhupāda attended the Vedanta Sammelan. There were thousands of people in the audience, and since most of them did not understand English, Prabhupāda spoke in Hindi. His presentation pleased everyone, and the committee members honored him by making him president of the Vedanta Sammelan.

Although the program was scheduled only for several hours in the morning and evening, Prabhupāda did not limit his preaching to these times; he preached every hour of the day. While he sat in his room, a constant stream of guests came to him, hundreds of pious Hindus seeking his blessings. Recognizing this vestige of Vedic culture, he pointed it out to his disciples. "Just see," he said, "how they treat a saintly person."

Prabhupāda also began receiving the usual flood of invitations to visit the homes of Hindu families. He accepted as many invitations as possible—more than possible, it seemed to his disciples.

Prabhupāda moved quickly. When the cars were ready, he would come out of his room and go, leaving behind anyone who wasn't ready. After each engagement, he would get into his car and go directly to the next. Latecomers would sometimes find he had already left. They would then jump into bicycle rickshas and try to catch him. A wrong direction or a missed turn might make them miss the next engagement. And when at last they would catch up, they would find Prabhupāda coolly, gravely in the midst of a lecture on *Bhagavad-gītā* or laughing and taking *prasādam* with his host.

Every day brought at least a half-dozen engagements—"Come to our temple for *darśana*," "Come to our house for *prasādam*." And whenever Prabhupāda would return to his *āśrama*, he would find a long line of guests waiting to spend a few moments with him.

None of the devotees could match Prabhupāda's pace and enthusiasm. His energy seemed never to wane. For his disciples, being invited insistently to take a full meal at half a dozen homes in one day was too much. They tended to overeat, and some of them got sick. But Prabhupāda knew how to handle the situation expertly. He would fully satisfy each host, speak about Kṛṣṇa consciousness, hold *kīrtana*, take a little *prasādam*, and move on.

One evening, in response to an invitation, Prabhupāda visited the home of Baladeva Indra Singh, a descendant of one of ancient Punjab's ruling families. Although nearing sixty, Mr. Singh was still a robust Punjabi *kṣatriya*, handsome, tall, and sporting a big black mustache. He showed Prabhupāda and his disciples through his elegant home, with its large portraits of ancestors, uniformed *kṣatriyas* with their helmets and swords. In the trophy room, which had many animal skins and stuffed heads mounted on the wall, Mr. Singh brought Prabhupāda and his disciples before his prize trophy, a large tiger's head. Prabhupāda approached closely. "You have killed this?" he asked.

"Yes," Mr. Singh replied. And he described the details of the hunt. The man-eater had killed many people in a nearby village, Mr. Singh explained. "So I went and shot it."

Prabhupāda's eyes widened, and he turned to his disciples. "Oh, very nice!"

Later, Prabhupāda sat in a chair, and Mr. Singh sat before him on the floor. He said something was troubling him. An astrologer had told him that in a previous lifetime, thousands of years ago, he had fought in the battle of Kurukṣetra—but on the side *against* Kṛṣṇa!

"That's not possible," Prabhupāda said. "Everyone present at the battle of Kurukṣetra was liberated. If you had actually been at the battle of Kurukṣetra, you would not still be within this material world." Mr. Singh wasn't certain whether to feel relieved or disappointed. But Prabhupāda assured him, "That's all right. Don't worry. Now you are a devotee of Kṛṣṇa."

When Prabhupāda asked Mr. Singh to become a life member of ISKCON, he agreed immediately. He confessed that when he had first invited Prabhupāda and his disciples he had actually been skeptical, but after being with Śrīla Prabhupāda for a few minutes, he said, all his doubts and suspicions had vanished. He would be happy to become ISKCON's first life member in Amritsar.

Although the devotees requested Prabhupāda to take fewer engagements, he would not slow down. It was his disciples, he said, who were finding the pace difficult. One night, after the eighth and final engagement of the day, Prabhupāda returned to his room just a little before midnight. For the devotees the day had been exhausting, and they were eager to get to bed as soon as possible. Noticing Prabhupāda's light still on, one of them went to his window. Prabhupāda was sitting at his desk, leaning back against the wall, listening to a tape recording of one of the talks he had given that day.

* * *

One afternoon Prabhupāda and his disciples went to see the famous Golden Temple of the Sikhs. A guide took them around and answered

Prabhupāda's questions. Sikh businessmen, the guide explained, maintained the temple and its expenses. The Sikhs pride themselves in the assertion that no one in Amritsar goes hungry, and they daily feed *dāl* and *capātīs* to ten thousand people. This interested Prabhupāda, and he observed their massive operation. He watched the group of men rolling *capātīs,* flipping them deftly through the air onto a giant griddle while other men, using long paddles, turned the *capātīs,* held them briefly over the hot coals, and then placed them in stacks. "This is how to distribute *prasādam,*" Prabhupāda said.

Prabhupāda signed the guest book "A. C. Bhaktivedanta Swami." Under *Religion* he wrote "Kṛṣṇaite." And under *Comments* he wrote "very spiritual."

Prabhupāda and his disciples visited Rāma-tīrtha-sarovara, the lake where in a bygone age the great sage Vālmīki had his *āśrama.* The terrain surrounding Rāma-tīrtha-sarovara was dry and rocky, and vegetation was sparse. As they stopped at the beautiful bathing *ghāṭa,* its steps leading down into the lake, the devotees were in a jubilant mood, happy to be on a field trip with their transcendental father and teacher. The peaceful lake and the beautiful *ghāṭa* seemed an ideal setting for being with Prabhupāda.

The devotees, who knew little of Lord Rāma, listened intently as Prabhupāda began to tell some of the pastimes of the Supreme Personality of Godhead in His incarnation of Lord Rāmacandra. During the last days of His earthly pastimes, Prabhupāda said, Rāma banished Sītā, His wife and eternal consort. Pregnant and alone, Sītā sought shelter at the *āśrama* of Vālmīki, where she soon gave birth to a son, Lava. Vālmīki created another son for Sītā from straw and named him Kuśa.

When Sītā learned that Rāma was sending a challenge horse throughout the world, she instructed her sons to catch the horse. In this way, she concluded, they would capture their father and bring Him before her. Unfortunately, while the boys were away on their mission, they learned that Lord Rāmacandra had departed from the world. Grief-stricken, they returned to Vālmīki. To mitigate the boys' anguish of separation, Vālmīki sang to them *Rāmāyaṇa,* the transcendental narrative of Lord Rāma's activities. One day, as Sītā was out walking, the ground opened before her, and she returned into the earth from which she had appeared.

These events, Prabhupāda explained as he stood with his followers by Rāma-tīrtha-sarovara, had happened no less than eight hundred thousand years ago. For the devotees, it was as if Prabhupāda had opened a new door to the spiritual world.

* * *

The organizers of the Vedanta Sammelan repeatedly asked Prabhupāda and his party to play a larger part in the *paṇḍāl* program. The scheduled discourses were mostly on Māyāvāda philosophy: God is impersonal, all religious paths are equal and lead to the Supreme One, all is one, we are all God. Such dry speculations could not hold the public's attention, and the Sammelan organizers daily requested the devotees to hold *kīrtana* in the *paṇḍāl.* But with so much other preaching, Prabhupāda preferred holding programs of his own in private homes around the city.

A devotee asked Prabhupāda about a Māyāvāda slogan he saw posted: *Tat Tvam Asi,* with the English translation underneath: "You are that too." This was a favorite saying of the impersonalists, who imagine that the living entity is God, Prabhupāda said. He explained elaborately the distinction between God and the living entity and told how God, when He appears, displays certain unmistakable characteristics that identify Him as the Supreme Personality of Godhead. "These *yogīs* will just talk and talk *Vedānta,*" Prabhupāda said. "It is simply mental speculation, and they never come to any conclusion. They will go on speculating for years and lifetimes, but we will realize God simply by eating." And from the plate of *prasādam* before him he took a sweet and popped it into his mouth.

In the midst of his activities in Amritsar, Prabhupāda continued to think of his spiritual children in various places throughout the world, and he regularly wrote them. To the devotees in Calcutta he wrote, "I am very much anxious to hear what you are doing there and if you have made any life members by this time." He asked them to register ISKCON with the government and try to establish a permanent center there.

To his disciples in Bombay he wrote, "I am very anxious to know your situation; whether you have removed to the Rama Temple or where you are stationed now." To Karandhara in Los Angeles he wrote,

> I hope everything is going on well with you in our Los Angeles World Headquarters.
>
> Please send me a report of your general activities. . . . and also your Governing Body Commission activities. Please offer my blessings to all the members of our Temples. How is the Deity worship being carried on?

Replying to Upendra in the Fiji Islands:

> Regarding worship of demigods, the whole Hindu society is absorbed in this business, so unless our preaching work is very vigorous it is very difficult to stop them.

And to Bhavānanda in New York:

> Please conduct the Samkirtan program regularly and that will give me great pleasure. Regarding our new temple in Brooklyn, Kṛṣṇa has given you very good chance to serve Him.

* * *

October 30, 1970

After ten days in Amritsar, Prabhupāda was on the train heading back to Bombay. He rode in a small first-class compartment with Guru dāsa, while the rest of his disciples rode in another part of the train. Prabhupāda's car, being close to the locomotive, caught soot from the engine's smoke stack, until he was soon flecked from head to foot with small black particles.

Yamunā: *We were traveling between Amritsar and Delhi, and I decided to go see how Śrīla Prabhupāda was doing, if there was anything he wanted (because sometimes when the train stopped he would ask for a devotee to purchase fresh fruit and other things from the vendors on the train platform). So Kauśalyā and I made our way through several cars to Prabhupāda's first-class compartment. He was lying back on several pillows with one knee up, looking like a monarch. He had a beautiful smile on his face.*

We paid our obeisances, and Śrīla Prabhupāda looked at us with a twinkle in his eye. "Is there anything hot to eat?" he asked. "What do you mean?" I said. "Do you want me to get your lunch, Śrīla

Prabhupāda?" "No," he said, "not that. Some rice, some hot rice." I said, "What do you mean, Śrīla Prabhupāda—from the train?" He said, "Well, no. If you can make me some hot rice." I said I would.

I had no idea how I was going to prepare hot rice for Śrīla Prabhupāda, but Kauśalyā and I found our way to the kitchen. Nobody was there, only two men dressed in black, turmeric-stained shorts, standing over the coal stove smoking cigarettes. I didn't know how to speak Hindi, but I said the best I could, "My Guru Mahārāja wants some cāvāl, *some hot rice."*

The men laughed at us as if we were crazy, and so I thought we had better find someone who would give us permission. But when we found the manager of the restaurant, he said, "No. Impossible. You can't cook in the kitchen." I said, "I'm sorry, this is for my Guru Mahārāja. There is no question of choice. I have said to him that I will fix rice, and I have to fulfill this." But again he said, "No, it is impossible."

I went and found the conductor of the train and explained the situation to him. "If I can't do this for my spiritual master," I said, "then I might as well jump off the train." The conductor took us very seriously and said, "Of course, of course, you can fix whatever you like in the kitchen."

So he brought us back to the kitchen and told the head of the kitchen as well as the head of the restaurant that he was giving us permission. The coal stove was gigantic, and I was completely unfamiliar with it. All sorts of aluminum pots and dishes were hanging around the kitchen. We cleaned out one of the pots as best we could, boiled the water, and put in the cāvāl. *We prepared a gigantic platter of very hot rice with butter, fresh lemon, salt, and pepper and carried it through the train to Prabhupāda's compartment.*

"Here's your rice, Śrīla Prabhupāda," I said as we entered. And his eyes lit up and opened wide. He gave a huge grin. "Oh, my goddesses of fortune have come," he said. "They have brought me my rice. Thank you very much. This is just what I wanted." He ate so much *from this huge plate. He took a little* kacaurī *and* purī *with it, and a little pickle. He was very pleased.*

That night the train pulled into the New Delhi station, with its scurrying crowds of passengers, hawking vendors, refreshment counters, newsstands, beggars, and coolies in their dingy red jackets. The stopover would be twenty minutes.

Suddenly a man appeared in Prabhupāda's compartment, identifying himself as D. D. Gupta. Although Prabhupāda had not met him before, they had corresponded. He was a Delhi man, not especially influential or wealthy, but he wanted to help. Offering Prabhupāda a box of sweets, he invited him to stay in Delhi. Prabhupāda, however, already had other plans and had even wired ahead to notify the devotees in Bombay of his arrival.

Prabhupāda looked over at Guru dāsa, who was feeling happy and especially blessed to have this intimate contact with his spiritual master. Twelve hours they had spent in the same compartment, eating together, talking together. Just minutes before, Prabhupāda had been stressing the importance of farming and explaining how the scarcity of food was due to mismanagement, not to lack of rain or arable land. Guru dāsa was happy, and he was looking forward to the next leg of the journey with Prabhupāda, anticipating the scenery and his return to Bombay.

"This man is inviting us," Prabhupāda said. "Get down and see what you can do."

"Get down?" There was hardly time to ask questions or discuss what to do in Delhi; the train would be leaving immediately. Guru dāsa said he would stay, but he would need help. He and Prabhupāda agreed on a team: Yamunā (Guru dāsa's wife), Girirāja, Durlabha, Bruce, and Gopāla. Guru dāsa ran to tell his wife and the *brahmacārīs* the news.

The devotees had little trouble picking up their light bags and getting off the train, but they felt sad to be leaving Śrīla Prabhupāda. As the train pulled away they offered obeisances outside Prabhupāda's window and waved to him, praying for his mercy. This was an austerity—perhaps a tiny drop of what Prabhupāda had gone through when he had first arrived in America.

* * *

Bombay
November 1970

For the next month, Prabhupāda and his disciples stayed at Manoharlal Agarwal's Sītā-Rāma temple in Chembur. Actually it was Mr. Agarwal's residence, but since he maintained the worship of Sītā-Rāma Deities he called his home Ram Sharanam, "under the shelter of Lord Rāma." Prabhupāda occupied one room, and his disciples two other rooms, with access to a kitchen and bath. The Sītā-Rāma temple and suburban neighborhood provided a peaceful atmosphere, and Prabhupāda returned to concentrated work on *Śrīmad-Bhāgavatam*, corresponding with ISKCON centers around the world and looking after the small group of disciples who were with him. He had great hope Kṛṣṇa would provide a way for ISKCON to become well established in India.

> We are just now receiving great publicity and it is reported that Bombay has now got its atmosphere filled with Krishna Consciousness. It is a fact, and the important members of the Bombay community are appreciating our Movement. . . .
>
> For the present I am more prominent than all swamis. People are appreciating—What are these swamis? They cannot go outside. There is a Bengali saying that a jackal is king in a small forest. The story is that a jackal became king in the forest by fooling the other animals for some time, but he remained always a jackal and his ruse was at last exposed.

Although Mr. Agarwal was honored that Prabhupāda had accepted his invitation and was now living as his guest, Prabhupāda knew that the situation would ultimately prove inconvenient for everyone involved. To open one's home to a dozen guests and feed them daily was a strain, even for a wealthy man; and for the devotees to live in those tiny quarters under the already trying conditions of irregular hours, frequent sickness, and tropical heat was not easy.

The solution, of course, was for the devotees to get their own place, an ISKCON center in Bombay. As a *sannyāsī*, Prabhupāda was prepared to stay anywhere, moving as often as necessary, accepting alms. He had lived that way for years before going to America. But now he had twenty spiritual children to support in India, and more on the way. They were not mature. He wanted them near him so that they could observe how he did things and imbibe the spirit of preaching in India.

When a Hindu organization in downtown Bombay requested a few devotees to attend a three-day program, Prabhupāda approved. But when the program was over and the leaders of the organization invited the devotees to stay on indefinitely, Prabhupāda said, "No. They will simply eat and sleep." Better for them to stay with him at crowded Ram Sharanam.

Mrs. Sumati Morarji, the wealthy director of Scindia Steamship Lines, had financed the printing of the third volume of Prabhupāda's *Śrīmad-Bhāgavatam* in 1964, and in 1965 she had provided him free passage to America. Now she invited Prabhupāda to speak at Scindia House, near Juhu Beach. Seated onstage, Prabhupāda and Sumati Morarji reminisced, celebrating Prabhupāda's success.

"I did not think you would come back alive," Mrs. Morarji said. "But I am so much pleased to see you." No longer was Prabhupāda the poor *sādhu* Mrs. Morarji had met six years ago. He was a success, and Sumati Morarji and her staff and friends were happy to hear about the Kṛṣṇa consciousness movement in the West.

Before Prabhupāda's lecture, Tamāla Kṛṣṇa formally introduced him to the audience. "Śrīla Prabhupāda left for the West five years ago from this city. He had almost no money. He went to New York, where he chanted Hare Kṛṣṇa in a park, underneath a tree. Soon he opened a temple, where he continued his chanting and held classes on Vedic philosophy. Many people came, and gradually he opened new centers: San Francisco, Montreal, Boston, and so on. Now he has many devotees and over forty temples. In each temple there is a full-scale program of *saṅkīrtana*, Deity worship, and *prasādam* distribution. India has sent many ambassadors and ministers to the West, but none of them can say that he made the Americans give up eating meat, fish, and eggs and got them to chant Hare Kṛṣṇa. Everyone is indebted to Śrīla Prabhupāda, because he came to relieve the suffering of all the fallen souls. . . ."

Prabhupāda sang three verses from the *Brahma-saṁhitā* and invited the audience to join in the chorus: *Govindam ādi-puruṣaṁ tam ahaṁ bhajāmi.* After speaking for half an hour, he accepted *prasādam* with Sumati Morarji and honored guests and dignitaries. He met Dr. C. Bali and his wife, the famous dancer and movie actress Vaijayanti Mala. He spoke only briefly with them, and they became life members of ISKCON.

Vaijayanti Mala: *Swami Prabhupāda made his preaching so simple that even a lay person would understand what our great philosophy and our great teachings meant. Not only was he propagating the great culture of our Lord Kṛṣṇa, but he was making the people of other parts of the world really understand its meaning and its significance. By his simple and yet very great teachings of Kṛṣṇa, he took this message so far and so wide that it's really a marvel that a person single-handedly could do so much. He not only preached and, you know, just talked about the whole thing, but he also established so many centers in so many parts of the world. This is really amazing that he could do it in spite of all difficulties. But his perseverance and his persistence, I think, kept him on.*

The public sensation of Prabhupāda's disciples chanting in the streets of Bombay and at the Sadhu Samaj had died down; the regular news coverage had stopped. Still Prabhupāda was sought after by many important people in Bombay. His accomplishments after five years in America commanded the esteem and attention of intelligent Indians, and daily he received respectable visitors who accepted him as the authority on Kṛṣṇa consciousness.

The Indians regarded Prabhupāda as unique. Even in a culture where *swamis* and holy men are commonly treated with respect, he was regarded as special. His visitors would beg him to come to their homes and sanctify them. And this was also in line with Prabhupāda's desire; he wanted to engage the Indians in chanting Hare Kṛṣṇa, hearing the philosophy of *Bhagavad-gītā*, and honoring the Lord's *prasādam*. He wanted them to appreciate the purity of the Kṛṣṇa consciousness movement, enlist as life members of ISKCON, and help him establish a large center in Bombay.

In preaching to Indians, Prabhupāda would often urge them to return to their all-but-forgotten spiritual culture. "Our culture is Kṛṣṇa consciousness," he said before a group of Bombay citizens. "But we are forgetting and becoming too materially absorbed. Lord Ṛṣabhadeva says that this is not good, because according to the law of *karma* you will have to take another body. But you don't have to give up your hard struggle for material life. Arjuna was not advised to do this. He remained in his position and executed Kṛṣṇa consciousness." Prabhupāda concluded, "I am begging. I have forty-two temples in the West, and in each one there are fifty to one hundred disciples. Thousands of books have to be printed. Please help me with this movement."

Manoharlal Agarwal, Prabhupāda's host at Ram Sharanam, would often sit with him for hours, inquiring about spiritual life. Mr. Agarwal was particularly interested in hearing of Prabhupāda's work in America: How had he transformed so many Christians into Rāma *bhaktas*? Had he been alone, or had there been helpers? How did he dress in America? What was his approach? Prabhupāda recounted his early preaching on the Lower

East Side of New York, and he explained how everything had happened by Kṛṣṇa's desire.

Mr. Agarwal doubted whether Westerners would be able to stay with Kṛṣṇa consciousness for very long. "Now in the radiance of your company," he said, "as long as you are here bodily and physically, they may continue to observe all these restrictions. But when your physical influence will not be there, one day when you will have to leave this world, then all these people that have come in contact with you, will they go bad?"

"No," Prabhupāda said firmly.

"Your claim is very tall," replied Mr. Agarwal. "Can you tell me what is the basic foundation of your claim?"

Prabhupāda reminded him that all his disciples had been initiated into the chanting of the Hare Kṛṣṇa *mantra* and that according to the Vedic scriptures the constant chanting of the Lord's holy name will save even the most fallen souls and protect them from falling again. Even after his passing away, Prabhupāda predicted, his disciples would not fall victim to *māyā,* as long as they continued their prescribed chanting.

One day Mr. Agarwal asked how long Prabhupāda and his disciples were planning to stay. Prabhupāda said that he was very happy staying where he was but would try to find a new place immediately. Mr. Agarwal insisted that he had no intention of asking Prabhupāda to leave; his home belonged to Prabhupāda, not to himself. He begged him to kindly continue to stay.

Prabhupāda said this reminded him of an incident from the *Caitanya-caritāmṛta,* and he told a story about Haridāsa Ṭhākura, the great devotee of Lord Caitanya. Haridāsa Ṭhākura used to live alone in a cave, where he chanted Hare Kṛṣṇa day and night. Many pilgrims would visit him, but when they learned that a python was also living within the cave, they became afraid. Although Haridāsa Ṭhākura was satisfied with his cave, he didn't want to inconvenience his visitors, so he said he would leave the cave that very day and not return again. Yet even as he spoke, the huge python came winding out from the back of the cave into the presence of all. Passing near Haridāsa Ṭhākura, the snake bowed his head to the ground and slithered away. The Supersoul within the heart of the python had impelled him to leave the cave so that Haridāsa Ṭhākura could remain.

Prabhupāda laughed as he told the story. "Agarwalji," he said, "you have said the same thing. You have said that you will go away and that we will stay. But no, no, we will go. We will go."

CHAPTER FIVE

"A Lot of Ground to Be Covered"

Indore
December 3, 1970

India continued to be like a dream for Prabhupāda's disciples, who gazed out the windows as the train moved them through India's unfamiliar rural world. The trackside bushes blossomed in yellow. Mile after mile of irrigated agricultural fields passed by—wheat, rice, sugarcane, and varieties of *dāl*. Small villages—mud-walled houses with straw roofs, or thatched walls with tile roofs—drifted peacefully by. An occasional village temple made of stone would rise above the surrounding simple structures. Cowherd boys with sticks tended their herds on the grassy banks of meandering streams. And the grazing cows, the oxen plowing in the ancient fields, the dung patties drying in the sun for fuel, the smoke rising from the cooking fires, and the smell of the warm earth—all were part of a peaceful, simple way of life the devotees were coming to appreciate through Prabhupāda's association.

Prabhupāda and his disciples were en route to Indore, a city of 475,000 in the central Indian province of Madhya Pradesh, thirteen hours northeast of Bombay. The directors of the Gita Jayanti Mahotsava, a festival to celebrate the teachings of *Bhagavad-gītā*, had invited Prabhupāda and his disciples to attend their convention and public meeting.

In Indore Śrīla Prabhupāda and his disciples settled into their quarters near the Gita Bhavan, the site of the Gita Jayanti Mahotsava. The directors of the convention had assigned Prabhupāda a bungalow with a lawn and garden and had provided nearby facilities for his disciples.

The devotees toured the grounds of the Gita Bhavan, noting the many swamis and *sādhus* who had arrived from various parts of India for the Mahotsava. They saw the large *paṇḍāl* and stage, the eye hospital run by the Gita Bhavan, and the diorama exhibit. The diorama exhibit they regarded as the kind of eclectic mixing of spiritual paths that Prabhupāda often referred to as "hodgepodge." Kṛṣṇa, Buddha, Jesus, Vivekananda, Ramakrishna, and demigods and animals were all on display. While admiring the energy and imagination that had produced such an exhibit, the devotees questioned the benefit of such a conglomeration.

On the first night of the festival Prabhupāda was scheduled as the last speaker. His disciples, who sat with him onstage, grew bored and restless from the ordeal of so many hours of Hindi speeches. And knowing that these speakers were presenting Māyāvāda misconceptions made the evening especially painful. Śrīla Prabhupāda sat sternly and waited, his hand in his bead bag, his head held high, his lips murmuring the Hare Kṛṣṇa *mantra.*

When Prabhupāda finally spoke, he began by explaining that in the West he was spreading the teachings of the *Gītā* as it is. *Bhagavad-gītā*, he said, could be properly understood only in disciplic succession, just as Arjuna, the original student of the *Bhagavad-gītā*, had understood it. The *Gītā* was for the devotee of Kṛṣṇa and should not be misinterpreted by nondevotees. To misinterpret the *Gītā*, he said, was to cheat in the name of religion. He also spoke strongly against pseudoincarnations.

Prabhupāda concluded his talk and asked his disciples to begin *kīrtana.* It was an ecstatic, spontaneous event, and Prabhupāda began dancing onstage along with his disciples. The crowd came to life and began clapping rhythmically. Haṁsadūta jumped down from the stage, still playing *mṛdaṅga*, and began inducing members of the audience to join in chanting and dancing. Several other devotees also jumped down, and soon hundreds of people had risen to their feet, swaying, clapping, and singing: Hare Kṛṣṇa, Hare Kṛṣṇa, Kṛṣṇa Kṛṣṇa, Hare Hare/ Hare Rāma, Hare Rāma, Rāma Rāma, Hare Hare. This was the real Gita Jayanti Mahotsava. The holy name of Kṛṣṇa was being sung, and everyone was happily united in the *kīrtana.*

Greatly pleased by the performance of Prabhupāda and his disciples, the *paṇḍāl* directors visited Prabhupāda the next day in his bungalow. Prabhupāda complained at having to wait so long before he could speak;

his disciples shouldn't be required to sit through hours of speeches in a language they couldn't understand. When Prabhupāda intimated that the speeches seriously deviated from the teachings of the *Gītā*, the director of the Gita Bhavan replied, "We do not favor any particular way. Followers of the Śaṅkara school and others also come to our institution. We do not subscribe wholly that Śrī Kṛṣṇa is the sole God or anything of the sort. There is a power behind Him . . ."

This remark drew fire from Śrīla Prabhupāda. What kind of glorification of the *Gītā* was this if the speakers did not accept Kṛṣṇa as He is explained in the *Gītā*? The *Gītā* declares Kṛṣṇa to be the highest truth: *mattaḥ parataraṁ nānyat.* Prabhupāda advised the directors of the Gita Bhavan to try to understand the meaning of *Bhagavad-gītā.* The directors did not change their opinion, but they were intelligent enough to see that Prabhupāda was a great *paṇḍita* and saint, and they listened respectfully. Nodding, they said they accepted his point of view.

After the men left, Prabhupāda continued, "They are thinking that there is something beyond Kṛṣṇa or that it is the spirit within Kṛṣṇa that we have to surrender to. But they do not know that the within and the without of Kṛṣṇa are all absolute, eternal, and full of bliss."

Prabhupāda said he could see that the organizers of the Gita Jayanti Mahotsava had invited him to draw larger crowds. But they would not make him sit again through all the Māyāvādī nonsense, he said. From now on, he would go with his disciples, speak, chant, and then leave.

The next night, however, despite promises by the *paṇḍāl* directors, Śrīla Prabhupāda again had to wait until the end of the program before he could speak and hold *kīrtana.* This night, the crowd was larger than before, and they were clearly waiting for Śrīla Prabhupāda and the foreign *sādhus.* When Prabhupāda's turn came at last, he spoke and then asked his disciples to begin *kīrtana.*

During the *kīrtana* one of the members of the Gita Bhavan gestured to the devotees to jump down into the crowd as they had done on the preceding night. But what had been a spontaneous event the night before could not be artificially staged simply as a crowd pleaser. The man, however, was insistent. He came forward to the edge of the stage, reached up, and began grabbing at the feet of the dancing devotees, trying to pull them into the audience. The devotees became annoyed. Grabbing indiscriminately, the man pulled at one of the women's *sārīs.* Śrīla Prabhupāda was also dancing, but when he saw this he rushed to the edge of the stage, swinging his *karatālas* toward the man's face and shouting, "Stop this!" The man retreated, and Prabhupāda and his disciples continued their *kīrtana.* Although little-noticed by the crowd, Prabhupāda's burst of lionlike ferocity had amazed his disciples.

The festival directors were once again pleased with Prabhupāda's lecture and *kīrtana.* But Prabhupāda sent them word that he would not again sit through the other lectures, waiting his turn to speak. He had wearied of hearing opinions on *Bhagavad-gītā* that avoided the conclusion of *Bhagavad-gītā*—surrender to Śrī Kṛṣṇa, the Absolute Truth. Some speakers made the *Gītā* an allegory, some said Kṛṣṇa was not an actual historical personality, and some simply took advantage of the *Gītā's* popularity to put forward their own political or social philosophies. A person with his own philosophy should write his own book, Prabhupāda said, not use as a vehicle for his own ideas the *Bhagavad-gītā,* a scripture worshiped by millions and respected throughout the world. Why should a conference under the name Gita Jayanti become a forum for speculative philosophies? *Bhagavad-gītā* states that the *Gītā* itself is the essence of knowledge, meant to benefit the entire world. To misrepresent the *Gītā,* therefore, was the greatest disservice. Prabhupāda felt that by sitting through such a program, he and his disciples were tacitly approving the blasphemous speeches.

On the third night of the festival, Prabhupāda and his disciples came early to the stage, having been promised by the festival directors that they would be first on the program. But when another speaker stood and began his discourse, Prabhupāda, followed by his disciples, stood and walked off the stage. The festival director was quite disturbed by this, since most of the audience had come especially for the *kīrtana.* He pleaded with Prabhupāda to return, but Prabhupāda refused. He did agree, however, to send his disciples every night; they would speak and hold *kīrtana.*

* * *

Śrīla Prabhupāda's disciples found the morning *Bhāgavatam* classes in Indore especially relishable. Not only was the setting intimate—ten devotees sitting with Prabhupāda in his room—but the *Bhāgavatam* story was intriguing, one they had never before heard.

"We are talking of Ajāmila, a *brāhmaṇa* residing in Kanyākubjā, presently known as Kanpur," Prabhupāda began, and he narrated the story of Ajāmila's life, pausing from time to time to read the Sanskrit text or to elaborate on the story and its lessons. Ajāmila, a young *brāhmaṇa*, had strictly followed the religious principles, until he became infatuated with a prostitute. As Prabhupāda lectured he focused on the bogus speakers at the Gita Jayanti Mahotsava.

"There are so many things to know, but these things are not being discussed here. It is very cheap to do whatever you like—you simply meditate and you become God. So much cheating is going on all over the world. The so-called *yogīs* say, 'You meditate, and as soon as you are realized, you become God.'

"The *Bhagavad-gītā* is being interpreted in so many different ways. And these so-called explanations are being accepted by the innocent public as authoritative knowledge. Someone is explaining that *kurukṣetra* means this body, and *pañca-pāṇḍava** means the senses. But this is not explaining. How can you explain the *Bhagavad-gītā* as it is when you do not understand it? Such an attempt is nonsense."

In his second lecture Prabhupāda narrated more of Ajāmila's life: his leaving his chaste wife and going to live with the prostitute, his adopting illegal means for supporting her, his having ten children by her and living sinfully until his eightieth year. This story took place, Śrīla Prabhupāda said, thousands of years ago. "At that time there was only one Ajāmila, but you will find many Ajāmilas like that at the present moment, because it is the age of Kali."

Ajāmila had great affection for his youngest son, Nārāyaṇa. And as Ajāmila lay on his deathbed and saw the agents of death approaching, he cried out for his son—"Nārāyaṇa!" Prabhupāda continued his story.

"He was just on the point of death, so—naturally he had affection for his son—so he was calling, 'Nārāyaṇa! Nārāyaṇa! Nārāyaṇa! Please come here! Please come here!' That is natural. I know my father—when he was dying, I was not at home. So he was living for one day to see me. He was always inquiring whether Abhay has come back. Like that. So father's paternal affection is like that, and similarly Ajāmila was calling, 'Nārāyaṇa! Nārāyaṇa!' "

Nārāyaṇa is also a name of Kṛṣṇa. And Prabhupāda said that,

*The five Pāṇḍava brothers, pure devotees of Lord Kṛṣṇa, are referred to in *Bhagavad-gītā*. They were the victors of the battle of Kurukṣetra.

according to *Bhagavad-gītā*, if a person remembers Nārāyaṇa, or Kṛṣṇa, at the time of death, he becomes liberated. One's mentality at death determines one's next birth. Because the devotee is Kṛṣṇa conscious, he enters the spiritual world at death; and because the materialist is absorbed in sense pleasure and mental speculation, he has to take birth after birth in the material world. Prabhupāda gave an example.

"One gentleman in Calcutta was a fairly big businessman. He was dealing in shares, stocks. So at the time of death he was crying, 'Kamarhati! Kamarhati!' So the result might be that he might have taken his birth as a rat in the Kamarhati mill. It is possible. At the time of death, whatever you think, that will carry you to your next type of body."

Because Ajāmila had called on the name of the Lord, even though referring to his son, he became purified of all sins. Yet because of his sinful life, the messengers of Yamarāja, the lord of death, also appeared, to take him for punishment.

"When Ajāmila was dying, he saw that there were three ferocious persons, very fearful persons, with ropes in their hands. Sometimes a dying man cries, because he sees somebody has come to take him to Yamarāja. He sees, and he is very fearful. So Ajāmila also became fearful. The assistants of Yamarāja have hair very curled, and the hairs on their bodies are standing. Now at the time of Ajāmila's death, the assistants of Yamarāja came to take him."

Prabhupāda paused. "We shall discuss sometime again." And he ended his lecture.

* * *

Prabhupāda began making life members in Indore by sending Haṁsadūta out alone. Haṁsadūta was inexperienced and even skeptical that anyone would pay the 1,111 rupees.

Haṁsadūta: *One day Prabhupāda told me to go to the market with a neighbor and take these books—he had three* Kṛṣṇa *books—and try to make some life members. Just show them the books, he said, and tell them this is a token of our work. Then ask them to please help our mission by becoming a life member for 1,111 rupees. I was thinking that no one was going to give one thousand rupees for two or three books, so I just didn't do anything about it. I just avoided the issue. The next day Prabhupāda gave me the same instruction, but again I didn't do anything. On the third day he said I had to go, so I went next door and got a man who took me to the cloth merchants.*

We went to the shop of the biggest cloth merchant in Indore. The man didn't speak English, so the neighbor who had accompanied me translated. I would say, "Tell him this. Tell him that." And the man would translate everything. After I had exhausted my presentation, I said, "Now ask him to give a check for 1,111 rupees." My translator relayed the message, and the merchant immediately took out his checkbook and wrote the check.

Then we visited another merchant, and the same thing happened—he immediately wrote a check. We went to another merchant, and he also became a life member. So I made three life members on the first day, and when I came back and told Prabhupāda, he was in ecstasy.

By sending disciples and by sometimes going out himself, Śrīla Prabhupāda soon had a dozen ISKCON life members in Indore. Prabhupāda, Haṁsadūta, and Girirāja visited the king of Indore and invited him to become a life member, but the king declined. The devotees were disappointed, and in the car on the way back to Gita Bhavan, Haṁsadūta asked Prabhupāda, "Did I say the right thing about the books?"

"My books are like gold," Prabhupāda replied. "It doesn't matter what you say about them. One who knows the value, he will purchase."

* * *

Because visitors often asked Prabhupāda and his disciples what they thought of various popular spiritual teachers, Prabhupāda gave his disciples hints on answering such questions. If the teacher was not a bona fide follower of Vedic scripture, Prabhupāda said, the devotee should reply, "Swami *who*?" By thus indicating that he had not heard of the particular teacher, he would minimize the teacher's importance. Then the devotee should ask, "What is this swami's philosophy?" When the person explained, the devotee could defeat the particular philosophy, without attacking the person.

India had many Māyāvādī *gurus*, Prabhupāda explained, and they often traveled in groups from one convention to another. Although each had his particular style, primarily they were interested in *capātīs*. "And for every *capātī*," he said, "there are many Māyāvādīs. So there is competition."

* * *

One of Prabhupāda's frequent visitors was Vairaghi Baba, an educated man who had visited America and who spoke fluent English. He regularly joined in the *kīrtana* with the devotees, chanting and dancing with them onstage, and when he visited Prabhupāda in his room he behaved with Prabhupāda in a familiar way—too familiar, Prabhupāda's disciples thought. But Prabhupāda tolerated him.

One day some devotees met Vairaghi Baba at a lunch engagement, and they noticed he was drinking tea. Almost naively, and yet with an air of challenge, one of the devotees asked why he was drinking tea. "Oh, I am an *avadhūta*," Vairaghi Baba replied. The devotees, who had never heard this word before, reported the incident to Prabhupāda. "*Avadhūta*," Prabhupāda explained, "means one who is beyond the regulative principles. Generally this refers to Nityānanda Prabhu."* Prabhupāda disapproved of Vairaghi Baba's tea-drinking and especially of his calling himself an *avadhūta*.

A small group of devotees were sitting with Prabhupāda in his room one afternoon. "Śrīmatī Rādhārāṇī's excellence was Her cooking," Prabhupāda said. "She could also sing and dance, but Her great service was Her cooking for Kṛṣṇa. Mother Yaśodā would ask Her personally to come and cook for Kṛṣṇa and the cowherd boys. So, all in a line, She would feed them *prasādam*."

An Indian lady came to the door, bringing an offering of *chidwa*—fried cashews, potatoes, and raisins, with spices. Śrīla Prabhupāda took some, then distributed the rest to the other devotees. "Do you like this?" he asked, turning to Yamunā.

"Oh, it is very, very tasty," she replied.

"Yes," he said, "you should learn to prepare this. I like it very much. My Guru Mahārāja was also fond of potato *chidwa*, and he would sometimes request it late in the afternoon. He was very fond of it."

"Śrīla Prabhupāda," a devotee asked, "may we publish pictures of you without *tilaka*?"

---

*An incarnation of Lord Kṛṣṇa who descended along with Lord Caitanya to spread the chanting of Hare Kṛṣṇa and deliver the fallen souls of this age. His supremely independent activities, without regard for rules and regulations that apply to human beings, made Him famous as an *avadhūta*. His unusual pastimes are relished by devotees and are not to be imitated.

"Yes," he replied, "my Guru Mahārāja has been recorded without *tilaka*. You have seen that picture where he is looking up from his books at his working table?"

"Yes," the devotee replied, "I have seen that picture. I have seen you look in that very same way, with the very same expression as in the picture of your Guru Mahārāja."

"You have only seen the glitter," Prabhupāda corrected. "He is the gold. I am only iron. Iron can never be gold. But you have seen the glitter of real gold."

One afternoon a renowned astrologer visited Prabhupāda and offered to read his palm. "No," Prabhupāda replied, "I am finished with that. But you may read my disciples' palms." The astrologer read the palms of the several devotees present, made his predictions, and then left. The devotees turned to Prabhupāda, wondering what to make of it. "As soon as you clap your hands in front of the Deities during *ārati*," Prabhupāda said, smiling, "all the lines of your palm are changed."

Śrīla Prabhupāda told his disciples a story about when he had lived in Vṛndāvana. A Bengali widow walked to the Yamunā River to take her bath every morning. And every morning without fail she would return with a pot of water for the Rādhā-Dāmodara *pūjārīs* to use in bathing the Deities. Prabhupāda said he would sometimes open the gate for the woman, since he also rose very early, and she would enter and wake the *pūjārī*.

"Although the Vṛndāvana nights are cold in the winter," Prabhupāda said, "the woman never once failed to come with the water. For this activity she will return back to Godhead. One who cannot rise early in the morning is not very serious about spiritual life. One must rise before the *brahma-muhūrta* hour—that is very auspicious. And one will take the trouble to do so if he is serious about spiritual life."

One day Prabhupāda was sitting outside near his bungalow, chanting on his beads, when an unknown man approached, calling out the names of Kṛṣṇa. Suddenly the man fell to the ground, rolling and crying, appearing to be in great ecstasy. Prabhupāda remained seated and observed the exhibition, but made no response. The man continued his crying and rolling and chanting; Prabhupāda now ignored him completely. After several minutes, the man got up and walked away, obviously disappointed.

Early one morning as Prabhupāda sat in his room with his disciples, a gentleman entered and tearfully announced that his mother was dying. The devotees, watching for Prabhupāda's reaction, saw him remain grave. He didn't try to reassure the man or preach to him, but made only a very mild comment. Prabhupāda was unpredictable. He was always Kṛṣṇa conscious, and he always acted in accord with *guru* and *śāstra*. But exactly how he would act in a given situation was unpredictable. Whatever he did, however, was Kṛṣṇa conscious and correct, and he was always instructing them by his example.

*　　　*　　　*

On Prabhupāda's last morning in Indore he continued the story of Ajāmila. He explained that because Ajāmila had uttered the holy name, he had immediately obtained salvation, even though he had been so sinful.

"So Ajāmila, at the time of his death, just remembered his youngest son, whose name was Nārāyaṇa. The very name of Nārāyaṇa has got the full potency of the Supreme Personality of Godhead, Nārāyaṇa. That is the secret of this *nāma-saṅkīrtana* movement. By chanting the holy name of Nārāyaṇa, you immediately contact with the Supreme Personality of Godhead. *Nāma*, the Lord's name, is not material—it is spiritual. Kṛṣṇa and Kṛṣṇa's name, there is no difference....

"In a very appealing voice Ajāmila began to ask his son Nārāyaṇa, 'Please come here. I am dying.' He was very afraid of the Yamadūtas.

"Kṛṣṇa sent the Viṣṇudūtas to give Ajāmila shelter. The Viṣṇudūtas looked just like Lord Nārāyaṇa, with four hands. With a grave voice, they said to the Yamadūtas, 'What are you doing? Stop! You cannot take this man to Yamarāja.' "

Prabhupāda ended his lecture—and his stay in Indore. Having accepted an invitation to travel to Surat in the state of Gujarat and hold Kṛṣṇa conscious programs, he and his disciples would be leaving shortly. Devotees from Bombay would also join them. Prabhupāda had come to Indore for the Gita Jayanti Mahotsava, but actually the Mahotsava was but a small part of his preaching in Indore. He had met hundreds of people, made life members and friends. He had touched their lives. His presence in Indore would leave a lasting impression.

Baba Balmukund: *I've seen many* sādhus *and great saints in this Gita Bhavan. I saw Śrīla Prabhupāda also in the same place. I was very much impressed by Śrīla Prabhupāda and his preaching. It was because Prabhupāda had revealed the reality about* bhakti, *because he was a pure* bhakta, *that he could change the people of the West and give them another dress, he could give them another diet, he could entirely change their culture and give them true* bhakti. *And this was the greatest thing Prabhupāda has done. Let the world say as it likes, but he has done a marvelous thing regarding Lord Kṛṣṇa's* bhakti. *What Swami Vivekananda, Swami Ram Tirtha, and others could not do, Śrīla Prabhupāda has done. It is a marvelous thing.*

* * *

Surat
December 17, 1970

It was like a dream come true. Thousands lined the street for many blocks, while the devotees, playing *karatālas* and *mṛdaṅgas* and chanting Hare Kṛṣṇa, made their way along. Spectators stood on rooftops or clustered at windows and doorways, while others joined the procession. The police had stopped traffic at the intersections, allowing only the *kīrtana* procession to pass. The earthen road, freshly swept and sprinkled with water, had been decorated with rice flour designs of auspicious Vedic symbols. Green, freshly cut banana trees adorned either side of the way. Overhead, women's *sārīs* strung like bunting across the narrow roadway formed a brightly colored canopy over the *kīrtana* party.

Mr. Bhagubhai Jariwala, Prabhupāda's host in Surat, had advertised the daily parade routes in the local newspapers, and now, day after day, the devotees were holding a *kīrtana* procession through various sections of the city. While more than twenty of Prabhupāda's disciples led the daily procession, thousands of Indians chanted, cheered, and clamored to see, and women threw flower petals from the rooftops.

Often the procession would have to stop as families came forward to garland the devotees. Sometimes the devotees would receive so many garlands that their blissful faces would be scarcely visible, and they would distribute the garlands to the people in the crowd. Never before had the devotees met with such a reception.

"It is a city of devotees," Prabhupāda said. He compared the people of Surat to dry grass catching fire. By nature they were Kṛṣṇa conscious, but the arrival of Śrīla Prabhupāda and his *saṅkīrtana* party had been like a torch, setting the city spiritually ablaze.

The entire population of Surat seemed to turn out every morning, as tens of thousands flocked at seven A.M. to the designated neighborhood. Men, women, laborers, merchants, professionals, the young, the old, and all the children—everyone seemed to be taking part. Cramming the streets and buildings, they would wait for the *kīrtana* party, and when the devotees arrived, everyone became joyous.

Prabhupāda attended only a couple of the morning processions, preferring to stay in his quarters at Mr. Jariwala's home. Each morning Prabhupāda would come out onto his second-floor balcony, just as the devotees were leaving. Although the mornings were cold and many of the devotees sick, seeing Prabhupāda on the balcony offering them his blessings eased their troubles. Prabhupāda would wave, and the devotees would set off down the street, chanting.

The devotees had no special paraphernalia other than *mṛdaṅgas* and *karatālas*—no flags, no marching band, no *ratha* (cart), just an enthusiastic *kīrtana* party. And there was no official *paṇḍāl*, no Sadhu Samaj, no Vedanta Sammelan, no Gita Jayanti Mahotsava—just an entire city of Kṛṣṇa *bhaktas* waiting eagerly for the American Hare Kṛṣṇa chanters.

To be worshiped for chanting Hare Kṛṣṇa was just the opposite of what the devotees had experienced in the West. In Hamburg, Chicago, New York, London, Los Angeles, the devotees had been insulted, threatened with arrests, assaulted, and ignored. Of course, sometimes they had been tolerated and even appreciated, but never honored.

The daily *saṅkīrtana* outing was exhausting, since the route was long and the stops frequent. Many of the devotees had sore throats from singing, and the usual digestive upsets persisted. But the devotees took everything as the mercy of Lord Caitanya, who was allowing them to engage a whole city in His *saṅkīrtana* movement.

Twenty devotees from the West had just arrived in Surat, as had an American photographer, John Griesser, on assignment for *Asia Magazine*. John went out every day to shoot the *kīrtana* processions, and as he did he felt himself becoming caught up in something much greater than a mere photo assignment.

The people of Surat, who considered themselves Kṛṣṇa *bhaktas* at heart, saw Prabhupāda as a great saint. And they saw his disciples, in whom they found the true Vaiṣṇava qualities, as saints also. The devotees' dress, behavior, and way of life showed pure *bhakti-yoga*, and their *kīrtana* was genuine worship of the holy name. By honoring the Lord's devotees, the people of Surat knew they were honoring Lord Kṛṣṇa Himself. Devotion to Kṛṣṇa was the heart of their own culture, yet they had never expressed it to such a degree as now.

After several days of *kīrtana* processions, the mayor of Surat, Mr. Vaikuntha Sastri, closed all schools and proclaimed a holiday throughout the city. Everyone was now free to celebrate the mercy of Lord Caitanya and chant Hare Kṛṣṇa. Signs throughout the city read, in Gujarati, "Welcome to the American and European Devotees of Krishna," and "Welcome to Members of the Hare Krishna Movement."

The devotees felt tired and blissful as they returned to Mr. Jariwala's home, and Prabhupāda was waiting for them. As soon as they saw him, they all bowed down.

Cidānanda: *Prabhupāda was at the foot of the stairs, greeting us. We were in complete bliss, with flower garlands all over us, big smiles on our faces. We were very happy that we had been so well received. It was as if Prabhupāda was standing there saying, "Just see how wonderful this Kṛṣṇa consciousness is! Just see how happy you are!" He was standing there smiling. He was so happy that we were happy.*

The devotees were not alone, however, as they returned to Mr. Jariwala's home, for hundreds of Indians thronged behind them, eager to see Śrīla Prabhupāda. Śrīla Prabhupāda, his disciples, and a clamoring crowd of Surat devotees squeezed tightly into Prabhupāda's room. The guests—those who got in—inquired about ISKCON and its activities, while those outside pushed to get inside. The crowd around the house grew so great that traffic couldn't pass. While Prabhupāda continued to answer questions inside, the crowd outside grew larger and more restless. By their good fortune, they had realized Prabhupāda's greatness, and they wanted to be with him. As their desire became stronger, their eagerness more intense, Prabhupāda got up from his seat and walked out to the balcony.

The crowd roared, "Hare Kṛṣṇa!" their arms upraised.

When Prabhupāda returned inside, the crowd remained unsatisfied, and he asked some of his disciples to try and pacify them. Several devotees went out to the people, answering their questions and telling them Prabhupāda would come out to see them again.

Bhagubhai Jariwala had come in touch with Prabhupāda's movement several years before in San Francisco, when he had donated a silver *mūrti* of Kṛṣṇa to the San Francisco temple. Now the Jariwala family, to accommodate their guests, had moved into modest quarters on the roof of their home and offered the rest of the house to Prabhupāda and his disciples. Hospitable hosts, they made the devotees feel welcome to stay forever.

At lunch and again in the evening, Prabhupāda would take *prasādam* with the devotees and guests, the devotees sitting in rows on the floor and Prabhupāda sitting at the head, in a chair at a table. Mr. Jariwala and his family would serve everyone. Often respectable citizens would also attend the lunches. Mr. Chandra Desai, the chief minister of Gujarat; Mr. Vaikuntha Sastri, Surat's mayor; the state education minister; and others attended.

The *prasādam* was the finest Gujarati cooking, and when a dish was particularly to Prabhupāda's liking he would ask one of his women disciples to learn from Mrs. Jariwala how to cook it. Honoring *prasādam* twice a day with Prabhupāda was another intimacy the devotees shared with their spiritual master in India. Had they been with him in any other part of the world, such intimacy would probably have been impossible.

Beginning at 4:30 A.M. Prabhupāda would hold *kīrtana* and *ārati* before Rādhā and Kṛṣṇa and lecture from *Śrīmad-Bhāgavatam*. His room would be filled with guests, including the members of the Jariwala family. Although at outside engagements Prabhupāda usually spoke Hindi, in these morning meetings he always spoke English, for his disciples. He continued lecturing on Ajāmila, focusing on Ajāmila's degradation due to bad association and on his deliverance by chanting of the holy name. To Śrīla Prabhupāda's disciples, who were all aspiring to chant Hare Kṛṣṇa purely and go back to Godhead, these topics were urgently relevant. He was speaking of them.

"Anyone who utters the name of Kṛṣṇa is immediately freed from all sinful activities. That is the power of Kṛṣṇa's name. The difficulty is that after being freed we again commit mistakes. Kṛṣṇa's name has got the power—as soon as you utter the name you immediately become freed from all contaminations. But if one thinks, 'I am chanting Hare Kṛṣṇa, so even if I commit sinful activities it will be counteracted by my chanting,' that is the greatest offense. Just like sometimes in Christian churches they go on Sundays and confess and they are supposed to be excused from sinful reaction. But again, after coming back from the church, they commit the same sin with the expectation that 'Next week when I go to the church I shall confess, and it will be counteracted.' This kind of understanding is prohibited. . . . If you accept spiritual life and at the same time go on committing sinful activities, then you will never be able to progress."

Prabhupāda's outdoor evening engagements were well attended. The city officials made one of Surat's main intersections a festival site, rerouted all traffic, and set up a stage and sound system. Thousands would gather nightly. The crowd was sometimes so large and excited that Prabhupāda would have difficulty speaking above the noise, so he would hold a *kīrtana.* In the quiet that followed, he would have one or two of his disciples speak. Then he would speak. If the audience again became noisy, he would again say, "All right, let us have *kīrtana.*" Or sometimes he would simply sit and distribute bits of crystalized sugar candy to the thousands who approached him to touch his lotus feet and take a piece of *prasādam.*

Girirāja: *All the area around this block was completely packed with people. They were all mad after Śrīla Prabhupāda and Kṛṣṇa consciousness. Although a very big area, still people were occupying every space available, perching on rooftops, looking out windows, sitting on odd cement boulders or blocks scattered here and there.*

Everything about Prabhupāda's program was completely satisfying to everyone. The old people liked it because there was the saintly figure of Śrīla Prabhupāda with his young foreign disciples. And the intellectuals liked it because Śrīla Prabhupāda was giving such sound philosophy. And the children liked it because they could run and dance and join in the kīrtana.

Mādrī dāsī: *At one program they mobbed us so, we couldn't even get out of the cars, they were so eager to see Śrīla Prabhupāda. There were so many people. Prabhupāda said, "All right, the next night will be a night for ladies only." So the next night only ladies came, but still it was just as packed, and Prabhupāda gave a wonderful lecture.*

Bruce: *One program was so noisy that no one stopped talking, so Prabhupāda just started chanting the* Brahma-saṁhitā. *That was the whole program. He just chanted the* Brahma-saṁhitā. *Then he gave up and went out.*

Cidānanda: *Before going out to attend these programs, Prabhupāda looked like a general getting ready to go out for battle. He would come out of his room, beautifully dressed and effulgent, ready to go out and fight* māyā. *There were thousands and thousands of people waiting. I didn't know what to make of it. I couldn't handle so many people. But Prabhupāda was waging war on* māya. *He was there to convince all these people, and the more people would come, the stronger he would get.*

Prabhupāda preached in the outlying villages also. He would ride in a car with Mr. Jariwala, several disciples, and his Rādhā-Kṛṣṇa Deities to Bardoli or Meol. The village dwellings were made of baked mud, with straw roofs and cow dung walls and floors. For Prabhupāda's visit the villagers drew rice flour designs on the ground outside their houses and lined their lanes with clay pots, plantain leaves, and coconuts.

Mr. N. D. Patel: *The people in my village were much impressed by the presence of Prabhupāda. They used to say that he has done miracles by chanting. "He is a miracle saint, no doubt," people were saying. "So many Western people have become devotees, just by chanting the name of the Lord." The people were very much impressed by Prabhupāda's practical way of* bhakti. *In his lecture Śrī Prabhupādajī created such a good impression, not only on Vaiṣṇavas but so many Christians, Parsis. Even some Muhammadan friends started believing in Lord Kṛṣṇa as the universal Godhead.*

With regards to all the saints, nobody has been able to spread this philosophy like this in the past. In our village we are already Vaiṣṇavas, of course, but we used to believe in Sūryajī, Durgā, Ṭhākurajī, and all these things. But after Prabhupāda's explanation of what is Gītā, *what is Lord Kṛṣṇa, we are chanting Hare Kṛṣṇa, Hare Kṛṣṇa, Kṛṣṇa Kṛṣṇa, Hare Hare/ Hare Rāma, Hare Rāma, Rāma Rāma, Hare Hare. After Prabhupāda conducted his discourse here in the village, the people were so impressed that even in his absence they chant the* mahā-mantra *loudly and they greet people with the words "Hare Kṛṣṇa, Hare Kṛṣṇa." At the time of departure the people wished every devotee and Prabhupāda with the words "Hare Kṛṣṇa!"*

When there were no outside engagements, Prabhupāda would sit in his room and receive visitors. To a member of Parliament who came to visit, Prabhupāda said that wherever he traveled he encountered the concept of India as a beggar, backward and poverty-stricken. Ambassadors from India, he said, had only reinforced that image by going to Western countries and begging, "Give me rice, give me money, give me alms." India, Prabhupāda explained, had the greatest wealth of spiritual culture and the knowledge of *Bhagavad-gītā*. Prabhupāda had taken this wealth to the West and given it away freely. He was not a beggar.

Yamunā: *During visiting hours, riding in the car, walking, standing, or sitting, Prabhupāda was chanting* japa *all the time in Surat. His fingers were always moving within his saffron bead bag. He was always a Vaiṣṇava—the pure devotee of Kṛṣṇa, well groomed, with beautiful, neat* tilaka *on, and his hand was always in his bead bag. As he was sitting to greet people, one would be struck by his inconceivable beauty. Śrīla Prabhupāda said persons who give themselves to others are called magnanimous. And this was how Śrīla Prabhupāda was during his pastimes in Surat. He was always delivering Kṛṣṇa to everyone he met. He affected people's hearts by his great potency.*

Every morning in *Śrīmad-Bhāgavatam* class Prabhupāda added another installment of the Ajāmila story. Sometimes he would refer to the degradation of Indian culture, citing specific examples he had seen during his India tour.

"Now I am very sorry to inform you that in your city I have seen two temples—they are known as Rama Mandir. But there is no Rāma. This cheating is going on, and you are accepting. There is no Rāma Deity worship, but a man's photo is there, Sri Rama. And people are so foolish they do not question why this is going on. In Indore I have been in the Gita Bhavan, and so many nonsense things are there. Another place I saw Gita Samiti, and there was not a single photograph of Kṛṣṇa, but a lamp is there. And this is in the name of *dharma*.

"Last night this boy informed me that *Bhagavad-gītā* is going to be distributed by some swami, but according to *Bhagavad-gītā* that swami is fool number one. He is distributing *Bhagavad-gītā*, and people are accepting and paying for it. This is going on. It is a very serious situation all over the world. In the name of *dharma* (religion), *adharma* (irreligion) is going on."

Just as Ajāmila had become degraded, Prabhupāda explained, Indian culture had also become degraded. The only hope was for people to return to their rightful position of Kṛṣṇa consciousness.

"So all over the world—not only in India—there cannot be peace unless you reform the whole social structure. And that can be done only by this movement, Kṛṣṇa consciousness. Now see how this man fell down. Lusty people—they don't care for society, they don't care for elderly persons, they do it in the road, in the street, on the sea beach, anywhere, in the cinema. These things are going on. It is advertised also in the cinema nowadays to attract people. Formerly in India it was not so. But they are introducing all of this nonsense to make people more lusty. To become lusty means he is going to hell. If you want to open the door to your liberation, then you should engage yourself in serving the *mahat*, the pure devotees. If you want to open the door to the hellish condition of life, then you mix with those who are too much attached to women."

He spoke of the slaughterhouse and continued to decry the public display of illicit sex. Regarding illicit sex, he said that what had been a rare incident in the time of Ajāmila was now a common affair.

"How can young people protect themselves? They are not trained up. This Ajāmila was trained up, and yet he fell down. I saw in many parks, such as Golden Gate Park, within the cars the young boys and girls . . . Now here it is said that this behavior is expected of the *śūdra*, not from the higher castes. So just try to understand. They are thinking that they are becoming advanced. But they are not becoming advanced. They are becoming degraded. The whole world is degraded, and India is also imitating their degradation. How, by degraded association, one becomes himself degraded—that this story will reveal."

Prabhupāda had accomplished in Surat what he had intended. He had given the holy name, and the people had embraced it. The people of Surat, though not prepared to alter their lives radically and live as ISKCON devotees, appreciated that Prabhupāda had turned Westerners into devotees of Lord Kṛṣṇa and that he was teaching the pure message of the scriptures and chanting Hare Kṛṣṇa. They had responded to Prabhupāda, not out of a dogma or ritual but out of an appreciation of the importance of spiritual life and a recognition that Prabhupāda and ISKCON were genuine.

For Prabhupāda's disciples, the visit to Surat had given them a glimpse of what the world would be like if everyone was a devotee.

* * *

Allahabad
January 1971

Kumbha-melā is the greatest congregation of human beings on earth. Every twelve years in Allahabad, *sādhus* and pilgrims from all over India gather at the Triveṇī, the confluence of the three holy rivers Ganges, Yamunā, and Sarasvatī. And at an auspicious time that assures the worshiper liberation from the cycle of birth and death, as many as fifteen million people enter the sacred waters. A smaller version, the Māgha-melā, takes place annually during the month of Māgha (December-January). January of 1971, however, happened to fall halfway through the twelve-year cycle from one Kumbha-melā to the next, and the Melā was known as Ardha-kumbha-melā. Millions would attend, and Śrīla Prabhupāda decided to take advantage of the opportunity and attend the Melā with his disciples to preach.

While his disciples took the train from Surat to Allahabad, Prabhupāda, accompanied by Tamāla Kṛṣṇa, Haṁsadūta, Nanda Kumāra, and others, went briefly to Bombay and then to Calcutta, where he satisfied himself that his shipment of books from Dai Nippon was safely stored at a Scindia warehouse. He also purchased twenty-four-inch brass Rādhā-Kṛṣṇa Deities to take with him to Allahabad. On January 11 he wrote,

> . . . tomorrow morning we are going to Allahabad to attend the Ardha Kumbha Mela festival. We shall be going all 40 strong devotees and there are an expected 7,000,000 going by there also for the month of Magh.

About twenty-five devotees had taken the train from Surat to Allahabad, and others, newcomers from the U.S. and England, would soon be arriving. After a twenty-three-hour train ride, the first group arrived. As they disembarked, they could see only fog. With the address of a *brahmacārī āśrama* where they were to stay until they could pitch their tents at the Melā site, they started forward.

The devotees knew little of what to expect as they crowded into several one-horse *ṭāṅgās* and proceeded toward the appointed *brahmacārī āśrama.* They had heard that the Kumbha-melā was the most auspicious time to bathe at the Triveṇī and that the water was icy cold. In the foggy morning, they saw pilgrims along the road, riders on camels, and guards carrying rifles. Reaching the *āśrama* at sunrise, they could see the sacred Ganges before them.

The next morning the devotees started for the pilgrimage site, joining the stream of pilgrims funneling toward the Triveṇī. As they passed the Ram Bhag train station, a sign read, "From this point the confluence of the holy rivers Ganges and Yamunā and the forts are five kilometers." Riding in bicycle rickshas, the devotees merged with the moving tide of pilgrims, and soon they saw before them, on what one week before had been an empty plain, a city of tents. From the small tents, big tents, and giant *paṇḍāls* with flags flying rose a dissonance of sounds—music, loudspeaker announcements in different languages, *bhajanas,* and the hum of prayers.

The devotees got down from their rickshas, paid their drivers, and proceeded ahead, moving with the flow of pilgrims. As they walked, the ground transformed from grass to sand to mud, and the amplified music and the din of *mantras* and chants increased. The entire way was lined by beggars with leprosy, elephantiasis, and deformities.

The Melā committee had given ISKCON a good location near one of the entrance gates, and a few of the experienced devotees engaged workers in setting up the tents. ISKCON's *paṇḍāl* was large and brightly colored, with three smaller tents close by—one for the men, one for the women, and one for Śrīla Prabhupāda. A flimsy shack of corrugated tin served as a kitchen. Prabhupāda was to arrive the next day, and the devotees worked quickly putting down hay and rolling out *darīs* (large carpets of coarse cotton fabric). The devotees would have to build their own fires, gather their own vegetables, wash their own clothes, and do everything for themselves—all in the middle of a cold, barren sand flat. It was a far cry from being served like princes at a life member's home.

The devotees were in the midst of a great religious festival and human spectacle, and without Prabhupāda most of them were bewildered by the strange sights and sounds. *Yogīs* sat all day in the same posture, while crowds stood watching. Trident-carrying Śaivites, with simple red cloth, *rudrākṣa* beads, and matted hair, sat smoking *gañjā*. A procession of elephants, followed by two long files of naked *sādhus*, strode by. An ascetic lay on a bed of thorns. And there were still others, extreme renunciants rarely seen by the rest of civilization. And of course the various Hindu sects abounded, their chants and prayers rising into the air to mingle with the morning mist and the smoke from the ten thousand campfires that clouded the sky above the city of tents.

When Prabhupāda arrived at the ISKCON camp the next day, the devotees were ecstatic. Eagerly they began to tell him of the bizarre sights of the Melā. One of them mentioned a *guru* riding on an elephant and added, "Actually, *you* should ride on the elephant."

"No," Prabhupāda replied, "I would put Rādhā and Kṛṣṇa there."

Prabhupāda's presence reassured his disciples, reminding them that spiritual life was neither exotic nor bewildering, but simple and practical. In Prabhupāda's presence the devotees' attractions to mystic *yoga*, Vedic rituals, and material blessings and benedictions vanished. They accepted that great spiritual benefit awaited the pilgrims at the Melā, but as Prabhupāda had said, "To go to a holy place means to find a holy person and hear from him. A place is holy because of the presence of the saintly persons." The devotees understood, therefore, that the greatest spiritual benefit lay in hearing from Śrīla Prabhupāda.

Sitting in his tent with his disciples, Prabhupāda explained the significance of Ardha-kumbha-melā. For millions of years, he said, this had been among the most sacred places in India. During the appearance of the tortoise *avatāra*, when the demons and demigods had been churning immortal nectar, a drop of that nectar had fallen here. Since then, every six and twelve years certain auspicious planets form a jug, and this jug, filled with immortal nectar, is said to pour that nectar upon the Triveṇī. Lord Rāmacandra and Hanumān appeared here in Allahabad, and here Lord Caitanya taught Rūpa Gosvāmī the science of devotional service. Prabhupāda said he had also lived in Allahabad with his wife and family, and Śrīla Bhaktisiddhānta Sarasvatī had initiated him at Allahabad's Rūpa Gosvāmī Gaudiya Math in 1932. As for the Melās, anyone who came and bathed at the auspicious times when the *prāṇa* was pouring down from the heavens was guaranteed either promotion to the heavenly planets or liberation.

John Griesser: *I talked with other so-called* gurus, *and they were very impersonal. They didn't seem to care so much for persons, especially Westerners. They had a dislike, sort of a disdain, even though occasionally some of them would have a Western disciple. Prabhupāda was completely different. He didn't seem so much concerned about externals, but was very concerned about a person's philosophy, his consciousness. And of course he always tried to inject Kṛṣṇa consciousness into everyone he met.*

Prabhupāda said that although most of the saints and *sādhus* present were inauthentic, many were perfect *yogīs*, some of them three and four hundred years old. These *yogīs*, from remote parts of India, would come out for the Melā and then return to seclusion. "I have personally seen," he said, "that they take bath in the Ganges and come up in the seven sacred rivers. They go down in the Ganges and come up in the Godāvarī River. Then they go down and come up in the Kṛṣṇā River, and go down, like that." The devotees, therefore, should respect everyone who attended the Melā.

"So actually it's true," one of the devotees inquired, "that just by bathing here they are liberated?"

"Yes," Prabhupāda said, "it's true. They come here for liberation. But we have not come for liberation. We have come to preach. Being engaged in Kṛṣṇa's unalloyed devotional service, we are already liberated. We are not interested in liberation. We have come to preach devotional service."

When Prabhupāda rose early the next morning, the temperature was near freezing. His tent had no heat. He walked to the *paṇḍāl* to lead the *kīrtana* at *maṅgala-ārati*, and as he sat on his *vyāsāsana* a disciple handed him his quilt, which he wrapped around himself. To rise and bathe in such cold was difficult for most of the devotees. A few went to the Ganges, others bathed at a nearby pump, and some refused to get up at all.

Girirāja: *The program was very rigorous, because it was bitterly cold at night and we were expected to get up at four o'clock in the morning and bathe and attend* maṅgala-ārati. *So a few staunch devotees like Tamāla Kṛṣṇa and Haṁsadūta got up early—by three or three-thirty—and walked all the way from our camp to the Ganges to take an early-morning bath. But those of us staying in the* brahmacārī *tent were not so staunch, and generally when it was time to get up at four o'clock it was so cold out that we preferred to remain in our sleeping bags.*

Śrīla Prabhupāda also started to notice that some of us were coming late to maṅgala-ārati *and that some of us were not coming at all. Prabhupāda became very upset about this, because he knew how important* maṅgala-ārati *was for us. So one morning, although he was a little frail in health, he got up at four o'clock and came out in his* gamchā, *sat down under the pump, and took that ice-cold bath early in the morning—just to encourage us to get up, bathe, and come to* maṅgala-ārati. *That had a very profound effect on all of us, and we felt so ashamed that we just couldn't sleep late any more.*

After *kīrtana* Prabhupāda lectured on *Śrīmad-Bhāgavatam*, resuming the story of Ajāmila. This particular story, with its glorification of the Lord's holy name, seemed especially relevant. The holy name was so powerful that by chanting only once Ajāmila had been saved. Chanting, therefore, was far more beneficial than the *prāṇa* coming down from the constellations.

Dawn came and the sky lightened—but only barely. A damp, heavy fog from the river, mingling with the smoke from the campfires, clung to everything. Rain began to fall. The devotees were unprepared for this weather. With food hard to get and cook and toilet facilities the crudest, the devotees wondered how they would last for the scheduled two weeks.

Prabhupāda, however, who shared with his disciples all these austerities, remained transcendental and apparently unaffected. If the sun peeked through the clouds, he would sit outside and take his massage. Then he would bathe himself, sitting in his *gamchā*, dipping his *loṭā* into warmed Ganges water, and pouring it over his body. He seemed so content, the devotees took heart. He wasn't complaining, so why should they?

Early in the morning, Prabhupāda took the devotees out chanting. He wore his gray woollen *cādar* and his swami hat strapped under his chin, and his disciples dressed in the warmest clothes they had—sweaters, hats, *cādars*. Prabhupāda led the party as they weaved and wandered through the densely populated tent city. The *kīrtana* was a joy to the other pilgrims. Ironically, amid such an exotic gathering of *yogīs,* renunciants, naked *sādhus,* and the like, Prabhupāda and his disciples created the greatest stir.

And they were preaching. Although other groups were uttering *mantras* or lecturing in their tents, there was nothing else like this. This was the only *saṅkīrtana,* and everyone welcomed it. With Prabhupāda stately but joyful at the head, the procession grew, and Indians joined the Western *sādhus* in chanting Hare Kṛṣṇa.

Prabhupāda sent the devotees out on *saṅkīrtana* each morning. As the *kīrtana* party roamed from camp to camp, many pilgrims would run up, offering prostrated obeisances, money, and respect. With strong, experienced street *kīrtana* drummers and chanters like Madhudviṣa, Dīnanātha, and Haṁsadūta leading the chanting party, the devotees would forget the cold and the austerity.

Prabhupāda stressed the importance of chanting; always there must be *kīrtana,* he said. Philosophy and lectures would not be as effective at such gatherings, because the common people would not understand. Lord Caitanya had never lectured in public, but always He had held *kīrtana.*

As a result of the devotees' *kīrtana,* thousands would stream into ISKCON's large *paṇḍāl* to see the Rādhā-Kṛṣṇa Deities and take *prasādam.* ISKCON had the only Kṛṣṇa Deity at the whole Melā, and thousands would line up to see Him. Prabhupāda would speak in English in the morning and in Hindi at night, and his evening *kīrtanas* in the *paṇḍāl* became a great success. The Western *sādhus* with the women and the little child were a great curiosity to behold.

Prabhupāda also arranged for mass *prasādam* distribution, and he assigned Revatīnandana and a few helpers to cook almost nonstop over two small wood fires in the kitchen shed. Some nights the devotees would cook vegetables and *halavā* or vegetables and *purīs* for as many as seven hundred people. ISKCON's impact on the Melā pleased Prabhupāda.

> In the meantime our program for touring India has been going with all success in every place we are invited. Now we have come to the Ardha Kumbha Mela at Prayag (Allahabad) and we have got undisputed prominence amongst all groups here in the large gathering.

Śrīla Prabhupāda's lectures on Ajāmila gave life to the cold and sometimes sick devotees. This opportunity to hear from Prabhupāda was the reward for all their austerities. In each morning class, Prabhupāda continued to stress the importance of chanting the holy names purely.

"The purification of one's chanting *hari-nāma* means as soon as you chant the holy name of Kṛṣṇa you will see the form of Kṛṣṇa, realize the qualities of Kṛṣṇa, remember the pastimes of Kṛṣṇa. That is pure chanting of Hare Kṛṣṇa *mantra.* That is stated in the commentary of Śrīla Jīva Gosvāmī—that a pure devotee who chants Hare Kṛṣṇa *mantra* immediately realizes the *nāma, rūpa, guṇa, līlā,** everything about Kṛṣṇa, simply by chanting the names. You will feel the form of Kṛṣṇa. You will remember all His qualities— 'Oh, Kṛṣṇa is so qualified; He is so magnanimous.' Then you will remember His *līlā,* pastimes—'Oh, Kṛṣṇa instructed Arjuna. Kṛṣṇa played with His cowherd boys. Kṛṣṇa had very nice talks with the *gopīs*, with His mother, Yaśodā.' These things you will remember. That is the actual perfection of chanting."

Prabhupāda reiterated that the only reason he had come with his disciples to the Melā was to glorify Lord Kṛṣṇa so that others could understand the importance of the Kṛṣṇa consciousness movement. But if the devotees were to successfully give Kṛṣṇa consciousness to others, they must first realize Kṛṣṇa themselves. It was possible, he said, to think of Kṛṣṇa always. He gave the example of the Indian women carrying big waterpots on their heads. Just as they have learned to keep their balance, in spite of all other movements, so a devotee, despite his activities and despite any mental agitation, should always remember Kṛṣṇa. And the best way to remember Kṛṣṇa is to practice always chanting the holy name.

"I remember one of our teachers in our school life instructed that if you always think, 'I shall pass my examination with distinction,' then you will pass in the first division. If you think, 'I shall pass my examination in the first division,' then you will probably pass in the third division. And if you think, 'I will somehow or other pass my examination in the third division,' then you will fail. This means that if you expect more than your capacity, then it may be possible that at the time of examination you will pass. So when chanting the Hare Kṛṣṇa *mantra,* Caitanya Mahāprabhu has said not that you chant only one hour—no. One should *practice,* and that practice was shown by Haridāsa Ṭhākura (who chanted almost twenty-four hours daily). But because we cannot, therefore we have to engage always in the service of Kṛṣṇa. That will make you remember Kṛṣṇa."

Prabhupāda said that the chanting of Hare Kṛṣṇa is exactly like a lion's

*Name, form, qualities, and pastimes, respectively.

roar. As a lion's roar frightens all small creatures, the chanting of Hare Kṛṣṇa ends all one's sinful reactions. He repeatedly warned the devotees, however, to avoid the most dangerous offense, that of committing sins on the strength of the holy name.

"But even if you fall down, there is no loss. That is the statement of Nārada. If one takes to Kṛṣṇa sincerely and executes devotional service but then again falls down, still he will come back. Just like we have practical experience. Some of our students have fallen down. But whatever sincere service he has rendered, that is his permanent credit. And one day he will be saved, just like Ajāmila."

On Prabhupāda's last day in Allahabad a Mr. Gourkishore visited him in his tent, inviting him to Benares. As chairman of the 456th annual festival commemorating Lord Caitanya's visit to Benares, Mr. Gourkishore wanted Prabhupāda to attend the festival as the honored guest. When Prabhupāda said he felt ill and that perhaps some of his disciples could go in his stead, Mr. Gourkishore persisted until Prabhupāda finally agreed. But first Prabhupāda wanted to visit Gorakhpur.

* * *

Gorakhpur
February 3, 1971

The Ardha-kumbha-melā over, some devotees went to Delhi, some to Bombay, and others to Calcutta. Prabhupāda and the remaining devotees went to Gorakhpur—a ten-hour journey on the antiquated meter-gauge railway. Prabhupāda had been invited by his only disciple in Gorakhpur, Dr. R. P. Rao (now Rāmānanda), a research chemist who had met Prabhupāda in San Francisco, taken initiation in 1967, and since returned to his family and four children to teach chemistry at Gorakhpur University.

Prabhupāda and his disciples moved into crowded quarters at Rāmānanda's modest home, and about one hundred people attended Prabhupāda's lecture that evening. Prabhupāda already had plans for a Rādhā-Kṛṣṇa temple on the Gorakhpur University campus as well as accredited courses and degrees in Kṛṣṇa consciousness—B.A., M.A., and Ph.D. He envisioned graduates going out to teach Kṛṣṇa consciousness in schools, colleges, and temples all over the world. He inspired Rāmānanda and a group of his friends to form a committee to introduce Kṛṣṇa consciousness within the university, and he initiated about one dozen disciples. Since they all professed to be following the rules against illicit sex, intoxication, and gambling and had been lifelong vegetarians, he waived the usual six-month trial period. He asked them to chant sixteen rounds daily and to make their city Kṛṣṇa conscious. In his absence they should maintain Rāmānanda's home as an active ISKCON center and try to establish courses in Kṛṣṇa consciousness at the university.

* * *

Benares
February 6, 1971

Mr. Gourkishore was counting heavily on Prabhupāda's participation in the upcoming celebration. The climax of the week-long observance of Lord Caitanya's visit to Benares would be a parade, Mr. Gourkishore said, and Prabhupāda and his disciples had an important part in it. Newspaper articles, handbills, and loudspeaker carts had announced throughout the city the presence of Śrīla Prabhupāda and his "foreign disciples." The devotees sensed they were being treated like entertainers, expected to perform as if under contract—but without salary.

On the day of the procession Prabhupāda rode in a silver chariot, the kind customarily used in extravagant wedding processions. The chariot was pulled by a pair of white horses, wearing silver crowns and decorative blankets. The leading float in the parade bore a six-foot statue of Lord Caitanya in yellow *nim* wood. Next followed a file of decorated elephants. One elephant carried a banner reading *Harer Nama Eva Kevalam*, one carried actors dressed as Lord Rāma and Sītā, another carried two actors dressed as Rādhā and Kṛṣṇa, who waved to the crowds, and another a picture of Lord Caitanya and His associates performing *saṅkīrtana.* Next came a decorated flatbed truck with children portraying Lord Caitanya and Lord Nityānanda, chanting and dancing. Then followed a series of professional *kīrtana* groups and Prabhupāda's "foreign disciples" dancing and performing *kīrtana.*

Behind the devotees, Śrīla Prabhupāda rode in his chariot. On either side of the chariot walked a devotee fanning Prabhupāda with a *cāmara* whisk, while Prabhupāda sat with his right hand in his bead bag, his left hand on his cane. He was dressed in silk, with pearl buttons on his *kurtā.*

A wide patch of sandalwood paste covered his forehead. He didn't wave or smile or turn to see the crowds, but sat calmly, chanting Hare Kṛṣṇa on his beads.

Following Prabhupāda's chariot was a *śāhnāī* group, several more *kīrtana* parties, and finally another statue of Lord Caitanya, carried by eight men.

The festival committee said three hundred thousand attended, double what they would have had without Prabhupāda and his foreign disciples. The procession was over, however, and as the star attraction, Prabhupāda had made his appearance and drawn a large crowd, and now nothing more was required. He felt tired. He and his disciples were taken to a nearby *dharmaśālā* and served a feast. Prabhupāda remained grave and as soon as possible returned to his quarters and his regular schedule.

A student at the University of Benares who had met Prabhupāda at the Allahabad Melā stopped by to visit. The boy's father had given him a biography of Lord Caitanya as a gift for Prabhupāda, and when the boy showed Prabhupāda a picture of his father, Prabhupāda said, "Yes, your father is a devotee. So why don't you also take initiation?"

The boy was hesitant. As he walked with Prabhupāda in the garden, Prabhupāda said, "You have got the seed of devotional service from your father, so you must now cultivate."

"But how can I shave my head?" the boy inquired. "I am a university student."

"No, it is a custom. You should shave once, and then you can keep short hair."

"But how can I wear *tilaka*? They will laugh at me."

Prabhupāda said the boy should not fear criticism. He should become a soldier of Kṛṣṇa. Just as the government honors its valiant soldiers, Kṛṣṇa rewards a devotee who accepts difficulties and criticism on His behalf.

"What about *guru-dakṣiṇā*?" the boy asked.

"*Guru-dakṣiṇā* is just a formality," Prabhupāda said. "It was a custom in olden days that when someone gets initiation, he goes to the various homes. It is a sign that you have become a servant of your *guru*, you are prepared to beg alms for your *guru*. It is whatever you give."

The boy returned home and told his father. The next day was an auspicious day, his father said—the appearance day of Lord Nityānanda.

A good day to receive spiritual initiation.

So the next day, on Nityānanda Trayodaśī, Śrīla Prabhupāda initiated the boy, giving him the name Nirañjana dāsa. When Prabhupāda asked Nirañjana if he had any questions, Nirañjana said he wanted to know his eternal relationship with Kṛṣṇa; was it as servant, as friend, as parent?

Prabhupāda replied that servitude was the common ground in all transcendental relationships with Lord Kṛṣṇa. By chanting Hare Kṛṣṇa, Nirañjana would become more and more purified and realize more and more his relationship with Kṛṣṇa. Nirañjana asked how he would understand his relationship.

"No, don't jump," Prabhupāda said. "You have some *śraddhā* (faith) from your father, and now you are associating with devotees and chanting. Gradually you will realize."

Nirañjana agreed to be patient.

Prabhupāda asked Nirañjana to arrange a lecture for him on campus, and Nirañjana, with the help of his uncle, a philosophy professor, got Prabhupāda a speaking engagement for his last morning in Benares.

On the day Prabhupāda was to leave, he met with John Griesser, the American photographer traveling with him and his party since Surat. John, who had shaved his mustache and thought a lot about his future, came to say good-bye—until Bombay, where they would meet again in a few weeks.

John found Prabhupāda in the courtyard, enjoying the sunshine and eating *gur* (date sugar) from a clay pot. Prabhupāda asked that the pot be broken and distributed to John and the other devotees present, and while John sat licking *gur* from a piece of clay pot, Prabhupāda talked about his boyhood in Calcutta.

John: *Prabhupāda was talking in his accented, rhythmic English about his boyhood days in Calcutta, and he described a gracious city, before the crowding and squalor of today. As a schoolboy he had seen splendid Victorian buildings of white marble, surrounded by stately lawns and trees.*

Suddenly Prabhupāda looked over at me and laughed. "So, John," he said, "I think Kṛṣṇa has captured you." I agreed. I had known it for quite a while, but now Śrīla Prabhupāda confirmed it.

When Prabhupāda was leaving Benares to return to Gorakhpur, many of his disciples went to the wrong train station. While Prabhupāda and a few followers waited at the correct train station, Kauśalyā asked him,

"How did you like it here in Benares, Śrīla Prabhupāda?"

"It is all right, " he said, indifferently.

"Did you have a nice rest?" she asked, trying to think of some positive aspect of the visit.

"Rest I can have any time," said Prabhupāda. "But I like to be with my devotees."

Surrounded by luggage, Prabhupāda sat on the bench, while Tamāla Kṛṣṇa and Śyāmasundara ran from the ticket office to the train and back. The train would leave soon. But where were the other devotees? Prabhupāda watched as his spiritual sons argued with the conductor, telling him the train couldn't go until the other devotees arrived. "They do not know what they are doing," Prabhupāda said, and he smiled.

* * *

Gorakhpur
February 10, 1971

On hearing that Prabhupāda wanted to preach in Gorakhpur, Hanuman Prasad Poddar, eminent head of the Gita Press publishing company, offered one of his properties, a two-story house (his former residence), known as Krishna Niketan. Mr. Poddar, who was bedridden in another house in Gorakhpur, had first met Prabhupāda in 1962, and he appreciated Prabhupāda's mission.

When Prabhupāda received permission to use the Krishna Niketan, he acted quickly. It was not proper, he said, that the Deities of Rādhā and Kṛṣṇa he had brought from Calcutta had been packed away in a trunk after the Ardha-kumbha-melā. They had already been worshiped, so Their worship should not be stopped. "The Deities have to be installed tomorrow," he said, and he put Kauśalyā and Nanda Kumāra in charge of the preparations.

Seeing that Nanda Kumāra and Kauśalyā needed more help, Prabhupāda called for all his disciples, and soon twenty American devotees were scurrying about, preparing for the next day's festival. Prabhupāda directed the devotees in cleaning the temple room from ceiling to floor and in building the altar. He asked Himāvatī to donate her fanciest *sārī*, which he hung like a curtain before the table that was to be the Deities' altar. The altar needed a backdrop, he said, and while Kauśalyā stood on the table he handed her pieces of colored fabric to arrange against the wall.

The backdrop completed, Prabhupāda took a rug a devotee had bought in Allahabad and placed it over the table-altar.

That night Prabhupāda surveyed the temple room. "Oh, it is very nice," he said. He retired to his room, and two devotees stayed up all night sewing clothes for Rādhā and Kṛṣṇa. The next morning the Deities were placed on the altar, and the devotees resumed Their worship, offering Them *prasādam* and *ārati* six times a day.

The devotees were living in an ISKCON temple atmosphere for the first time since they had arrived in India, and their lives became regulated and secure. The weather warmed, and the devotees—many of whom had exhausted their health in Allahabad—felt relief. The Gorakhpur temple was situated on several acres of agricultural land outside the city; it was a peaceful place. During the day Prabhupāda would rest, as the sunshine came through the window and warmed his body.

In the evenings guests would come for *kīrtana* and Prabhupāda's lecture. Speaking on the Sixth Canto of *Śrīmad-Bhāgavatam*, Prabhupāda referred repeatedly to Śrīdhara Svāmī's commentary, from the twelfth century.

Śrīdhara Svāmī said that simply by chanting—without any regulative principles—one becomes liberated. So how is that? Śrīdhara Svāmī replies, also, that there are regulative principles. The idea is that chanting of the holy name is so powerful that it can immediately liberate the chanter. But because we are prone to fall down again, therefore there are regulative principles. . . .

"Morning, noon, and evening, we should daily chant Hare Kṛṣṇa *mantra* with devotion and faith. By doing this, one can avoid volumes of miserable conditions of life—simply by chanting. So one should be so much careful and faithful. You should know that as soon as you are chanting, Kṛṣṇa is dancing on your tongue. Therefore, how much careful and respectful we should be."

Each night Prabhupāda would take the commentaries of Śrīdhara Svāmī as his text.

"So Śrīdhara Svāmī gives this example, that without knowing that there is a very nice medicine a man takes so many thousands of medicines. Similarly, the great stalwart leaders of religious principles, without knowing this Hare Kṛṣṇa *mantra*, take so many troublesome ritualistic ceremonies.

Actually, there is no need. The whole thing is—Śrīdhara Svāmī is giving the stress very strongly—that you can simply chant Hare Kṛṣṇa *mantra* without understanding any ritualistic ceremonies. . . ."

Śrīdhara Svāmī's commentary was filled with quotations from various scriptures about the supreme benefit of chanting the holy names of Kṛṣṇa.

"Then Śrīdhara Svāmī says, *akhila-ceṣṭitam.* That means that any endeavor for pushing on Kṛṣṇa's glories, that is as good as chanting the holy name. When you go out for canvassing, for pushing on this movement, people might think that you are not chanting. But suppose you are canvassing for a life member—that topic is also as good as chanting Hare Kṛṣṇa *mantra*, because it is *akhila-ceṣṭitam.* One's life must be dedicated simply for Kṛṣṇa's service."

Speaking before his Indian audiences, Śrīla Prabhupāda also told about his preaching in the West. One evening he gave a personal history, describing how his spiritual master, on their first meeting, had immediately told him to preach Lord Caitanya's message to the English-speaking world.

"At that time I argued with him that we are a dependent nation, and who is going to hear about our message? So he defeated my argument. Yes. He was a learned scholar. So what I was? I was a tiny boy. So I agreed that I was defeated." Prabhupāda laughed softly.

Prabhupāda told about his business years in Allahabad and how he again met his spiritual master and became initiated. He told of starting *Back to Godhead* in 1944, of taking *sannyāsa,* and of finally traveling to America in 1965. He mentioned his struggles in New York City and how the first boys had joined him when he started his movement in a storefront on Second Avenue.

"So practically we began work from 1968. In 1966 I started, but in '67 I became very much sick, so I came back to India. And again I went there in 1968. Practically this propaganda work began vigorously from 1968. From '68, '69, '70, and this is '71. So three, four years, all these branches have grown up, and now practically throughout the whole continent of Europe and throughout America they know what is Hare Kṛṣṇa movement, due to our propaganda."

Early each morning before sunrise, Prabhupāda would sit in the temple room before his disciples and lecture from *Śrīmad-Bhāgavatam.* And each morning the lights would go out, leaving everyone in darkness. It was a typical Indian power failure, and Prabhupāda would stop lecturing while a devotee lit two candles by his *vyāsāsana* and two candles on the altar. Long shadows would mix with the luminous gold of the Rādhā-Kṛṣṇa Deities, and Prabhupāda, wearing spectacles and holding open the *Śrīmad-Bhāgavatam* in his hand, would appear wonderfully mysterious.

One morning Śrīla Prabhupāda sang a new song, *Jaya Rādhā-Mādhava.*

"I will teach you this song," he said. Reciting the first line, he had the devotees repeat it again and again. One line at a time, he went through the song.

jaya rādhā-mādhava kuñja-bihārī
gopī-jana-vallabha giri-vara-dhārī
yaśodā-nandana braja-jana-rañjana
yāmuna-tīra-vana-cārī

They should know it, he told them, by the next morning.

Only a few devotees managed to memorize the song, so the next morning Prabhupāda went through it again, line by line. During the evening lecture he explained the meaning of the song.

"*Jaya rādhā-mādhava kuñja-bihārī.* Kṛṣṇa is enjoying in Vṛndāvana. That is the real picture of God—simply enjoying. The *vṛndāvana-līlā* of Kṛṣṇa is the perfect presentation of the Supreme Personality of Godhead—He is simply enjoying.

"All the inhabitants of Vṛndāvana—the *gopīs*, the cowherd boys, Mahārāja Nanda, Yaśodā—*everyone* is simply anxious how to make Kṛṣṇa happy. They have no other business. The residents of Vṛndāvana have no other business than to satisfy Kṛṣṇa, and Kṛṣṇa has no other business. *Yaśodā-nandana braja-jana-rañjana yāmuna-tīra-vana-cārī.* He is acting as the little son of Yaśodā. And His only business is how to please the residents of Vṛndāvana.

"*Yaśodā-nandana braja-jana-rañjana yāmuna-tīra-vana-cārī.* He is wandering in the forest of Vṛndāvana on the bank of the Yamunā. This is the actual picture of the Supreme Personality of Godhead.

"But Brahmā, Indra, big, big demigods, they are also bewildered. They are sometimes mistaken how this cowherd boy can be the Supreme Personality of Godhead. Just like some of us think like that. But those who are thinking like that, for them also there is manifestation of Kṛṣṇa's supremacy. *Gopī-jana-vallabha giri-vara-dhārī.* Although He is engaged in pleasing the residents of Vraja, when there is need He can lift up the Govardhana Hill at the age of seven years. Or He can kill the Pūtanā at the age of three months.

"So many demons used to visit daily. Kṛṣṇa used to go with the calves and cows, with His friends in the forest, and every day Kaṁsa used to send a demon to kill Him. Aghāsura, Bakāsura, Dhenukāsura—so many.

"So also, Kṛṣṇa is playing just like a cowherd boy. His supreme mercy as the Supreme Personality of Godhead is never absent there. That is God. God is not created by meditation. God is God. God is never manufactured. We should know this."

On the third morning after introducing *Jaya Rādhā-Mādhava,* Prabhupāda again sang it with the devotees responding. Then he began to explain it further. Rādhā-Mādhava, he said, have Their eternal loving pastimes in the groves of Vṛndāvana.

He stopped speaking. His closed eyes flooded with tears, and he began gently rocking his head. His body trembled. Several minutes passed, and everyone in the room remained completely silent. Finally, he returned to external consciousness and said, "Now, just chant Hare Kṛṣṇa."

After this, the Rādhā-Kṛṣṇa Deities of Gorakhpur became known as Śrī Śrī Rādhā-Mādhava.

Kauśalyā would regularly wash the temple floor while Prabhupāda gave his *Śrīmad-Bhāgavatam* lecture. One morning Prabhupāda interrupted his lecture. "Just see this girl," he said—Kauśalyā was down at the other end of the room, scrubbing. "This is first-class service."

The next day Prabhupāda called Kauśalyā forward. "Every morning you are washing the floor so nicely," he said, "but this morning you are washing the floor like a crow takes a bath." Prabhupāda shook his hand, as if flicking water about. "You do not know how to wash the floor. I am going to show you." Prabhupāda came down from his *vyāsāsana* and walked to the other end of the room, followed by all the devotees.

"Where is your bucket?" Kauśalyā brought over her bucket. Prabhupāda asked for a rag. She gave him hers. He then crouched down and started scrubbing. "This is how you wash the floor," he said, "—with lots of water. And you do it a section at a time." It should be done in two stages: first with a wet rag, and then with a wrung rag.

The devotees stood in amazement, watching. Several times Prabhupāda repeated the procedure, washing a section of the floor and then drying it, careful not to touch the clean area with his feet. "See?" he said. "That is expert."

When Tamāla Kṛṣṇa requested Prabhupāda to move on to Bombay and bigger preaching, Prabhupāda replied, "Let us see if Kṛṣṇa wants us to have this place." Haṁsadūta also became restless to preach, and Prabhupāda sent him with a group of *brahmacārīs* to Aligarh and Agra.

Little appeared to be happening in Gorakhpur, but Prabhupāda had plans. He was still negotiating with the university authorities for land for constructing a temple.

> If we are successful in our attempt, it will be unique in all the world and soon more and more college campuses will follow. . . . And if we can establish a seat of Krishna Consciousness then students may take their doctorate degree in Krishna Consciousness and go out and preach all over the world.

Prabhupāda had three goals: to reach the Gorakhpur university students, to introduce *kīrtana* into the factories, and to introduce *kīrtana* into the homes. The main obstacle was lack of commitment from the local people. Many were willing to attend his evening lectures, but to actually surrender time, money, and energy in the service of Kṛṣṇa was more difficult. At least the Rādhā-Kṛṣṇa temple was lively, and Prabhupāda hoped the directors of Gita Press would turn the Krishna Niketan building over to ISKCON permanently.

Prabhupāda continued lecturing, morning and evening. For three consecutive evenings he spoke on a single verse of *Caitanya-caritāmṛta*, defeating the Māyāvāda arguments that the Absolute Truth is ultimately impersonal Brahman.

"The Māyāvādī philosophers say that the Absolute is impersonal and that there is no different energy. So Caitanya Mahāprabhu's challenge is that the Absolute Truth has got multienergies. Suppose someone has a big business, a big factory. So if the proprietor says, 'I am all-pervading over this factory,' that is correct. Take, for example, Birla. They say, 'Birla's factory.' Birla's name is there. Although Birla is a person and he is not personally present in that factory, everyone says, 'Birla's factory.' That means Birla's money, Birla's energy, is there. If there is any loss in that factory, the suffering goes to Birla. Or if there is any gain in the factory, the profit goes to Birla. Therefore Birla's energy is there in the factory. Similarly, the whole creation is a manifestation of Kṛṣṇa. Everything there is Kṛṣṇa, His energy. He is represented by His energy. That is called simultaneously one and different, *acintya-bhedābheda-tattva.*"

Discussing preaching in America, Prabhupāda said the Western world was ninety-nine percent in the modes of ignorance and passion. Although America was the richest nation on earth, its youth were becoming hippies, much to the dismay of parents and government leaders. So despite their wealth, they were unhappy. They were ripe, however, for understanding spiritual knowledge.

"This is the causeless mercy of Lord Caitanya. Now you can see that these boys, when they are chanting—how they are in ecstasy. They are immediately on the transcendental platform. Not only here, everywhere they are chanting—in every temple. The advantage of these boys and girls is that they have no hodgepodge in their head. They directly accept Kṛṣṇa as the Supreme Personality of Godhead, and they directly accept the instruction of Lord Caitanya. Therefore they are making advancement. Their fortune is that their brain is not congested with hodgepodge ideas. They have given up all other occupations and accepted Kṛṣṇa as the Supreme Personality of Godhead. So in India we can also do that. What is the difficulty? We must do this. Just accept this: *kṛṣṇas tu bhagavān svayam.** And surrender unto Him."

Prabhupāda celebrated the appearance day of Śrīla Bhaktisiddhānta Sarasvatī in Gorakhpur. At the morning gathering he said, "We should honor this day and very respectfully pray to Bhaktisiddhānta Sarasvatī Gosvāmī that 'We are engaged in your service, so give us strength. Give us intelligence. We are being guided by your servant.' So in this way we have to pray. And I think in the evening we shall distribute *prasādam.* There will be so many guests coming, so they can be distributed *prasādam.*"

Prabhupāda said life members and other friends should be invited for the flower offering at noon. One of the devotees asked about the feast.

*"Kṛṣṇa is the Supreme Personality of Godhead." (Bhāg. 1.3.28)

Prabhupāda: "Feasting means *purī* and *halavā* and a vegetable and chutney. That's all—four things. Make it simple."

Tamāla Kṛṣṇa: "Prabhupāda? You want us to offer a feast to your Guru Mahārāja at noontime? A special plate of feast?"

Prabhupāda: "Not a special plate. The process is that whatever we offer to the Deity, that is offered to *guru*. And *guru* offers to his *guru*. In this way, it goes to Kṛṣṇa. We don't directly offer to Rādhā-Kṛṣṇa. No. We have no right. Nor does Kṛṣṇa accept in that way. The pictures of the *ācāryas*—why are they there? Actually you have to offer the plate to your *guru*, and he will offer to his *guru*, he offers to his *guru*, his *guru*. In this way, it will go to Kṛṣṇa. That is the process. You cannot directly approach Kṛṣṇa or predecessor *ācāryas*. That is not possible."

One day Prabhupāda visited Hanuman Prasad Poddar. Mr. Poddar had been gravely ill for some time, but he was able to sit up and speak briefly with Prabhupāda. As the pioneer of the *Kalyana* magazine, which printed installments of the *Mahābhārata* and other Vedic classics, Hanuman Prasad Poddar was a world-famous patron of Indian religious thought. His inexpensive Hindi *Bhagavad-gītā* translation had been distributed by the millions, so that even a poor man could have a copy of *Bhagavad-gītā*. Mr. Poddar had been a friend to Prabhupāda when in 1962 Prabhupāda had come to him in Gorakhpur and shown him his manuscript for the first volume of the *Śrīmad-Bhāgavatam*. Appreciating the importance of the work, Mr. Poddar, by his word of approval, had helped Prabhupāda get a donation for its printing from the Delhi industrialist Mr. Dalmia. Now, almost ten years later, Prabhupāda was showing Mr. Poddar his recently published books *Kṛṣṇa, the Supreme Personality of Godhead, Teachings of Lord Caitanya, The Nectar of Devotion,* and his magazine *Back to Godhead.* Mr. Poddar was impressed, and he and Prabhupāda exchanged their sincere appreciation of each other's work.

Mr. Suryakant Fogla: *Hanuman Prasad Poddar was my grandfather. He was very much ill at the time Prabhupāda came here to meet him in his bedroom upstairs. There are certain things which cannot be explained, but they were talking in the language of their eyes. My grandfather expressed some gratitude, some affection, some regard by his eyes, and Prabhupāda's reply was also in the same way. The appreciation from both sides could easily be seen and appreciated by the persons who were present. A lot of Prabhupāda's disciples were there, and everyone was almost in tears when those two saints, great people, met and talked to each other.*

They were talking about the spiritual world, and they were praising each other for their deeds. My grandfather also was saying that what Prabhupāda has done, it is unforgettable for anyone of the world. Because to take our Indian culture to Western countries—the credit entirely goes to our beloved Prabhupāda. And he was the only person who took Rādhā-Kṛṣṇa and the holy name outside—in such a way that nobody else could and will be able to in the future.

Since Mr. Poddar was ill and weak, Prabhupāda left after about half an hour. Prabhupāda had spent two weeks in Gorakhpur, and now he was eager to go to Bombay. Leaving two disciples behind to attend to the Deity worship and continue preaching in Gorakhpur, he left.

* * *

ISKCON's Bombay headquarters was a four-room flat on the seventh floor of the Akash-Ganga Building. Rent was nearly three thousand rupees a month, and the devotees had no guaranteed monthly income. Yet because the building was in a vital, prestigious location, Prabhupāda had taken the risk. Such a headquarters would be a necessary base for the preaching he wanted to do in Bombay, and his next preaching would be a grand eleven-day *paṇḍāl* program. "If you are going to hunt," Prabhupāda said, "then you should hunt for a rhinoceros. In that way, if you don't succeed, everyone will simply say, 'Oh, it couldn't be done anyway.' But if you do succeed, then everyone will be surprised. Everyone will be amazed."

As Prabhupāda revealed his plans for a gigantic *paṇḍāl* festival, the devotees became keenly aware that Prabhupāda's inspiration was motivating all their preaching; without him they could never attempt anything so bold and ambitious as a giant *paṇḍāl* festival in Bombay. Often "the American and European disciples" had been billed along with him, as if of equal importance, but the devotees saw themselves as only foolish servants trying to help the genuine pure devotee of the Lord. Although Prabhupāda credited his disciples, his disciples knew that Prabhupāda was Kṛṣṇa's empowered representative. He was their authority and personal link to Kṛṣṇa; his words and actions evinced full transcendental potency. As Kṛṣṇa was unlimited, Śrīla Prabhupāda, Kṛṣṇa's dearmost friend, was entitled to demand unlimited service on Kṛṣṇa's behalf. In the service of Kṛṣṇa, no project was impossible. *Impossible,* Prabhupāda said, was a word in a fool's dictionary.

But as Prabhupāda unfolded his plans for the *paṇḍāl* festival, the devotees doubted: How could they ever raise the money? How could they erect such a huge tent? Where would they get so much food? And who would cook it? Prabhupāda seemed amused at their doubts. "You are all Americans," he said. "So what is the use of being American unless you do something wonderful?"

A Bombay *paṇḍāl,* Prabhupāda said, would be the perfect way to link America's ingenuity with India's spirituality. He gave the example of a blind man and a lame man. Although separately they are helpless, by cooperating—the blind man carrying the lame man on his shoulders, and the lame man giving directions—the two can work successfully. America, because of materialism and ignorance of God, was blind. And India, because of foreign invasions, poverty, and misinterpretations of Vedic knowledge, was lame. America had technological advancement and wealth, and India had spiritual knowledge. The job of the Kṛṣṇa consciousness movement was to combine the two strengths and uplift the world. And one practical application would be the Bombay *paṇḍāl* festival.

Prabhupāda divided the work, assigning Śyāmasundara to publicity, Tamāla Kṛṣṇa to the *paṇḍāl* arrangements, Girirāja to fund-raising, and Madhudviṣa to the scheduled programs onstage. Catching Prabhupāda's spirit of "shooting the rhinoceros," Śyāmasundara organized a massive publicity campaign, with giant posters and banners strung across the streets, announcing "His Divine Grace A. C. Bhaktivedanta Swami Prabhupāda will speak in English language about the science of God. Prasadam distribution and bhajan singing will be led by his American and European bhaktas—Hare Krishna Festival at Cross Maidan—March 25 to April 4."

Girirāja: *Śrīla Prabhupāda took Bombay by storm. The whole city was alive with excitement about the Hare Krishna Festival. We had banners at all the major intersections in Bombay. We had posters up on all the walls, many posters on every wall, and we had very big advertisements in the newspaper, with a beautiful picture of Śrīla Prabhupāda superimposed over a globe, and the words* Bhagavat Dharma Discourses: A Hare Krishna Festival. World Preacher of Bhakti Cult, His Divine Grace A. C. Bhaktivedanta Swami.

Day by day the momentum grew more and more, and every day something new was happening. Finally, in the last two days, we got a huge billboard at Victoria Train Station, the busiest intersection of downtown Bombay. By then everyone knew so much about the festival and where it was going to be and everything that all this billboard said was Hare Krishna *in huge letters. By then everyone knew, so just these two huge words* Hare Krishna *was enough.*

Then Śyāmasundara had arranged for a big helium-filled balloon that was attached to a very long rope at the Cross Maidan site. That balloon just hovered over the city, and there was a streamer attached to the balloon, saying Hare Krishna Festival. *It was real American ingenuity, flair, and dynamism.*

Inspired by Śyāmasundara's lead and taking up a spirit of competition, the other devotees worked at their projects with great enthusiasm. When Prabhupāda called a meeting of the local ISKCON life members and supporters, the turnout was disappointing—only about a dozen. And even those, on hearing the proportions of Prabhupāda's plan, became hesitant. The festival would cost more than one hundred thousand rupees! Although some life members doubted whether the devotees could actually execute such a large production, a handful of stalwarts—Sadajiwatlal, Chandulal Bahl, Kartikeya Mahadevia, Kailash Seksaria, Ramchand Chabria, G. D. Somani, and others—vowed they would do their best to help raise the funds.

Prabhupāda remained actively involved, and he warned his disciples to be wary of cheaters during their business transactions. Every night the devotees would report to him, and he would ask about many details. He wanted the best location, the best work, and the best price. He wanted to know everything: What about the cooking area? Are all the devotees working to their full capacity? Is the mailing list complete? Have the invitations been sent? What about the latrines? What was the cost for the sound system? He scrutinized every detail with sharp, critical intelligence.

Girirāja's fund-raising work was going well. He had donations solicited from businessmen and had printed a souvenir pamphlet. But he was feeling a strain, and he came to Prabhupāda for solace. "Can we use force in Kṛṣṇa consciousness?" he asked.

Prabhupāda frowned. "No. We cannot use force."

"But what if we see one of the workers is lazy on the job and not doing what he is supposed to?"

"No,"Prabhupāda replied. "We can never use force."

"Well, what about in making life members?"

"Force we cannot use," Prabhupāda repeated. "But we can trick them." He told a story about a boy who didn't want to do arithmetic; as soon as the teacher wrote *one plus one* on the board, the boy would balk. So the teacher drew a picture of a cow on the board and asked the boy, "If a man has one cow and then he buys another cow, how many cows will he have?" The boy answered, "Two." Thus the teacher began teaching him arithmetic, even though he was unwilling to learn.

"So people may be averse to serving Kṛṣṇa," Prabhupāda explained, "but we can trick them and get them to serve without their knowing it. But we can never use force. These people are all businessmen. They are always calculating profit and loss. But they are also pious, and they want to go to Kṛṣṇa. So you have to convince them that by giving this money they will gain so much by coming closer to Kṛṣṇa. And that is the truth. When they are convinced, then they will give."

Prabhupāda had ordered from Jaipur two sets of large white marble Deities (paid for by a donation from R. D. Birla). One set was to be installed in the Bombay temple and the other worshiped at the *paṇḍāl* and later sent to one of the temples in the West. But the devotees were anxious that the Deities be finished and shipped on time. And there were other sources of anxiety, right up until the very day of the festival. *Paṇḍāl* construction, *prasādam* distribution, seating arrangements, sound systems—whether these things would be ready on time and whether there would be enough money remained uncertain. But under Prabhupāda's direction the devotees worked steadily, with firm faith in Kṛṣṇa.

And all turned out successful, with ten thousand people attending the first day and twenty thousand that night. The devotees, including those just arrived from the West, numbered about a hundred, and the large stage easily accommodated them, with ample space for dancing *kīrtanas*. Onstage, within a gorgeous, golden-domed altar, surrounded by profuse flower arrangements, stood Rādhā and Kṛṣṇa. Prabhupāda's large red *vyāsāsana*, covered by a canopy, stood at stage center. Also onstage was a display of Prabhupāda's books. The tall and spacious *paṇḍāl*, built to hold more than thirty thousand, was lined with fluorescent bulbs, and the stage glowed with colorful flashing lights.

The program was *kīrtana*, *prasādam*, a lecture, and slides, more *kīrtana*, and more *prasādam*. And the Bombayites—devotees at heart, despite their sophistication and Westernization—loved these very things: Rādhā and Kṛṣṇa, *kīrtana*, and *prasādam*. And that all this was being presented by Westerners made the *paṇḍāl* especially attractive.

The cooks prepared *prasādam* at the *paṇḍāl* site, cooking over a hard coal fire and using big paddles to stir *kicharī* and *halavā* in woks eight feet across. Each night the devotees would serve thousands of plates.

Prabhupāda's appearance in the evening was always the high point. He would sit on his *vyāsāsana*, little Sarasvatī would walk out and garland him, and the crowd would cheer. He would wait for the crowd to quieten, which never happened. So he would just begin speaking, his voice ringing over the powerful sound system. He titled his first lecture "Modern Civilization Is a Failure, and the Only Hope Is Krishna Consciousness."

Prabhupāda sat, eyes half closed in concentration, addressing the largest audience that had ever assembled to hear him. His speaking was particularly forceful, as he glorified Kṛṣṇa and criticized the enemies of Kṛṣṇa. He spoke against governments that were not Kṛṣṇa conscious and against *gurus* who neglected the worship of Kṛṣṇa. He stressed the necessity of teaching Kṛṣṇa's message to the whole world, while his Godbrothers from the Bombay Gaudiya Math sat in the audience, listening respectfully.

"And you are practically seeing that all over the world these *Bhagavad-gītā* principles—Kṛṣṇa, the Supreme Lord—is being accepted. All these boys and girls who are dancing in Kṛṣṇa consciousness—four years ago, four years back, they never heard of Kṛṣṇa. Of course, some of them knew *Bhagavad-gītā*, because *Bhagavad-gītā* is very widely read. But because *Bhagavad-gītā* was not properly presented, although for the last hundred or two hundred or more than that years *Bhagavad-gītā* is widely read all over the world, there was not a single Kṛṣṇa *bhakta*. But since *Bhagavad-gītā* is being presented as it is, within four years there are hundreds and thousands of Kṛṣṇa *bhaktas*. That is our point, that you present the thing as it is, without any adulteration. . . .

"So it is our mission. It is India's culture. People are hankering after this culture, Kṛṣṇa culture. So you should prepare yourself to present *Bhagavad-gītā* as it is. Then India will conquer all over the world by this Kṛṣṇa culture. Rest assured. But we are hankering after help from others. Our government men go there in America: 'Please give us wheat. Please give us money. Please give us soldiers.' Simply begging business. But here is a thing which you can give to them. Simply begging does not glorify your country."

Girirāja: *Prabhupāda was preaching forcefully to the people of Bombay, and every evening the* paṇḍāl *was packed with at least twenty thousand people. Śrīla Prabhupāda would preach so strongly, emphasizing following religious principles. He knew that these people are Hindus but they are not following these principles. Prabhupāda was speaking so powerfully that I knew that what he was saying would be hard for many of the audience to accept.*

"We have something to give to the whole world. That is Kṛṣṇa consciousness. . . . Why you neglect this treasure of Vedic knowledge? And the summarized knowledge is *Bhagavad-gītā*. So if we simply try to understand *Bhagavad-gītā* as it is, we understand immediately the science of God. And because we are all parts and parcels of God, we are actually hankering after uniting with God. That is our seeking. *Ānandamayo 'bhyāsāt*. God is *ānandamaya* (by nature, full of pleasure), and we, being part and parcel of God, or Kṛṣṇa, we are also *ānandamaya*. But we are seeking *ānanda* (pleasure) in a different atmosphere, in the material atmosphere. Therefore we are being baffled. The only remedy is that you take to Kṛṣṇa consciousness and you will be happy. So it is the duty of every Indian to understand this science."

Girirāja: *At that time I was thinking that if Prabhupāda had wanted to flatter the audience or compromise his philosophy, he could have attracted millions of followers. But because he was preaching so boldly and forcefully without compromise, many of the audience did not like it, because it was a challenge to their sense gratification and to their sentiment.*

"This is a science. It is not a dogmatic, bluffing thing. It is a science, and spoken by the Lord Himself, and understood by all the *ācāryas*. Kṛṣṇa says, *ācāryopasanam:* we have to understand things through the *ācāryas*. *Ācāryavān puruṣo veda:* one who is not following the footsteps of the *ācāryas*, he cannot understand anything. Kṛṣṇa also says, *tad-vijñānārtham*. That is said in the *Kaṭhopaniṣad: tad-vijñānārthaṁ sa gurum evābhigacchet*. Kṛṣṇa says, *tad viddhi praṇipātena paripraśnena sevayā*. So everywhere the same instruction is there, 'You approach a person who is coming in disciplic succession—*evaṁ paramparā-prāptam*—and try to learn *Bhagavad-gītā* as it is.' Your life will be sublime. Your life will be successful. That is our mission."

Girirāja: *The fact is that people were wild about Prabhupāda and ISKCON. One night we showed slides of the Ratha-yātrā in San Francisco, and the audience was going wild. In front of ten thousand people Prabhupāda announced that we will hold Jagannātha Ratha-yātrā in Bombay, and everyone started to cheer and applaud.*

Day after day, the *paṇḍāl* festival was a success. Bombay's most important citizens came and were impressed. White-shirted businessmen and their well-groomed wives joined in the chanting. For hundreds of thousands of Bombay citizens, coming to the Cross Maidan to attend an evening *paṇḍāl* program was easy enough. Some were intent on listening to the lecture and inquiring deeply into devotional service, others came mostly to see the Deity, take *prasādam*, or appreciate the *kīrtana*. In any case, A. C. Bhaktivedanta Swami Prabhupāda and the Hare Kṛṣṇa devotees were a refreshing addition to the life of the city. It was the biggest public event in Bombay.

One evening Prabhupāda conducted a Vedic marriage ceremony and an initiation before thousands of people. The marriage was arranged between Vegavān, who was Swedish, and Padmavatī dāsī, who was Australian. They completely enchanted the whole audience—she with her ornate red *sārī* and Indian jewelry, including a nose ring, and he with his nice white *dhotī* and *kurtā* and clean-shaven head. Six *brahmacārīs* were initiated at that time also.

Girirāja: *The audience was impressed. First of all they were amazed just to see foreign devotees, foreign* sādhus. *Then, on top of that, to see them being initiated, and even more than that, being married in front of ten thousand people—it was overwhelming. So during the ceremony, as Śrīla Prabhupāda made the boy and girl husband and wife, he mentioned that she was from Australia and he was from Sweden. Then Śrīla Prabhupāda said, "This is the real United Nations," and everyone burst into applause. It was the most glamorous, wonderful program.*

The final night of the festival, the devotees carried the Deities of Rādhā and Kṛṣṇa in a palanquin to the seaside. Prabhupāda spoke and held *kīrtana* before a crowd of twenty-five thousand.

The next day, The *Indian Express* reported, "FITTING FINALE TO HARE KRISHNA FESTIVAL."

> It was a grand, fitting finale to the 11-day Hare Krishna festival which attracted thousands of devotees at Cross Maidan in South Bombay.
>
> The decorated murtis of Radha and Krishna were taken in procession on a regal ratha from the venue through Dirgaum Road to Chaoupatty in the evening.

> Dozens of nama-sankirtana mandalas from all over the city spearheaded the procession with loud and ecstatic chanting of the Hare Krishna maha-mantra, followed by His Divine Grace A. C. Bhaktivedanta Swami Prabhupada in an elegant horse-drawn coach chanting. Crowds chanted Hare Krishna on the road sides as the ratha was pulled by devotees along the route.
>
> At Chaoupatty the four-foot-tall Deities, splendidly dressed and decorated with jewels and garlands, were displayed on Their magnificent "simhasana" (throne) donated to the Hare Krishna movement by Madhav Baug and Mumba devi temples.
>
> During the celebrations Prabhupāda spoke from the Gita and Srimad-Bhagavatam daily, morning and evening. More than thirty of his foreign disciples conducted kirtana, aratika, and film shows in the specially erected pandals.
>
> Prabhupada will deliver his final public message to the citizens before leaving in a few weeks on a preaching tour of the major cities of Russia.

Bombayites would not soon forget the Hare Kṛṣṇa festival, and a letter from Prabhupāda to the ISKCON life members pledged that it had been only the beginning.

> By the Grace of Their Lordships Sri Sri Radha and Krishna our recent festival in Cross Maidan Exhibition Ground has been counted a grand success, and quite noticeably the spirit of bhakti has been actively revived in Bombay. My blessings go especially to all of you who have joined with us in service.
>
> As you may know, my plan is to establish in this most auspicious city a unique International Krishna Conscious Training Centre, where hundreds of persons from abroad may be educated in the Vedic way of life, while at the same time Indian boys and girls may be trained up for *prachar* (preaching) work in foreign countries. We will construct classrooms, workrooms, dormitories, kitchen for large-scale public *prasad* distribution, a lecture hall, library, and a beautiful temple for the glorification of Radha and Krishna.
>
> We are on the threshold of bringing this important project to fruition, and we are very excited to inform you the progress made in this respect.
>
> You will agree with me that your active participation and your direct involvement in this is most essential, and hence I appeal to you to spare your valuable time for Krishna and make it a point, inspite of your extremely busy life, to extend your unstinted co-operation. It is proposed to hold a meeting on Monday, the 26th April 1971, at 6:30 p.m., "Akash

> Ganga,'' 7th floor, 89 Bhulabhai Desai Road, Bombay-26, to discuss and to finalise plans to channel our united energies to achieve the goal. It will also be a great opportunity for like-minded Krishna devotees to meet, to have darshan of the deities, and to exchange views and suggestions to make rapid progress in spiritual life.
>
> I very much want to meet you again, so kindly make it a ''*must*'' to attend our meeting; there is a lot of ground to be covered to spread Krishna Consciousness to millions and millions of our slumbering brothers and sisters!

That so many were accepting ISKCON and the *saṅkīrtana* movement as bona fide testified to the purity of Śrīla Prabhupāda's presentation of Lord Kṛṣṇa's teachings. His teachings were not sectarian; they were meant for everyone all over the world. He was teaching love of Kṛṣṇa, the universal principle for all humanity. In his lectures at the *paṇḍāl* he had lamented that although India was known as the land of religion, where God consciousness had traditionally permeated society, India's leaders were becoming atheists and communists. Whether Indians, polluted by the madness for sense gratification and confused by a hodgepodge of pseudoreligious teachings, could still recognize and adopt the real thing remained to be seen. But at least in Bombay, the *paṇḍāl* program had had a great effect—of that Prabhupāda felt satisfied.

The program had been the same program he had introduced everywhere: chanting, dancing, taking *prasādam*, worshiping the Deity, hearing about Kṛṣṇa. It was Lord Caitanya's program, adapted slightly according to the particular circumstances—but Lord Caitanya's program nonetheless. This *saṅkīrtana* was the only possible remedy for the disease of modern society. Yet people were reluctant to take the remedy. Prabhupāda, therefore, had ''labeled the bottle.'' The medicine was unchanged, but he had labeled it attractively: a gala evening of entertainment, music, and refreshments, featuring the youth of America and Europe transformed into Vaiṣṇavas.

The labeling was simple, nondeceptive; everyone in Bombay knew well that the Hare Kṛṣṇa *paṇḍāl* festival was a product of their own Vedic heritage. They were fully aware that the Hare Kṛṣṇa leader was a great *ācārya* in the ancient tradition. But it had come to them in such a spectacular and attractive way that they had become caught up in it.

Madhudviṣa: *No one really thought Prabhupāda was leaving India. In India Prabhupāda was the cutting edge of the whole movement. He was the force. Things were moving because of Prabhupāda. In the Western world Prabhupāda would give the idea, and the devotees would expand on it; Prabhupāda was the overseer, but he didn't have such an integral, active part in the West. But in India Prabhupāda was right in the thick of it. He was checking the accounts. He was so much involved in the Indian scene that Ṛṣi Kumāra, the Bombay treasurer, would have to go to Prabhupāda every other day and show him the accounts. He was very much involved in everything. The whole movement in India depended on Prabhupāda. Because of this, no one thought that Prabhupāda would really leave us.*

CHAPTER SIX

Jet-Age Parivrājakācārya

May 1971

Śrīla Prabhupāda prepared for extensive world travel. Although his itinerary was indefinite, his general plan was to travel widely for a few months, then tour the U.S., visit London, and then return to India. He had sent disciples to Australia and Malaysia, and he wanted to visit them. He also wanted to go to Moscow and was awaiting a letter of permission from the Soviet government. As he had spread his movement in America, visiting major cities and preaching and then stationing a few faithful disciples there to carry on, he now expanded his field to include the whole world.

Śrīla Prabhupāda's traveling was in the mood of Nārada Muni, the eternally wandering devotee. In the First Canto of *Śrīmad-Bhāgavatam*, Śrīla Prabhupāda had translated Nārada Muni's words:

> I travelled all over the earth fully satisfied and without being proud or envious. . . . I do travel everywhere, by the Grace of the Almighty Vishnu either in the transcendental world or in the three divisions of the material world without any restriction because I am fixed up unbroken in the devotional service of the Lord. I do travel as abovementioned by constantly singing the glories of the Lord in transcendental message by vibrating this instrument of Vina charged with transcendental sound and given to me by Lord Krishna.

And in his *Bhāgavatam* purports, Śrīla Prabhupāda had explained,

> It is the duty of a mendicant to have experience of all varieties of God's creation as *Paribrajakacharya* or travelling alone through all forests, hills,

> towns, villages etc. to gain faith in God and strength of mind as well as to enlighten the inhabitants of the message of God. A Sannyasi is duty bound to take all these risks without any fear and the most typical Sannyasi of the present age is Lord Chaitanya Who travelled in the same manner through the central India jungles enlightening even the tigers, bears, snakes, deers, elephants and many other jungle animals.

In the age of Kali, Prabhupāda had explained, *sannyāsa* is especially difficult. If, however, one did take *sannyāsa,*

> One who may take the vow of renunciation of family life may not imitate the *Paribrajakacharyas* like Narada or Lord Chaitanya but may sit down at some holy place and devote the whole time and energy in hearing and repeatedly chanting the holy scriptures left by the great Acharyas like the six Gosvamins of Vrindaban.

Yet Prabhupāda was traveling as a mendicant missionary, *parivrājakācārya.* Having already attained the advanced stage wherein the pure devotee resides in Vṛndāvana and chants Hare Kṛṣṇa incessantly, he was now traveling for the good of the whole world. He, like Nārada, was traveling to all parts of the world. As a news writer in India had appropriately titled him, he was "a jet-age *parivrājakācārya.*"

A few *brahmacārīs*, each only recently initiated by Śrīla Prabhupāda, had been preaching alone on the tropical peninsula of Malaysia for several months. With nearly a million Indians in Malaysia, many of them wealthy and influential, the *brahmacārīs* were meeting with success. During one program at a Hindu temple in Kuala Lumpur, a South Indian doctor and his lawyer wife expressed their appreciation of the devotees and offered to donate a house and some land to ISKCON. When the devotees visited the property and found that the offer was serious, they informed Prabhupāda, who decided to visit.

Prabhupāda, accompanied by his disciple Vegavān, flew from Bombay to Kuala Lumpur. Since he planned to go next to Sydney and install Rādhā-Kṛṣṇa Deities in the new temple there, he carried the Deities with him, the same Rādhā and Kṛṣṇa who had presided at the Bombay *paṇḍāl.* Lord Kṛṣṇa rode in a wooden box in the plane's luggage compartment, and Śrīmatī Rādhārāṇī, wrapped in cloth, rested on Vegavān's lap.

Within a brief time after Prabhupāda's arrival at Kuala Lumpur, he was lecturing before a large audience at his host's home.

> I'm very glad to inform you that we have reached Malaysia very shortly, that on my arrival there was a nice meeting, and then we have come outside the city. Yesterday I was very busy all day.

For two days Prabhupāda stayed in the home of a wealthy Sindhi merchant of Kuala Lumpur. The house was large and luxurious, with thick carpets and large mirrors. But when Prabhupāda learned that his hosts were meat-eaters, he refused to eat anything except fruit and milk, even though his disciples offered to cook for him. His disciples, having traveled throughout Malaysia, considered eating at the homes of meat-eaters permissible, as long as the devotees could prepare their *prasādam* in pots not used for cooking meat. But Prabhupāda's standard was higher.

One room in the house held a large collection of marble Deities, about fifty sets of Lakṣmī-Nārāyaṇa and Rādhā-Kṛṣṇa Deities in rows. It appeared to be more of a collector's display than worship, however, and Prabhupāda was unimpressed.

Prabhupāda lectured at the Kuala Lumpur town hall and the Lakṣmī-Nārāyaṇa temple, mostly to Indians. He explained that people could be united only on the spiritual platform. "Look at the United Nations," he said. "They are adding more and more flags. And there are only more and more wars. This Kṛṣṇa consciousness movement will be the real United Nations." Prabhupāda had brought with him slides of ISKCON's activities, and he had one of his disciples narrate a slide show, coaching him on what to say. When a slide appeared of Ratha-yātrā in London's Trafalgar Square, Prabhupāda prompted the devotee, "Now it's no more Lord Nelson. Now it's Lord Jagannātha."

When Prabhupāda met the couple offering the land, he discovered that the agreement had certain important conditions. The doctor and his wife said that they would give ISKCON a large piece of land near the main highway and that their own construction company would build the temple. Within two years, however, if the company hadn't completed the building, the doctor and his wife would reclaim the property. Always eager to consider any serious donation of land, Prabhupāda accepted the conditional offer. But he knew that such offers were usually too conditional.

Already the doctor and his wife had hinted of "Indian *brāhmaṇas*" running the temple and of ISKCON's having only a side altar.

One evening as Prabhupāda talked with the doctor, a gynecologist, the talk turned to birth control. Prabhupāda explained its sinfulness, and he gave an example. If someone poisoned the air in the room he and the doctor were sitting in, then they would have to leave the room or die. Similarly, Prabhupāda explained, contraception meant to poison the womb, denying a soul its rightful shelter.

Like Prabhupāda's previous host, the doctor ate meat, although the devotees had been pushing him to give it up. Prabhupāda was gentle. "Try to stop eating meat," he urged. It was Ekādaśī, and Prabhupāda decided to fast from all food, again showing extreme reluctance to eat in the home of a meat-eater.

* * *

Sydney
May 9, 1971

The Sydney devotees weren't ready for Prabhupāda. An early telegram had informed them he was coming, but a later telegram had said, "Prabhupāda not coming now." A third telegram had come, announcing that Bali-mardana, the Australian G.B.C. secretary, was coming. When a fourth telegram had stated only "Arriving" and the date and flight number, the devotees had presumed this referred to Bali-mardana, not to Prabhupāda. The devotees had taken a small garland and had gone to meet the plane, and when the doors to the customs area opened and Prabhupāda himself walked out, they were flabbergasted.

A white attaché case in his left hand, a cane in his right, a lightweight *cādar* around his shoulders, Śrīla Prabhupāda entered the airport. Reporters, on hand to interview Bali-mardana, came eagerly forward, one of them inquiring why Prabhupāda had come to Australia.

Replying softly, Prabhupāda said he traveled everywhere, just as a salesman travels everywhere. A salesman looks for customers wherever he can find them, and Prabhupāda was traveling, searching for anyone intelligent enough to accept his message. "There is no difference in coming to Australia," he said. "The governments have made a demarcation—'This is Australia'—but we see everywhere as the land of Kṛṣṇa."

One of the devotees hurried to phone the temple—Prabhupāda was coming!

Like Prabhupāda's original temple at 26 Second Avenue in New York, the Sydney temple was a one-room storefront on a main business thoroughfare. On the storefront's plate glass window, one of the devotees had painted a picture of Rādhā and Kṛṣṇa. Prabhupāda entered the room and found it bare, except for a simple wooden altar with three-inch Jagannātha deities, and a big cloth-covered *vyāsāsana.* An old rug hid the floor. The blue haze hanging in the air was smoke from the downstairs kitchen, where a devotee was frantically burning cumin seeds to spice Prabhupāda's lunch.

Prabhupāda remained grave as he walked deliberately to the rear door and looked outside. But when he saw garbage and boards stacked high against the building, his gravity turned to sternness. "What is all this?" he asked. Someone tried an explanation. Unsatisfactory. A devotee brought a glass of milk. "Too hot," Prabhupāda said, and the devotee took it away.

Prabhupāda sat on the large *vyāsāsana.* He looked around the room at each face. None of the fifteen or so devotees had ever seen him before, and only a handful had been initiated (by mail). They were untrained. The carpet was dirty, he said; it should be replaced. And why were there no flowers on the altar? He had brought Rādhā and Kṛṣṇa Deities, but before the devotees could begin Their worship, everything must be very clean. The devotees would have to become *brāhmaṇas* before they could worship Rādhā and Kṛṣṇa.

These devotees, Prabhupāda saw, knew little of Kṛṣṇa consciousness. The devotees who had come to Australia originally, Upendra and Balimardana, had opened the center and left, returning but rarely. Thus an entire temple of inexperienced devotees had been virtually left on its own. Since none of the Sydney devotees could lecture well, the daily classes had consisted of readings from Prabhupāda's abridged *Bhagavad-gītā As It Is,* the only book they had. Yet their firm faith in Prabhupāda compensated for their lack of training. They accepted him as a pure devotee directly in touch with God, and they accepted his books as truth and Kṛṣṇa as the Supreme Personality of Godhead. But many practical things they didn't know, such as how to cook, lecture, and worship the Deities. They knew Prabhupāda wanted them to chant Hare Kṛṣṇa publicly and distribute *Back to Godhead* magazines to the people of Sydney, and this they did daily. Despite frequent arrests, they continued with their *saṅkīrtana.* Sincerity they had. They only lacked training.

A devotee brought Prabhupāda his lunch, poorly cooked—the *capātīs* half burned, half raw, the vegetables wrongly spiced. Prabhupāda rebuked the cook, "If you didn't know how to cook, why didn't you tell me? I can show you." And he went into the kitchen. One of the cooks had tried to make *kacaurīs* and had failed. Although she knew that the dough had to be rolled thin, the filling put in just right, and then the edges folded over precisely, neither she nor any of the other devotees had been able to do it. Prabhupāda, using the same dough and filling, demonstrated the art and made perfect *kacaurīs.*

The devotees explained their difficulty in making *capātīs.* There was no flame on their electric stove. The *capātīs* always came out dry or raw or burned and never puffed up. The excuse only annoyed Prabhupāda, however, who showed exactly how to make *capātīs* that puffed up every time—even on an electric burner. Then he taught the cooks a simple vegetable dish, advising as he cooked. After he left the kitchen, the devotees tried the *capātīs* again. They wouldn't puff. It seemed a magical art only Prabhupāda knew.

Śrīla Prabhupāda had his reasons for bringing Rādhā and Kṛṣṇa to Australia—some of them apparent, others so deep that only he and Rādhā and Kṛṣṇa could understand them. Of course, he was always expanding his movement, of which Deity worship was an important part. So that was one reason for bringing Rādhā and Kṛṣṇa to Australia: to strengthen the devotees and establish more solidly his movement there.

And Prabhupāda loved these Deities. They had presided over the Bombay *paṇḍāl,* and when They hadn't been onstage he had kept Them in his room, where he could look at Them during the day. He had brought Them from Bombay to Malaysia to Sydney, and now he proposed to install Them in this fledgling ISKCON center. But the infinite purity of his heart and the depth of his determination to risk anything for Their Lordships Śrī Śrī Rādhā and Kṛṣṇa are unfathomable. Śrīla Prabhupāda's activities are most grave, and their deeper meaning eludes an observer. Of Lord Caitanya, Kṛṣṇadāsa Kavirāja wrote, "I do not know the deep meaning of Śrī Caitanya Mahāprabhu's activities. I am just trying to describe them externally."

When Prabhupāda came to the temple to perform the initiation ceremony and Deity installation, the devotees weren't ready. Only one small vase of flowers decorated the almost bare altar, and the devotees had not made garlands for the Deities. Prabhupāda was displeased. The small temple was packed, however, and guests and devotees crowded the open doorway and peered through the front window. TV crews filmed the action under hot lamps.

While devotees hurriedly strung garlands for the Deities, Prabhupāda performed the initiation ceremony. There were fifteen initiates in all. To some devotees he gave first initiation, to some second initiation, and to others both first and second. Then he lovingly bathed the forms of Rādhā and Kṛṣṇa and performed the fire sacrifice. While dressing the Deities, he remarked that Their clothes had been poorly made and that the devotees should make new ones immediately. He named the Deities Śrī Śrī Rādhā-Gopīnātha.

Vaibhavī: *He initiated everyone in the temple, anyone who was there—even one boy who had just joined that week and had only come across Kṛṣṇa consciousness the week before, and people who weren't living in the temple, just anyone who was there and somehow serving. He wanted Kṛṣṇa consciousness to be established in Australia, so he just initiated everybody. He gave first and second initiations at the same time, because, having installed the Deities, there had to be some* brāhmaṇas.

But we didn't know anything. We weren't even ready. The altar wasn't finished. Prabhupāda explained to me that we had to string flowers for a garland—the Deity was supposed to wear one. I was running up and down the street trying to find some flowers and get some thread and make a garland.

Same with the sacred thread. There were no sacred threads. Prabhupāda gave the men a sacred thread at brāhmaṇa *initiation, but no one really knew what it was. So I had to run and buy some string. And while Prabhupāda was initiating people, I was sitting there in the arena making sacred threads, copying the one that Bali-mardana had taken off himself.*

I made five of them, and then I was next. After the sacrifice, and after I came out of Prabhupāda's room, where he'd given me the Gāyatrī mantra, *the other devotees said, "You're a* brāhmaṇa *now. So you have to have a sacred thread, too." They told me to make one for myself, which I didn't, because someone told me later a woman wasn't supposed to wear one. We just didn't know much.*

At Sydney Grammar School, an elite school for boys, Prabhupāda led his disciples and a group of students in a *kīrtana* procession through the schoolyard. About two hundred boys and several teachers took part, some children frolicking and laughing, some singing the *mantra,* some soberly following the procession, as the teachers smiled and watched. The procession ended in a large room with a row of chairs in the front. Prabhupāda sat in the headmaster's elaborately carved thronelike seat in the center and began playing *karatālas,* continuing the chanting of Hare Kṛṣṇa. Seeing only a few students responding, he stopped and looked around at the children sitting before him.

"So you are all beautiful boys. Why you do not join us in chanting Hare Kṛṣṇa? Is it very difficult? Will you not try to chant? Hare. Say *Ha-re.*"

A few children: "Hare."

Prabhupāda: "All of you chant, Hare."

The children, weakly: "Hare." Some giggled.

Prabhupāda led them through the *mantra,* one word at a time. Still some children were reticent.

Prabhupāda: "There are only three words: *Hare, Kṛṣṇa,* and *Rāma.* Is it very difficult? Chant again—Hare."

Children: "Hare."

Teasing and prodding, Prabhupāda coaxed them. "Oh, you cannot chant? You are all dumb?" The children broke into laughter. "How is that? Three words you cannot chant? Oh, that is very astonishing. Chant! *Hare*!"

"Hare."

"*Kṛṣṇa!*"

"*Kṛṣṇa!*"

Prabhupāda began rhythmically ringing his *karatālas,* the children following him as he sang: Hare Kṛṣṇa, Hare Kṛṣṇa, Kṛṣṇa Kṛṣṇa, Hare Hare/ Hare Rāma, Hare Rāma, Rāma Rāma, Hare Hare.

After a short time Prabhupāda brought the *kīrtana* to a close. Sitting in the beautiful ornate chair, he smiled at the children. "Three words: *Hare, Kṛṣṇa,* and *Rāma.* Do you know what is God? Can any of you stand up and tell me what is God?"

There was silence, then whispering. Finally, one twelve-year-old boy stood. His schoolmates applauded and laughed.

"Oh, thank you," Prabhupāda said. "Come here."

The boy approached.

"Do you know what is God?" Prabhupāda asked.

"Yes," the boy replied. "God is self-realization, and God is found in the unconscious mind."

"Thank you."

Again the children applauded.

"No, wait. Don't go away," Prabhupāda said. "Now you must explain what you mean. What is self-realization?"

Boy: "It is tapping the powers of the unconscious mind and seeing yourself . . ."

Prabhupāda: "Do you think the mind is unconscious?"

Boy: "The mind is unconscious."

Prabhupāda: "To understand the unconscious, you have to find out what is consciousness."

Boy: "I'm not talking about consciousness—the *un*consciousness."

Prabhupāda: "Unless you know consciousness, how can you describe unconsciousness?"

Boy: "The unconsciousness. The id."

Prabhupāda: "Unconsciousness is the negative side of consciousness. So you should explain what is consciousness. Then we can understand unconsciousness."

Boy: "Consciousness?"

Prabhupāda: "Yes. Try to understand what is consciousness. Then you will understand what is unconsciousness. Consciousness is spread all over the body. Suppose I pinch any part of your body. You feel some pain. That is consciousness. This feeling of pain and pleasure is consciousness. But that consciousness is individual. I cannot feel the pains and pleasures of your body, neither you can feel the pains and pleasures of my body. Therefore, your consciousness is individual and my consciousness is individual. But there is another consciousness, who can feel the pains and pleasures of your body and who can feel the pains and pleasures of my body. That is stated in the *Bhagavad-gītā.*

"You have heard the name of *Bhagavad-gītā*? You? Any of you?"

Another boy: "Yes."

Prabhupāda: "Who says yes? Please come here. Thank you. Very good. At least one of you knows what is *Bhagavad-gītā*. In the *Bhagavad-gītā* it is stated that . . ." And Śrīla Prabhupāda proceeded to explain the difference between the material body and the soul and between the individual souls and the Supreme Soul, Kṛṣṇa.

"You are individual knower of your body. I am knower individually of my body. So everyone is knower of his own body. But there is another person, who says, 'I know everything of everyone's body.' Just like I know something of my body, or I know something of this world. Similarly, there is another *ātmā* (soul), supreme *ātmā,* who knows everything of this universe. He is sometimes called God or the Paramātmā or Kṛṣṇa, whatever, according to different language."

After describing the soul's intimate relationship as an eternal servant of Kṛṣṇa and the soul's suffering caused by forgetting that relationship, Prabhupāda concluded his lecture.

"These teachings should be introduced in every school and college so that from the very beginning children understand what is God, how great He is, how we are related with God, and how we have to live.

"So our movement, Kṛṣṇa consciousness, is teaching that thing. Don't think that it is a sectarian religion. We are making people God conscious. It doesn't matter to what religion you may belong. If by following the principles of religion one becomes advanced in God consciousness, that is first-class religion. That is our motto, and we are preaching all over the world.

"Therefore, I request your teachers here to make the students from the beginning God conscious. Then their future life will be very peaceful, prosperous, and hopeful. Thank you very much. Hare Kṛṣṇa."

Prabhupāda also agreed to speak at Wayside Chapel, a center in downtown Sydney ministering to drug addicts and prostitutes. A Wayside sponsor met Prabhupāda at the temple and accompanied him to the Chapel. The sponser, a long-haired young man in hippie dress, boasted of how Wayside Chapel helped drug addicts. Prabhupāda, however, took it that he was saying the Chapel supplied drugs to the addicts.

At Wayside Chapel a skeptic in the audience challenged Prabhupāda. Prabhupāda had explained that the chanting of the holy names of God was the only way to actually help people, but the cynic challenged, "What good actually is this chanting of Hare Kṛṣṇa?"

"It saves you from death!" Prabhupāda answered forcibly.

May 12, 1971

In his quarters in Sydney, Prabhupāda wrote the Preface to the upcoming edition of *Bhagavad-gītā As It Is*. The Macmillan Company had now agreed to print the unabridged manuscript. The contract was signed, the book was being readied for printing; only the Preface remained to be written.

Prabhupāda wrote in his Preface that although he was known for starting the Kṛṣṇa consciousness movement in America, actually "the original father of this movement is Lord Kṛṣṇa Himself." Giving all credit for his own achievements to his spiritual master, Prabhupāda said that the only qualification he himself had was that he had tried to present *Bhagavad-gītā* as it is, without adulteration.

> Instead of satisfying his own personal material senses, he (a person) has to satisfy the senses of the Lord. That is the highest perfection of life. The Lord wants this, and He demands it. One has to understand this central point of *Bhagavad-gītā*. Our Kṛṣṇa consciousness movement is teaching the whole world this central point, and because we are not polluting the theme of *Bhagavad-gītā As It Is*, anyone seriously interested in deriving benefit by studying the *Bhagavad-gītā* must take help from the Kṛṣṇa consciousness movement for practical understanding of *Bhagavad-gītā* under the direct guidance of the Lord. We hope, therefore, that people will derive the greatest benefit by studying *Bhagavad-gītā As It Is* as we have presented it here, and if even one man becomes a pure devotee of the Lord we shall consider our attempt a success.

As Prabhupāda explained in his Preface, he was publishing the full *Gītā* manuscript "to establish the Kṛṣṇa consciousness movement more soundly and progressively." He would do this by presenting transcendental literature like *Bhagavad-gītā*. But he would also have to go, as Lord Caitanya has said, "to every town and village"—either personally or through his agents, his disciples. And wherever he went, he would preach *Bhagavad-gītā* to whoever would listen.

Tomorrow Prabhupāda would leave Australia for a big *paṇḍāl* festival in Calcutta, then on to Moscow, Paris, Los Angeles . . .

Lord Kṛṣṇa states in *Bhagavad-gītā* that no servant is more dear to Him than one who teaches *Bhagavad-gītā* to the devotees. And Prabhupāda, in all his activities—whether writing a Preface, lecturing to the prostitutes and drug addicts, teaching a disciple to cook *capātīs* without burning them, or planning grand projects yet to come—was always teaching *Bhagavad-gītā* and therefore was always the dearest servant of Lord Kṛṣṇa.

Prabhupāda stood before the Deities of Rādhā-Gopīnātha with folded hands. After less than a week in Sydney, he was leaving. He knew that the devotees here were not up to the standard required for worshiping Rādhā and Kṛṣṇa. And he knew he was taking a risk, entrusting Their worship to neophyte disciples. Yet as an empowered *ācārya* and as the representative of Lord Caitanya, he had to implant Kṛṣṇa consciousness anywhere it might take root. The world was in desperate need. If his disciples followed the process he had given them—chanting, hearing, observing regulative principles—he knew they would quickly become purified.

He had given an analogy: Although in material life a man must first become a highly qualified lawyer before sitting on the judge's bench, in Kṛṣṇa consciousness a sincere devotee is first allowed to "sit on the bench," to become a *brāhmaṇa*, and later, by the mercy of the holy name and the spiritual master, he becomes qualified. The devotees in Sydney, however, were particularly immature, and Prabhupāda made an extraordinary request of Rādhā-Gopīnātha: "Now I am leaving You in the hands of the *mlecchas*. I cannot take the responsibility. You please guide these boys and girls and give them the intelligence to worship You very nicely."

* * *

Calcutta
May 13, 1971

Prabhupāda arrived just in time for the ten-day Calcutta *paṇḍāl* festival. On his orders, Girirāja and Tamāla Kṛṣṇa had come to organize the festival, just as they had the one in Bombay. Prabhupāda had written to Jayapatāka Swami, president of ISKCON Calcutta,

> In the San Kirtan festival pandel if a very big kitchen arrangement can be made, then we shall distribute prasadam daily. Try to make this arrange-

ment. Puri, halevah, kitrie—whatever can be arranged as much as possible. Tamal Krishna and Giriraj have all the ideas.

Attendance surpassed that of the Bombay *paṇḍāl,* with twenty to thirty thousand people attending daily, including ministers of Parliament and other distinguished speakers. It was one of the biggest religious functions Calcutta had ever seen; the whole city became aware of the strength of the Hare Kṛṣṇa movement.

In the early afternoon the devotees would begin selling Prabhupāda's books from a booth, performing *kīrtana* onstage, and distributing *prasādam* to the masses. Around 6:30 the evening program would begin with a long, intense *kīrtana*, which would increase in its fervor as Prabhupāda arrived for the evening *ārati* before the Deities of Rādhā and Kṛṣṇa. Prabhupāda would lecture, sometimes in Bengali and sometimes in English. Afterward the devotees would show slides of the Kṛṣṇa consciousness movement around the world, and Prabhupāda would answer questions from the audience. After the program, people would push forward to receive a morsel of the *prasādam* that had been offered to the Deity.

Naxalite terrorists threatened Prabhupāda's life. These young Communist terrorists, who had been active in Calcutta during Prabhupāda's visit of 1970, had never disturbed him until now. Their tactic was to approach prominent businessmen in their homes or on the street and coerce them into cooperation with Naxalite political objectives. If a businessman refused, the Naxalites would burn his home or place of business or even assassinate him. The Naxalites, who were eager for all of Bengal to turn from their religious traditions and embrace communism, saw Prabhupāda rekindling the religious spirit in Calcutta. Prabhupāda's tremendous crowd-gathering *paṇḍāl*, they concluded, was undermining the principles of communism.

"Fly or Die," read the note Prabhupāda received. He informed the police, who regretted their inability to help. The whole of Calcutta, they said, was in terror of the Naxalites. Prabhupāda, however, refused to be intimidated; he would not fly. Even if they were to attack him, he said, what better way for a Vaiṣṇava to leave his body than while preaching the glories of the Lord?

The next night as Prabhupāda came before the crowd to speak, he noticed a group of rowdy young men, Naxalites, near the stage. They were protesting the preferential seating of certain dignitaries onstage. When one young radical shouted that the radicals themselves wanted to dance onstage, the devotees invited them to join in a *kīrtana*. The Naxalites backed down, but continued shouting and disrupting the meeting. They began banging the seats of the wooden folding chairs, calling out Naxalite slogans, and threatening to burn the place down. Others in the audience began talking nervously among themselves, increasing the commotion. In a vain attempt to bring order, some of the devotees threatened the dissenters. Pushing and scuffling broke out in the audience.

"*Cintāmaṇi-prakara-sadmasu kalpa-vṛkṣa-/ lakṣāvṛteṣu surabhīr abhipālayantam . . .*" Prabhupāda's voice rang over the powerful loudspeaker system. Appearing uninterested in the crowd, depending only on Kṛṣṇa, he began singing prayers from *Brahma-saṁhitā,* and within minutes everyone quieted. Those who wanted to leave left, and those who wanted to stay sat down. The crowd subdued, Prabhupāda lectured.

Several more "fly or die" notes came, and the Naxalites returned the next night, threatening again to burn the *paṇḍāl*. "Call them," Prabhupāda said. "I will meet with them." The devotees thought it unsafe, but Prabhupāda insisted. In a small room behind the *paṇḍāl*, Prabhupāda spoke with the hostile youths. They were angry and disrespectful at first, but as Prabhupāda explained to them the Vedic concept of communism—with Kṛṣṇa at the center—he caught their interest. They agreed to allow Prabhupāda's meetings to continue without any further disruptions.

Acyutānanda Swami: *The last night of the ten-day* paṇḍāl *program was a grand finale, with over forty thousand people attending. I had just stepped out to get sugarcane juice. The* paṇḍāl *was completely packed when I left, but when I got outside, I saw rivers of people flowing through the four main gates into the* paṇḍāl *tent. I thought this must be Kṛṣṇa's mystic power, because the tent was already packed and still thousands of people were entering it. I thought that Kṛṣṇa must be unlimitedly expanding the dimensions of space.*

The climax of the evening was a big procession, beginning at the *paṇḍāl* and going up Park Street to the ISKCON temple on Albert Road. The Deities of Rādhā-Govinda rode on a palanquin to the temple, where They were placed on the altar. After an *ārati* in the temple, the remaining crowd dispersed.

Acyutānanda Swami was standing next to Prabhupāda that night in the Calcutta temple. "Prabhupāda," he said, "someone put Kṛṣṇa's flute in backward." Prabhupāda looked. It *was* backward. "Kṛṣṇa is all-powerful," he said, turning to Acyutānanda Swami. "He can play from the back end also."

Śrīla Prabhupāda was still striving for a plot of land in Māyāpur. Having abandoned the idea that his Godbrothers in Māyāpur might help, he had been working through Bengali friends in negotiating with Muslim farmers in Māyāpur. On returning from Australia, Prabhupāda had sent Tamāla Kṛṣṇa to Māyāpur with orders not to come back until he had purchased land. Tamāla Kṛṣṇa's mission was successful, and after six days he returned to Prabhupāda in Calcutta, having purchased nine *bighās,* three acres, in Māyāpur.

Conceiving the value of Māyāpur was difficult for the devotees, however. One devotee journeyed from Calcutta to see the new ISKCON property and on returning asked Prabhupāda, "What are we going to do there? It's just a big empty field. Nothing is there."

"Because there are no factories and cars," Prabhupāda replied, "therefore you think there is nothing to do. But we are going to chant Hare Kṛṣṇa in Māyāpur. We will build a big temple there, and all the devotees in the world can go out and chant Hare Kṛṣṇa in the place of Lord Caitanya's birth." On May 28 Prabhupāda wrote,

> You will be glad to learn that we have purchased about five acres of land in Mayapur, the birthsite of Lord Chaitanya, and we have proposed to hold a nice festival there from Janmastami day for two weeks. At that time the foundation stone will be set down. I wish that all our leading disciples come to India at that time. There are 50 branches, so at least one from each branch should attend the function.

* * *

June 1971

For months Prabhupāda had been planning to visit Moscow. Aside from his desire to preach to the Russian people, he had a specific meeting in mind with a Russian Indology professor, G. G. Kotovsky. Professor

Kotovsky headed the department of Indian and South Asian studies at Moscow's U.S.S.R. Academy of Sciences, and Prabhupāda had been corresponding with him for a year.

Kṛṣṇa dāsa in West Germany, with the help of a Dr. Bernhardt of the University of Hamburg, had obtained the names of other Russian scholars of Indology. A letter to Kṛṣṇa dāsa in December of 1970 had revealed Prabhupāda's plans for preaching in Russia.

> I am very encouraged to see your enthusiasm for preaching this message to the Russian people, and your idea to send letters with the help of Dr. Bernhart is very good. He is a big scholar and he also appreciates our movement. So if you arrange a tour of Russia for me, I am prepared to accept. Let us see what Krishna desires.... If we can go to Russia with our World Sankirtan Party, I am certain that it will be very much appreciated and people will see the real peace movement is chanting process—chanting the Holy Names Hare Krishna, Hare Krishna, Krishna Krishna, Hare Hare/ Hare Rama, Hare Rama, Rama Rama, Hare Hare. So try for it.

Śrīla Prabhupāda had coached Kṛṣṇa dāsa on how to best cultivate the Russian Indologists.

> You can ask them some questions like: What is the ultimate goal of life? What is your ideal ultimate goal of life? What is the difference between animal and human life? Why is religion accepted by all kinds of civilized societies? What is your conception of the original creation? In this way questions may be put to find out what is their standing. We do not grudge an atheist provided he has got some philosophical standing. In this way try to elicit some answers from the Professors. If you can finally establish one Moscow center, it will be a great credit to you. So far studying Russian language, it is not necessary, but if you do so it is all right. I want very much a center in Russia, so for the time being I shall desire that Moscow Center.

In March 1971, Professor G. G. Kotovsky had replied to Kṛṣṇa dāsa's letter.

> I thank you for your information about Swami Bhaktivedanta's lecturing tour. If he would come to Moscow, the Soviet scholars doing research in ancient Indian culture would be very happy to meet him in the Institute of Oriental Studies, USSR Academy of Sciences. I would be thankful to

> you for your information on the dates of Swami Bhaktivedanta's arrival and stay in the USSR.

Śrīla Prabhupāda had personally replied to Professor Kotovsky.

> . . . it was understood that you and your university are interested in hearing about Krishna culture and philosophy. This ancient Krishna culture and philosophy is the oldest in the world or in the universe. At least from a historical point of view it is not less than 5,000 years old.
>
> Perhaps you may know that I have started this cultural movement since 1966 and it is already spreading all over the world. Krishna culture is so popular in India that even the government attracts many foreigners by Air India time table to visit Vrindavan, the land of Krishna culture. Enclosed please find one page from the latest Air India time table (April 1971) wherein the Krishna culture is depicted for general attraction.
>
> My life is dedicated to spreading this Krishna culture all over the world. I think if you give me a chance to speak about the great Krishna culture and philosophy in your country, you will very much appreciate this simple programme with great profit. This culture is so well planned that it would be acceptable by any thoughtful man throughout the whole world.

Having preached a year in the Eastern Hemisphere, Prabhupāda was eager to return to the West, and he planned to fly to Moscow and on to Europe. For Prabhupāda and his traveling companions, Śyāmasundara and Aravinda, getting tourist visas for Russia was simple. They would take a five-day, government-controlled tour, with every activity planned by the Soviet Tourist Bureau and everything paid for in advance.

Captain Lal, the pilot of the flight to Moscow, considered Prabhupāda an important passenger and came back to visit him during the flight. They spoke of Prabhupāda's movement, his chances for lecturing in Moscow, and of Bombay, where Prabhupāda was trying to purchase land. Captain Lal invited Prabhupāda to the cockpit, and Prabhupāda came and sat behind the captain, asking technical questions about the equipment and the flight. Prabhupāda and Captain Lal agreed to meet again in Moscow.

Prabhupāda, his secretary, and his servant cleared Soviet customs and immigration quickly and smoothly, and a government tourist guide escorted them by limousine to the Hotel National. The hotel, near Red Square, Lenin's Tomb, and the Kremlin, was expensive but plain. Prabhupāda found his room dingy and cramped, with barely space for a bed and two chairs. The room for Śyāmasundara and Aravinda was far away, and Prabhupāda decided that Aravinda should share the room with him instead, crowding Prabhupāda's room all the more.

Aravinda told the hotel manager that they would not eat the hotel fare, but would have to cook their own meals. The manager refused at first, but finally allowed them use of the maid's kitchen.

That problem solved, the next was getting food. Prabhupāda sent Śyāmasundara out. Across the street, Śyāmasundara found a milk and yogurt store, but he returned to Prabhupāda's room without any fruit, vegetables, or rice. Prabhupāda sent him out again, and this time Śyāmasundara was gone practically all day, returning with only a couple of cabbages. Prabhupāda sent him out the next day for rice. When Śyāmasundara returned with rice after several hours, Prabhupāda saw that it was a poor North Korean variety, very hard. Prabhupāda asked for fruit, but Śyāmasundara had to hike for miles through the city to find anything fresh—a few red cherries. Wherever Śyāmasundara went, he would have to stand in long queues to purchase anything. Usually, however, someone in the queue would notice that he was a tourist and bring him to the front of the line. Everything Śyāmasundara purchased was with coupons.

Prabhupāda remained peaceful and regulated, keeping to his daily schedule. He would rise early and translate, and in the cool of early morning he would go out for a walk through the all-but-deserted streets. Prabhupāda, wearing a saffron *cādar,* strode quickly, Śyāmasundara sometimes running ahead to photograph him.

As they would pass Lenin's Tomb a queue would already be forming. "Just see," Prabhupāda commented one morning, "that is their God. The people don't understand the difference between the body and the spirit. They accept the body as the real person."

Prabhupāda appreciated the sparseness of the traffic—some trolleys and bicycles, but mostly pedestrians. As he walked among the old, ornate buildings, he saw elderly women hosing the wide streets—a good practice, he said. The Russian people appeared to live structured, regulated lives, much more so than the Americans. These simple, austere people, unspoiled by the rampant hedonism so common in America, were fertile for Kṛṣṇa consciousness. But devoid of spiritual sustenance, they appeared morose.

Prabhupāda had Śyāmasundara arrange a meeting with Professor Kotovsky and invite Captain Lal to come along. The tourist bureau provided a car and guide, and Prabhupāda and his party rode outside the city to Professor Kotovsky's office in an old white brick building at the Academy of Sciences.

When Prabhupāda arrived, the middle-aged Russian professor, dressed in a gray suit, got up from his cluttered desk and welcomed Prabhupāda into his small office. Professor Kotovsky appeared a bit hesitant, however, more cautious than in his letters. When Śyāmasundara mentioned Prabhupāda's eagerness to lecture before interested scholars at the Academy, Professor Kotovsky flatly refused—it would never be allowed. Prabhupāda was disappointed.

The next moment, however, Prabhupāda seemed unaffected and began speaking in his humble, genteel manner, sitting in a straight-backed office chair beside Professor Kotovsky, who sat at his desk. Śyāmasundara turned on the tape recorder, which the professor eyed cautiously but didn't object to.

Prabhupāda: "The other day I was reading in the paper, *Moscow News*. There was a Communist congress, and the president declared that, 'We are ready to get others' experiences to improve.' So I think the Vedic concept of socialism or communism will much improve the idea of communism."

Professor Kotovsky listened intently and politely as his foreign visitor explained how the *gṛhastha* in Vedic culture provides for everyone living in his house—even for the lizards—and how, before taking his meal, he calls in the road to invite any hungry person to come and eat. "In this way," Prabhupāda explained, "there are so many good concepts about the socialist idea of communism. So I thought that these ideas might have been distributed to some of your thoughtful men. Therefore I was anxious to speak."

Professor Kotovsky's academic interest was piqued. "You know, it is interesting," he said, his articulate English heavily accented. "As it is here in our country, there is now great interest in the history of old, old thought." He described the accomplishments of his colleagues and himself, particularly a booklet they had recently prepared highlighting Soviet studies in Indology. He said he would like to give a copy to Prabhupāda.

Professor Kotovsky: "You will be interested to discover that we published not all but some *Purāṇas,* then some parts of the *Rāmāyaṇa,* eight volumes in Russian of the *Mahābhārata,* and also a second edition of the *Mahābhārata,* translated by different people in full and published. *Manu-smṛti* is also translated in full and published with Sanskrit commentaries. And such was the great interest that all of these publications were sold in a week. They are now completely out of stock. It is impossible to get them in the book market, after a month. Such a great interest among reading people here in Moscow and the U.S.S.R. towards ancient Vedic culture."

Prabhupāda: "Among these *Purāṇas,* the *Śrīmad-Bhāgavatam* is called the *Mahā-purāṇa.*" And he told of his own translation of *Śrīmad-Bhāgavatam,* "the ripened fruit of the Vedic desire tree." He would show some volumes to the professor if he was interested.

Professor Kotovsky said the Moscow and Leningrad libraries had nearly all the major texts of Indian culture in Sanskrit. These libraries housed not only ancient texts but more recent literature as well, comprising an up-to-date study of Hinduism.

"Hinduism," Prabhupāda interrupted, "is a very complex topic." And they both laughed. Professor Kotovsky acknowledged that Hinduism was more than a religion; it was a way of life. But Prabhupāda explained that the name Hindu was actually a misnomer. The real term to explain Vedic culture was *varṇāśrama.* Briefly Prabhupāda described the four orders: *brāhmaṇa, kṣatriya, vaiśya,* and *śūdra.*

Professor Kotovsky: "You have told that in any society there are four divisions, but it is not so easy to distinguish. For instance, one can group together different social classes and professional groups into four divisions in any society. There is no difficulty. The only difficulty is, for instance, in socialist society, in our country and other socialist societies, how can you distinguish productive group and workers?"

Prabhupāda welcomed the professor's questions, although grounded in Soviet socialist vested interests. Prabhupāda considered the professor not so much an academician as a pawn of the Soviet university system; much as one political power tries to understand its adversary, the professor was inquiring into Indian culture so that his government might penetrate it with their own ideology. Behind Professor Kotovsky's apparent interest in Vedic culture, Prabhupāda could see the view of the Socialist party, a view diametrically opposed to Vedic philosophy. Nevertheless, Prabhupāda tactfully continued to present Kṛṣṇa consciousness in accord with *paramparā*, and he tried to convince Professor Kotovsky through scripture and logic.

Quoting *Bhagavad-gītā*, a *śāstra* with which the professor was familiar (in his own way), Prabhupāda described Lord Kṛṣṇa as the creator of the four divisions of society. Professor Kotovsky immediately countered with the theory of the Soviet scholars that the *varṇāśrama* divisions were a recent addition to Vedic culture. He also again registered his opinion that the divisions of *varṇāśrama* had no meaning within socialism.

Professor Kotovsky: "There is a great distinction between socialist society and all societies preceding socialism, because in modern Western society you can group all social and professional classes in the particular class divisions—*brāhmaṇas, kṣatriyas, vaiśyas* (or factory owners), and *śūdras*, or menial workers. But here we have no *vaiśyas*. Because we have administrative staff in factories, managerial staff—you can call them *kṣatriyas*—and then *śūdras*, the workers themselves, but not this intermediate class."

Prabhupāda: "That is stated, *kalau śūdra-sambhavaḥ*. 'In this age, practically all men are *śūdras*.' That is stated. But if there are simply *śūdras*, then the social order will be disturbed. In spite of your state of *śūdras*, the *brāhmaṇas* are there. That is necessary. So if you do not divide the social order in such a way, then it will be chaos. That is the scientific estimation of the *Vedas*. You may belong to the *śūdra* class, but to maintain the social order you have to train some of the *śūdras* to become *brāhmaṇas*. It cannot depend on the *śūdras*."

Prabhupāda gave his standard analogy, comparing the social body to the human body. All the parts are necessary, not only the legs but the belly, the arms, and the head. "Otherwise," he said, "it will not work properly. As long as this is going on, there will be some disturbance."

Modern society's missing point, Prabhupāda said, was an understanding of the purpose of human life. "They do not know what is the next life," he said. "There is no department of knowledge or scientific department to study what is there after finishing this body."

Professor Kotovsky objected—politely, completely. "Swamiji," he said, "when the body dies, the owner also dies." Prabhupāda marked his reply. The learned professor, head of the department of Indian studies in the

Soviet Academy, was caught in a classic moment of ignorance. His concept of who he was was no more advanced than an animal's.

"No," Prabhupāda quickly replied. "This fact you must know. Why is there no department of knowledge in the university to study this fact scientifically? That is my proposition. That department is lacking. It may be as you say, it may be as I say, but there must be a department of knowledge. Now recently a cardiologist, a doctor in Montreal and Toronto, has accepted that there is a soul. I had some correspondence with him. He strongly believes that there is a soul."

Prabhupāda continued to build his argument: "We accept knowledge from authority." The professor countered that everything had to be accepted on the basis of empirical evidence. But then, in midsentence, he stopped arguing and inquired, "Have you many branches of your society in the world?"

Prabhupāda began speaking about ISKCON, with its sixty-five branches all around the world, and of how he was going next to Paris, where his disciples had recently acquired a new center, and of how the American boys and girls especially were joining his movement. He told of the four prohibitive rules (no meat-eating, no illicit sex, no intoxication, and no gambling) and of the books he had published. As Prabhupāda described the workings of his movement, Professor Kotovsky nodded approvingly.

When Prabhupāda returned to comparing Kṛṣṇa consciousness to communism, he concluded that the two philosophies were in agreement. And both stressed surrender to an authority. The devotee surrenders to Kṛṣṇa, the communist to Lenin.

Prabhupāda: "Our life is by surrender, is it not? Do you disagree with this point?"

Kotovsky: "To some extent you surrender."

Prabhupāda: "Yes. To the full extent."

Kotovsky: "You have to surrender to the society, for instance—the whole people."

Prabhupāda: "Yes, to the whole people or to the state or king or government or whatever you say. The surrender must be there. It may be different."

Kotovsky: "The only difficulty is we cannot have surrender to government or to a king. The principal difference is of surrender to a king, who is a single person, or to the whole society."

Prabhupāda: "No, that is a change of color only. But the surrender is there. The principle of surrender is there. Whether you surrender to monarchy, democracy, aristocracy, or dictatorship, you have to surrender. That is a fact. Without surrender there is no life. It is not possible. So we are educating persons to surrender to the Supreme, wherefrom you get all protection. Just like Kṛṣṇa says, *sarva-dharmān parityajya.* So surrender is there. No one can say, 'No, I am not surrendered to anyone.' The difference is *where* he surrenders. And the ultimate surrendering object is Kṛṣṇa. Therefore in *Bhagavad-gītā* it is said, *bahūnāṁ janmanām ante jñānavān māṁ prapadyate:* 'After surrendering to so many things, birth after birth, when one is factually wise he surrenders unto Me.' "

Professor Kotovsky agreed. But surrender had to be accompanied by revolution, he said. The French Revolution, for example, was a revolt against one kind of surrender, and yet the revolution itself was another surrender, surrender to the people. "So it is not enough to come full stop," the Professor argued. "Surrender is to be accompanied with revolt against surrender to other people."

Prabhupāda: "Yes, the surrender will be full stopped when it is surrender to Kṛṣṇa. That is full stop: no more surrender. Other surrender you have to change by revolution. But when you come to Kṛṣṇa, then it is sufficient—you are satisfied. Just like—I give you one example. A child is crying and people change laps: 'Oh, it has not stopped.' But as soon as the baby comes to the lap of its mother. . ."

Kotovsky: "It stops."

Prabhupāda: "Yes, full satisfaction. So this surrender, the changes will go on in different categories. The sum total of all these surrenders is surrender to *māyā* (material illusion). But the final surrender is to Kṛṣṇa, and then you will be happy."

After only three days, Prabhupāda's mission in Moscow seemed finished. The meeting with Professor Kotovsky over, what was left? The government would allow nothing else. It had not allowed him to bring in books, and now he had been refused the opportunity to speak publicly. Foreigners were not to talk with the Russians. He could go nowhere, unless on an accompanied tour. So with no preaching and no prospects, he stayed in his cramped room, taking his massage, bathing, accepting whatever food Śyāmasundara could gather and cook, dictating a few letters, chanting Hare Kṛṣṇa, and translating *Śrīmad-Bhāgavatam.*

Prabhupāda took a guided tour of Moscow, riding with other tourists on a crowded bus. He saw elderly Russians going to church, armed guards stationed at the door; and he surmised that the guards were to prevent the younger generation from entering to worship. He soon tired of the tour, however, and the tour guide got him a taxi and instructed the driver to return him to the Hotel National.

Śyāmasundara continued to spend most of his day looking for fresh food. Hearing that oranges were available at a certain market across town, he set out across the city. With his shaved head and his white *dhotī* and *kurtā* he drew stares from everyone he passed, and as he was returning, after dark, uniformed men wearing red armbands accosted him, taking him to be a local deviant. Grabbing him, they pinned his arms behind his back and shouted at him in Russian. Śyāmasundara caught the word *dakumyent* ("document, passport"). He replied, "*Dakumyent,* hotel! Hotel!" Realizing Śyāmasundara was a tourist, the officers released him, and he returned to the hotel and informed Prabhupāda of what had taken place. "There is no hope in Russia without Kṛṣṇa consciousness," Prabhupāda said.

Once Śyāmasundara was standing in line at the yogurt store when a man behind him asked him about *yoga*. "I really want to talk with you," the man said, and he gave Śyāmasundara his name and address and a time they could safely meet. When Śyāmasundara told Prabhupāda, Prabhupāda said, "No, he is a policeman. Don't go."

Standing at his window, Prabhupāda glimpsed a parade in nearby Red Square—troops, tanks, artillery, and missiles parading through the streets. By always preparing for war, Prabhupāda said, the Russian leaders kept the people motivated and thus avoided a revolt. He compared warlike Russia to the *asuras* (demons) in the ancient Vedic histories like *Śrīmad-Bhāgavatam.*

One day two young men, one the son of an Indian diplomat stationed in Moscow, the other a young Muscovite, were loitering near Red Square when they saw an amazing sight. Out of the usual regimented routine of city traffic, a tall young man with a shaved head, a long reddish ponytail, and flowing white robes approached. It was Śyāmasundara. Familiar with Śyāmasundara's dress, the son of the Indian diplomat stopped him. Śyāmasundara smiled, "Hare Kṛṣṇa, brother." And he began talking with the Indian, whose name was Narayana. The Russian, Ivan, knew a little English and followed the conversation as closely as he could. The talk grew serious.

"Why don't you come up and meet my spiritual master?" Śyāmasundara asked. Honored, the boys immediately accompanied Śyāmasundara to the Hotel National. When they arrived, they found Prabhupāda seated on his bed, aglow and smiling, Aravinda massaging his feet. Śyāmasundara entered, offering obeisances before Prabhupāda. Ivan was completely fascinated.

"Come on," Prabhupāda said, and the three of them sat at Prabhupāda's feet. Turning first to Narayana, Prabhupāda asked his name and his father's occupation. Narayana liked Prabhupāda and offered to bring him green vegetables; his father, being highly placed at the Indian Embassy, had produce flown in from India.

Ivan was interested even more than his Indian friend, and Prabhupāda began explaining to him the philosophy of Kṛṣṇa consciousness, while Narayana helped by translating. Ivan inquired with respect and awe, and Prabhupāda answered his questions, teaching as much basic information about Kṛṣṇa consciousness as was possible in one sitting. Prabhupāda explained the difference between the spirit soul and the body and described the soul's eternal relationship with Kṛṣṇa, the Supreme Personality of Godhead. He spoke of *Bhagavad-gītā*, of his network of temples around the world, and of his young men and women disciples all practicing *bhakti-yoga*.

Prabhupāda mentioned his desire to preach in Russia, which was a great field for Kṛṣṇa consciousness because the people were openminded and hadn't been polluted by sense gratification. He wanted to introduce Kṛṣṇa conscious literature in Russia through a library or a reading room or in whatever way possible. Kṛṣṇa conscious philosophy, he said, should be taught to Russia's most intelligent people, but because of government restrictions it would have to be done discreetly. Devotees would not be able to sing and dance in the streets, but they could chant quietly together in someone's home. Prabhupāda then began singing very quietly, leading the boys in *kīrtana*.

Ivan's taking to Kṛṣṇa was like a hungry man's eating a meal. After several hours, however, he and his friend had to go. They would return the next day.

Śyāmasundara began spending time with Ivan and Narayana. Ivan, a student of Oriental philosophies, was very intelligent and eager to know what was going on in the outside world. He was fond of the Beatles, and Prabhupāda told him of his association with George Harrison and John Lennon. Ivan and Śyāmasundara had long talks about the ambitions and hopes of young people outside Russia, and Śyāmasundara explained to him how Kṛṣṇa consciousness was the topmost of all spiritual paths. Śyāmasundara also taught him basic principles of *bhakti-yoga*, such as chanting the prescribed sixteen rounds of *japa* daily, and gave him his own copy of *Bhagavad-gītā As It Is*.

Prabhupāda showed Ivan how to prepare *capātīs* and rice and asked him to give up eating meat. Joyfully, Ivan accepted the chanting, the new way of eating—everything. Ivan was being trained so that after Prabhupāda left, Ivan could continue on his own. Ivan would be able to feel himself changing and advancing in spiritual life, and after practicing for some time he could be initiated. Ivan said he would tell his friends about Kṛṣṇa consciousness. With only two days left in Moscow, Prabhupāda taught Ivan as much as he could. In this young Russian's eagerness and intelligence, Prabhupāda found the real purpose of his visit to Russia.

Prabhupāda gave the analogy that when cooking rice the cook need test only one grain to determine whether the whole pot of rice is done. Similarly, by talking with this one Russian youth, Prabhupāda could tell that the Russian people were not satisfied in their so-called ideal land of Marxism. Just as Ivan was keenly receptive to Kṛṣṇa consciousness, millions of other Russians would be also.

Cāṇakya Paṇḍita says that one blooming flower can refresh a whole forest and that a fire in a single tree can burn the whole forest. From the Marxist point of view, Ivan was the fire that would spread Kṛṣṇa consciousness to others, thus defeating the communist ideology. And from Prabhupāda's point of view, he was the aromatic flower that would lend its fragrance to many others. Prabhupāda's visit to Russia was no obscure interlude, but had become an occasion for planting the seed of Kṛṣṇa consciousness in a destitute land.

Śrīla Prabhupāda had brought the movement of Lord Caitanya to yet another country. Caitanya Mahāprabhu Himself had predicted that the *saṅkīrtana* movement would go to every town and village, yet for hundreds of years that prediction had remained unfulfilled. Prabhupāda, however, in the few years since his first trip to America in 1965, had again and again planted Lord Caitanya's message in one unlikely place after another. And of all places, this was perhaps the most unlikely; during a brief, government-supervised visit to Moscow, he had planted the seed of Kṛṣṇa consciousness within the Soviet Union. He was like the needle, and everyone and everything connected with him was like the thread that would follow.

Professor Kotovsky had remarked that Prabhupāda's stay in an old-fashioned hotel would not prove very interesting. But Prabhupāda, unknown to Professor Kotovsky, was transcendental to Moscow or any other place in the material world. Prabhupāda had come to this place, and Kṛṣṇa had sent a sincere soul to him to receive the gift of Kṛṣṇa consciousness. This had happened not by devious espionage against the Soviet government but by the presence of Kṛṣṇa's pure devotee and his natural desire to satisfy Kṛṣṇa by preaching. In response to Prabhupāda's pure desire, Kṛṣṇa had sent one boy, and from that one boy the desire would spread to others. Nothing, not even an Iron Curtain, could stop Kṛṣṇa consciousness. The soul's natural function was to serve Kṛṣṇa. And Kṛṣṇa's natural will was to satisfy the pure desires of His devotee.

In a farewell letter to Professor Kotovsky, Prabhupāda tried to encourage further correspondence.

> You wanted to see the manuscripts of my lectures, therefore I am sending herewith an *Introduction* to the lectures, and if you so desire I shall be glad to send essays on these subjects:
>
> 1. Vedic Conceptions of Socialism and Communism
> 2. Scientific Values of Classless Society
> 3. Knowledge by Authoritative Tradition

In a letter to Tamāla Kṛṣṇa, Prabhupāda summed up his Moscow visit.

> The city is well-planned. There are big, big houses and roads and at day time the streets are busy with buses, cars, and underground trains which are far better than American or English. The underground streets are very neat and clean. The surface streets are also daily washed. But there is some difficulty in collecting vegetarian foodstuffs; still we are cooking our meals by the cooker which has saved our lives. We talked with one big professor Mr. Kotovsky, and Shyamsundar talked with many great writers and

musicians. Two boys are working with us; one Indian and one Russian. So there is good prospect for opening a center, although the atmosphere is not very good. The embassy was no help. So our visit to Moscow was not so successful, but for the future, it is hopeful. Tomorrow I go to Paris for one day, then to S.F. Rathayatra and then I shall come back to London.

* * *

Paris
June 25, 1971

Śrīla Prabhupāda was lying on the couch in the conference room of the Indian Tourist Office, having just come from Orly Airport. Two disciples, Ārādhana and his wife, Śantanu, had come with him in the taxi and were the only others in the room. Since there was to be a press conference later, Prabhupāda said he wanted to rest, and he closed his eyes.

At the airport, Paris immigration officials had detained Prabhupāda while some thirty European devotees, none of whom had ever met him, had waited anxiously. They had glimpsed him as he had walked from the plane to the terminal building, and they had watched him carrying his *sannyāsa-daṇḍa* with umbrella strapped to it. He had waved to them, holding up his bead bag. But then he had been kept from them, just beyond a thin wall, until finally, after two hours, Paris immigration had allowed him through.

The Paris devotees had not arranged a car for Prabhupāda, so when he had asked for one, several devotees had run off to hail a taxi. When the taxi had arrived, Prabhupāda, along with Ārādhana and Śantanu, had started for the Indian Tourist Office, leaving the others to join him later.

After a brief rest, Prabhupāda opened his eyes and saw Ārādhana, Śantanu, and Śyāmasundara in the room. The other devotees and the press would be arriving soon. As Prabhupāda sat up, Śantanu offered him some mango, and Śrīla Prabhupāda smiled.

Yogeśvara: *I sat outside the door to Prabhupāda's room, eating the peel of the mango Prabhupāda had eaten. My heart was pounding, and I had no idea what it was going to be like after having been initiated for a year and a half and having never met my spiritual master personally—but now knowing that he was just behind that door!*

Then Śyāmasundara opened the door and peered out and saw me sitting there. He stuck his head back inside the door and said, "There's a devotee here. Shall I let him in now, Śrīla Prabhupāda?" I peeked around the door, and Śrīla Prabhupāda, who had been lying down on the couch, was now sitting up with his hand on his knee very solidly, with a royal, majestic look. He responded to Śyāmasundara's question by motioning with his hand that we could all come in. It was the first perfect thing I had ever seen in my life—that one gesture. So I came in and immediately fell flat on the floor. And then I understood that "Now I am with my spiritual master."

Gradually the devotees began arriving from the airport, and they came into Prabhupāda's room. The press also arrived, as Prabhupāda spoke warmly and pleasantly with his followers, encouraging them in their preaching and telling them of his own recent preaching in Moscow. Hardly any of the devotees had ever been with their spiritual master before, and Locanānanda began introducing them to Śrīla Prabhupāda.

Hari-vilāsa: *I arrived late, and when I came in I was mixed up with surprise, with elation, with egotistical pride, and with amazement that the Lord's pure devotee was there. I walked in with Ghanaśyāma, the boy who had started translating some of Prabhupāda's books into French. The room was almost filled, and Ghanaśyāma immediately sat down in the back. I was the president of the temple, and I was very proud and puffed up about it. So I made my way all the way up to the front, where Śrīla Prabhupāda was, and I sat down right next to him. I looked at him, expecting him to look at me and smile or something, some recognition. But he didn't look at me at all.*

Locanānanda was introducing all the devotees to Prabhupāda. Locanānanda said, "This is Ghanaśyāma. He is the translator." Prabhupāda said, "Where is he?" And everyone looked around to Ghanaśyāma in the back. Prabhupāda said, "Let him stand up, please." Ghanaśyāma stood, and Prabhupāda looked at him and smiled and said, "Oh, thank you very much."

Right then I felt a little funny. I sat there wondering, "What have I done? I've walked all the way up to the front, and I'm expecting so much recognition."

Then Locanānanda said, "This is Hari-vilāsa. He is the president of the temple." Prabhupāda didn't even look at me. And I knew, yes, I had made a big mistake. I began to realize, "This is my spiritual master."

Because immediately he had acted in such a way as to point out a great fault in me.

Reporters began their questioning, and Prabhupāda patiently answered them, taking advantage of their sometimes superficial questions to elaborate on the philosophy of Kṛṣṇa consciousness and explain the Kṛṣṇa consciousness movement. The conference ran one hour.

As Prabhupāda left the Indian Tourist Office he found that there was no car to take him to the temple. While several devotees ran around trying to find a taxi, Prabhupāda waited, standing before a sidewalk café.

Thinking that Prabhupāda must be tired from the rigorous press conference and his long flight from Moscow, one of the devotees asked, "Śrīla Prabhupāda, would you like to sit here for a minute?" And the devotee pulled one of the café chairs out away from its table.

"What is this place?" Prabhupāda asked.

"This is a sidewalk café," the devotee replied.

"What do people do here? Do they smoke and drink?"

"Yes, Śrīla Prabhupāda, it's a café. They serve alcoholic beverages."

"No," Prabhupāda replied. "*Guru* cannot sit in such a place."

When Prabhupāda reached the temple, he bathed and took *prasādam.* The next day he was scheduled to leave for Los Angeles, and his one day in Paris was filled with outside engagements. He rested and again went out to preach.

The devotees had rented the Olympia Theater, a large auditorium meant to seat more than two thousand. But because the devotees had advertised Prabhupāda's lecture only two days in advance, only forty people attended. Prabhupāda was undaunted, and he lectured and held *kīrtana.* Afterward he went to a television studio for an interview.

By the time Prabhupāda returned to the temple, it was one in the morning. Śyāmasundara told the devotees, who had all accompanied Prabhupāda during the day, that they should rest a full six hours before rising. But the next morning Prabhupāda rose as usual, and at five o'clock he was demanding to know why there was no *maṅgala-ārati.* He sent his servant to wake the devotees, and as the devotees were hurrying to the temple room to begin their morning worship Prabhupāda was going out on his morning walk.

Accompanying Prabhupāda on his walk were Śyāmasundara, Aravinda, and the Paris temple president, Hari-vilāsa. The spring morning was sunny, and Prabhupāda, walking with his cane, appeared noble. "Śyāmasundara,"

Prabhupāda asked, "Why are all the householders in *māyā*?" When Śyāmasundara couldn't reply, Prabhupāda said, "That's all right. That is their position—to be in *māyā*."

He said that when he had gone to America his plans had been to make *sannyāsīs,* but when he saw the free mixing of the sexes in the West he had decided to let his disciples first get married and have a child, and then the wife could go to Vṛndāvana with the child, and the husband could take *sannyāsa.* Prabhupāda laughed. Man becomes entangled by his family, he said—by his home, his bank account, his animals, and so many other attachments.

Near the end of his walk, Prabhupāda spoke specifically of Paris. "Three things are prominent here," he said, "wine, women, and money. What do you think, Hari-vilāsa? Is this a fact?"

Hari-vilāsa replied, "Yes, Prabhupāda, this is definitely a fact—wine, women, and money."

Prabhupāda said that although these attachments were very strong, the Kṛṣṇa consciousness movement could overcome their influence.

Prabhupāda said that the houses in the Paris suburb, with their attractive fenced-in yards, were excellent. But everything was being wasted for sense gratification. Although a French gentleman may have such a first-class house, garden, wife, bank account, and car, he has no spiritual knowledge. Therefore, he would always remain attached to his first-class possessions, and at the end of his life his great attachment would lead him to take birth as a cockroach or rat or dog within that same house.

As Prabhupāda and the devotees continued walking, Prabhupāda asked Hari-vilāsa how he thought the temple's preaching was faring. Hari-vilāsa said he thought it would be successful but that it might be a good idea to make extra income by starting a business.

"Your business is preaching," Prabhupāda said. "If there are some householders, they can do business."

When Prabhupāda and his party arrived at the temple, they found the devotees eagerly waiting for Prabhupāda's morning *Bhāgavatam* lecture. But there was no time. Prabhupāda had to leave at once for the airport. He was returning to America.

CHAPTER SEVEN

"This Remote Corner Of the World"

Although Śrīla Prabhupāda had been away from America for a year, his Kṛṣṇa consciousness movement had flourished, by Kṛṣṇa's grace, and the devotees' attachment for him had grown. His disciples, having heard reports and seen photos of his triumphant tour of India, had felt inspired to increase their own preaching. In each American center new devotees had been joining and were learning Prabhupāda's teachings from the senior devotees. Already accepting Śrīla Prabhupāda as their spiritual master, hundreds of newcomers were eagerly awaiting initiation.

How different from Prabhupāda's first arrival in America, alone in 1965. Walking the cold streets with no money and no temple, he had been ignored. Sometimes he had thought of quitting, taking a boat back to India. But he had maintained absolute faith. And now, less than six years later, in dozens of ISKCON centers throughout America, hundreds of disciples worshiped him and would throng ecstatically to receive him.

Los Angeles
June 26, 1971

When Prabhupāda had left Los Angeles a year ago, the political turmoil there had troubled his mind, but on returning he found the devotees recovered. Faithfully they were executing his orders to chant publicly, distribute *Back to Godhead* magazine, and worship the Deity of Rukmiṇī-Dvārakādhīśa. In the gorgeously decorated Los Angeles temple, Prabhupāda performed a large initiation ceremony, accepting dozens of new disciples.

On June 27 Śrīla Prabhupāda traveled from Los Angeles to San

Francisco for the fifth annual Ratha-yātrā. Two hundred followers met him at the airport.

"How many devotees do you have?" a reporter asked.

"Unlimited," Prabhupāda said. "Some admit and some don't admit. Admit you are a servant of Lord Kṛṣṇa, and your life will be a success."

After two days in San Francisco, Prabhupāda returned to Los Angeles and on July 16 flew to Detroit. Bhagavān dāsa, Prabhupāda's Governing Body secretary for the Midwest, had preached vigorously in his zone, opening centers in St. Louis, Chicago, and other cities. Almost three hundred devotees, most of whom had never seen Prabhupāda, assembled at the Detroit airport to receive him.

Sureśvara: *Devotees had come from all over the midwestern U.S. and eastern Canada to greet Śrīla Prabhupāda at Detroit's Metro Airport. A red and gold throne stood in the center of the reception room, and the devotees were chanting Hare Kṛṣṇa and dancing, awaiting Prabhupāda's arrival. When the plane finally landed, all bliss broke loose. The disembarkation dolly joined the plane, but we couldn't see Śrīla Prabhupāda. I became anxious—when would he enter the room? Suddenly a cry went up, and I looked around. Devotees were bowing down.*

Urukrama: *Śrīla Prabhupāda entered the room as bright as the sun, and everyone immediately prostrated themselves on the floor. Not like the other times when we bowed down together, but this was like an overwhelming force hit us and we were being thrown to our knees. When I stood up, I couldn't believe my eyes. There was Prabhupāda! Almost everyone in the room was crying.*

Indradyumna: *My first glimpse of Prabhupāda was through the lens of my camera, and I thought he looked just like he did in his pictures. I had only seen him in pictures, and now he looked just like the pictures, only moving. All the devotees began to cry and fall to the ground. It was a transcendental, emotional thing. I was looking, watching all the older devotees—how much love they had for Śrīla Prabhupāda. And I was feeling unqualified and sinful.*

Urukrama: *Prabhupāda appeared powerful, yet at the same time delicate and soft, like a very wonderful flower. As he moved along very slowly, the devotees lined up and made an aisle for him to walk. He walked up to Kīrtanānanda Mahārāja, put a garland around him, and embraced him. Kīrtanānanda Mahārāja was crying tears of ecstasy, and he looked like a little boy next to his father. Then Prabhupāda went to Bhagavān and patted him on the head. Then he embraced Bhagavān, who also began to weep like a little boy who has just seen his father after a very long time.*

Viśvakarmā: *I arrived late. When I got there, I was afraid to look at Śrīla Prabhupāda, because I felt too fallen to look upon the pure representative of the Lord. So I stayed behind a wall of devotees, afraid to look. Finally, I realized this is ridiculous, as the perfection of the eyes is to behold the form of Kṛṣṇa's pure devotee. I raised my head, and I saw him sitting on his* vyāsāsana, *drinking a cup of water. Never had I seen anyone drink water like that—without touching the goblet to their mouth. The water poured from the cup like a shining silver stream, straight into Śrīla Prabhupāda's mouth and throat, and he finished the water in a few swallows. He appeared to be a grand sage from the spiritual realm, and as everyone chanted, he looked around at the devotees, smiling with great pleasure. Everyone was overwhelmed with transcendental joy, and I joined with over half the devotees in weeping.*

Prabhupāda began speaking.

"This is very satisfactory that so many devotees, boys and girls, are taking part in this great movement, Kṛṣṇa consciousness movement. It is a very important movement, because it is correcting the human civilization. It is a great defect in the modern civilization—people are accepting this body as self. And based on this mistake in the foundation, everything is going wrong. Accepting this body as the self is the beginning of all problems. The great philosophers, scientists, theologians, and thoughtful men do not know what is the defect.

"Recently I was in Moscow. So I had a nice talk with a professor of Indology, Professor Kotovsky. He was speaking that, 'Swamiji, after this annihilation of this body, everything is finished.' So I was astonished that a learned professor, posing himself in a very responsible post, had no idea about the soul and the body—how they are different, how the soul is migrating from one body to another. . . ."

As Prabhupāda spoke, a voice announced over the public address system that the departure lounge had to be cleared for the next flight. "They are speaking about ourselves?" Prabhupāda asked. "We shall stop? All right. Let us go."

That evening, in the temple room of Detroit's ISKCON center, Śrīla Prabhupāda sat on his *vyāsāsana* before the deities of Lord Jagannātha,

Subhadrā, and Balarāma. While a devotee led the *kīrtana*, Prabhupāda played his *karatālas*, looking around the room at his disciples. He was nodding his head, pleased to see them dancing and chanting. After the *kīrtana*, he lectured.

"Just see how their characters are being formed, how they are becoming purified, how their faces are becoming brighter. It is practical. So our request is, take full advantage of the center—you come here. It is being guided by one of my best disciples, Bhagavān dāsa. So he and others will help you. Please come regularly to this temple and take advantage of it."

After his lecture, Prabhupāda asked for questions. Bahulāśva raised his hand. "Śrīla Prabhupāda, what is the thing that will please you the most?"

"Chant Hare Kṛṣṇa," Prabhupāda replied, and the devotees spontaneously cried out, "Jaya! Jaya!"

Prabhupāda: "That is the simplest thing. You are chanting. I am very much pleased. That's all. I came to your country to chant that you would chant also along with me. You are helping me by chanting, so I am pleased.

"But this tendency is very nice, that you want to please me. That is very good. And to please me is not very difficult. Caitanya Mahāprabhu said that 'Under My order, every one of you go preach and become spiritual master.' And what is that order? The order is, 'Whomever you meet, you talk to him about Kṛṣṇa.' "

Prabhupāda emphasized that if one wanted to preach and represent Kṛṣṇa, then he could not change the message of Kṛṣṇa, but must repeat what Kṛṣṇa says. "I have come here for the first time," Prabhupāda continued, "but before me, Bhagavān dāsa, he has organized. And what is his credit? He has presented things as I told him. That's all. This is wonderful. In Los Angeles also a program is going on very nicely. My disciple in charge there is Karandhara. He is present here. He is simply doing what I instruct, and he is doing very nicely—first class. Everyone who comes, they come and are enchanted by the temple, with the activities, with the disciples. So this is the way. This is called *paramparā* system. Don't concoct."

As Prabhupāda was leaving the temple that evening, the mother of one of his disciples approached him. "You know," she said, "these boys actually *worship* you!"

"Yes," Prabhupāda said, "that is our system. I am also worshiping my Guru Mahārāja." The devotees around Prabhupāda looked at one another and smiled. Although the woman had tried to make it appear extraordinary that Prabhupāda's disciples worshiped him, Prabhupāda had taken it casually. One *must* worship the *guru*. It was the Vaiṣṇava standard and nothing to wonder at.

* * *

Śrīla Prabhupāda had so many centers in the U.S. that to visit each one was not practical. During his year in India, many new centers had opened—on the West Coast, in Florida, Texas, the Midwest, the East. Prabhupāda said he had more establishments than a wealthy businessman, and more residences. Were he to stay at each of his "houses," he quipped, he couldn't visit them all in a year. And especially to Indian audiences he would cite the monthly expenditures for his centers.

Though proud of ISKCON's growth, Prabhupāda was never proud on his own account; he never considered using ISKCON for his own enjoyment. Whenever he visited a center, his quarters were usually an apartment arranged at the last minute, often fraught with annoyances like noisy neighbors and incompetent cooks. At seventy-five years, his constant traveling was hardly an arrangement for his health and comfort.

Prabhupāda never felt complacent over the small success his society enjoyed, nor would he claim the credit for that success. Rather, he said, it was due to the mercy of his spiritual master and the previous spiritual masters. ISKCON still had but little influence in the world; people considered it a small, exotic religious sect. But by the blessings of the previous *ācāryas*, it was growing. Prabhupāda was initiating more and more disciples, and the potential was unlimited.

One of Lord Caitanya's chief followers, Jīva Gosvāmī, had warned that a spiritual master should not accept many disciples; many neophyte disciples would bring suffering to the spiritual master. Yet on Prabhupāda's U.S. tour during the summer of 1971, he initiated more disciples than ever before. As Lord Caitanya's empowered representative, he wanted to increase the number of devotees more and more. He was aware of the risk, but he was also aware of the great need. As he had written in *The Nectar of Devotion,*

> The one point is that without increasing the number of disciples, there is no propagation of the cult of Kṛṣṇa consciousness. Therefore, sometimes even at a risk, a *sannyāsī* in the line of Lord Caitanya Mahāprabhu may

accept even a person who is not thoroughly fit to become a disciple. Later on, by the mercy of such a bona fide spiritual master, the disciple is gradually elevated. However, if one increases the number of disciples simply for some prestige or false honor, he will surely fall down in the matter of executing Kṛṣṇa consciousness.

Śrīla Prabhupāda's test of a prospective disciple's readiness for initiation was standard: the candidate must have followed the four rules and chanted sixteen rounds daily for at least six months and have the recommendation of the temple president and local G.B.C. secretary. Prabhupāda accepted anyone who fulfilled these conditions, and he expected the disciple to remain sincere and true to the vows of initiation.

Despite Prabhupāda's growing number of disciples, he intimately touched each of their hearts. Although a few disciples enjoyed extended association with him, most of his hundreds of disciples saw him only from afar. Yet each of them was certain that Prabhupāda was his own. Each could say "my spiritual master." Each could say "Prabhupāda" and feel close to their dearest friend and well-wisher, the one who was saving them from death. They knew that Prabhupāda was the direct representative of Kṛṣṇa and the most empowered *ācārya* of Lord Caitanya's message. Those who were sincere knew without doubt that their connection with Prabhupāda was transcendental, not to be interrupted or limited by physical or geographical considerations. If they surrendered to Prabhupāda's orders, Kṛṣṇa within their hearts would help them advance. If they were sincere, Kṛṣṇa would help them become better disciples of Śrīla Prabhupāda.

The devotees' love for Prabhupāda was not a vague sentiment. He was engaging them in Kṛṣṇa's service, and they were directly experiencing the transcendental results. Only a devotee, however, could understand Śrīla Prabhupāda's personality or the depth of his disciples' attraction for him or the debt they owed him. No wonder onlookers at the Detroit airport had not understood the apparently delirious devotees in their blissful reception of Śrīla Prabhupāda.

* * *

New York City
July 19, 1971

After Detroit, Prabhupāda visited Boston and then flew to New York, where another large group of devotees had gathered. The *New York Daily News* covered his airport arrival with photos and an article: "Swami, How They Love You."

Bhavānanda, the New York temple president, had decorated the temple room of the Brooklyn center with bright colors. Prabhupāda's *vyāsāsana* was a special creation of plaids, stripes, and checks in fuchsia, lime, black, white, and red. Prabhupāda liked it very much.

Two hundred devotees—many having waited for more than a year to be initiated—converged on the Brooklyn temple, and Prabhupāda held initiations for five consecutive days, initiating around two dozen disciples each day. One after another, the young men and women would approach Prabhupāda on his multicolored *vyāsāsana* to receive their initiation beads and spiritual names. Those receiving the *brāhmaṇa* initiation went one by one to see Prabhupāda in his room and receive the Gāyatrī *mantra.*

Madhumaṅgala: *I went to Prabhupāda's room and offered obeisances. "Come here," he said. So I went and sat close to him. He began teaching me the Gāyatrī* mantra, *and I was looking up at him. The sun was right behind his head. He looked like a mountain, like the Himalayas, and I was like a mole, a stone. He was very big, and I seemed very insignificant.*

Rikthānanda: *Prabhupāda turned to face me, and his eyes seemed like limitless pools of an entrancing liquid. I knew he was focused always on Kṛṣṇa, and his eyes were a reflection of that happiness. He said something to me, and I said, "No, sir." Saying "sir" to him seemed natural, and he seemed to be happy that I had said it. Then in a very clear, soft, steady voice, he began to teach me the Gāyatrī* mantra. *Then he took the sacred thread and put it around my neck and across my shoulder, very gracefully and with such precision in his movements. "Now," he said, "you are a* brāhmaṇa."

Daivī-śakti: *Prabhupāda had the Gāyatrī* mantra *written on a small piece of paper, and as he was teaching it to me he had his eyes closed. I would repeat it word for word after him. When he got to the third line, however, instead of saying* gurudevāya *he said the word from the fifth line. I didn't know whether to follow what he had said or just say what was on the paper. So I said what was on the paper, and then Prabhupāda immediately realized what he had done and changed it. But I suddenly realized that the perfect chanting of* mantras *was not so significant. Prabhupāda was fully absorbed in thinking of Kṛṣṇa, and although there may have been some apparent flaw in his pronunciation, he was perfect, regardless. I saw that the real perfection of devotional service was to follow Prabhupāda.*

After I received my Gāyatrī mantra, *I asked Prabhupāda if I could ask him some questions, and he said yes. "Śrīla Prabhupāda," I said, "I haven't been able to serve you in rapt attention. What can I do to serve you?" I was praying he would give me a special service to do for him personally. "Chant Hare Kṛṣṇa," was all he said.*

"Is there anything more?" I asked. He said, "Are you married?" I said, "Yes." So he said, "Serve your husband."

I said, "My husband and I don't get along." So he said, "Be a pūjārī*—there are so many things."*

His answer seemed to solve all my difficulty. First and foremost was to chant Hare Kṛṣṇa. And in addition to that, there are so many other services. If you don't do one of them, then go on to the next one—"There are so many things." When he said those words, it relieved all my anxiety.

In New York Prabhupāda lectured gravely and authoritatively from *Śrīmad-Bhāgavatam*, stressing surrender to Kṛṣṇa through surrendering to the Kṛṣṇa consciousness movement. Unlike any other *Bhāgavatam* lecturer, Prabhupāda was able to offer a movement, a society, and a way of life that were fully Kṛṣṇa conscious and that gave any interested person practical entrance into the devotional service of the Lord.

Someone asked how a person who had been very sinful could be relieved of his *karma*, and Prabhupāda replied simply, "Come and live with us. That's all. Is it very difficult? Our students—they are living with us. You simply come and live with us, and you are free from all *karma*. Is it difficult? Then do that. We shall give you food, we shall give you shelter, we shall give you nice philosophy. If you want to marry, we shall give you a good wife. What do you want more? So come and live with us. That's all."

Prabhupāda stressed this same point in his lectures: if a person seeking spiritual fulfillment lived and served with the ISKCON devotees, even material fulfillment would come.

"These Kṛṣṇa conscious boys and girls—in sixty centers—they are living in the best houses. They are eating the best food. They are in the best consciousness. They have got the best hope. Everything best. Their feature of body is best. What material happiness do you want more than this?

They have got wife, children, happiness, home—everything full. So material happiness is nothing to a Kṛṣṇa conscious person. Material happiness will roll at his feet, saying, 'Please take me, please take me.' There is no need of asking for it. Simply be steady and ask Kṛṣṇa, 'Please engage me in Your service.' Then your satisfaction will automatically come. Don't bother for material happiness."

Nanda-kiśora asked, "What happens to a person out on the street if we just give him one Simply Wonderful* or some *prasādam*?"

Prabhupāda: "Then it is wonderful—simply wonderful. (The devotees laughed.) He has not tasted such wonderful sweet in his life. Therefore, you give him wonderful, and because he is eating that wonderful sweet, one day he will come to your temple and become wonderful. Therefore it is simply wonderful. So go on distributing this Simply Wonderful. Your philosophy is simply wonderful, your *prasādam* is simply wonderful, you are simply wonderful. And your Kṛṣṇa is simply wonderful. The whole process is simply wonderful. Kṛṣṇa acts wonderfully, and it is acting wonderfully. Who can deny it?"

Kīrtanānanda Mahārāja: "Prabhupāda is simply wonderful."

While Prabhupāda continued in New York, poised to leave for London in a few days, his secretary mentioned that many U.S. centers were still vying for his presence. Prabhupāda casually remarked that if any center could arrange a good lecture program and pay his travel expenses plus one thousand dollars, then he would go there before leaving for London.

Hearing this, the devotees in Gainesville, Florida, determined to meet Prabhupāda's transcendental challenge. The temple president, Hṛdayānanda, assigned an uninitiated devotee, David Liberman, to find a sponsor at the University of Florida willing to pay one thousand dollars for Prabhupāda to come and speak. David visited every student organization on campus until he found a donor.

Prabhupāda agreed to come, even though his secretary informed him that the flight would lay over two hours in Atlanta and then continue to Jacksonville, a one-and-a-half-hour car ride from Gainesville.

* * *

*A sweet made from powdered milk, butter, and sugar and offered to Lord Kṛṣṇa.

Atlanta
July 29, 1971

The ten residents of the recently opened Atlanta temple arranged to receive Prabhupāda during his layover at the Atlanta airport. They prepared a large feast and decorated the Eastern Airlines V.I.P. lounge with fruits, flowers, and garlands.

Bill Ogle: *Although Śrīla Prabhupāda was not big physically, he immediately captured the consciousness of the entire Atlanta airport when he entered. Everyone was watching as he walked, with his head held high, his cane moving gracefully with every step. The airport is one of the busiest in the country, but everyone who saw Prabhupāda looked at him in amazement. Airport officials voluntarily began clearing a path for Prabhupāda to walk. But what was even more amazing was that he was so submissive to such insignificant disciples as we.*

Prabhupāda entered the V.I.P. lounge with his disciples and about twenty Indian guests. Confronting the portable *vyāsāsana* atop a marble table, Prabhupāda declined; the seat seemed unsteady. But the devotees assured him that it was sturdy, so Prabhupāda climbed up, sat down, and began leading a *kīrtana.* After speaking for about fifteen minutes, Prabhupāda concluded his lecture.

"This is not sentimental chanting, but it is based on the soundest philosophy, Vedic literatures. We have got so many books, and you can buy them in our book store. Where is the book store?"

There was a long pause. The devotees had remembered fruits, flowers, the chair, the feast, invitations to the Indians—but they had forgotten Prabhupāda's books. Prabhupāda continued to wait for an answer to his question, until finally the senior disciple, Janamejaya, replied, "Prabhupāda, we usually have a book store."

"Hmm" was all Prabhupāda said. Again a long silence. "So," Prabhupāda said, looking to the audience, "any questions?"

Prabhupāda chatted with the Indians, asking their names and where they were from in India. Most of them were young men with families and treated him respectfully, like a grandfather or a revered swami. One Indian man, about thirty-five, mentioned that he was getting his Ph.D. in biology.

"Oh, biology," Prabhupāda said. "Hmm, poor frogs." Everyone in the lounge—except the biologist—burst into laughter.

"No, no," the biologist protested, embarrassed. "Why 'poor frogs'?"

"Because you are killing," Prabhupāda said.

"But it is for the advancement of knowledge," said the biologist. "So it is worthwhile. It is for the advancement of knowledge."

"All right," said Prabhupāda, "if I ask you now, will you give your body for the advancement of knowledge?" Everyone in the room began to laugh.

"Yes! Yes, I would!" the man replied. But the more he protested, repeating, "Yes, I would!" the more ridiculous he seemed, and the harder everyone laughed.

"How many species of life are there?" Prabhupāda asked.

"Fifty million," the biologist replied.

"Oh?" said Prabhupāda. "You have seen them all?"

"No."

"How many have you seen?"

"Perhaps five thousand."

"And you are wrong," Prabhupāda said. "There are 8,400,000 species of life. We have scientific knowledge from the *Vedas*."

Bill Ogle: *After Prabhupāda took* prasāda, *we performed a play for him. The play was "The* Brāhmaṇa *and the Cobbler." I played Viṣṇu. It was terrible. I had to be Viṣṇu, and my wife had to be Lakṣmī. I was lying down as Lord Viṣṇu, and my wife was massaging my feet. Prabhupāda kept looking at me, and I thought he must be thinking, "Who is this rascal playing Viṣṇu?" My feeling was, "This is not very good. I shouldn't be doing this." I was very embarrassed to be in front of Prabhupāda like that.*

Jayasena was Nārada Muni, and he offered obeisances about a hundred times throughout the play. Because Prabhupāda was there, Jayasena was constantly offering obeisances to everyone and anything. So although he was playing Nārada Muni, he offered obeisances to the cobbler. But some of the Indians spoke up. They were a little taken aback that Nārada Muni, such a great saint, was offering obeisances to a cobbler, who is ordinarily a very low-class person.

So at this point Prabhupāda interrupted and began to explain. "Actually," he said, "it is all right that Nārada Muni has offered obeisances to the cobbler, because the cobbler is a Vaiṣṇava. Any Vaiṣṇava can receive obeisances, more than a brāhmaṇa.*" He continued, narrating the play. He told the story, and we continued acting. It was ecstatic.*

As Prabhupāda was leaving the lounge to board his flight for Jacksonville, a lady in a wheelchair, the mother of one of the devotees in Atlanta, raised herself up and threw herself at Prabhupāda's feet. With tears in her eyes, she cried out, "I am dying of cancer. Save me! Save me!" Śrīla Prabhupāda bent down and put his hand on her head. "That is all right," he said comfortingly. "That is all right."

As Prabhupāda, garlanded with red roses and magnolias, walked down the corridor toward his plane, the devotees thought that Prabhupāda appeared majestic, like a king. He emanated a golden effulgence, and he seemed powerful, yet humble. The devotees felt spiritual strength and pledged to follow Prabhupāda's teachings. They last glimpsed him walking across the airfield toward the small plane that would take him to Jacksonville. His saffron silk *dhotī* and *kurtā* blowing in the breeze, he turned to them and waved.

* * *

Gainesville
July 29, 1971

Śrīla Prabhupāda asked how fast the car was going and how long it would take them to get to Gainesville. Sixty-five miles per hour, the driver said; it would take an hour and a half. Prabhupāda observed the scenery along the highway—pine forests, marshes, exotic birds, an occasional armadillo foraging near the highway. Lotuses and lilies grew wild in the canals along the roadside, and bright sunshine warmed the clear air.

Gainesville was a side trip for Prabhupāda, a special day of preaching. He had left Śyāmasundara, his secretary, in New York and brought with him only Aravinda, his servant. He had come for a day to bring the mercy of Lord Caitanya to yet another city. When the devotees had picked him up at the airport, he had appeared grave. But on catching sight of the devotees he had smiled wonderfully, and then, turning to Hṛdayānanda, he had asked, "Which way?" He was like a transcendental fighter, asking to be pointed toward the battle.

Prabhupāda walked along a flower-sprinkled pathway and into the temple, a rented house near the University of Florida campus. In the temple room he stood a moment, studying a crude but sincerely executed painting of Lord Caitanya and His associates. Hṛdayānanda asked Prabhupāda if he would like to rest, and he nodded. While the devotees performed *kīrtana*, Prabhupāda retired to his room, returning later to sit on the large blue velvet *vyāsāsana* in the small temple room. In addition to Prabhupāda's disciples from Gainesville, Miami, Tallahassee, and New Orleans, many university students and other guests were also present.

"It is so nice to see so many young boys and girls here," Śrīla Prabhupāda began, "in this remote corner of the world, so far away from the birthplace of Lord Caitanya."

Prabhupāda lectured about the saving grace of chanting the holy name of the Lord. One of his disciples, he said, had been present when his mother was dying. "Because he had been telling her about Kṛṣṇa and Hare Kṛṣṇa, she said to her son in her last words, 'Where is your Kṛṣṇa? Is He here now?' And then she died." For her uttering the holy name and thinking of Kṛṣṇa, Prabhupāda said, she would go to the spiritual world.

After Prabhupāda finished his talk, a girl reporter from the university newspaper raised her hand. "I see almost all young people here," she said. "Why is that?"

Prabhupāda replied with a question: "Why are there so many young people in the university?'

The girl reflected a moment, "Well . . . I guess that's the age for education."

"Yes," Prabhupāda said, "so this is the age for Kṛṣṇa consciousness. You cannot teach an old dog new tricks."

The engagement for which Prabhupāda had come, and for which the University of Florida was paying a thousand dollars, was to be that afternoon on campus at the Plaza of the Americas. When Prabhupāda arrived, several hundred students were gathered near the temporary stage, sitting casually on the grass, lounging beneath the fragrant magnolia trees. The sky was overcast, and rain threatened.

As more students gathered, the crowd grew to five hundred. Then just as Prabhupāda was about to speak, a light drizzle began to fall, and Hṛdayānanda came onstage to hold an umbrella over Śrīla Prabhupāda.

Prabhupāda, sitting on his *vyāsāsana*, said softly into the microphone, "Someone is smoking," and the students politely extinguished their cigarettes. No sooner did Prabhupāda begin his lecture, however, than a dog started yapping. Prabhupāda paused. "Who is that dog?" he asked. When the dog persisted, Śrīla Prabhupāda said, "He also wants to talk." Finally the barking stopped, and so did the rain. But Hṛdayānanda continued to hold the umbrella over Prabhupāda's head.

While riding in the car back to the temple, Prabhupāda asked to hear the tape recording of his lecture. When he heard the dog barking at the beginning of his talk, he laughed.

"Prabhupāda," Hṛdayānanda said, "your lecture was wonderful. Everyone liked it. The students liked it, the devotees liked it, the professors liked it."

"All right," Prabhupāda said. "Hare Kṛṣṇa."

Śrīla Prabhupāda's day of preaching was not over yet. Next was an evening television interview.

The interviewer had done some preparatory reading, and he introduced Śrīla Prabhupāda by first describing who Kṛṣṇa was, according to Vedic literature, and how Śrīla Prabhupāda was in the disciplic succession from Lord Caitanya. When the interviewer asked Prabhupāda for an introductory statement, Prabhupāda explained, "The Kṛṣṇa consciousness movement is trying to invoke in all people the original consciousness that we are a part and parcel of Kṛṣṇa."

When the interviewer asked Prabhupāda, "Who is your spiritual master?" Prabhupāda lowered his head humbly and stated the full name of his Guru Mahārāja, "Oṁ Viṣṇupāda Paramahaṁsa Parivrājakācārya Bhaktisiddhānta Sarasvatī Gosvāmī Mahārāja Prabhupāda."

The interviewer, however, seemed bent on controversy. "In what way, sir, may I ask, did you think and do you think right now that the teaching of love of God that you are preaching is different and perhaps better than the teachings of love of God that were being conducted in this country and have been conducted in the rest of the world for centuries?"

Śrīla Prabhupāda: "This teaching is the most authorized. That is a fact. We are following in the footsteps of Lord Caitanya. He is accepted by us, according to the authority of Vedic religion, to be personally Kṛṣṇa Himself. For example, you are the expert in this establishment. If someone is doing something under your guidance and if you personally teach him,

'Do like this,' that is very authorized. So when Lord Caitanya taught God consciousness, God Himself was teaching."

Prabhupāda had answered positively, avoiding the sectarian dispute the interviewer had invited. Yet repeatedly the interviewer tried to involve him in a controversy. He seemed to want Prabhupāda to appear arrogant, sectarian, and anti-American. Prabhupāda, however, insisted he was not opposed to any other religion and that anyone in the world could chant the name of God as it appeared in his religion.

Interviewer: "But there must have been an element of dissatisfaction on your part with the way Godhead was being professed in this part of the world before you came. Otherwise, there would have been no sense in your being here."

Śrīla Prabhupāda: "It is not just this part of the world. Practically every part of the world has very little interest in God. They have more interest in dog."

Prabhupāda's answers were strong and philosophically strong. The interviewer, trying his professional best, again attempted to find some fault.

Interviewer: "It seems to me, sir, as interpreted in your writings, that there is a very high emphasis placed on the relationship between the individual and God."

Śrīla Prabhupāda: "Yes. That is found everywhere."

Interviewer: "Yes, but you place more emphasis on that relationship than on the relationship between one individual and another. Am I right in that?"

Śrīla Prabhupāda: "We have to establish, first of all, our lost relationship with God. Then we can understand what is our relationship between one individual and another. If the central point is missing, then there is practically no relation. You are an American, and another is an American, and both of you feel American nationality because the center is America. So unless you understand God, you cannot understand who I am, nor can I understand who you are."

Interviewer: "I think that in this part of the world, in the Western world, we place a great deal of emphasis on religion in the ways it gets one man to deal with another man—the ethic of religion. Now in the Kṛṣṇa consciousness movement . . ."

Śrīla Prabhupāda: "We are not concerned how one man deals with another man."

Interviewer: "Isn't that part of your Kṛṣṇa consciousness movement?"

Śrīla Prabhupāda: "No, this is not important. Because we know as soon as one knows how to deal with God, he will automatically deal very nicely with others."

Interviewer: "But let's take the Christian religion for an example. You know the ten commandments? There is a heavy emphasis in the ten commandments on the relationships between one human being and another: 'Thou shalt not steal. Thou shalt not kill.' You know, that sort of thing."

Śrīla Prabhupāda: "But I say that Jesus Christ never said and never meant that 'Thou shalt not kill' refers to only human beings. Where is that evidence? Jesus Christ never said that 'Thou shalt not kill' refers only to human beings. Thou shalt not kill any animal."

Interviewer: "Any life?"

Śrīla Prabhupāda: "Any life. That is religion."

Interviewer: "It has never been interpreted that way."

Śrīla Prabhupāda: "You have interpreted it differently, but he said, 'Thou shalt not kill.' He never said, 'Thou shalt not kill amongst human beings.' Why do you interpret it that way?"

Prabhupāda had given the TV interviewer the very thing he was after, controversy, but because it was not desirable controversy the interviewer promptly dropped it. Instead, he asked Prabhupāda how one could recognize a true follower of Kṛṣṇa consciousness by his behavior.

"He'd be a perfect gentleman," Prabhupāda said, "that's all.... Therefore, I prohibit my disciples to eat meat."

Interviewer: "To eat meat?"

Śrīla Prabhupāda: "Yes. And therefore I prohibit illicit sex life. Therefore I prohibit intoxication. They do not even smoke, what to speak of other intoxication."

When Prabhupāda said that whoever observed these four rules would become a perfect gentleman, the interviewer asked whether there was a place for women in the religion. Prabhupāda replied that women and men had the same rights and followed the same principles. The interviewer asked whether Prabhupāda was encouraged or discouraged, and Prabhupāda said he was encouraged because so many devotees were joining. The interviewer doubted that many were joining, since out of two hundred million Americans, only two dozen devotees were present in the TV studio. "When you sell diamonds," Prabhupāda replied, "you cannot expect that everyone will purchase."

As a final question, the interviewer asked if Prabhupāda had any major complaints about American society.

Śrīla Prabhupāda: "I have no complaint. These boys and girls are very nice. I am, rather, encouraged that these boys and girls are hankering after something nice. They are frustrated. So now, since they have the best thing, they are coming."

The interviewer asked Śrīla Prabhupāda and his followers to chant Hare Kṛṣṇa, and within half a minute they were off the air. The hot studio lights went out, and the engineers started talking among themselves. The interviewer bid Śrīla Prabhupāda a polite farewell—he had no intention of continuing their talk—but Śrīla Prabhupāda continued preaching. On-camera or off-camera made no difference to him. He saw the interviewer not merely as a television personality but as someone to receive Kṛṣṇa's mercy.

The two had been sitting very closely for the interview, and Prabhupāda now leaned toward the interviewer and said, "Let me ask you one question. If you have some disease and you want to cure this disease, what is the best way to go about it? By asking a friend or by going to a medical doctor and asking how to cure this disease? Would you go to a friend?"

The man replied, "Yes." Prabhupāda shook his head, "You would go to a friend?" Again the man said, "Yes."

The interviewer was not concentrating, so Prabhupāda patiently repeated his example. "Try to understand," he said. "If you have some disease, then would you go to a medical doctor or would you go to a friend?" The man could not grasp the point, so Prabhupāda answered, "No, you would not go to a friend. You would go to a physician—one who knows the answer. That is the spiritual master." They talked a while longer, and finally Prabhupāda and the devotees left.

It was almost midnight, and Prabhupāda went to his room. When he had first arrived in Gainesville he had agreed to initiate the five eligible candidates and had even taken their *japa* beads. But now the day had passed, there had been no initiation, and Prabhupāda still had five strands of beads. Joseph and Sam, who had come all the way from New Orleans, and David Liberman and his wife, Adrienne, and a Gainesville boy named Gary were all in anxiety. They had stayed up, talking among themselves, wondering whether Śrīla Prabhupāda would hold an initiation ceremony in the morning, before he left.

Aravinda told them there would be no time for a ceremony in the morning, but that he would ask Śrīla Prabhupāda when they could have their beads back. He went to Prabhupāda's room, leaving the devotees to sit and talk about Śrīla Prabhupāda. When Aravinda returned, he surprised everyone by announcing, "Prabhupāda is going to give you your beads now. He is going to give you your initiation in his room." The devotees excitedly hurried to Śrīla Prabhupāda's room.

Prabhupāda sat on his bed. He wore no shirt, only his *dhotī*, which he had pushed up high on his thighs and tucked under himself, like a loincloth or *gamchā*. His body was smooth and glowing. The devotees sat on the floor around his bed while he held their beads in his hands and chanted.

Prabhupāda handed Gary his beads. "So your name is now Dharma dāsa. This means 'one who is a strict follower of all religious principles.' "

Dharma: *I was actually very nervous, and I was practically shaking, because I was afraid I would do something wrong in front of Śrīla Prabhupāda. I was so nervous practically I couldn't even hear properly. But I was very happy to have been accepted by Śrīla Prabhupāda. I knew, of course, there was no question of ever leaving the movement now. I never wanted to leave anyway, but now this was official. Even if I had considered it before, now there was no question of it.*

Then there was Joseph from New Orleans. "What is his name?" Prabhupāda asked Aravinda. Aravinda read from a sheet, "Bhāgavata dāsa." Prabhupāda smiled and said, "Oh, Bhāgavata dāsa. Very good. There are two things. There is the book *bhāgavata—Śrīmad-Bhāgavatam* and *Bhagavad-gītā*—and the person *bhāgavata*, who follows perfectly those teachings. He is a living manifestation of the book *bhāgavata*. And you are Bhāgavata dāsa. That means you are the servant of the book *bhāgavata* and the person *bhāgavata*.

Bhāgavata: *I always wanted a name that meant I was the servant of the* guru. *So when I heard this, I was very happy. Prabhupāda started to hand me my beads, but then he pulled them back and asked, "And what are the four regulative principles?" So I told him, and he said, "Very good."*

Then he went to hand me my beads again, but again he pulled them back. He asked, "How many rounds do you chant?" I was very proud, because I had been chanting twenty rounds a day for about five months, so I sat up real straight and said, "You're supposed to chant sixteen rounds a day, Śrīla Prabhupāda. But I chant twenty."

Śrīla Prabhupāda just turned away from me and said, "That's all right." It was like he was saying, "Don't get puffed up." Then he turned to me and said, "Here are your beads."

Handing Dave his beads, Prabhupāda said, "Your name is Amarendra. This means 'the best of the immortals.' " He named Adrienne "Gāyatrī dāsī" and Sam "Suvrata."

When Suvrata stood and Prabhupāda noticed he was not wearing neck beads, he withheld the chanting beads and said, "You have no neck beads? Where are your neck beads?" Prabhupāda turned to Bhāgavata dāsa. "You also have no neck beads?" Bhāgavata thought that Prabhupāda was going to take his chanting beads back, so he hid them against his stomach. Then Prabhupāda turned to the senior devotees in the room, criticizing. "What is the matter with you?" he said sternly. "You are leaders, and you don't know these things? Don't you know that you must put neck beads in giving initiation?"

The senior devotees were frightened by Prabhupāda's anger. "We are sorry, Prabhupāda," someone said. "Tomorrow for the fire *yajña* they will have neck beads."

"Yes," Prabhupāda said, "you cannot do the fire *yajña* without neck beads. They must have neck beads."

Although it was midnight, Prabhupāda asked if the devotees had any questions. Bhāgavata dāsa raised his hand. "How is it that we are on a transcendental platform but sometimes we are affected by the three modes of nature?"

"It is just like you are on a boat," Prabhupāda replied. "If you are on the boat, then I cannot say you are not on the boat. Is it not? So you are on the transcendental boat. Therefore, you are on the transcendental platform. You cannot say that you are not. But the waves are coming, and they are rocking the boat." Prabhupāda gestured with his hands like a boat rocking. "So the waves of the material nature are coming," he continued, "and they are rocking the boat. But when you become an expert boatman, then even in the greatest storm you can stay steady and steer the boat, and it will not rock."

"Well, how does one become an expert boatman?" Bhāgavata asked.

"You become expert," Prabhupāda replied, "by becoming enthusiastic, sincere, confident, determined, and patient." Seeing Bhāgavata's anxious face, Prabhupāda added, "And you must be patient. Everything will come in due course."

Sitting informally on the bed, in his abbreviated *dhotī*, Prabhupāda had answered Bhāgavata's questions in such a way as to fully satisfy all the devotees. The devotees were already satisfied just to be with Prabhupāda, but by his answers to their questions not only they but all devotees could take encouragement and be satisfied. They would tell the others what he had said, and everyone would cherish these instructions of Śrīla Prabhupāda.

Amarendra also had a question. Amarendra was intense and impassioned, and so was his inquiry. Before becoming a devotee, he had been a leader of campus radicals. Now he wanted to bring that same intensity to bear in spreading Kṛṣṇa consciousness. "Śrīla Prabhupāda," Amarendra asked, "how can we make them take to this Kṛṣṇa consciousness? What can we say when we go to preach to people? What can we say that will make them take it?" His voice was heavy and forceful, demanding action.

"You simply ask them to please chant Hare Kṛṣṇa," Prabhupāda replied. "Whether they take or not, that is their business. That is between them and Kṛṣṇa. But you have done your business. You have done your duty for Kṛṣṇa by simply asking them, 'Please chant Hare Kṛṣṇa.' "

"How do we take our minds away from *māyā* and bring them to Kṛṣṇa?" Rādhā-vallabha asked.

"You must *drag* the mind," Prabhupāda said. "You must *drag* the mind back to the sound vibration of Hare Kṛṣṇa, Hare Kṛṣṇa, Kṛṣṇa Kṛṣṇa, Hare Hare." And again he repeated, "You must *drag* the mind back to the sound vibration."

"All right." Prabhupāda looked around. "You are satisfied now?"

The devotees responded, "Yes, Śrīla Prabhupāda. Thank you very much." Then they all left. It had been the greatest day and night of their lives, they all agreed, and they would never forget it.

While Prabhupāda rode to the Jacksonville airport in a car with a few disciples, the other devotees followed in their van, bringing the *vyāsāsana* from the temple for Prabhupāda to use at the airport. Śrīla Prabhupāda closed his eyes and rested as he rode, and the devotees in the back seat of his car ate the remnants of his *prasādam*.

Hṛdayānanda: *It was my idea to bring Prabhupāda's* vyāsāsana *to the airport. I was thinking, "How can my spiritual master sit in the same seats that* karmīs *sit on?" It just seemed impossible. How could Prabhupāda put his lotus body, how could he sit, on the same seats as the* karmīs? *I was very agitated by that. Amarendra had built the* vyāsāsana, *and he used to build everything like a tank. The* vyāsāsana *must have weighed several hundred pounds. It took four or five devotees to carry it.*

So Prabhupāda arrived first, and the vyāsāsana *wasn't there. By the time he got to his boarding gate and the* vyāsāsana *still wasn't there, I was in anxiety, because I didn't want him to sit in a regular seat. I thought it would be a great offense on my part. Then as I looked down the long, long airport corridor, I saw six* brahmacārīs, *half of them without their shoes on, lugging Prabhupāda's* vyāsāsana *down the corridor. It was such an absurd scene. Prabhupāda just stood there looking in disbelief and disgust, and finally several sweating, groaning* brahmacārīs *came and dropped the* vyāsāsana *down in front of Prabhupāda. Prabhupāda just looked at it with disdain, walked past it, and sat down in the ordinary seat.*

While most of the devotees sat at Prabhupāda's feet, chanting the *Gurv-aṣṭaka* prayers to the spiritual master, Hṛdayānanda was preaching to the people who were standing and watching the spectacle. He had some of Śrīla Prabhupāda's books, and he was trying to distribute them. Prabhupāda gave more attention to this preaching than to the devotees seated at his feet.

* * *

Having visited half a dozen cities in a little more than a month's time, Śrīla Prabhupāda was planning next to visit London. Clearly, his field had become the entire world. And his traveling was the practical enactment of his conviction that Kṛṣṇa consciousness should be given to people everywhere.

By Prabhupāda's wide traveling and bold preaching, the old idea that the *Bhagavad-gītā* and Kṛṣṇa were only for the Hindus had become an anachronism, a prejudice. Barriers of race, religion, nation, sex, class—all were now down. The Hindu saying that a swami should not cross the ocean had become a superstition, intended perhaps to protect lesser swamis but certainly never to restrict the message of the Absolute Truth from being spread.

Caitanya Mahāprabhu's express desire was that in every town and village of the world His name be heard, and no Vedic injunction could prohibit that. Of course, the Vedic literatures advised a devotee to live in a secluded place and avoid worldly men and women, and they advised a devotee not to disturb the minds of innocent persons or preach to the faithless. According to one Vedic injunction, a devotee should not even see the face of a nonbeliever. Such rules and regulations, however, intended mainly for the protection and purification of the neophytes, were superseded by a stalwart *ācārya* acting on the higher principle of compassion.

And in support of that higher principle Lord Kṛṣṇa had promised, "My devotee shall never be vanquished." The surrendered preacher, taking up Lord Caitanya's highest order, would be immunized against contamination, despite regular contact with worldly persons. Even at the risk of his own spiritual life, the preacher approached worldly people, and in return Kṛṣṇa protected him.

Prabhupāda was merciful to everyone, everywhere. Therefore he was *jagad-guru,* the spiritual master for the entire world. To become *jagad-guru* didn't mean to claim that one was better than everyone else or that he was the best *guru* in the world. *Jagad-guru* meant that, like Nārada Muni, a preacher of Kṛṣṇa consciousness went everywhere, preached everywhere, and had disciples everywhere. And Śrīla Prabhupāda did that.

On arriving at one U.S. airport, Śrīla Prabhupāda had mentioned that *yogīs* had formerly traveled in three different ways: by flying carpet, by pigeons, and by *mantra.* "Then why have you come today on American Airlines?" the reporter had challenged. "Just to be one with you," Śrīla Prabhupāda had said, smiling.

But that Prabhupāda had come by jet instead of by some extraordinary mystic power was actually no less miraculous. The miracle was that he was always traveling and that wherever he went he spoke the message of Kṛṣṇa consciousness, created faith in the faithless, and transformed the low-grade persons of Kali-yuga into pure Vaiṣṇavas.

Śrīla Prabhupāda, in addition to his selfless, compassionate traveling, was also offering volumes of transcendental literature. His disciples in sixty-five centers around the world were gratefully accepting their role of assisting him, assuring him that they were able to preach to the people in their areas and that he should feel confident to go on opening new frontiers of Kṛṣṇa consciousness and presenting more and more transcendental literature. His disciples especially wanted him to have time for translating *Śrīmad-Bhāgavatam*, because he had told them that that was his desire. Often he said that if he could simply spend time translating

Śrīmad-Bhāgavatam he would stop traveling. He could not stop traveling for very long, however. Even if he found enough peace and a suitable place for concentrating on the *Bhāgavatam,* duty would call; again he would have to travel—to see new people, to introduce *saṅkīrtana* in a new place, to insure that his movement was progressing smoothly.

Prabhupāda, therefore, had developed a routine of translating *Śrīmad-Bhāgavatam* anywhere he went, for at least a few hours a day. He had a briefcase with Sanskrit *Bhāgavatams* and commentaries and a suitcase with a dictating machine. Wherever he was, he would rise in the middle of the night, sit at his desk with his dictating machine and Sanskrit and Bengali volumes, and take up where he had left off, translating the verses into English and composing his Bhaktivedanta purports. Thus his busy traveling and his translating were able to go on simultaneously.

CHAPTER EIGHT

In Every Town and Village

London
August 1971

From Florida, "this remote corner of the world," Prabhupāda returned to New York and after three days flew to London. There he became ill. On August 14 he wrote to Tamāla Kṛṣṇa,

> I am sick here since the last four days. There is no sunshine. Almost always there is darkness and rain. So it has affected my health, because I am already rheumatic.

Prabhupāda said he wanted to retire from traveling and management: "This body is old, it is giving warning." But he didn't have sufficient confidence that his leading managers could push on—without his pushing them.

Prabhupāda complained to his secretary, Śyāmasundara, criticizing him and the other zonal secretaries for not producing and distributing his books on a large scale. "Why are there no books?" Prabhupāda demanded, and Śyāmasundara cringed, unable to give a satisfactory answer. Śyāmasundara said he would immediately write to his Godbrothers on the Bhaktivedanta Book Trust.

"Why have a book trust?" Prabhupāda argued. "What have they done? There is no stock of big books. * There are no literatures in foreign languages after years of promises and plans. Why hasn't the unabridged *Bhagavad-gītā As It Is* been printed yet?"

---

* *Teachings of Lord Caitanya; The Nectar of Devotion; Śrīmad-Bhāgavatam; Kṛṣṇa, the Supreme Personality of Godhead.*

"Well," Śyāmasundara replied, "because they . . ."

"No! It's *your* responsibility," Prabhupāda yelled. "Why haven't *you* done it?" Prabhupāda chastised his G.B.C. secretaries around the world through the one secretary before him. The G.B.C.'s duties were to see that Prabhupāda's books were always in stock, that *Back to Godhead* magazine was being published regularly, that accounts were being paid regularly, and that the devotional life in the temples was healthy.

"Our business is how to expand," said Prabhupāda, "—how to introduce Kṛṣṇa consciousness into educational circles. Let any philosopher, scientist, or educationist come—we have got enough stock. But this sleeping, this leisurely work will not do. They can learn activity from an old man like me, because my determination is like this: If I die working, it is a great credit. Just like a marshal, if he dies on the battlefield, it is his credit. Arjuna was told, 'Even if you die, you are still the gainer.'

"This slow process of printing is the most condemned position. Why should I go on translating when you cannot print? You say, 'Retire and translate.' But why should I translate? No one will ever see it! I can give you volumes. There is Dai Nippon, who will print in Japan on credit, so why don't you print? Always, 'It is to be done. It is to be done.' That's all. And big men complaining, 'Either he goes or I go.'

"This restlessness, this diversion has to stop. When the father is providing, it is the duty of the son to serve. I am the father. I am giving you everything. Why don't you serve me by printing these books? If one book only is read and understood, that is sufficient to make him Kṛṣṇa conscious. Don't you see how important it is?

"They are always asking me, 'Is such-and-such book bona fide?' They can't even take the time to read one of my books, and still they ask for one of my Godbrothers' books. How will things go on? First Canto of *Śrīmad-Bhāgavatam* is not even edited or corrected, what to speak of printed. So many books unprinted. So tell them: From the book fund not a farthing should be for eating."

One day Advaita, the manager of ISKCON Press, called from New York with some good news: in a week they would be sending Dai Nippon the negatives for five big books. ISKCON Press had also sent a shipment of the German *Īśopaniṣad* to Europe. And other foreign-language books were forthcoming. Prabhupāda was pleased, and Śyāmasundara informed his G.B.C. Godbrothers.

> Needless to say, this was just the medicine required to treat Prabhupāda's slackening faith in us. Things are looking up, but still Prabhupāda encourages us all to write up these reports and get a clear all-around picture of the total book situation.

Although Prabhupāda's health was still weak, he felt heartened to hear that his books were being printed, and he continued with his translation and commentary of *Śrīmad-Bhāgavatam.*

Raṇacora: *One night I was up very late, one o'clock in the morning. As I came in I saw that Prabhupāda's lights were on in his front room, and I could hear his voice speaking into the dictating machine. I came up the stairs, being as quiet as I possibly could so Prabhupāda wouldn't know that I was up so late. But as I passed his door I couldn't resist the temptation to just stop and listen for a while. I tried looking through the keyhole, but I couldn't see anything. So I just listened to Prabhupāda's voice as he was dictating* Śrīmad-Bhāgavatam.

Then all of a sudden he stopped. I supposed he was just thinking about what he was going to say next. But then I got the feeling that he knew I was out there, listening through the door. I became frightened and went up the stairs as quietly as I could, although the stairs creaked. Everyone was asleep—not only the temple, but practically the whole city of London—at one o'clock in the morning. But Prabhupāda was awake and translating. He had been speaking quietly, but with a voice of great strength and determination. All during the day he was under pressure to organize things and see people, and yet at night, the one time when he could have some peace and quiet, he was up dictating.

In London Prabhupāda began a book on the Western philosophers, beginning with Socrates. Every morning Śyāmasundara would present a synopsis of a major philosophy to Prabhupāda, and for several hours Prabhupāda would discuss the philosopher's major points from the light of Kṛṣṇa consciousness. Daily Śyāmasundara was busy transcribing the morning discussions and preparing the next philosopher.

On August 14 Śrīla Prabhupāda observed Janmāṣṭamī, the birthday of Lord Kṛṣṇa. On the next day, Prabhupāda's own seventy-fifth birthday, a paperback book of collected homages by his disciples arrived. Many of the Vyāsa-pūjā homages praised Śrīla Prabhupāda for his extensive traveling to deliver fallen souls all over the world and for the vast scope of his merciful preaching.

> This year you have been traveling to India personally speaking and managing ISKCON and showing us the meaning of *ācārya* by example. And now you are traveling and inspiring the devotees and centers in the U.S. and Europe.
>
> At Vyās Pūjā time we, your intimate children, are gathered at your feet to tell you our feelings as best we can. By your blessing, we can go forth from this Vyās Pūjā gathering of 1971 and, all devotees together as one great ISKCON, without faction, truly perform the work with our thoughts, words, and deeds. Let us go and distribute this literature of Śrīla Prabhupāda's—Kṛṣṇa's message—kindly delivered to the Western countries. Let us cooperate without ill feelings among ourselves. Let us very strictly observe all the regulative principles and stay as pure representatives. Let us celebrate pure *saṅkīrtana* and magazine distribution to please you. All glories to Śrīla Prabhupāda!
>
> All your disciples pray that you will remain in our presence for many years to come, and by our cooperation you will be able to spend time writing volumes of *Bhāgavatam* while we carry on the program and mission of your Guru Mahārāja.

Prabhupāda's ill health continued.

> I was sick for four or five days; now I am a little better but the disease is prolonging in a different way. I cannot sleep at night more than 2 hours and during the day sometimes I am feeling some dizziness. Otherwise everything is all right. I am chanting Hare Krishna as usual and writing my books regularly.

Śyāmasundara: *Aravinda and I were sleeping right outside of Prabhupāda's room. I was on a lower bunk bed, and I heard "Śyāmasundara." It was a really urgent sound, and I woke up so hard that I hit my head on the bunk above. I ran into Prabhupāda's room. As I was opening the door, he collapsed in the doorway. I caught him. He felt so light, like a little doll, and his face was gray. I took him over to his bed and thought, "Oh, my God, what's going on?"*

He was shivering. I turned the electric heater way up and put it next to his bed. I covered him with a lot of blankets and waited. He was just still. His eyes were closed.

Finally he said, "Śyāmasundara, go get me some black pepper." He described how to make a black pepper paste. "Rub it on my forehead," he said. So I ran down to the kitchen and prepared it and came up and put it on his head. I asked him, "Are you . . . what's wrong?" I don't believe he made a response. He closed his eyes and appeared to be asleep.

I slept there by him on the floor for a while. At some point in the night, he said, "You may go back to your room. I'll be all right." He stayed in bed until about eight or nine o'clock the next morning. And then he was just completely well, like nothing had happened. His spirit was so strong that although he had encountered devastating blows to his body, he had come right out of it. I could tell it wasn't a physical event. He had made a full recovery from what must have been something close to death.

* * *

One day while meeting with an Indian man, a Mr. R. B. Pandya from Mombassa, East Africa, Prabhupāda mentioned his illness. Mr. Pandya said he owned a house on the ocean at Mombassa, where it was always sunny and warm, with pleasant sea breezes—a perfect place for Prabhupāda to recover his health. Mr. Pandya invited Prabhupāda to go and live there as long as he liked. Taking the offer seriously, Prabhupāda began to think of going to Africa—not only for health, but for preaching. Three months ago he had sent Brahmānanda Swami and Jagannivāsa to East Africa, so a visit there would encourage them as well as enable Prabhupāda to work personally at expanding the Kṛṣṇa consciousness movement on the African continent. Prabhupāda sent Bhavānanda and Nara-Nārāyaṇa from London to Mombassa to see if it would really be possible for him to stay there as Mr. Pandya had suggested.

When Bhavānanda and Nara-Nārāyaṇa arrived, Brahmānanda Swami, who had been struggling in East Africa with only one assistant, was delighted to see them and to hear that Prabhupāda was coming soon. Previously, Brahmānanda Swami had been preaching in Florida, and Prabhupāda had written him to go to Pakistan. Immediately he had gone, along with one assistant, Jagannivāsa, flying to Paris and then taking the Orient Express through Eastern Europe. On hearing that war fever was building in Pakistan, Prabhupāda had sent a second letter to Brahmānanda Swami in Florida, advising him not to go to Pakistan. But Brahmānanda Swami had never received the letter. En route to Pakistan, while holding public *kīrtana* in Turkey, Brahmānanda and Jagannivāsa had been arrested and detained for several days on suspicion of being Christian missionaries.

Finally, Brahmānanda and Jagannivāsa had arrived in Pakistan, where students had spit at them, accused them of being spies, threatened them, and called them names. Several times people on the street had rubbed the Vaiṣṇava *tilaka* off the devotees' foreheads and warned them not to show themselves in public or they would be stabbed. Local Hindus had warned the devotees to leave as soon as possible, and so they had reluctantly decided to go to Bombay to see Prabhupāda.

Meanwhile, in Bombay Prabhupāda had read in an Indian newspaper that Pakistani soldiers in Dacca had killed four Hare Kṛṣṇa missionaries. "I am very much anxious to know about Brahmānanda," Prabhupāda had written. "The day has been full of anxiety with this bad news, and still it is going on."

When Śrīla Prabhupāda had heard that Brahmānanda Swami had actually arrived in Bombay, he had asked to see him at once. Like a father recovering his lost child, Prabhupāda had embraced him. "You risked your life just on my order," Prabhupāda had said. After some days Prabhupāda had told Brahmānanda Swami, "You should go to Africa. If you go, then we will be on all the continents."

Now, after preaching in Africa, Brahmānanda Swami eagerly awaited the visit of his beloved spiritual master.

* * *

Nairobi
September 9, 1971

As Śrīla Prabhupāda disembarked in Nairobi from the East African Airlines 747 jet, he wore a wool *cādar* over his shoulders and carried the same white vinyl attaché case he had taken with him all over the world. Flanked by his secretary and servant, he walked with his cane across the airfield toward the terminal building. Inside, he sat on a cloth-covered chair and joined in the *kīrtana*, while Indians and Africans gathered around to watch.

Kul Bhusana, a journalist and friend of Brahmānanda Swami's, approached Prabhupāda with questions. He asked Prabhupāda what he had come to teach, and Prabhupāda answered, "Modern civilized man has forgotten his relationship with Kṛṣṇa, or God, and is therefore suffering. Whether you are Hindu, Muslim, or Buddhist, that doesn't matter. Unless you reestablish your relationship with God, you cannot be happy."

"Have you come only for Hindus?" asked Mr. Bhusana.

"No," Prabhupāda replied, "for everyone."

Mr. Bhusana: "East Africa, especially Kenya, is one of those countries which enjoys a great amount of racial harmony in brotherhood of man. What is your special message you can bring to Kenya?"

Śrīla Prabhupāda: "That brotherhood of man can be complete when they are in God consciousness. Otherwise, it will again break."

Mr. Bhusana: "So your disciples will be making special efforts to reach the Africans rather than confine themselves to the Hindus? That is very important here in this country."

Śrīla Prabhupāda: "Our method is the same. But the method is so powerful that it appeals to everyone. We do not have to convey a new method for a new place. The method is the same—universal. It will appeal to everyone."

After spending one night in Nairobi, Prabhupāda and his party flew the next day in a small propeller aircraft to Mombassa. Mr. Pandya was away, and his family, although not very enthusiastic, opened their home to Śrīla Prabhupāda. The large house was of contemporary design, with rounded corners, porthole windows, and a spacious living room with a veranda facing the ocean.

Prabhupāda, standing by the window in his room, beheld an aquamarine sea, a cloudless blue sky, and a white sandy beach fringed with palms. Turning back toward Brahmānanda Swami and the others, he said, "Brahmānanda told me that this was one of the most beautiful places in the world. Now I see he is correct."

Prabhupāda had come with a chronic cough, but walking on the beach and relaxing in the Mombassa sunshine, he soon recovered his health. Prabhupāda maintained his program begun in London of daily dialogues with Śyāmasundara concerning the Western philosophers. Chronologically he had proceeded from Socrates to Descartes.

Śyāmasundara: "He is saying, 'I think, therefore I am.' First of all, he has discovered that 'I am.' This was his innate basis for truth. In his time there was no real authority."

Prabhupāda: "But this is not big knowledge. Long, long ago there were many who could understand 'I am.' This is called *ātmānaṁ manyate jagat:* a fool thinks all others are fools. He is not the first man to realize the identification of the self. Kṛṣṇa says *aham. Aham evāsam evāgre:* 'I existed in the beginning, and when everything is finished, I shall continue to exist.' This we also say. 'I existed before this body was created, and I shall exist when the body is annihilated.' This conception of *I* is there in God; it is in me. Then where is the new thing?

As soon as he felt better, he was ready to preach. Mombassa, he said, was a small place, and Nairobi, the capital, would be better for preaching. So he returned to Nairobi.

Nairobi
September 18, 1971

In Nairobi Śrīla Prabhupāda demonstrated how a *sannyāsī* should preach. For one month he strictly followed Vedic tradition by staying only three days or less in the home of each of his Indian hosts. Then, although his hosts always provided him good food and comfortable accommodations, he would move on to the next place. This was the rule for *sannyāsīs*, Prabhupāda said; it kept them from becoming attached to bodily comforts and from inconveniencing their hosts.

For Śrīla Prabhupāda to practice these rudimentary lessons of *sannyāsa* was, of course, unnecessary, for he was a *paramahaṁsa*, a *sannyāsī* in the highest order of Kṛṣṇa consciousness. His body, mind, and words being totally engaged in Kṛṣṇa's transcendental service, he was automatically detached from material comforts. Nevertheless, he followed the Vedic system, just to instruct his disciples by his example. He was following the system of *madhukarī*—named for the bee, which takes only a little pollen from a flower and then goes on to the next. This system of brief visits also enabled Prabhupāda to involve more families in Kṛṣṇa consciousness and to honor the abundance of invitations.

Wherever Prabhupāda went, he was undisputably the *guru*, the venerable *sādhu*. Yet he would deal intimately with his hosts, developing friendships and behaving practically like an elder member of the family. His hosts would offer him the best room in their home, usually their own bedroom, and the lady of the house, along with her assistants, would cook elaborate meals. Prabhupāda's natural Kṛṣṇa conscious bearing was commanding, and his behavior was always aristocratic; yet his hosts were charmed by his humility. Quickly he was becoming the friend and Vaiṣṇava *guru* of many families in Nairobi.

Prabhupāda's behavior in Nairobi was instructive for the few Western disciples who accompanied him. On one occasion a Mr. Devaji Dhamji invited Prabhupāda to bless the temple room in his home. Prabhupāda entered, and Mr. Dhamji offered him a deerskin to sit on. "We do not sit on deerskin," Prabhupāda said. "It is pure, but our Vaiṣṇavas don't wear them or sit on them. That is for the *yogīs*."

Bhavānanda: *Mr. Dhamji invited Prabhupāda to sit on a sofa, which had been covered by a clean white cloth. Prabhupāda sat down, and they bathed his feet. This was the first time I ever saw anyone bathe Prabhupāda's feet. They bathed his feet with milk and then with water and rose petals. Then they put* candana *on his feet, then red* kuṅkuma *powder, rice powder, and jasmine flowers. His toes were red from* kuṅkuma, *and grains of rice and little white jasmine flowers just stayed on his feet. And then he gave a talk. I had never noticed the* guru's *feet up until that time. That was the first time I realized that the feet of the* guru *are special. And they are astoundingly beautiful.*

Prabhupāda wasn't satisfied preaching only to the Indians. He wanted to preach to the Africans. Indians and Africans were completely segregated. But since a Kṛṣṇa conscious person does not make distinctions based on the body, Prabhupāda said the Indians had a duty to share their spiritual culture with the Africans.

Prabhupāda impressed on Brahmānanda Swami that his first duty in Africa was to give Kṛṣṇa consciousness to the Africans. Because of bad experience in Turkey and Pakistan, Brahmānanda Swami had been reluctant to hold public *kīrtanas* in Nairobi. Besides, the Africans spoke mostly Swahili; they were culturally different and usually too poor to buy books, so Brahmānanda Swami didn't know how to preach to them effectively. Going to the Indians had been easy and natural.

But Prabhupāda wanted the Africans. "It is an African country," he said simply. "They are the proprietors. We should be preaching to them."

As with everything else in Kṛṣṇa consciousness, Prabhupāda demonstrated how to do this also. He got the use of a Rādhā-Kṛṣṇa temple in a predominantly African downtown area. The temple had a hall with doors opening onto the busy street, and Prabhupāda instructed the devotees to hold *kīrtana* in the hall, keeping the doors open. The devotees did as he asked, and in five minutes the hall began filling up with people. It was a shabby area of town, and the people who entered were illiterate and dirty. But they were curious, and they happily joined in the *kīrtana*, smiling, clapping, and dancing.

Brahmānanda Swami left the hall and went to the nearby house where Prabhupāda was staying. "The place is filled with people," Brahmānanda Swami said, "but it's not necessary for you to come. We can carry on and do the program ourselves."

"No," Prabhupāda said, "I must go."

Brahmānanda Swami tried to discourage him.

"No, I must go," Prabhupāda repeated. "Are you going to take me?"

When Brahmānanda Swami arrived with Śrīla Prabhupāda, the hall was even more crowded than it had been a few minutes before. Prabhupāda, in his silken saffron robes, appeared effulgent as he entered the dingy, poorly lit auditorium. As he walked the crowd parted, leaving an aisle for him to pass among them, and they watched him curiously. Onstage Prabhupāda led a *kīrtana* and lectured. Although the Swahili-speaking audience was unable to understand Prabhupāda's lecture, the people were respectful. And the *kīrtana* they loved.

Members of the Indian community had been apprehensive of Prabhupāda's opening their hall to the Africans, and some of them had attended to see what would happen. Observing Prabhupāda's compassionate program, however, the Indians were impressed. Such an apparently simple program had the spiritual potency to erase cultural boundaries.

This should be Brahmānanda Swami's mission in Africa, Prabhupāda insisted—offering Kṛṣṇa consciousness to the Africans. And the program should be simple: distributing *prasādam*, distributing free books, and chanting Hare Kṛṣṇa with drums and *karatālas*. Kṛṣṇa consciousness should not be just another Nairobi Hindu religious society. The Hindus should take part by donating money, but Brahmānanda Swami's preaching and recruiting should be among the Africans.

When several black American disciples joined Prabhupāda in Nairobi, Prabhupāda told them, "Four hundred years ago your ancestors were taken away from here as slaves. But ah, just see how you have returned as masters!"

Prabhupāda also organized Nairobi's first outdoor *kīrtana* performance. The devotees went to Kamakunji Park's largest tree, a historical landmark connected with Kenyan independence. As they stood chanting beneath the tree, a large crowd gathered, and many began chanting. Some even danced in a sort of tribal shuffle. One young man stepped forward and offered to translate Brahmānanda Swami's speech into Swahili. The devotees distributed sweet *bundi,* and the people in the crowd really enjoyed themselves. The whole affair was a great success.

Rushing back to Prabhupāda, Brahmānanda Swami reported on the wonderful *kīrtana* in the park. Brahmānanda felt the same emotion as in 1966 when he had reported to Prabhupāda the success of the first *kīrtana* at Washington Square Park in New York City. Now, as then, Brahmānanda Swami had followed Prabhupāda's instructions, and the results had been successful. Prabhupāda, by his personal example and by his pushing Brahmānanda Swami, had within a few days changed the emphasis of preaching in Africa—from Indians to Africans.

The night of Śrīla Prabhupāda's lecture at the University of Nairobi, two thousand African students filled the auditorium, with hundreds more standing outside to look in through the doors and windows. First Prabhupāda had Bhūta-bhāvana, a black American disciple, deliver a short introduction, using some borrowed Swahili phrases. "*Harambay,*" he began—which means "Welcome, brothers. Let us work together." Then Prabhupāda spoke.

"The whole world is simply hankering and lamenting. You African people are now hankering to be like the Europeans and Americans. But the Europeans have lost their empire. They are now lamenting. So one party is hankering, and one party is lamenting. . . .

"We have come to these African countries to invite all intelligent Africans to come and understand this philosophy and distribute it. You are trying to develop yourselves, so develop very soundly. But don't imitate the Americans and Europeans, who are living like cats and dogs. Such civilization will not stand. The atom bomb is already there. As soon as the next war breaks out, all the skyscraper buildings and everything else will be finished. Try to understand from the real standpoint, the real view of human life. That is the Kṛṣṇa consciousness movement, and we request you to come and try to understand this philosophy. Thank you very much."

The audience burst into applause, giving Prabhupāda a standing ovation. This response proved once again that Kṛṣṇa's message spoke to the heart; it was for all people, regardless of their political, geographic, or social predicament. When Prabhupāda had first landed at the Nairobi airport, he had assured the reporter that he would be preaching to the Africans. And now he was. He was delivering to the Africans the same message and the same process of devotional service he had delivered to the Americans. What the Americans wanted and what the Africans wanted could be realized only in Kṛṣṇa consciousness. Kṛṣṇa consciousness would work anywhere, if sincere and intelligent persons would only come forward and help distribute it.

Prabhupāda continued with outside speaking engagements. While appearing on the popular TV show *Mambo Leo,* Prabhupāda displayed a painting of Lord Caitanya dancing and chanting with His devotees. The interviewer asked Prabhupāda why only Caucasians appeared to be in the picture. "Well, there are many colors in India," Prabhupāda replied.

"And who is the central figure here?" the interviewer asked.

"This is Śrī Caitanya Mahāprabhu," Prabhupāda replied. "He is God."

"He cannot be God!" the large, burly interviewer retorted. "What do you mean He is God? This is a human being."

But Prabhupāda became even more aggressive than the interviewer. "Why do you say He cannot come as a human being? Why God cannot come as a human being?"

In another of his many Nairobi lectures, Prabhupāda stressed that peace was possible only on the spiritual platform. Kṛṣṇa consciousness alone would unite the present factions.

"For instance, in Africa the Indians may be satisfied with their own methods, but the Africans are not satisfied. So if one is dissatisfied in material life, then another is satisfied—and there will be disturbance. But if you come to the Kṛṣṇa conscious platform, if you engage yourself in the transcendental loving service of the Supreme Personality of Godhead, then your mind and soul will be fully satisfied."

Prabhupāda went on to explain his plans for helping Africans.

"We have come to Africa to educate the people—not only Indians or the Hindus, but also the native people, the local population. I am glad that our people are going to *saṅkīrtana* party in the streets, as we go everywhere—in London, in New York, and all the big cities of the world. We are trying to lead our *saṅkīrtana* parties through the streets, and the local African boys and girls and gentlemen are gathering. They are receiving this movement.

"So there is every possibility of spreading Kṛṣṇa consciousness everywhere. This movement has come here, so I request that those who are present try to cooperate with the Kṛṣṇa consciousness movement. And I am sure that the African boys and girls will take part in it, as you have experienced. We have a great many African boys and girls as our students in America, so there is no difficulty.

"It is not that because one is very busy, therefore he cannot serve God. Or that because one is poor, or black, or white, that he cannot serve God. No. Anyone who takes to the process of pure devotional service will never be checked."

Prabhupāda also asked his audience to help the devotees establish a center in Nairobi.

"We must have a place to stay. Unless we stay, how can we prosecute the movement? Therefore, help us immediately. Give us a place and see how things improve. You have already tested this movement and found that it has been successful all over the world. Why not in Africa? We are not a sectarian group. We don't consider whether one is African or American."

In Nairobi Prabhupāda heard of a new law in Tanzania that after ten years all private property would automatically become the property of the state and that the owner would be entitled to only a ten-percent reimbursement. This was a typical Kali-yuga law, Prabhupāda remarked. The state passes a law with no reasoning and no benefit for the people. The state should protect the people, Prabhupāda said. In Vedic history, during the misrule of the demoniac king Veṇa, the sages and *brāhmaṇas* had become very disturbed and had punished him; the *sādhus'* duty was to make sure the kings ruled justly. But today, nowhere in the world were political affairs in order. There was no sane philosophy to guide society.

"We must begin to interfere," Prabhupāda urged his disciples. "Now we are five hundred men, and we each have fifty years. So think of what we can do. But you must become dedicated as I am. Sometimes a Vaiṣṇava is criticized as doing nothing. But Arjuna and Hanumān were Vaiṣṇava warriors. When the high-court judges wear *tilaka*, then we are successful—my Guru Mahārāja said that. My Godbrothers were for getting temples, some rice, eating a little, chanting. But for us—first we work, then *samādhi*."

The word *samādhi* technically refers to a state of trance, in which one is completely absorbed in Kṛṣṇa and forgets the material world and all material desires. Generally, *samādhi* is thought of in terms of secluded meditation; a highly advanced *yogī* goes to a solitary, peaceful place and meditates or chants constantly. But Prabhupāda demonstrated by his life's example that the world situation was too urgent for a devotee to retire and meditate. Rather, a devotee should labor hard to increase the Kṛṣṇa consciousness movement. This would benefit both the devotee and the masses. Prabhupāda's disciples, therefore, as servants of their spiritual master, should work now; and later, perhaps in old age and spiritual maturity, they could retire to a holy place to constantly chant and hear about Kṛṣṇa.

Prabhupāda emphasized work. Yet what was that work? At least for Śrīla Prabhupāda, propagating Kṛṣṇa consciousness was *samādhi* itself. *Samādhi* didn't have to be limited to sitting in a solitary place. The full meaning of *samādhi* implied complete absorption in the loving service of Kṛṣṇa, with the senses, mind, and intelligence fixed in trance. Thus in *samādhi* one could be active—traveling, preaching, distributing *Back to Godhead* magazines, chanting in the streets. If a devotee always thought of Kṛṣṇa and worked on behalf of Kṛṣṇa, then he was the topmost *yogī*. This had also been Lord Kṛṣṇa's advice to Arjuna: "Remember Me, and at the same time fight." Śrīla Prabhupāda was the emblem of active *samādhi*—always hearing about, glorifying, and remembering Kṛṣṇa, and always fighting as a soldier on behalf of Lord Caitanya.

Prabhupāda's preaching in Nairobi had been especially active. He had established Kṛṣṇa consciousness in a new city, setting the example for Brahmānanda Swami to emulate, showing the standard for spreading Kṛṣṇa consciousness throughout the continent. And Śyāmasundara was keeping his G.B.C. Godbrothers informed of Prabhupāda's amazing activities.

> The pace has been lightning fast, and His Divine Grace is opening up yet another vast theater of operations. The people are thronging with curiosity and serious questions. . . .

> Prabhupāda, after finishing one late-night preaching marathon, asked for food and remarked, "You see, I am hungry. Keep me talking—that is my life. Don't let me stop talking. . . ."

But Nairobi was only one city in one country on one continent, and Prabhupāda's desire was to see Kṛṣṇa consciousness in every city, town, and village in the world. How could he do it in one lifetime—traveling to every city in the world, printing and distributing books in every language, constructing fabulous temples? He couldn't. But he wanted to do as much as possible in whatever time Kṛṣṇa allotted to him, to insure that the Kṛṣṇa consciousness movement would survive. He criticized the politicians' typical attitude that unless they themselves remained active everything they had worked for would crumble. Such politicians were always reluctant to retire, preferring to remain in office until their last breath. Prabhupāda, however, had no personal ambition, and he knew that results were awarded by Kṛṣṇa. As a true *sannyāsī*, he had renounced the world and worldly ambition. But he had not become lazy.

He was executing his mission at an advanced age, and Lord Kṛṣṇa was rewarding his attempts. Prabhupāda, therefore, in a mood of reciprocating with Kṛṣṇa, kept working to expand the Kṛṣṇa consciousness movement. Knowing that Lord Kṛṣṇa wanted the world flooded with love of God, Śrīla Prabhupāda had earnestly tried to do it, beginning in a storefront in New York City. And Kṛṣṇa had responded, sending him a few men and enough money to pay the rent. Then Śrīla Prabhupāda had attempted to do more, and again Kṛṣṇa had responded. Thus a second ISKCON center and a third and a fourth and more had sprung up, and book printing had begun. Śrīla Prabhupāda, in his mood of loving reciprocation with Kṛṣṇa, just kept attempting more and more.

Now it was no longer simply one person's work; Śrīla Prabhupāda was entrusting the work to his disciples. And those disciples, if they were actually to help, would have to adopt Prabhupāda's selfless dedication.

As they tried to follow him in his expansive plans, however, their minds faltered. For a handful of devotees to maintain even one temple in one city was a big job, yet Prabhupāda was doing this a hundred times over. He wanted the movement he had started to continue for thousands of years, and he was confident that as long as his followers remained pure, working within the guidelines he had given, they would be successful.

Although the present age of Kali was the worst of all ages, in which people had little or no interest in spiritual life, Prabhupāda had faith in the past *ācāryas'* predictions that Kṛṣṇa consciousness was destined to enter a golden age of worldwide influence. True, it was the worst of times; yet by the influence of the holy name of Kṛṣṇa it would become the best of times. The chanting of the holy name was the religion of the age; the people of Kali-yuga could find deliverance simply in chanting Hare Kṛṣṇa.

Śrīla Prabhupāda's activities show he was empowered by Kṛṣṇa. This is evident from his childhood, when at the age of five he held a Ratha-yātrā festival, and it is certainly evident from these years, 1968 to 1971, when he actively expanded his Kṛṣṇa consciousness movement. Prabhupāda compared ISKCON to the Varāha incarnation of Kṛṣṇa, who at first had been no bigger than a thumb but had quickly expanded to half the size of the universe.

ISKCON's rapid growth was not simply due to rapid communications and modern travel, nor to its founder-*ācārya's* material organizational abilities. Prabhupāda, judged materially, was not a likely person to conduct a worldwide movement, to travel vigorously, to write volumes of books, and to train thousands of disciples on every continent. He was satisfied with a simple, regulated life, and he disdained all such cultural items as music, fashion, sports, politics, art, food—anything not related to Kṛṣṇa. He worked and traveled out of an intense desire to benefit the world with real culture, to implant spiritual culture in what to him was the desert of a materialistic society.

Therefore, accepting that Prabhupāda was not materialistically ambitious, we can understand his proclivity for worldwide propaganda and dissemination of a spiritual movement as entirely transcendental. He was acting solely to carry out the desires of Lord Kṛṣṇa, the Supreme Personality of Godhead.

Śrīla Prabhupāda saw himself as a servant of his spiritual master, Śrīla Bhaktisiddhānta Sarasvatī, whose message he was carrying. That message, which was also the message of Lord Kṛṣṇa, had come down through disciplic succession: "We are all spiritual souls, eternal servants of the Supreme Personality of Godhead, Kṛṣṇa. We have now fallen into forgetfulness and are suffering birth after birth in this material world. By chanting Hare Kṛṣṇa, we can revive our lost relationship with God."

With Prabhupāda's first success in America, a few of his Godbrothers in India had minimized his work. Bhaktivedanta Swami, they had said, happened to have a temperament suited to mixing with lower-class Western youth. The fact, however, as Prabhupāda's own experience testified, was that the young people among whom he preached were not particularly receptive, nor had he arrived timely and welcomed, simply to discourse on *Śrīmad-Bhāgavatam* to throngs of submissive disciples. He had been successful because of his great patience, tolerance, and compassion.

It was not, therefore, the advent of the jet plane (although Prabhupāda gladly took advantage of it), nor was it happenstance, nor luck, nor even a social or historical phenomenon that enabled Śrīla Prabhupāda to spread Vedic culture from East to West and back again. No. It was the will of Kṛṣṇa and the sincerity of His servant.

Caitanya-caritāmṛta states that unless one is possessed of *kṛṣṇa-śakti*, special power from God, one cannot propagate the chanting of the holy name.

kali-kālera dharma—kṛṣṇa-nāma saṅkīrtana
kṛṣṇa-śakti vinā nahe tāra pravartana

"The fundamental religious system in the age of Kali is the chanting of the holy name of Kṛṣṇa. Unless empowered by Kṛṣṇa, one cannot propagate the *saṅkīrtana* movement." (Cc. *Antya.* 7.11) This verse describing Lord Caitanya Mahāprabhu also describes Lord Caitanya's servant, Śrīla Prabhupāda. Had Śrīla Prabhupāda not been empowered by Kṛṣṇa, he could not have inspired so many people to accept the chanting of Hare Kṛṣṇa.

According to Vedic literature, when a person has extraordinary spiritual endowment, *kṛṣṇa-śakti*, he is known as a *śaktyāveśa-avatāra*. Although the word *avatāra* generally refers to incarnations of God Himself, the term *śaktyāveśa-avatāra* refers to an individual empowered by God to enact the mission of God in this world.

Śaktyāveśa-avatāras and their particular functions are mentioned in the Vedic literature. For example, the emperor Pṛthu possessed the *śakti* for God conscious administration; the four Kumāras possessed the *śakti* of transcendental knowledge; and Nārada Muni possessed the *śakti* of devotional service. Lord Buddha, whose name and activities are described in *Śrīmad-Bhāgavatam*, is also a *śaktyāveśa-avatāra*, and even other divinely empowered personalities outside the Vedic culture, such as Jesus Christ and Muhammad, are accepted by Vaiṣṇava *ācāryas* as *śaktyāveśa-avatāras*.

Śrīla Prabhupāda's activities during the years 1968 through 1971 establish him as a *śaktyāveśa-avatāra*, and he fulfills the predictions of the scriptures.

pṛthivīte āche yata nagarādi grāma
sarvatra pracāra haibe mora nāma

"In all the villages and towns all over the world, everywhere, the *saṅkīrtana* movement of Lord Caitanya will be preached."

Even from the viewpoint of religious history, Prabhupāda's preaching was a fulfillment of the mission of Lord Caitanya, who had appeared in West Bengal about five hundred years before Kṛṣṇa consciousness came West. The Vedic literature and the Vaiṣṇava *ācāryas* concur that Lord Caitanya is the original Supreme Personality of Godhead, Kṛṣṇa Himself, appearing in this age as a pure devotee of the Lord. And just as Lord Kṛṣṇa appeared with His plenary expansion Lord Balarāma, Lord Caitanya appeared with Lord Balarāma's incarnation for Kali-yuga, Lord Nityānanda.

Śrīla Prabhupāda can be appreciated not only generally, as the empowered representative of God, but specifically, as the manifestation of Lord Nityānanda. According to Gauḍīya Vaiṣṇava philosophy, Lord Kṛṣṇa manifests Himself to the souls of ordinary men through Lord Nityānanda. The individual soul requires the help of God to realize God. This help comes by the causeless mercy of Lord Nityānanda, who is therefore known as the original *guru*. Although Lord Nityānanda is the direct expansion of Lord Caitanya, His pastime is to serve Lord Caitanya by redeeming the fallen souls.

Lord Nityānanda and His representative, the spiritual master, do not alter the scriptures or the teachings of Lord Kṛṣṇa but make them more accessible and understandable. Lord Caitanya commissioned Lord Nityānanda to preach the holy name at everyone's door, and Lord Nityānanda's exemplary mood of vigorous, compassionate preaching was also the mood of Śrīla Prabhupāda. As Śrīla Prabhupāda imparted this mood to his disciples, they in turn went out into the streets of cities around the world to distribute to everyone the mercy of the holy name of God.

Lord Nityānanda is especially renowned for saving two drunkard brothers, Jagāi and Mādhāi, even though they had assaulted Him when He had attempted to bless them with the holy name. In Lord Nityānanda's time, Prabhupāda on several occasions explained, there were only one Jagāi and Mādhāi, but now the whole world is filled with Jagāis and Mādhāis. And Prabhupāda was recruiting his disciples from these Jagāis and Mādhāis. Śrīla Prabhupāda fully displayed Lord Nityānanda's compassion in taking all risks and freely giving the holy name.

Even Lord Nityānanda Himself, during His appearance in India, did not approach as many fallen souls as Śrīla Prabhupāda, nor did He approach souls in such degraded conditions of life or in so many rejected parts of the world. But He has done so now, through His representative Śrīla Prabhupāda. As the recipient of the combined mercy of Gaura-Nitāi (Lord Caitanya and Lord Nityānanda), Śrīla Prabhupāda blessed the world with love of God.

Śrīla Prabhupāda, however, never described himself as a great empowered personality, either in public or among his disciples. But he stressed that he was in disciplic succession, carrying the authorized knowledge. And he encouraged his disciples to take the same position: "We want to create many pure devotees, so that other people will benefit by their association. In this way, the number of pure devotees increases."

Prabhupāda knew well that propagating Kṛṣṇa consciousness was not a professional business. Although in India many professionals spoke or wrote on *Śrīmad-Bhāgavatam* to earn their livelihood, they could not convert materialistic people to devotional service. Only a pure devotee could change the materialistic heart.

Prabhupāda did not even conclude that *he* was a pure devotee, only that he was the servant of a pure devotee, Śrīla Bhaktisiddhānta Sarasvatī, his Guru Mahārāja.

Prabhupāda prayed that before he left the world he could create a living family of pure devotees to spread the *paramparā* teachings of Kṛṣṇa consciousness and protect them from being changed or obscured. He emphasized that all the preachers of the Kṛṣṇa consciousness movement could become pure devotees by following the regulative principles, avoiding sinful life, and regularly chanting Hare Kṛṣṇa. Only in this way, he said, could the devotees have an effect on others.

October 18, 1971

Having spent a busy five weeks in Africa, Prabhupāda was ready to travel on to India. His plan was to visit Bombay, Calcutta, and Delhi.

He had made a strong beginning for ISKCON in India—with land in Māyāpur and centers in Bombay, Calcutta, and New Delhi, and he had groups of disciples strategically located in other parts of India. Indians were recognizing ISKCON and appreciating its festivals, *kīrtanas*, and *prasādam*. Life members were offering service and being benefited, they were receiving and reading ISKCON publications, and they were helping support the ISKCON centers.

And this was only a start. To get a foothold—anywhere, whether in India, Africa, America, or Russia—was certainly a great accomplishment. But a foothold was not enough. Although much had been done to establish the mission of Lord Caitanya, much more remained to be done. Preaching Kṛṣṇa consciousness was not a job that at some point would be completed.

Of course in one sense it was already complete and perfect. Prabhupāda's preaching had always been successful, even when he had struggled alone in India to make his message heard through *Back to Godhead* magazine, the League of Devotees, and his translations of *Śrīmad-Bhāgavatam*. He had always remained fixed in the transcendental order of his spiritual master and Kṛṣṇa; therefore, he had been successful. The Kṛṣṇa consciousness movement was already complete, and now, by the will of its author, Lord Caitanya Mahāprabhu, this completeness was becoming manifest. But the work, the ecstasy, the *samādhi* of selflessly and single-pointedly serving that mission was unending and ever unfolding. Now there was a foothold in Africa. Tomorrow he would fly to Bombay, where Kṛṣṇa had already allowed him a foothold. And, as Kṛṣṇa desired, he would continue to travel and to send his devotees and his books and his message until he reached every town and village in the world.

Appendixes

BOOKS by His Divine Grace A.C. Bhaktivedanta Swami Prabhupāda

Bhagavad-gītā As It Is
Śrīmad-Bhāgavatam, cantos 1–10 (30 vols.)
Śrī Caitanya-caritāmṛta (17 vols.)
Teachings of Lord Caitanya
The Nectar of Devotion
The Nectar of Instruction
Śrī Īśopaniṣad
Easy Journey to Other Planets
Kṛṣṇa Consciousness: The Topmost Yoga System
Kṛṣṇa, the Supreme Personality of Godhead (3 vols.)
Perfect Questions, Perfect Answers
Teachings of Lord Kapila, the Son of Devahūti
Transcendental Teachings of Prahlāda Mahārāja
Teachings of Queen Kuntī
Kṛṣṇa, the Reservoir of Pleasure
The Science of Self-Realization
The Path of Perfection
Life Comes From Life
The Perfection of Yoga
Beyond Birth and Death
On the Way to Kṛṣṇa
Rāja-vidyā: The King of Knowledge
Elevation to Kṛṣṇa Consciousness
Kṛṣṇa Consciousness: The Matchless Gift
Search for Liberation
Geetār-gan (Bengali)
Vairāgya-vidyā (Bengali)
Buddhi-yoga (Bengali)
Bhakti-ratna-bolī (Bengali)
Back to Godhead magazine (founder)

A complete catalog is available upon request.

Bhaktivedanta Book Trust
3764 Watseka Avenue
Los Angeles, California 90034

Significant Events in the Life of Śrīla Prabhupāda

14 Dec. 1967	San Francisco temple on Frederick St. Returned to America from India after four and a half months of preaching and recuperating from heart attack.
Jan. 1968	Los Angeles temple on West Pico Blvd. Interviewed by *Life* magazine.
May 1968	Boston, temple on Glenville Ave. Lectured at Harvard and M.I.T.
June – Aug. 1968	Montreal temple on Park Ave. Sent six disciples (three married couples) to preach in London.
Sept. – Oct. 1968	Visited ISKCON centers in Seattle and Santa Fe.
Oct. 1968 – Mar. 1969	Los Angeles temple on La Cienega Blvd. Introduced more regulated Deity worship and weekly festivals.
Dec. 1968	Began work on *The Nectar of Devotion* and *Kṛṣṇa, the Supreme Personality of Godhead.*
May 1969	Columbus, Ohio. Appeared onstage with Allen Ginsberg at Ohio State University and led 2,000 students in ecstatic *kīrtana.*
May – June 1969	First visit to the New Vrindaban farm community in West Virginia.
23 June 1969	Los Angeles temple on La Cienega Blvd. Installed Deities of Rādhā-Kṛṣṇa.

26 July 1969	Presided over San Francisco Ratha-yātrā.
Aug. 1969	Visited ISKCON center in Hamburg, Germany.
11 Sept. 1969	London arrival. Resided at Tittenhurst, John Lennon's Ascot country estate.
Sept.–Oct. 1969	Lectured at Camden Town Hall. Gave a series of lectures at Conway Hall. Lectured at English Speakers Union. Appeared on TV talk show "Late Night Line-Up." Traveled to Amsterdam for TV appearance.
30 Oct. 1969	Oxford Town Hall lecture.
3 Nov. 1969	Moved from Tittenhurst to an apartment on Baker Street, near the Bury Place temple.
Dec. 1969	Moved into Bury Place temple. Received $19,000 donation from George Harrison for publishing Vol. I of *Kṛṣṇa, the Supreme Personality of Godhead.* Acquired Rādhā-Kṛṣṇa Deities for Bury Place temple.
14 Dec. 1969	Inaugurated first Gauḍīya Vaiṣṇava temple in London and installed Deities of Rādhā and Kṛṣṇa.
21 Dec. 1969	Boston temple on Beacon St. Visited ISKCON Press.
Jan.–July 1970	Resided at Los Angeles temple on La Cienega Blvd.
25 Feb. 1970	Los Angeles. Appearance day of Śrīla Bhaktisiddhānta. Moved into temple on Watseka Ave., ISKCON world headquarters and model for all ISKCON temples.
5 July 1970	San Francisco Ratha-yātrā.

July 1970	Awarded *sannyāsa* order to several disciples.
28 July 1970	Formed the Governing Body Commission (G.B.C.) of ISKCON.
29 July 1970	Formed the Bhaktivedanta Book Trust (BBT).
Aug. 1970	Hawaii, enroute to India. Tokyo. Instructed disciples on proper observance of Vyāsa-pūjā. Wrote letter to New Vrindaban, resolving the growing misconception of the spiritual master's position. Made contract with Dai Nippon Printing Co.
29 Aug. 1970	Calcutta. Instituted ISKCON Life Membership program.
Oct. 1970	Bombay. Home of Mr. Kailash Seksaria on Marine Dr. Chowpatti Beach *paṇḍāl,* Sadhu Samaj. Developed Bombay Life Membership.
late Oct. 1970	Amritsar. Preached at the Vedanta Sammelan. Daily accepted numerous invitations. Enlisted life members. Visited Golden Temple of the Sikhs. Visited Rāma-tīrtha-sarovara, *āśrama* of Valmīki Muni.
20 Nov. 1970	Bombay. Resided at Sītā-Rāma temple in Chembur. Invited by Sumati Morarji to speak at Scindia House.
3 Dec. 1970	Indore. Gita Jayanti Mahotsava. Established Life Membership.
17 Dec. 1970	Surat. Resided at home of Mr. Bhagubhai Jariwala. Daily *kīrtana* processions through city. Citywide holiday proclaimed.

	Preached in outlying villages.
Jan. 1971	Bombay and Calcutta.
Jan. – Feb. 1971	Allahabad. Attended Ardha-kumbha-melā.
Feb. 1971	Gorakhpur. Resided at home of disciple Dr. R. P. Rao. Formed committee to introduce Kṛṣṇa consciousness within Gorakhpur University.
Feb. 1971	Benares. Attended festival of Lord Caitanya's visit to Benares and rode in the procession in a silver chariot.
Feb. – Mar. 1971	Gorakhpur. Resided at second home of Hanuman Prasad Poddar. Introduced the song *Jaya Rādhā-Mādhava.* Negotiated with university authorities for land for constructing an ISKCON temple. Met with Hanuman Prasad Poddar, head of Gita Press.
Mar. – Apr. 1971	ISKCON center at the Akash-Ganga Building. *Paṇḍāl* at Cross Maidan with nightly attendance of 20,000. Revealed plan for Bombay center in letter to life members.
4 May 1971	Visited Kuala Lumpur, Malaysia, and lectured at the Town Hall. Lectured at Lakṣmī-Nārāyaṇa temple.
9 May 1971	Sydney. Brought and installed Śrī-Śrī Rādhā-Gopīnātha. Performed initiations.
May 1971	Sydney Grammar School engagement.

	Lectured at Wayside Chapel, a rehabilitation center in downtown Sydney.
12 May 1971	Wrote Preface to *Bhagavad-gītā As It Is.*
13 May 1971	Arrived in Calcutta for a ten-day *paṇḍāl.* Naxalite youths threatened his life. Lectured to more than 40,000 at *paṇḍāl's* grand finale and led a procession to ISKCON temple on Albert Road, where he placed Rādhā-Govinda on the altar.
May 1971	Purchased land in Māyāpur through disciple Tamāla Kṛṣṇa.
June 1971	Moscow. Met with Indologist Professor G. G. Kotovsky. Instructed a Russian youth, Ivan, in Kṛṣṇa consciousness.
25 June 1971	Paris press conference. Olympia Theater television interview.
26 June 1971	Los Angeles initiations.
27 June 1971	San Francisco. Fifth annual Ratha-yātrā festival.
Summer 1971	Initiated several hundred disciples in Los Angeles, Detroit, and Brooklyn. Gainesville. Lectured at University of Florida. Television interview.
Aug. 1971	London. Serious illness. Stressed displeasure at delayed book publication.
Sept. 1971	Nairobi. Interviewed by reporters. Mombassa. Recovered health in home of Mr. Pandya.

Sept.–Oct. 1971	Nairobi. Set example for *sannyāsī* by staying three days or less in the home of each host. Stressed preaching to the Africans. Organized Nairobi's first outdoor *kīrtana* at Kamakunji Park. Lectured at University of Nairobi to 2,000 students. Appeared on TV show *Mambo Leo.*
19 Oct. 1971	Departure for Bombay.

Sanskrit Pronunciation Guide

Throughout the centuries, the Sanskrit language has been written in a variety of alphabets. The mode of writing most widely used throughout India, however, is called *devanāgarī,* which means, literally, the writing used in "the cities of the demigods." The *devanāgarī* alphabet consists of forty-eight characters, including thirteen vowels and thirty-five consonants. Ancient Sanskrit grammarians arranged the alphabet according to practical linguistic principles, and this order has been accepted by all Western scholars. The system of transliteration used in this book conforms to a system that scholars in the last fifty years have accepted to indicate the pronunciation of each Sanskrit sound.

The short vowel **a** is pronounced like the **u** in b**u**t, long **ā** like the **a** in f**a**r, and short **i** like the **i** in p**i**n. Long **ī** is pronounced as in p**i**que, short **u** as in p**u**ll, and long **ū** as in r**u**le. The vowel **ṛ** is pronounced like the **ri** in **ri**m. The vowel **e** is pronounced as in th**e**y, **ai** as in **ai**sle, **o** as in g**o**, and **au** as in h**ow**. The *anusvāra* (**ṁ**), which is a pure nasal, is pronounced like the **n** in the French word *bo***n**, and *visarga* (**ḥ**), which is a strong aspirate, is pronounced as a final **h** sound. Thus **aḥ** is pronounced like **aha**, and **iḥ** like **ihi**.

The guttural consonants—**k, kh, g, gh,** and **ṅ**—are pronounced from the throat in much the same manner as in English. **K** is pronounced as in **k**ite, **kh** as in Ec**kh**art, **g** as in **g**ive, **gh** as in di**g h**ard, and **ṅ** as in si**ng**. The palatal consonants—**c, ch, j, jh,** and **ñ**— are pronounced from the palate with the middle of the tongue. **C** is pronounced as in **ch**air, **ch** as in staun**ch-h**eart, **j** as in **j**oy, **jh** as in he**dgeh**og, and **ñ** as in ca**ny**on. The cerebral consonants—**ṭ, ṭh, ḍ, ḍh,** and **ṇ**—are pronounced with the tip of the tongue turned up and drawn back against the dome of the palate. **Ṭ** is pronounced as in **t**ub, **ṭh** as in ligh**t-h**eart, **ḍ** as in **d**ove, **ḍh** as in re**d-h**ot, and **ṇ** as in **n**ut. The dental consonants—**t, th, d, dh,** and **n**—are pronounced in the same manner as the cerebrals, but with the forepart of the tongue against the teeth. The labial consonants—**p, ph, b, bh,** and **m**—are pronounced with the lips. **P** is pronounced as in **p**ine, **ph** as in u**ph**ill, **b** as in **b**ird, **bh** as in ru**b-h**ard, and **m** as in **m**other. The semivowels—**y, r, l,** and **v**—are pronounced as in **y**es, **r**un, **l**ight, and **v**ine respectively. The sibilants **ś, ṣ,** and **s**—are pronounced, respectively, as in the German word **s***prechen* and the English words **sh**ine and **s**un. The letter **h** is pronounced as in **h**ome.

Glossary

A

Ācārya—one who teaches by example.

Ārati—a ceremony for worshiping the Deity of the Lord with offerings of food, lamps, fans, flowers, and incense.

B

Balarāma—the first expansion of Lord Kṛṣṇa, appearing as His elder brother.

Bhagavad-gītā—"Song of God"; the essential summary of spiritual knowledge spoken to Arjuna by the Supreme Lord, Śrī Kṛṣṇa.

Bhajana—worship of God by the chanting of His holy names.

Bhakti—devotion to the Supreme Personality of Godhead.

Brahmacārī—a celibate monk; the first of the four *āśramas,* or spiritual orders of life.

Brahma-muhūrta hour—an auspicious hour before sunrise.

Brāhmaṇa—an intelligent man who understands the spiritual purpose of life and can instruct others; the first Vedic social order, or *varṇa.*

Brahma-saṁhitā—a Vedic scripture describing Lord Kṛṣṇa, the Supreme Personality of Godhead.

C

Cādar—a blanket or cloth used to cover the upper part of the body.

Caitanya Mahāprabhu—the *avatāra* of Lord Kṛṣṇa in this age whose mission is to teach love of God through the chanting of His holy names.

D

Dharmaśālā—an inexpensive residence set up especially for pilgrims.

Dhotī—the standard Indian men's garment, a simple piece of cloth wrapped around the lower body.

G

Gamchā—a short cloth wrapped around the lower part of the body.

Gañjā—marijuana.

Gauḍīya Vaiṣṇava—a follower of Lord Kṛṣṇa (Viṣṇu) in the line of Lord Caitanya Mahāprabhu.
Gopīs—the cowherd girls of Vṛndāvana, who are the most advanced and intimate devotees of Lord Kṛṣṇa.
Gṛhastha—one who is practicing spiritual life while living with wife and children; the second *āśrama,* or spiritual order.
Gurukula—the school of the spiritual master.

H

Halavā—a dessert made from toasted grains, butter, and sugar.
Hari Bol—"Chant the names of Lord Hari!"

I

ISKCON—the International Society for Krishna Consciousness.

J

Jagannātha—"Lord of the universe"; a special Deity of Lord Kṛṣṇa, originating in Orissa on the east coast of India at Purī.

K

Kali-yuga—the present age of confusion and quarrel, which began five thousand years ago.
Karatālas—sacred hand-cymbals.
Karma—fruitive action, for which there is always a reaction, good or bad.
Kicharī—a cooked preparation made from rice and lentils.
Kīrtana—glorification of God, especially by the chanting of His holy names.
Kṛṣṇa-bhakti—*See: Bhakti*
Kṣatriya—the administrative and protective occupation according to the system of social and spiritual orders.

L

Loṭā—a waterpot.

M

Maṅgala-ārati—the first worship ceremony of the day, observed before sunrise.

Mlecchas—meat-eaters.
Mṛdaṅga—a sacred drum, made of clay, used in *kīrtana.*

N

Nārada Muni—the sage among the demigods, who is the son of Lord Brahmā and the spiritual master of Vyāsadeva.
Navadvīpa—the holy birthplace of Lord Caitanya Mahāprabhu, in Bengal.

P

Paṇḍāl—a tent.
Prāṇa—the life air within the body.
Prasādam—food spiritualized by first being offered to the Supreme Lord for His enjoyment.
Pūjārī—priest.
Purī—the abode of Lord Jagannātha, in Orissa (on the east coast of India); also, puffy wheat bread fried in ghee.

R

Rādhā(rāṇī)—the eternal consort of Lord Kṛṣṇa and manifestation of His internal pleasure potency.
Rādhāṣṭamī—the appearance day of Rādhārāṇī, Kṛṣṇa's eternal consort.
Rāsa dance—Kṛṣṇa's pastime of dancing with the *gopīs.*
Ratha-yātrā—the annual cart festival of Lord Jagannātha.
Rudrākṣa beads—chanting beads used by devotees of Rudra (Lord Śiva).

S

Sādhu—a saintly person.
Śāhnāī—an oboelike musical instrument.
Samosā—a fried pastry, stuffed with spiced vegetables.
Sandeśa—a sweet prepared from milk curd.
Saṅkīrtana—congregational chanting of the holy names of the Lord, the recommended process of *yoga* for this age.
Sannyāsī—one in the *sannyāsa* (renounced) order.
Sārī—the standard garment of women in Indian society, a single piece of cloth covering the entire body.
Śāstra—scripture.
Śikhā—the tuft of hair remaining on the back of the shaven head of a Vaiṣṇava.

Subhadrā—the younger sister of Lord Kṛṣṇa and personification of His spiritual potency.

T

Ṭāṅgā—a horse-drawn cart.
Tilaka—sacred clay marking the body of a devotee as a temple of God.

V

Vaiṣṇava—a devotee of Viṣṇu (or Kṛṣṇa).
Vyāsāsana—the honored seat of the spiritual master.

Index

When footnotes are referred to in the index, they are indicated by a number followed by an asterisk.

A

Abbey Road, recording studios on, 31–32
Absolute Truth. *See:* Kṛṣṇa; Supreme Lord
Academy of Sciences, U.S.S.R., 210, 213–17
Ācarati defined, 38
Ācārya(s)
Prabhupāda as, 232, 248
See also: Spiritual master(s); *specific spiritual masters*
Ācāryavān puruṣo veda
quoted, 189
Ācāryopasanam
quoted, 189
A.C. Bhaktivedanta Swami. *See:* Prabhupāda, Śrīla
Acintya-bhedābheda-tattva philosophy, 182
Acyutānanda dāsa
in Calcutta, 117–19, 208–9
dancing in *kīrtana,* 11
in Māyāpur, 125
Prabhupāda &, 117, 119
quoted on Calcutta *paṇḍāl* program, 208
sannyāsa requested by, 119
as swami, 208–9
Acyutānanda Swami, 208–9
See also: Acyutānanda dāsa
Adānta-gobhir viśatāṁ tamisram
verse quoted, 39
Adharma defined, 164
Adrienne, 243, 245
See also: Gāyatrī dāsī
Advaita dāsa, 83, 84, 252
Africa,
devotees in, 257–61, 264–65
Nairobi. *See:* Nairobi
Prabhupāda in, 257–65
Prabhupāda invited to, 255
segregation in, 259
Swahili language prominent in, 259
Africans, Prabhupāda's preaching to, 259–63
Agarwal, Mr. Manoharlal, 141–45
Aghāsura, 180
Agra, devotees in, 181
Aham evāsam evāgre
quoted, 258
Ajāmila, story about, 150–52, 156, 160, 163, 164, 169, 170–71, 172
Ajanta Caves, 68
Akash-Ganga building, temple in, 184
Akhaṇḍānandajī, Swami, 129
Akhila-ceṣṭitam defined, 178
Aligarh, devotees in, 181
Allahabad
bathing at, 165, 166, 168
Caitanya in, 167
Kumbha-melā in. *See:* Ardha-kumbha-melā
Prabhupāda in, 165–72, 178
Rāmacandra in, 167
Rūpa Gosvāmī Gaudiya-math in, 167
Rūpa Gosvāmī in, 167
Allen Ginsberg, 12–13
Altar(s)
in Beacon Street temple, 82
in Tokyo temple, 110
in Watseka temple, 89
Amarendra dāsa, 245, 246
See also: David Liberman
Ambassadors from India, 163
America
compared to blind man, 185
compared with India, 185
people of, compared with Russians, 212
Prabhupāda's tour in 228–47
See also: Prabhupāda, *in specific cities*
youth in, 182
See also: specific cities in America
Amrita Bazar Patrika, 120

E

F

G

H

I

J

K

L

M

O

P

T

Z

The Author

Satsvarūpa dāsa Goswami was born on December 6, 1939, in New York City. He attended public schools and received a B.A. from Brooklyn College in 1961. Then followed two years as a journalist in the U.S. Navy and three years as a social worker in New York City.

In July 1966, he met His Divine Grace A. C. Bhaktivedanta Swami Prabhupāda, and he became his initiated disciple in September of that year. Satsvarūpa dāsa Goswami began contributing articles to *Back to Godhead,* the magazine of the Hare Kṛṣṇa movement, and later became its editor in chief. In August 1967 he went to Boston to establish the first ISKCON center there. Satsvarūpa dāsa Goswami was one of the original members selected by Śrīla Prabhupāda to form the Governing Body Commission of ISKCON in 1970. He remained as president of Boston ISKCON until 1971, when he moved to Dallas and became headmaster of Gurukula, the first ISKCON school for children.

In May 1972, on the appearance day of Lord Nṛsiṁhadeva, he was awarded the *sannyāsa* (renounced) order by His Divine Grace Śrīla Prabhupāda and began traveling across the United States, lecturing in colleges and universities. In January 1974 he was called by Śrīla Prabhupāda to become his personal secretary and to travel with him through India and Europe. In 1976 he published *Readings in Vedic Literature,* a concise account of the Vedic tradition. The volume is now being studied at various American universities. In 1977 Śrīla Prabhupāda ordered him to accept the duties of initiating *guru,* along with ten other senior disciples. He is presently preparing further volumes of the biography of His Divine Grace A. C. Bhaktivedanta Swami Prabhupāda.

SRINIVASA dasa